FOR ADULT
USERS ONLY

Everywoman: Studies in History,
Literature, and Culture

Susan Gubar and Joan Hoff
General Editors

The Dilemma of Violent Pornography

FOR ADULT USERS ONLY

EDITED BY
Susan Gubar and
Joan Hoff

INDIANA UNIVERSITY PRESS

Bloomington and Indianapolis

MANUFACTURED IN THE UNITED STATES OF AMERICA

Library of Congress Cataloging-in-Publication Data

For adult users only.

   (Everywoman : studies in history, literature,
and culture)
   Includes index.
   1. Pornography—Social aspects—United States.
2. Women—United States—Crimes against.   3. Obscenity
(Law)—United States.   4. Violence—United States.
I. Gubar, Susan, 1944–   .   II. Hoff,
Joan, 1937–   .   III. Series: Everywoman.
HQ471.F67   1989   363.4'7'0973   88-45499
ISBN 0-253-32365-7
ISBN 0-253-20508-5 (pbk.)

1 2 3 4 5 93 92 91 90 89

Contents

FOR ADULT
USERS ONLY

Introduction

SUSAN GUBAR AND JOAN HOFF

I

After one hour on the highway that has taken you out of the Indianapolis airport and southward toward the outskirts of Bloomington, you might heave a sigh of relief at the sight of an array of roadsigns which includes billboards for Jackson Heights Apartments and Knight's Inn, intimations for the lyrically inclined (or for a visitor familiar with the boroughs of New York) of a courtly and courteous Queens in the middle of the middle of the country. And if you drive beyond a sculpture representing the unity of women and men, blacks and whites, Eastern and Western peoples, you can travel through a blooming town—lit with tiny white lights strung around the Courthouse during the winter or festive with flower boxes set around the renovated buildings of the central square in the summer—into a campus where you will find precisely such Queens' gardens: in the shasta daisies intermixed with huge elephant ears behind the house of the president of Indiana University; in the shadowy woods between science and humanities buildings, woods dotted by circuitous brick paths that lead past an Adam and Eve caught by their creator in a moment of eternal longing; in arboreta and quadrangles adjacent to the ivy-covered limestone auditoriums, within which you can hear the Beaux Arts Trio or watch Bobby Knight's Hurryin' Hoosiers. At least one option in the endlessly inventive speculations about the etymology of the word "Hoosier"—the one that claims early settlers asked, "Whose here?"—suggests that this green and pleasant land offers a sparsely populated enclave in which you can break away from the getting and spending of urban centers to participate in a secluded but rigorous physical and ethical culture. Indeed, even the phrase "college town" evokes the cultural benefits of a great institution of higher education combined with the friendly safety of village life.

Given this pastoral atmosphere, it comes as something of a shock to learn that Bloomington—like so many other college towns and like so many of the large cities in America—has recently experienced what one might call an epidemic of violence against women. On the day when this introduction was begun, February 7, 1988, the headline in the *Sunday Herald-Times* read, "Woman fatally beaten; son charged." A story followed the next day with the explanation by the accused James Keith Arthur that a snake had entered his sixty-seven-year-old mother's body and that to his mind, therefore, Mabel Arthur "was in control of the demon or she is the demon herself. . . ." A retiree who lived alone in a trailer, Mabel Arthur had received numerous injuries, including the skull fracture that apparently caused her death. The second page of the Sunday paper—usually devoted to lesser local police work—included an account about an unnamed woman "forced to engage in sexual behavior with a male acquaintance who had accompanied her in a car to a remote area southwest of Bloomington."

Nor is this kind of violence, which has resulted in the formation of a women's crisis center, limited to the town half of a town-gown community that in other respects prides itself on sensitive and mutually beneficial interaction between civic and academic populations. On the contrary, a number of campus problems, ranging from sexual harassment to date rape and assault, explain why the Indiana University Police Department has worked with the Office of Women's Affairs and specifically with its newly instituted Personal Safety Commission to promote better lighting and more emergency telephones in remote areas, lock-up policies for co-ed dormitories and locker rooms, a chauffeuring service to transport late-night scholars from, say, the library back to the residence halls, and workshops for the concerned about self-defense as well as the widespread distribution of whistles.

Perhaps the impossibility of disentangling town from gown problems, as well as the dreadful frustrations confronting law-enforcement agencies, is even more disturbingly illuminated by the tragic death in 1986 of Ellen Marks than it is by the fates of Mabel Arthur and the nameless abducted woman. An English graduate student who had dropped out of the program, Marks lived on the so-called wrong side of the tracks, in a section of town once dubbed "Pigeon Hill," where she was known as a weaver (there was a loom inside her makeshift home) and a flutist (she played for the kids on the street). Specifically, she inhabited what the newspaper described as a discarded freight box, occasionally using the water of neighbors, sometimes taking shelter and food at a nearby Christian community center. After her body was found—her hands and head had been cut off and her torso had been thrust into a plastic garbage bag—telltale signs led the police to a rooming house where they gathered evidence that resulted in the murder indictment of a tenant, a part-time clerk in a 7-Eleven store, who was later convicted. Not only was the community horrified by the dismemberment and specifically by the absence of Marks's head and hands (which were never found) and the removal of her heart, liver, and sexual organs (which were cut out with a mysterious surgical precision that evoked shades of the turn-of-the-century killer Jack the Ripper); it was also shocked to discover that some three years previously an acquaintance of the accused had brought a letter composed by the defendant to the police, a letter describing just such a grisly scheme. At that time, the police explained, the evidence was not incriminating enough for legal action to be taken because the writing of a letter does not constitute a crime.

It is a far cry from sexist jokes in classrooms or even professorial requests for sexual favors in exchange for grades (both considered forms of sexual harassment) to the assaults suffered by Mabel Arthur and Ellen Marks. Yet, despite the bucolic atmosphere of Bloomington, all these threats to women's safety and to their sense of security ominously prove that paradise has not been regained, even in this green place. For both the town and the university, the fact that Bloomington functions as a microcosm of the society at large remains a touchy subject, one that could frighten parents so badly that they might veto the second largest residential campus in the country and instead send their children to smaller schools that set (and can enforce) more rigid regulations over student life. Not only could the community suffer dire economic hardship from publicity and incidents of molestation, harassment, rape, and battery, but just such publicity might paradoxically and tragically multiply the crimes it means to counter. In addition, as on all college campuses, students seeking freedom of inquiry feel themselves to be at odds with other undergraduates arguing for protective security measures and with an administration that attempts to curtail the eruption of sexual violence by eradicating those activities—in particular, alcohol consumption and the viewing of X-rated films—which might spawn such violence.

Of course, these divided points of view reflect national debates, but they illustrate even more vividly the statewide concern that surfaced when, in June 1984, Indianapolis became the only community in the United States actually to adopt a statute making pornography a violation of women's civil rights. The pornography controversy struck even closer to home in the fall of 1984, when the Indiana University dean of students in Bloomington imposed a temporary ban on the showing of X-rated films for recruitment purposes by fraternities or for general entertainment purposes in dorms and when Judge Sarah Evans Barker struck down the proposed Indianapolis antipornography ordinance. Among other things, the latter decision made Indianapolis a national focal point on this issue, as litigation continued throughout 1985 and into 1986. In March 1985, the Indiana University Faculty Council responded to the campus controversy over X-rated films by endorsing the education of the student body about pornography and by creating a Task Force on Pornography to begin that process. It was in this context that a multidisciplinary faculty seminar on violence and pornography—out of which most of the essays in this volume evolved—was funded by the Indiana University dean of the faculties.

There are, of course, many ways to study sexual violence against women. But one way that seemed particularly feasible, given the holdings of the Kinsey Institute for Research in Sex, Gender, and Reproduction, was to analyze those materials most centrally concerned with this subject matter, namely, those movies, books, magazines, paintings, and photographs loosely grouped around the term "pornography" as well as the approaches of various academic disciplines to social problems associated with the pornography industry. In particular, members of the seminar focused weekly discussions on the nature and effects of violent pornography. Our undertaking was generated as a response to local events more than by any assumption that pornography was necessarily the cause of tragedies like those suffered more recently by Mabel Arthur and Ellen Marks. But by examining explicit representations of male violence against women, the members of the seminar attempted to investigate (1) cultural artifacts eerily similar in both plot and imagery to those events traumatically affecting abused women; (2) how past examples of pornography compare with present ones; (3) the relationship between those materials and the material conditions of too many women's lives; and (4) current philosophical and legal debates among feminists about the status and effects of violent pornography and specifically those arguments between civil libertarians and pro-ordinance activists which crystalized a rift in feminism that divided our own group of participants.

Using the perspective of our different disciplines—history, literary criticism, religious studies, ethics, political science, journalism, law, and psychology—we met at The Kinsey Institute throughout the fall of 1985 and through most of the spring of 1986 primarily to discuss the second, third, and fourth of these questions. Has contemporary pornography evolved into more violent forms than those which prevailed in earlier time periods? Is there an established link between, for example, so-called snuff movies or advertisements displaying mutilated women and real-life crimes against women? If so, are there legal, economic, or educational measures that could effectively regulate private production or public consumption of such materials? Almost all of our presentations and discussions explicitly analyzed the research of such different theorists as the historian Michel Foucault, the poet-polemicist Susan Griffin, and the psychologist Edward Donnerstein in order to focus on these topics. However, it may have been the first subject—the disquieting parallels between representations of sexual abuse and the fates of such women as Mabel Arthur and Ellen Marks—that was, on the one hand, so awful as to be unspeakable and, on the other hand, the secret cause of the concern that drew us together.

II

When Mabel Arthur's son explained that a demon had possessed his mother, his image drew on an identification of women with serpents that clearly goes back as far as Eve's alliance with Satan in Eden and forward to such imaginative works as Coleridge's "Christabel" and Keats's "Lamia," two Romantic poems that portray the mesmeric power of glitteringly seductive and snakey sorceresses. But more contemporary (and seemingly more realistic) works provide analogues for the brutal beating Mabel Arthur experienced, at the same time that they demonstrate why such violence—not overtly sexual in nature—needs to be contextualized in terms of the unnamed woman whose abduction and forced compliance in sex acts were also described in the February 7, 1988, edition of the *Sunday Herald-Times*. The intensity of the present tense in James Keith Arthur's claim about his dead mother—that "She was in control of the demon or she *is* the demon herself"—raises a question about whether Mabel Arthur would have been assaulted if she had not been born female. Two films especially popular among undergraduates and undoubtedly typical of numberless others could be said to elaborate on the murderous motives of Mabel Arthur's son.

In *Blue Velvet* (1986), a crazed man tortures a woman whose child he has kidnapped and whom he calls "mommy" when he repeatedly batters and rapes her. Pumping himself up by breathing through a sinister oxygen mask, the character portrayed by Dennis Hopper reduces his "mommy" to a fleshy thing presumably because he is still traumatized by the otherness of the first woman in his life, his mother. Even his antagonist, the ethical hero of this movie, becomes threateningly enthralled by the seductive sensuality of the maternal *femme fatale* and must defend himself against her eroticism by aligning himself with a suburban teen queen. If in *Blue Velvet* men's anxious sense of the omnipotence of the mother fuels masculine violence against the female, in *Angel Heart* (1987) a seemingly angelic man discovers his own diabolical instincts, which are stimulated by and enacted on powerful women. This hallucinogenic movie depicts a white woman's heart cut out of her body and a black woman either fucked to death by a man who uses his penis as a weapon or shot to death by a phallic gun inserted into her vagina. The Faustian protagonist discovers what he has repressed—that he had made a pact with the Devil—only after he realizes that the madman who cut out the white woman's heart and who ejaculated blood instead of semen into the black woman's body is either himself or the Devil with whom he has bargained. But because the two women are associated with demonic rituals, the "black magic" of voodoo, each is presumed to be a signature of his damnation and an appropriate victim of his fallen depravity.

Both *Blue Velvet* and *Angel Heart* evince a fascination with bloody body parts that permeates the letter written by the man who may have spent three years planning to dismember Ellen Marks: in the first case, the ears that the psychopath slices off his victims as well as the mouths which he stuffs with pieces of blue velvet; in the second, the heart and vagina attacked by the satanic Angel. Just as important, though, is the sense running through so many contemporary films that a woman like Marks—that is, a woman who lives a life outside societally approved proprieties and pieties—actively complies in making herself vulnerable to inevitable attacks. A riff on the cliché that the abused woman must have "wanted it" or that the "crime" constituted by her unconventional lifestyle is to be blamed for the "punishment" she receives, this script surfaces even in the most sophisticated films about sexual violence: in *Dressed to Kill* (1980), for example, where the bored wife played by Angie Dickinson discovers, after searching out and finding an erotic adventure, that she will be murdered in an elevator by a man aroused by her sensuality; or in *Crimes of Passion* (1984), where a businesswoman psychologically unstable enough to spend her evenings playing the part of a whore called China Blue with a succession of perverse clients must confront a demented preacher who brandishes a steel dildo.

By presenting scenes of helpless women tormented by a predatory, sadistic phallicism, *Blue Velvet, Angel Heart, Dressed to Kill,* and *Crimes of Passion* meditate on precisely those scripts that led to the abducted woman's enforced compliance in sexual behavior and that destroyed both Mabel Arthur and Ellen Marks. Significantly, too, all four of these movies depict male violence against women as a source of male sexual satisfaction. But, to return to the other questions which formed the substance of the conversations in our seminar, do such portrayals differ in essential ways from earlier depictions of sexuality? Are such representations of abuse themselves abusive? And do they promote sexual violence? In their defense, after all, it could be argued not only that all four movies are cautionary tales—monitory stories about the inexplicable evil that lurks in the hearts of men—but also that all draw on historically established aesthetic traditions to deal with the perversity of a culture that identifies sex with death—eroticism with murder—and that fixates men on a model of masculinity that deforms or defeats male maturity.

Indeed, the central characters of both *Blue Velvet* and *Angel Heart* are shown to experience themselves as men haunted by a sense that they have been constructed by powerful, primary female figures: the first by his "mommy" and the second by women crafty in the life-and-death mysteries of voodoo. To the extent that *Blue Velvet* and *Angel Heart* suggest that masculine rage at the omnipotence of the mother inexorably leads to a slippage between conceptualizations of male potency and of male domination, both films could be said to critique socially constructed definitions of masculinity. Similarly, the male psychopaths in *Dressed to Kill* and *Crimes of Passion*—the former a crazed psychiatrist, the latter a psychotic preacher—wreak vengeance against women because of a self-loathing identified with their attraction not only to female impersonation but to the "feminine" within both of them. To the extent that *Dressed to Kill* and *Crimes of Passion* echo Hitchcock's classic *Psycho* in their attempts to define transsexuality as a tragic schism between male desire to be the woman and male hostility toward the woman who is biologically female, both might be viewed as sympathetic portrayals of the double bind of women destined to be loved and hated, pursued and persecuted, imitated and immolated.

All four of these movies also have what we would ordinarily call aesthetic ambitions, signaled through a number of technical and literary strategies: *Blue Velvet* sardonically displays and parodies the facile message that "normalcy" and "good" will triumph through a trite parable told by the stereotypical teen queen about the robins that return to a regenerated suburbia in the spring; *Angel Heart* exploits surrealistic images of water turning into blood within the framework of a plot drawn not only from *Faust* but also from *Oedipus* (the detective who discovers he is the criminal; the hero who unwittingly commits incest); *Dressed to Kill* counterpoints nightmare visions with waking realities to blur the distinction between mimesis and fantasy; and *Crimes of Passion* flashes shots of works of art—Japanese prints, René Magritte's *The Rape*, Gustav Klimt's *The Kiss*—to emphasize both the long history of erotic imagery and its commonality with or difference from the disturbing pictures generated by the story line. Not only in their deployment of discernibly artistic motifs but also in moralistic conclusions that demonstrate the self-destructiveness of coercion, all four of these movies would seem to distinguish themselves from hard-core pornography.

Or do they? Couldn't it be argued that, by endowing these films with special intensity in their effects, such artistry makes them even more dangerous? Couldn't it be claimed, too, that their moralistic conclusions are merely tacked on and that, further, they merely reinforce a hegemonic ideology that instructs vulnerable women to seek the help of protective men? Certainly when *Blue Velvet, Dressed to Kill,* and *Crimes of Passion* manage to conclude in a happily-ever-after, they end by reestablishing stable heterosexual asymmetries, so that we are left to speculate that the blurring of gender lines and the sexperimentation that supposedly characterize psychosis can be sanitized, if and only if men are on top of women clearly marked as male property. The adolescent who liberates "mommy" from sexual slavery in *Blue Velvet* ends up ensconced with his teen queen at a family barbeque; the son of the murdered Angie Dickinson in *Dressed to Kill* catches the transsexual psychotic and manages to redeem the prostitute who feared his mother's fate; and Bobby, who extricates himself from his frigid wife in *Crimes of Passion,* salvages China Blue from her unwholesome decadence by teaching her the wonders of straight sex. In the films that "solve" the problem and "save" the heroines, therefore, the saviors are all younger, "healthily heterosexual" men, the implication being that women need to rely on male protection from sexual violence, which is frequently inflicted by and thereby associated with homosexual or transsexual men. How different, then, are these comparatively ambitious films from *Deep Throat* or *Debbie Does Dallas?*

III

Released with an "R" rating that means all viewers under seventeen years of age must be accompanied by an adult, all four of these films were shown not in movie houses or drive-ins specializing in X-rated material but in neighborhood theaters. Significantly, two of them—*Angel Heart* and *Dressed to Kill*—appear in uncut versions (which would not have received an "R" rating) on the shelves of local video shops. Clearly, however, they are meant "for adult users only," the cautionary slogan on the signs of countless pornography stores throughout the United States. The title of this collection attempts to draw attention to the problems posed by the mass distribution of sexually explicit, violent works since the 1960s and by largely ineffectual restrictions placed upon them, restrictions based on very different, earlier forms of pornography. Who are "adults," when pornographic materials—prominent especially in video shops—are no longer limited to certain age groups? Can the readers of books and the viewers of movies be said to be "users"? Should one limit access to the "use" of certain types of explicit sexual representations and, if so, how? Is it possible to determine which sorts of these materials are "only" pornographic?

This series of questions is related to another set of issues that concerned the Indiana University seminar. What do the history and literary history of pornography and the control of pornography tell us about the current debate between civil libertarians, who invoke the First Amendment to protect pornographers' "freedom of speech," and pro-oridinance activists, who claim that pornography represents a "clear and present danger" to women? Does the relationship between religion or ethics and sexual iconography illuminate the odd coupling between (some libertarian) feminists and pornographers, on the one hand, and (some pro-ordinance) feminists and Christian fundamentalists, on the other? Have public-policy decisions about sexually violent material been as legally effective as they could be? Most important, do representations of abusive men and abused women psychologically desensitize men and render women more vulnerable to the horrors suffered by Mabel Arthur and Ellen Marks? Precisely these concerns were addressed by both local campus and community groups in Bloomington as well as through the legal debates in Indianapolis and elsewhere as the city's ordinance made its way on appeal to the Supreme Court of the United States.

In the seminar, one factor emerged very clearly from our talks: not all of the disciplines represented had an equal interest or stake in the contemporary ramifications of violent pornography. History, literary criticism, and religious studies seem to gravitate toward an analysis of past sexual portrayals of women in a search for noncontemporary meanings that could help clarify present concerns, while such action-oriented fields as law, journalism, clinical psychology, and political science engage the practical consequences of pragmatic decision-making. In addition, probably the most disheartening (as well as enlightening) realization to emerge from the Indiana University seminar was not only how relatively intransient the perspectives of our respective disciplines were but also how little our discussions and arguments changed opinions in the course of the two semesters. At one level, therefore, the seminar reflected a cross section of America. At cocktail parties, in bars, around the dinner table, and in many other social settings across the country, mentioning the word pornography often sets off explosive conversations on all sides of the issue. As Justice Potter Stewart suggested more than twenty years ago, no one can define pornography, but everyone knows what it is when they see it and especially when they begin to argue about it. Thus, the debates that animated but split our interdisciplinary group of scholars continue to rage throughout our society.

Both the fate of the Indianapolis statute, which defined pornography as a form of sex discrimination and hence a violation of women's civil rights, and the stalemate in the current women's movement, which divides feminists equally committed to women's rights, illuminate the problems our seminar set out to confront. The approach of the Indianapolis City-County Council (and of other cities such as Minneapolis and Cambridge that have considered similar legislation) was novel because obscene material has traditionally been subject to criminal, not civil, law. Supporters wanted pornographic material removed from the purview of the First Amendment, which was designed to permit the un-fettered interchange of social or political ideas. Since the primary function of the First Amendment is to protect communication, proponents of the Indianapolis antipornography ordinance maintained that pornography "is no more the communication of ideas than segregation is." Carrying this analogy further, the defendants in *American Booksellers Association, Inc., v. Hudnut* argued that while it is still possible in the United States to *advocate* "separate but equal" treatment as an example of protected speech, the *practice* of segregation is not a form of protected speech. Thus, espousing the subordination of women to men is protected, but the "practice of subordinating women through pornography is not and can be validly proscribed."

Although the city ordinance attempted to define pornography as a form of sex discrimination and a violation of women's civil rights, in August 1985, the U.S. Court of Appeals for the Seventh Circuit in Chicago upheld a 1984 ruling against the ordinance by the U.S. District Court for the Southern Division of Indiana. Subsequently, on February 24, 1986, without issuing an opinion, the Supreme Court affirmed the rulings of these lower federal courts that declared the Indianapolis antipornography ordinance unconstitutional because it violated the First Amendment right of free speech. The various decisions in *American Booksellers Association, Inc., v. Hudnut* did not settle the issue among feminists. While accepting the premises of the Indianapolis ordinance—namely, that "depictions of subordination tend to perpetuate subordination"—the Seventh Circuit Court of Appeals held that no legal definition of pornography had been put forth that did not violate free speech under the Constitution. Since this decision, the Attorney General's Commission on Pornography issued a report in July 1986, which has only exacerbated the disagreements among scholars and feminists alike, for it declared categorically that pornography plays a leading role in causing "sexual violence, sexual aggression or unwanted sexual coercion," despite the ambiguity of social-science research on this causal relationship.

That the contributors to this volume often found themselves unable to change their own or their colleagues' minds about the significance of pornography in today's society remains one sure sign of the recalcitrance of this subject. After all, it addresses some of the most troubling and important societal issues: free speech versus civil rights, "high" versus "low" culture, and individual versus community rights. Some groups feel that pornography stimulates sexual responsiveness, whereas others claim that it anesthetizes or perverts sensuality. Some theorize that all forms of sexuality and pornography should be free from any restrictions if participants are consenting, equal adults, but others speculate that there can be no consensual equality in relationships or representations based on the domination or objectification of women. At the same time, the status of pornography engages disparate interdisciplinary points of view: the definitional controversy about whether "erotica" can be disentangled from pornography; male as compared to female responses to—or authorship of—pornographic materials; Freudian or non-Freudian psychological models; imitative versus cathartic sociological paradigms. Finally, arguments between those who believe that public policy cannot reflect private morality and those who argue that personal behavior is inexorably patterned on political programs lead to conflicting points of view about the actual or optimum interaction between the government of a democratic society such as the United States and the sexual expectations of its individual citizens in the last decades of the twentieth century.

Therefore, of all the problems currently facing the women's movement, pornography may be potentially the most divisive and debilitating since the fifty-year debate over protective legislation and the ERA, begun in the 1920s. Unlike Betty Friedan, who in 1985 warned against the "preoccupation with pornography and other sexual diversions that do not affect most women's lives" and who in 1981 categorically asserted that "Porn doesn't really hurt anybody," many American feminists claim that the issues of pornography in particular and of sexuality in general represent the last frontiers in women's struggle to achieve true liberation and equality. These feminist thinkers and activists, who disagree about the nature and impact of pornography, nevertheless believe that regardless of sexual preference, each individual woman must at some time in life face her own private sexual existence and evaluate how it enlarges or diminishes her other roles and functions in society.

By concentrating on the current split within the women's movement over pornography, we tend to forget that when the antipornography campaign began in the late 1970s, there was widespread consensus. A general belief that somehow pornography contributed to violence toward women was heightened by the view that it was not even very sexually stimulating because so much of it was aimed at arousing a predominantly male audience. Since then, one group of feminists has decided that depictions of sexual submission can be either pleasurable or a form of sex education for women while another has continued to emphasize the harmful subordination of women in most pornography. Vocal members of the women's movement have been polarized into two factions—those who think pornography liberates or enlightens and those who argue it degrades or humiliates contemporary American women—and this opposition shows few signs of abating in the near future.

Aligning themselves with civil libertarians, represented primarily by the American Civil Liberties Union, the women who make up the Feminist Anti-Censorship Taskforce (FACT) oppose legislation against pornography largely on First Amendment grounds. They also question whether images can be said to cause acts, and whether allying with right-wing fundamentalists on antipornography ordinances is wise from a political perspective. They oppose all forms of censorship, even as they argue that banning pornography would not solve the problem of widespread violence against women. On the other side are Women Against Violence in Pornography and the Media (WAVPM), Women Against Violence Against Women (WAVAW), and Women Against Pornography (WAP). These national groups point to recent sociological and psychological data suggesting a positive correlation between viewing violent sexual acts against women and perpetrating such abusive acts. Although they are not always in agreement about whether both hard-core and soft-core, violent and erotic, pornography are equally responsible for dehumanizing women, they view both types as the erotization of male power. Consequently, antipornography activists believe that representations of the sexual subordination of women lower male inhibitions toward violence against women as well as the collective civil status of women.

Unfortunately, this serious disagreement among feminists has been framed and fanned by escalating violence against women in the United States. Furthermore, except for those acts covered by criminal law, too much verbal and physical abuse remains an unpunished social "problem." Obviously most pertinent here is the fact that, despite the efforts of law-enforcement agencies to hire women and to refrain from "blaming the victim," most experts believe that only one out of approximately nine rapes gets reported. Even so, statistics now reveal that in the United States one rape occurs every three minutes and that domestic violence kills ten women each day. Clearly, much of the physical harm women endure takes place in the home—most often inflicted by male relatives and acquaintances or men with whom they are intimately involved. Between random violence on the streets, sexual harassment on the job, and abuse at home, what are women to do?

IV

All of the essays in this volume necessarily engage the problem of defining pornography to determine its relationship to violence against women. Those in the first half of the book go on to present historically oriented portraits of the polarizing impact of pornography in contemporary society. Those in the second half attempt to resolve some of these current divisions. A number of issues not developed in this collection remain of crucial importance for further study. As our discussion here of the "black magic" in *Angel Heart* and of the transsexuality in *Dressed to Kill* and *Crimes of Passion* intimates, especially significant would be an examination of the racial and nonwestern meanings of violent pornography as well as its impact on the images and realities of homosexual and transsexual men and women. In an effort to cover other relevant subjects not fully developed during the months that our seminar met, we have solicited essays for this volume on the 1986 Commission on Pornography (by Edna Einsiedel), on the status of "pornography as a legal text" (by Robin West), and on hard-core movies (by Linda Williams). Taken together with the papers contributed by members of the seminar, all of the articles provide a multidisciplinary outlook that is grounded in their authors' common commitment to feminist goals, although each primarily uses the methodology developed by one or two fields.

Interestingly, there are no distinctive methodological differences between the two sets of essays. Both sections of *For Adult Users Only* reflect recently developed approaches in the humanities, as well as in social-science theories and techniques, and to varying degrees all of the articles have been shaped by modes of investigation introduced into academic inquiry by earlier women's studies scholars. For example, Mary Jo Weaver's essay in the first section synthesizes feminist thinking about traditional Christianity and pornography, concluding provocatively (and yet somewhat hopefully) that, "while one must choose between eros and pornography . . . , one does not necessarily have to choose between Christianity and eros." Likewise, in the second section Linda Williams ends her essay on the evolution of content in pornographic films with the assertion that, despite increased violence in pornographic representations, their diversity contributes to the defeat of what she calls "a phallic economy." Edna Einsiedel also finds hope in the lessons learned to date about the relationship between social-science data and public policy as represented in the controversial 1986 *Report* by the Attorney General's Commission on Pornography. In addition, critical deconstruction and speculative reconstruction can be found in each section into which this collection is divided, particularly in the essays by Robin West and Richard Miller. Their two pieces reflect the most profound levels at which there is little agreement on the subject of violent pornography among adult users and adult opponents of such material as well as their legal representatives. At the same time, West and Miller offer strategies for greater intellectual understanding (if not juridical resolution) of this mass social phenomenon.

In general, the essays in the first section demonstrate that there have always been adult users, and each tries to explicate the origins and meanings of sexually explicit discourse for widely diverse authors and audiences, ranging from the classical Greeks to the Victorians, from medieval mystics to modern religious groups, from early twentieth-century artists in the *avant garde* to recent mass moviegoers, from social scientists attempting to influence public policy to feminists envisioning an ideology for the future. While it is possible to construct a time line or chronology from the first to the second section, readers will find only two overarching theses linking the thoughts in the two parts of this book: the subordination of women in most pornographic representations and the relatively recent transformation of pornography from an elite to a popular form of entertainment whose cultural ramifications we have difficulty understanding, regardless of the restricted or unrestricted availability of such material in various time periods, including our own. Thus, the first group of essays addresses the ways in which adult use of pornography has changed and transformed itself over time to fit the particular socioeconomic, aesthetic, religious, and legal needs of Western culture.

The second half of this collection contains suggestions about the problems posed by the first set of essays, solutions that are not entirely consistent with one another. This should come as no surprise, given the multiple emotional and intellectual responses that pornography evokes. Doris-Jean Burton's essay about public attitudes toward pornography clearly does not reflect the reactions of those trying to evolve the regulations and legal procedures discussed by David Pritchard and Lauren Robel, or the attitudes of the filmmakers analyzed by Linda Williams. In fact, opinions among community leaders and members of what is called the "legal elite" often vary from public sentiment when it comes to tolerating pornography. As of the mid-1980s, for example, 52 percent of the public in a *Newsweek* poll felt that magazines showing nudity should not be publicly displayed; 47 percent wanted magazines picturing adults having sexual relations banned; 73 percent wanted magazines depicting sexual violence censored; and over 60 percent wanted both movies and videocassettes featuring sexual violence banned. At the same time, leaders in local communities and in the legal profession generally disagreed with the censorious views held by the public respondents (many of whom were, no doubt, consumers of the material they wanted to restrict). Forty-eight percent of community leaders and 67 percent of lawyers polled thought that the majority of pornographic films (regardless of how distasteful their content) were "mostly harmless"; and only 35 percent of the community leaders and 20 percent of the lawyers questioned believed that there was any connection between violent sex crimes and pornography, compared to 53 percent of the general public.

Such wide divergences between public and elite opinion account for the difficulty of recommending widely acceptable legal policies to deal with contemporary forms of pornography. Most encouraging in terms of potential public approval and most practical, perhaps, of all the suggestions in this section are those contained in the article by Margaret Intons-Peterson and Beverly Roskos-Ewoldsen. Picking up on one of the social-science lessons noted by Einsiedel earlier, they deal with educational techniques for mitigating the effects of violent pornography on adolescents and adults. After reviewing the latest literature on violent pornography, this essay documents both large and small group methods for debriefing those who encounter the myriad forms of pornography in contemporary society. Both David Pritchard and Lauren Robel consider other constructive ways in which public policy can be informed by current legislation and litigation relating to such material; however, they argue against creating false expectations about what political bodies at the local, state, or federal levels can or should do to remedy the current dilemma that violent pornography poses for American society as long as there are such diverse mass and elite opinions on the topic.

While the second section of this collection does not end on a note of unanimity or with a single set of recommendations, then, the essays within it do attempt to move the debate beyond the various stalemates described in the first section. Providing diverse analyses and opinions from many different disciplinary points of view, the contributors to this collection are agreed that the topic of pornography should not be swept under the rug because of its obvious divisiveness. *For Adult Users Only* is literally meant to be "used" by all its readers, as they attempt to sort out their own thoughts and attitudes on this important end-of-the-century topic.

Those members of the IU seminar who composed their work in the context of discussions held at The Kinsey Institute are indebted to a number of vocal participants: June Reinisch, the director of The Kinsey Institute; Stephanie Sanders, assistant to the director of The Kinsey Institute; Douglas Freeman, the head of collections at The Kinsey Institute; David Rogers, the artist-in-residence at The Kinsey Institute; Christie Pope, a colleague in Women's Studies and Afro-American Studies; Elyce J. Rotella, a member of the Economics Department at Indiana; Kathy Davies, a graduate student in English; Kathleen McHugh, a graduate student who shared her video project on the effects of broaching the ethical repercussions of pornography in the undergraduate classroom; and Robin Sheets, whose willingness to commute from the University of Cincinnati helped enliven our discussions. A number of nonparticipants also provided important insights into our investigations, most especially Sandra M. Gilbert, Phyllis Klotman, Noretta Koertge, Marjorie Lightman, Jan Sorby, and Jayne Spencer. All of us, moreover, are grateful to Anya Royce, Indiana University dean of the faculties, for funding our endeavor.

Although we write in the hope that our work will contribute to shaping a society in which both Mabel Arthur and Ellen Marks could have lived out their lives, most of us recognize the long history not only of sexual violence but also of the inadequacy of those measures taken to curtail it. When, in the summer of 1913, an Indiana University freshman named Helen Murphy left a dance in the Student Building with one Thomas Stineburg, her efforts to struggle against his assaults left her face so severely bruised that, after crawling back to the building to get help from a roommate, she could not open her swollen eyes to identify the culprit brought to her by the police later that night. As the journalist Rose McIlveen has recently shown, the Pan-Hellenic Council of Young Women responded to the battering of Helen Murphy by deciding in October of that year to limit physical contact during social events by approving only those dances (the hesitation waltz and one-step, without the dip) in which the couple's arms were extended. The assumptions upon which the council based its judgment and the nature of its action would seem ludicrous, were it not for the image of Helen Murphy inching her way blindly across the campus on hands and knees.

Nor is it yet clear what is to be done. Participants in the IU seminar initially thought we would reach agreement on a specific set of recommendations for understanding past stalemates over pornography and for ending the current one. This proved an impossible task. However, we continue to believe that women's studies scholars, feminists, and concerned citizens must move beyond the current pornography debate—beyond the deadlocked civil libertarian and civil rights arguments—if Bloomington and the culture it inevitably reflects are ever to be made safe for women.

PART ONE

Past Debates and Present Stalemates

1

Why Is There No History of Pornography?

JOAN HOFF

A funny thing happened to pornography on its way through time. It has come so quickly out of the shadows of antiquity into the glare of today's headlines that we have anachronistically assumed that pornography's present prominence must somehow represent a continuation from the past without bothering to find out whether, indeed, its history is related to its contemporary manifestations. Little of a chronological nature has been written about pornography that attempts to explain how it passed from obscurity in ancient times into a contemporary mass phenomenon without acquiring either a history or a legal definition. Most existing "histories" of pornography or eroticism, such as those by Brusendorff and Henningsen (1961–63), Gillette (1965), and Lo Duca (1966), were written before the methodological and theoretical advances associated with the new social history that evolved at the end of the 1960s. Consequently, these older works consist primarily of unanalytical descriptions of sex practices (and punishments) and old sexual stereotypes about repression versus liberation based on random secular or religious examples from art and literature. New social-history techniques and the insightful Foucauldian view of sexuality as "an expression of complex dynamic power relations in society" do not yet prevail in more recent sexual histories.[1] As a result, there is no truly synthetic, interpretative history of pornography or eroticism.

The 1986 *Report* of the Attorney General's Commission on Pornography (AGCP), for example, concluded that "the history of pornography still remains to be written." This same report stated that "to understand the phenomenon of pornography, it is necessary to look at the history of the phenomenon itself . . . [but] commissioning independent historical research was far beyond our mandate, our budget, and our time constraints. . . ." The 1970 President's Commission on Obscenity and Pornography, which had a budget sixteen times larger

17

than the AGCP (after taking into account the impact of inflation on the difference between $500,000 and $2 million), also failed to authorize such a historical study (AGCP, 1986, 1:222–225, 233 [quotation]). Why? Simplistic and often contradictory answers abound because liberal assumptions dominate most legal and historical research in the United States. They range from the implicit notion that pornography is too trivial (or too dangerous) a subject, to the explicit assertion that existing descriptions of sexual practices and of attempts to regulate such practices and writings about them are sufficient.

Several basic reasons for the lack of a history of pornography belie these standard liberal rationalizations. Many other feminists have already detailed the androcentric and misogynistic qualities of liberalism present in the writings of John Locke and Jean-Jacques Rousseau (Okin, 1979; Clarke, 1979; Butler, 1978; Brennan and Pateman, 1979; Lahey, 1984–85; and Nicholson, 1983, 1986). I will build upon, but not reiterate, them in this attempt to explicate why there is no history of pornography. In particular, I will rely throughout this essay on the connections that feminist scholars have made between these traditional liberal theories and "contemporary attitudes toward freedom of speech and pornography" (Lahey, 1984–85, 657). As long as male freedoms under liberalism continue to be dependent upon the sexual and psychological inequality of women, and as long as the basic freedom of speech is still primarily a male monopoly, women will not experience full freedom of expression in American society, especially in matters involving their sexuality. Because pornography challenges the traditional assumptions of both legal liberalism and historical liberalism,[2] most American historians and lawyers have tended to bring their respective talents to bear primarily on critical appraisals of the variety of attempts to censor pornography; they have not sought to understand it as a historical and cultural phenomenon.

In trying to make this tentative history of pornography more than a documentation of censorship, I have been greatly influenced by the critical legal studies movement[3] and by two very different writers: Michel Foucault and Mikhail Bakhtin. I begin my reconstruction of the history of pornography with an examination of the word itself and of related terms such as erotic, grotesque, and obscene. This etymological approach best reflects the basic underlying attitudinal responses that accompanied what Foucault has called the "invention" of sexuality (Foucault, 1980b, 68–69).

Beginning in the seventeenth century, according to Foucault, a sense of sexuality slowly emerged in the Western World. Not until the nineteenth century, however, did women (and to a lesser degree children) become institutionalized repositories of sexuality in medical, psychological, and socioeconomic studies. As a result, sexuality (and adolescence) became problematized for society, and the word pornography (the word erotica did not yet exist) came into common usage. Most important, this final transformation of sex into sexuality through pseudoscientific discourses in the nineteenth century made it possible for "woman" to be viewed as the source of all repressed sex, waiting to be heterosexually liberated by male psychiatrists beginning with Freud (Foucault, 1980a, 115–31).

For Foucault, the modern concept of sexuality and the changing meanings of pornography are the intellectual children of the nineteenth century.[4] Sex, as biology, was separated from all other epiphenomena. The epiphenomenon of sex became the new sexuality divorced from public ritual and restricted to personal, private relationships. Consequently, "a uniform [male] truth about sex," *scientia sexualis,* finally emerged supreme in the nineteenth century (Foucault, 1980b, 69). As a result of elaborate discourses, a private concept of sexuality gained prominence, with its accompanying antonyms of decency and obscenity (AGCP, 1986, 240–48; Kendrick, 1987). Sexuality came to focus on behavior in an exclusively personal relationship based on shared standards. Psychiatrists, pedagogues, economists, and literary figures quickly constructed an entire bourgeois "machinery for producing true discourses" on sexuality, "situated at the point of intersection of a technique of confession and a scientific discursivity" (Foucault, 1980b, 68). By the end of the nineteenth century, this transformation of sex into sexuality was reinforced by the resurrection of the word pornography, more easily produced and distributed pornographic publications because of technological improvements, and increased prostitution, which, in turn, triggered private antipornographic movements in the name of moral purity and the sanctity of the family.

As of 1900, Victorian society had also created various "acceptable" disguised propornographic representations of women, often in the form of grotesque circus or theatrical performances (Fiedler, 1978). This is why I have found Bakhtin's ideas about the grotesque images in Rabelais's writings extremely useful for understanding the more bizarre representations of women in most pornography over time, but especially in the current violent variety. Bakhtin, like Foucault later, sensed that some fundamental shift in Western thinking began to take place in the seventeenth and eighteenth centuries that culminated in the nineteenth's affecting sexual practices, and the literary images of such practices. Bakhtin described this change from a literary perspective in his work on Rabelais.

> In the second half of the eighteenth century an essential change took place in literature, as well as in the field of aesthetic thought. . . . Unlike the medieval and Renaissance grotesque, which was directly related to folk culture and thus belonged to all people, the Romantic genre acquired a private "chamber" character. It became, as it were, an individual carnival, marked by a vivid sense of isolation. The carnival spirit was transposed into a subjective, idealistic philosophy. It ceased to be the concrete (one might say bodily) experience of the one, inexhaustible being, as it was in the Middle Ages and the Renaissance. (Bakhtin, 1984, 35)

Bakhtin convincingly argued that the degrading physical and symbolic aspects of the carnival motif in Rabelais nonetheless contained life-giving characteristics of Renaissance folk culture and folk humor. In fact, he demonstrated that renascent themes often prevailed in such examples as those showing "two bodies in one: the one giving birth and dying, the other conceived, generated, and born" (Bakhtin, 1984, 26). In contrast, the shift to modern forms of the grotesque has meant that the body in various stages of reproduction, disintegration, and death has become separated from reality—no longer serving any vital or comic functions. As Mary Russo has paraphrased Bakhtin: "The privatism and individualism of this later humor [made] it unhumorous or regenerative and lacking in communal hilarity" (M. Russo, 1986, 218). These initial (and continuing) shifts in physical and symbolic representations of the grotesque reflected not only changes in the political economies of Western nations but also evolving sexual relationships within families, from an emphasis on reproduction to personal intimacy to individual pleasure (D'Emilio and Freedman, 1988). At the same time, new literary and social views about sexuality (of which the grotesque was but one part), served to criticize, disguise, and ultimately to justify emerging economic, political, and family structures. In a word, male sexual discourses began to change between two and three hundred years ago in ways so subtle and yet far-reaching that we are just beginning to understand their origins and gender implications for women.

Subsequently, in the twentieth century, sexuality became a primary form of personal identity and "a means of controlling and administering social relations" (Myers, 1987, 14). Beginning with Freudian concepts, sex education and contraceptive movements developed that ostensibly liberated women from unwanted consequences of heterosexual relations while simultaneously making them more sexually available; then came propornographic movements spearheaded by writers and lawyers in the 1920s and 1930s, leading to the creation and extolment of a genre of writings and movies known as erotica. Finally, since World War II, degradation of women in both literature and films had become an increasingly common manifestation of commercialized sex, culminating in the present trend toward more and more violence against women in pornography. This "capitalist seizure of sexuality" (D'Emilio and Freedman, 1988, 360) represents the ultimate perversion of Bakhtin's concept and definition of the grotesque. Instead of remaining a rather esoteric and aberrant component of past sexual representations, the grotesque dominates contemporary forms of pornography. As the ultimate in the commercialized form of "eroticization of [male] dominance and [female] submission" (MacKinnon, 1987, 50), pornographic grotesqueness may well become the common denominator of sexuality by the end of this century.

Only after the invention of modern sexuality by male bourgeois culture in the last half of the nineteenth century was the term pornography resurrected from linguistic neglect. Walter Kendrick has presented an interesting etymological analysis of the word pornography in *The Secret Museum*. In this 1987 work, he begins by noting, as have many others, that the Greek *pornographos* meant writing about (or by) prostitutes (Hyde, 1964; Gillette, 1965; Cotham, 1973; Barry, 1979). Since this definition so little resembles modern usage, Kendrick points out that in 1909, when the *Oxford English Dictionary (OED)* finally reached the letter "P," the first meaning cited came from an 1857 medical dictionary. It referred to "public hygiene" descriptions of prostitutes or prostitution. The second *OED* definition sounded a little more like some modern ones: "descriptions of the life, manners, etc., of prostitutes and their patrons; hence, the expression or suggestion of obscene or unchaste subjects in literature or art." (Kendrick, 1987, 1–2).

It should be noted that this definition *did not distinguish between varieties of pornography. In particular, it made no distinction between pornography and erotica.*[5] Thus, the word pornography rose reluctantly from its ancient Grecian origins to the obscurity of medical dictionaries, archeological digs, and museum catalogues in the eighteenth and nineteenth centuries, to largely ignored English language dictionaries of the early twentieth century, where it was used to describe *all* explicit sexual depictions in art and literature, to its currently perplexing status as a mass phenomenon without a definition.[6] Only in the twentieth century was "erotica" coined as a euphemism for pornography.

Because no history of pornography exists to provide a causal model explaining its changing forms over time (Stone, 1985), there are myriad nonhistorical and nonlegal definitions of the term, particularly in the twentieth century. Before and after the invention of sexuality, definitions of pornography ranged widely and appear to be based on several different variables, such as class, gender, education, sexual experience, and historical period. Although no one generic or legal definition yet exists in Western culture, all describe intimate physical contact based on subject-object relations. This means that most pornographic representations of heterosexual (and homosexual) relations share one (usually unstated) commonality: namely, female sexual subordination, or the subordination of the person playing the "feminine" role in sexual relations (Kappeler, 1986; A. Dworkin, 1981, 1987; MacKinnon, 1984, 1987; and West, 1987).

Not surprisingly, few women attempted to define either pornography or erotica before the 1960s. Writing in 1929, Virginia Woolf dispassionately tried to distinguish between two types of indecent books, using criteria that actually presaged the "average citizen" or community standards test that the Supreme Court finally endorsed in the 1970s.

> There are books written, published and sold with the object of causing pleasure or corruption by means of their indecency. . . . There are others whose indecency is not the object of the book but incidental to some other purpose—scientific, social, aesthetic, on the writer's part. The police magistrate's power should be definitely limited to the suppression of books which are sold as pornography to people who seek out and enjoy pornography. The others should be left alone. Any man or woman of average intelligence and culture knows the difference between the two kinds of books and has no difficulty in distinguishing one from the other. (Kendrick, 1987, 195)

Early male definitions of pornography, stemming from the late nineteenth through the first half of the twentieth century, often conveyed a sexist indifference or a laissez-faire attitude. In 1882 Oscar Wilde lectured a New York audience that there was no such thing as immoral or moral writing; only things that were "well written or badly written" (Seldes, 1985, 450). Or, as Somerset Maugham put it: "Pornography rather than brevity is the soul of wit" (*Gentlemen in Parlour,* 1930, xii). Henry Miller, of course, blithely wrote off the entire subject, saying that "the nature of the meaning of pornography is almost as difficult as talking about God" (Leach, 1975, 15–16). Only slightly less sexist and self-interested definitions have come from archivists, historians, and social scientists. "Pornography must be important, or it would not be so prevalent," according to librarian Ervin Gaines. "It has some meaning in our lives that we do not understand." For historian Richard Randall, it is "the most familiar and the most elusive of concepts in law and social life" (Leach, 1975, 16).

The same year that Virginia Woolf calmly divided "indecency into two classes," D. H. Lawrence, in his essay "Pornography and Obscenity," vehemently denied that either word could be defined. What is pornography to one man [*sic*] is the laughter of genius to another," he asserted. "The same with the word obscene: nobody knows what it means." Simultaneously, he ranted against the "mob-habit" of "common individuals" preventing artists like himself from exploring sexual subjects. Convinced that his writing was neither pornographic nor obscene, he nonetheless said: "But even I would censor genuine pornography, rigorously. It would not be very difficult. . . . genuine pornography is almost always underworld, it doesn't come into the open. . . . you can recognize it by the insult it offers, invariably, to sex." Yet Lawrence also insisted that "if a woman hasn't got a tiny streak of harlot in her, she's a dry stick as a rule," and called all those "ordinary, vulgar people" who were not as sexually enlightened as himself "perverts" (*This Quarter,* 1929, 17, 21, 22, 24, 25).

At the heart of Lawrence's egoistic discussion of pornography and that of so many other male writers and jurists from the 1930s down to the present is that there was "dirt," that is, "ugly, squalid dirty sex" as determined by "mob-reaction," and then there was "art." It is the idea that while "all pornography is obscene, not all that is obscene is pornography" (*This Quarter,* 1929, 21, 25; Cotham, 1973, 43). Male arrogance on the subject of pornography with respect to its meaning for, and impact on, women has been epitomized by two kindly old gentlemen in the last twenty years. Futile but determined attempts have been made, for example, to give Justice Potter Stewart legal and intellectual credit for saying in *Jacobellis v. Ohio,* 378 U.S. 184, 197 (1964):

> I have reached the conclusion . . . that under the First and Fourteenth Amendments criminal laws in this area are constitutionally limited to hard-core pornography. I shall not today attempt further to define the kinds of material I understand to be embraced within that shorthand description; and perhaps I could never succeed in intelligently doing so. *But I know it when I see it,* and the motion picture involved in this case is not that. (*AGCP,* 1986, 1:259, emphasis added)

"As a father and grandfather," Senator Barry Goldwater noted a decade later in a less quoted, but no less inane, non sequitur, "I know, by golly, what is obscene and what isn't" (Leach, 1975, 15). Another prevalent notion in most male definitions of pornography between the 1920s and 1960s was the belief that "art [meaning erotica] soothes and pornography excites" (Cotham, 1973, 43). In the last twenty years the conflation of sex with violence in most hard and much soft pornography has eliminated the soothing qualities from even those films and novels praised for their artistic or redeeming social value.

What do these changing definitions of pornography mean? First, the early English definition of pornography in the nineteenth century did not make the modern distinction between good and bad, or hard and soft pornography. *All literature and art treating sexually explicit subjects were simply called pornography.* Thus, the current insistence that erotic and pornographic depictions are qualitatively different is a recent and arbitrary linquistic convention with little etymological or historical validity. Second, the different definitions of pornography in this century are directly related to evolving definitions of erotica.[7] In other words, the invention of sexuality is "behind" all past and present debates over definitions of pornography and erotica in the United States.

This definitional confusion, especially the latest one over the meaning of grotesque representations of female mutilation, represents a convoluted historical and cultural evolution that has yet to be untangled. While I agree with Beatrice Faust that the issue of pornography should not be reduced to a passionless semiotic exercise (Faust, 1981), it is helpful to consider recent semiotic extensions of Bakhtin's concept of the grotesque. Mary Russo, for example, has semiotically analyzed why it is considered so shameful for a woman to make "a spectacle out of herself" (Russo, 1986, 213). She has suggested that the cultural price one pays for being a woman in Western society is to suffer from a marginality that at times can be overcome only through gender masquerading or other carnivalesque behavior that would otherwise be considered unacceptable. If the human body is viewed as a symbolic sign or microcosmic system representing the prototype of larger socioeconomic and political units, then the "female body as grotesque" is a threat to patriarchy when pregnant, aging, aggressive, or ugly (but not when being hacked into pieces or otherwise mutilated in violent pornography). There are a number of historical examples of the "unruly or carnivalesque woman" inciting riots and other unacceptable behavior (Russo, 1986, 214, 216; Davis, 1965). More often, however, men disguised as women (or as American Indians, in the case of the Boston Tea Party) used the ruse of temporary transvestism to demonstrate or riot for their own causes.

Some of the earliest American grotesque examples of this type of "shameless woman" can be found in the popular David Crockett narratives. These writings about violence and sex were designed to reassure male writers and readers in the face of the insecurity generated during the period in U.S. history known as the Age of Jackson. Carroll Smith-Rosenberg has analyzed the mythical and symbolic significance of various Davy Crockett almanacs published from the 1830s through the 1850s by arguing that "the physical body frequently serves as a symbol for the body politic." By expanding Foucault's argument and distinguishing even more rigorously than he does between the author and the audience in sexual discourse, Smith-Rosenberg has discovered, for example, that the most cannibalistic, scatological, masturbatory, racist, sexist, and violent episodes of the Crockett comic almanacs were primarily published in eastern, urban cities for consumption in the West. At the same time, however, male moral reformers on the East Coast were writing plays and lectures that preached the virtues of health reform, temperate drinking and sex habits, and, for young men and women, the glories of submitting to patriarchal domination.

Violence permeates all of the sexual imagery in the Crockett narratives, according to Smith-Rosenberg, particularly the scenes describing the "thinly veiled male homosexuality." Like the perennial Peter Pan, at one level Crockett represented the living nightmare of the writers who were part of the emerging American bourgeois: the sexually irresponsible male adolescent as male adult. The glorification of violence and male individualism took many forms in these Crockett narratives, including female representations that presaged pornographic cartoons and comic books. Women, for example, were often not given names and were grotesquely portrayed in comic fashion as the opposite of eastern gentility, with its outward show of prudishness. "Ugly, boisterous, and autono-mous," yet sexually active, they "bundled" with frontiersmen like Crockett on a moment's notice. They were, in essence, an early pornographic fantasy version of uninhibited western women, created by the same class of men who were imposing the "rigid proprieties" of the "Cult of True Womanhood" on eastern women. In particular, their clothing ridiculed, through bad imitation, the bourgeois woman's dress and manners. The wife of one character "wore a bearskin petticoat, an alligator's hide for an overcoat, an eagle's nest for a hat with a wild cat's tail for a feather . . . [and] sucked . . . rattlesnake's eggs" to improve her breath (Smith-Rosenberg, 1985, 106–108).

From the Middle Ages to the Age of Jackson, the carnival and the grotesque came to represent fewer positive forms of antisocial grotesque behavior for women. According to Bakhtin, the Romantics failed to revive an authentic version of the grotesque by the end of the nineteenth century, and several spin-offs evolved into feeble efforts to counter the rigid and sterile aspects of the new sexuality. Hysterical and mad women, after all, became the focus of much early psychoanalysis, complete with photographs or drawings of such women in ugly, contorted poses. These portrayals are sometimes remarkably similar to the histrionic antics of actresses in the legitimate theaters, women in burlesque shows (precursors of contemporary strip-tease acts), and, of course, circus performers. Like Davy Crockett's women, such females could make public spectacles of themselves with impunity (unlike the hysterical nineteenth-century housewife, or today's shopping-bag ladies) because it was entertainment "ar-ranged by and for the male viewer" (Brusendorff and Henningsen, 1983; M. Russo, 1986). Overacting, even gender cross-dressing, faked or real nymphoma-nia, garish prostitute costumes—all were not only tolerated but actually encour-aged by Victorian society—because they represented grotesque images of women created and controlled by men. The same can be said of the booming business in prostitution at the end of the century and, to a lesser degree, perhaps, about the female freaks in the sideshows that accompanied the traveling circuses and carnivals (D'Emilio and Freedman, 1988; Fiedler, 1978).

In general, the Victorians proved particularly adept at creating acceptable grotesque disguises or masks for pornographic representations of women. Leslie Fiedler, for example, has pointed out that "the sense of the pornographic [was] implicit in all Freak shows," so popular at the turn of the century. What he has called the "Eros of Ugliness" prevailed in the form of bearded ladies, fat women (and anorexic men), and other varieties of malformed living and dead human specimens. In our craze for physical perfection and sanitation, we tend to forget that "all Freaks [were once] perceived to one degree or another as erotic" (Fiedler, 1978, 18, 137). Instead, we have little trouble today identifying violence as erotic. With the demise of the popularity of freaks among heads of state, as well as among the population at large in Western nations between the two World Wars, died the last vestiges of the futile Romantic revival of "Renais-sance definitions of the human and of standards of normality" (Fiedler, 1978, 329). Moreover, the "mask" of the sideshow, not unlike film and videocassettes, was as much a participatory as a pictorial experience. All such masks contain a mesmerizing, addictive quality, which accounts, in part, for their attraction, influence, and social acceptability.

In this century acceptable forms of the grotesque have increasingly reflected only the most negative residue of the Victorian variety, without any of its sadly comic, sympathetic portrayals of both female and male freaks with their an-omalous sexuality. From the bound breasts and compulsory heterosexuality of the 1920s flappers, to the muscularly sexy "Rosie the Riveters" of the Second World War, or today's anorexic and bizarrely dressed high-fashion models—all have represented acceptable grostesque images of women—as have, of course, prostitutes through the ages. In contrast, unacceptable grotesque images that have been feared and ridiculed by American men range from the unmarried woman reformer of the late nineteenth and early twentieth centuries, to the frigid, 1950s housewife suffering from the feminine mystique, to the sexually liberated female flower child or bra-burning civil rights and antiwar demonstrator of the 1960s, and finally, the lesbian separatists. As forms of the grotesque unacceptable to the male hierarchy, these women were caricatured in the past as ugly, often hysterical, misshapen misfits, and more recently as ugly little old ladies in tennis shoes or ugly, protesting women in combat fatigues. Today, the most unacceptable grotesque women are the uncontrollable, unruly, "ugly" radical feminists because of their refusal to accept "man-made" definitions about female sexuality and women's appropriate place or role in society (Myers, 1987).

What better way to try to contain the *ugliest* and most threatening faction within the Second Women's Movement (to say nothing of the moderates) than to begin to dismember, maim, and kill *beautiful* women in pornographic novels, magazines, films, and videocassettes? If women will not accept various con-tradictory male definitions of the feminine as hysterical, nymphomaniacal, dependent, pain-loving, or seductively passive, then use physical or psychological media violence against the best and the brightest among them. Grotesque fantasies have often been used for symbolic and political purposes (Fiedler, 1978). Therefore, the subliminal message of the sexual violence so characteristic of much contemporary pornography is clearly one of attempting to terrorize women into either compliance, silence—or both. "With lovers like [these] men," asks Susanne Kappeler, "who needs torturers?" (Kappeler, 1986, 214; MacKinnon, 1987; A. Dworkin, 1981, 1987).

The medium is, indeed, the message, and even in its mildest forms the message is unmistakable. "A feminine woman defines herself almost exclusively by her relationship to man, and is sculpted accordingly," proclaimed a columnist in a 1981 issue of *The American Spectator*. "A woman's trust consolidates the man's dominance. Without it, the male tends to lose his masculinity. Ever since women decided not to trust men," the writer continued equally illogically, "there has been a marked increase in pederasty." And why have modern women begun to distrust men, you might ask? Because "a few ugly women who could not get men to like them decided to change something that is . . . unchangeable . . . man and woman." This article concluded by saying that "America's liberated women are the ugliest" and then proceeded to list some of the most moderate reformist leaders of the Second Women's Movement in order of their ugliness (Theodoracopulos, 1981). If there is to be a renascent grotesque in the Bakhtinian sense of the word, it will have to come from women, as Kathy Myers has argued (Myers, 1987). But the odds are not good.

Violent pornographic representations of women in the mass media have become the acceptable grotesque of the last quarter of the twentieth century. They are supported by gay sadomasochists and those suffering from a terminal case of legal and historical liberalism—often in the name of feminism. "S/M eroticism. . . . is the quintessence of nonreproductive sex," according to Pat Califia. "An S/M scene can be played out using the personae of . . . Nazi and Jew, white and Black, straight man and queer, parent and child, priest and penitent, teacher and student. . . . However," she adds, "no symbol has a single meaning. Its meaning is derived from the context in which it is used" (Califia, 1981, 32). This kind of relativism prevails in defense of sexual violence in the contemporary grotesque (Griffin in Lederer, 1980; Myers, 1987; A. Russo, 1987). Violent sex has no meaning at all, or it can mean anything. Such relativism on the part of sadomasochists and liberal legal feminists is compounded by false consciousness about the emancipating, antisocial aspects of sexual diversity and a misunderstanding about the meaning of the erratic nature of law enforcement against all forms of pornography over time.

Historically, we know, for example, that despite state and religious proscriptions, the authority of both institutions tolerated a wide range of sexually explicit representations from antiquity up to the nineteenth century. In colonial America there were some statutes that criminalized immorality, blasphemy, and heretical actions associated with them, but they did not primarily focus on materials dealing with sex. This remained true during the first decades of the new republic after the Constitution of 1787 officially separated church and state, because "pure sexual explicitness, while often condemned, was not . . . taken to be a matter of governmental concern" (AGCP, 1986, 242). Beginning in the nineteenth century private organizations and individuals supporting social concepts about decency and obscenity dominated attempts to regulate sexually explicit material (D'Emilio and Freedman, 1988). Before then protection of state authority and religious values formed the basis for such erratic regulation of immoral, but not usually sex-oriented, material as existed.

In the course of the last century certain individuals such as Anthony Comstock decided to ban all sexually explicit materials on grounds unrelated to state security or religious integrity. Instead, Comstock and others argued that sexually explicit materials were lewd, indecent, and obscene. Even after the passage of the federal "Comstock" law in 1873 and similar state statutes, courts quickly became confused over what obscenity meant, so enforcement remained highly idiosyncratic and only as effective as fanatics like Comstock could make it (AGCP, 1986, 233–44). During the progressive reform period of the early twentieth century, Margaret Sanger ran afoul of the Comstock Law in her attempt to disperse birth-control information to private individuals. These campaigns have actually strengthened, rather than weakened, the sexualization of society because they have encouraged the capitalist and patriarchal principles upon which nineteenth-century sexuality was based (D'Emilio and Freedman, 1988). Such campaigns have futilely attempted to solve a sexual societal problem through behavior modification of *individuals*—not through structural or collective attitudinal change. Moreover, these early sex-reform crusades in the United States—both for and against obscene materials—also failed to curb the simultaneous development of "acceptable" public forms of pornography under the guise of nineteenth-century versions of the grotesque that accompanied the increase in pornographic representations at private levels of society (Fiedler, 1978).

Then gradually during this century, such individual crusades gave way as the legal system and government focused on sexually explicit material much more systematically than ever before. But this time, it was not at the instigation of secular or religious zealots. Instead, the current government and juridicial interest in obscene materials originated with the free expression of concerns of the "lost generation" of post–World War I writers and liberal lawyers. Beginning in the 1920s and 1930s, U.S. intellectuals began to make highly subjective distinctions between erotica and pornography that had no historical or etymological rationale. They automatically assigned a reputable (and primarily heterosexual) past to the former, but not to the latter. Although this attempt to distinguish between the two is at most an arbitrary and artificial product of three generations of writers, literary and theater critics, and journalists, it has so captured the imagination of the liberal establishment that its relatively recent arbitrary and self-interested origins have been obscured.

These private literary definitions, having little to do with moral purity or sex education, were soon thrust into the public arena of the courts, as all literature became more professionalized and academicized between the two World Wars.

From the time that intellectuals successfully separated pornography from erotica, the statutory definition of obscenity narrowed, and enforcement of laws regulating obscene materials diminished (Kendrick, 1987). Two common themes linked opinions of the literary giants and academic experts of these decades to the nineteenth-century moral reform movements and legislation: one was the acceptance of objectification, and hence subordination, of women in most sexually explicit material (Capland, 1987; Kappeler, 1986), and the other was the continuing focus of the courts on obscenity, not pornography per se. (Some feminists also now maintain that "true" erotica consists of "sexually explicit materials premised on equality," and thus advocate the creation of a feminist erotica [Klausner, 1984–85, 734 (quotation); and Myers, 1987]. Unfortunately, all the examples of this type of material available in contemporary American society could fit on the head of a pin.)[8]

From the 1920s to the mid-1970s, most descriptions of sexually explicit material distinguished pornographic fantasy from erotic realism, thus reifying their own arbitrary distinction by successfully insisting that the latter contained "acceptable" violence toward, and degradation of, women. This standard distinction between the "fantastic" characteristics of pornography, as opposed to the "realistic" aspects of erotica, was quickly picked up and capitalized upon by pornographers as a way to maximize sales. The distinction was based on how physically bruised or bloody women emerged from batterings, or if they actually became pregnant as the result of rape. It was claimed by aficionados of sexually explicit materials that pornographic fantasies never left marks or ruined the lives of individual women through unwanted pregnancies or permanent bodily disabilities, while erotically realistic representations made the reader or viewer only too painfully aware of the physical and psychological damage done (Cotham, 1973). Thus, it was argued that erotica was capable of teaching lessons and stimulating discussions about sexuality. Unlike pornography, its main purpose or function was not simply sexual arousal. If it is true, as Ralph Ginsberg once remarked, that "Every nation gets the pornography it deserves" (Gillette, 1965), then the current brand of violent sexually explicit material in the United States represents the ultimate in liberal *realistic fantasy*.

What I am suggesting is that if this concept of realistic fantasy were employed along with Foucault's hypothesis about power and sexuality, and Bakhtin's literary theory about the grotesque, to write a history of the legal and cultural functions of pornography, it would show that there has been an *inverse relationship between the actual existence of daily physical violence and degradation in the daily lives of women and men since the Middle Ages and the amount of sexual violence and degradation in contemporary pornography*. As life has become ostensibly more humane, individualistic, democratic, and physically pleasant, pornography has become more dehumanized and depersonalized. It represents gratuitous violence that has no personal reality base for the vast majority of Americans who vicariously experience it every day through movies, television, and videocassettes. Although some proporn advocates argue that we are becoming inured or indifferent to such sexual violence (Ellis et al., 1986;

Soble, 1986), the latest psychological studies cited by the 1986 *Meese Report* indicate that movies and television have become more and more violent to satisfy heightened demand.

Under these conditions of mass distribution, *pornography cannot be passed off as offensive, but ineffectual, "bad art" imitating life;* it has become an attitudinally addictive way of life for millions of Americans. No longer the self-indulgent novels and art of the very rich, or the pool-hall and barber-shop escapist paperbacks of the poor, it is now an international business devoted to creating and distributing sexual fantasies that negatively affect attitudes toward women across all class lines. As the misogynist opiate of the last quarter of the twentieth century, pornography serves so many public and private purposes that despite numerous laws, including but not limited to those specifically dealing with obscenity, it has never been systematically prosecuted at any level. Yet pornographic fare in film and video cassettes no longer consists primarily of the silly and repetitious sex vignettes between ordinary and not so ordinary looking bodies of the early "stag" films. Nor is it any longer an extension of "girly" vaudeville shows. It is an $8 billion industry that represents in living color brutally detailed scenes that more often than not combine sex and violence into realistic fantasy.

During the late 1960s and early 1970s, the cultural and legal climate was such that pornographic fantasy and erotic realism merged with a vengeance in literature and films into what I call "pornrotica," happily escaping both definition and prosecution under obscenity laws. Pornrotica is *any representation of persons that sexually objectifies them and is accompanied by actual or implied violence in ways designed to encourage readers or viewers to assume that such sexual subordination of women (and children or men) is acceptable behavior or an innocuous form of sex education.* I prefer this terminology and definition because they more accurately convey the historical blurring or merging of the meanings of erotica and pornography rather than the conventional wisdom about the differences between them.[9] It is also essential in the 1980s that any definition of pornrotica recognize the close association in mass-distributed movies and videocassettes between sex and violence—most of which is directed *against* women *by* men.

At almost exactly the same time, that is, beginning in the 1970s, analytical and descriptive literature on pornography fundamentally changed. Up to then it consisted of writings by mostly liberal males exulting over the greater freedom of expression that the courts had endorsed. Their statements extolled the good that would redound to society from more sexually explicit material; there was little or no mention of gender distinctions. Before 1965, male-oriented depictions of sex were the norm of pornography, and early studies logically noted that women were not stimulated by it as much as men. Its male orientation was rationalized because of the presumed catharsis it offered to men, thus protecting women and children and marriage from perversions and attack (Leach, 1975; Hughes, 1970; Diamond, Russell, Bart, and Jozsa in Lederer, 1980; Gillette, 1965; Michelson, 1971; Thompson 1979; Brusendorff and Henningsen, 1983). Figures from Denmark and other Scandinavian countries purporting to support this position have since been proven wrong, but this is essentially the position of the 1970 President's Commission on Obscenity, whose recommendations both the Democratic Congress and Nixon condemned (Diamond in Lederer, 1980; Klausner, 1984–85; Grossman, 1985; *New York Times*, July 30, 1986, A22). Thus, until the late 1970s, authors of books about sex practices and literary examples of erotica seemed content with this plethora of meanings, their implicit acceptance of male domination in sexual relations, and the cathartic rationale for pornography.

As if being an orphan of history and an abandoned child of literature were not enough, pornography has been assigned bastard status as well by lawyers who have, since the 1960s, claimed that the term cannot be legally defined. By the late 1970s most lawyers had also accepted the almost unenforceable tripartite definition of what constitutes obscene material, stemming from the 1957 and subsequent 1973 Supreme Court decisions in *Roth v. United States* and *Miller v. California* (now further complicated by the 1987 decision in *Pope v. Illinois).*[10] Neither sexologists nor lawyers seriously attempted to come up with a historically comprehensive or accurate definition of pornography because, among other things, they were not concerned about gender as a category of analysis.

Without gender analysis, no analysis or definition of pornography will expose its basic sexism or its function as an ideological representation of patriarchy and an exercise in the "practice of power and powerlessness" (MacKinnon, 1985, 21). Therefore, pornrotica can no longer be arrogantly neglected by liberals or inadequately regulated by conservatives prosecuting under statutes and legal interpretations about proof, discovery, and immunity meant to apply in criminal obscenity cases. Clearly, a new legal and cultural analysis of pornography that accurately reflects its etymology and history as a social phenomenon is essential.[11]

Although obscenity and pornography are two quite different concepts, they, along with the word "erotica," are often used interchangeably by scholars and laymen alike.[12] The word obscene is derived from the Greek for "filth." Thus, the term (along with obscenity laws) continues to suggest that "sex is dirty" and that sexual materials are "behind-the-counter" items. Original anti-obscenity statutes were meant to cover sexually explicit material when it promoted "excessive" arousal or excitement (traditionally in males) through candid portrayals of nudity and illegal or unnatural acts. Not only does pornography have a very different etymological origin from obscenity, but its prurient appeal is not based exclusively on graphic depictions of sexual organs or sexual acts that stimulate men. Such representations reflect lingering puritanical and Victorian tenets about sex and women that were exacerbated by the invention of sexuality in the nineteenth century, with all of its misogynist and pseudoscientific overtones.

The current legal definition of obscenity not only reveals increasingly outmoded male views about sexuality and consensual aspects of sex but also makes the determination of what is obscene rest on subjective literary and/or community judgments that cannot be effectively applied and have little relevance for evaluating or regulating what I am calling sexually violent pornrotica. In this sense, the antipornography ordinances proposed by such feminists as Andrea Dworkin and Catharine MacKinnon are more realistic than the moral and literary definitions of obscenity that have been handed down in the *Roth, Miller,* and *Pope* decisions based on vague male notions about immorality, prurient interest, and patent offensiveness (Klausner, 1984–85; Elmer, 1987–88).

Since the Second World War, pornrotica has obtained an unofficial sanction within the legal system as one of the forms of protected speech under the First Amendment, and an unofficial position as one of the most powerful legal texts of contemporary patriarchy, a topic that Robin West's chapter in this collection discusses in detail. At the moment, the American Civil Liberties Union (ACLU) insists that a legal definition of pornography would be an exercise in both futility and folly, given the current conservative climate in the United States. The ACLU places itself in direct opposition to those feminists who argue that the violent and misogynistic nature of modern pornography makes it a major cause of continued sex discrimination and battering of women (and children). While pornrotica has become a litmus test of free expression for liberals, radical feminists claim that it is a form of sex inequality and that its very existence harms women by maintaining a patriarchal status quo and by projecting a subordinate and degrading view of women that often equates violence with virility for men and pain with pleasure for women.[13]

The essential male definition of obscenity is now meaningless for regulating the current flood of sexually violent pornography on the market and for figuring out whether this kind of material harms women in contemporary American society. In fact, "many sexually explicit materials that current law would classify as obscene would not be prohibited by anti-pornography laws," according to the *Harvard Law Review,* "because such materials do not present a false and damaging image of women" (p. 474). In other words, what is obscene to the radical right is not pornographic to the radical left (MacKinnon, 1987, 150). Even the much-maligned Meese Commission's report stated that most nonviolent and nondegrading obscene material is probably not very harmful to women or society but noted that this category of sexually explicit material "is in fact quite small" compared to what is currently available (AGCP, 1986, 277–351, 355 [quotation]). Moreover, past and present legally defined obscenities have always carried with them the connotation that they somehow offended or were outside the moral boundaries or propriety of society (Klausner, 1984–85).

The same cannot be said of mass-distributed forms of pornography. They are right smack in the middle of the most respected communities—in supermarkets, bookstores, movie theaters, malls, and video rental outlets. There is little "outsidedness" about the bulk of the mainstream material now flooding the country. Pornrotica is no longer "just a private secret abuse," as Catharine MacKinnon has noted. "Now pornography is publicly celebrated. . . . sexual terrorism has become democratized [and]. . . . available [even] to its victims for scrutiny and analysis . . ." (MacKinnon, 1987, 151.) So both in quantity and quality there is a difference in kind rather than simply in degree between past obscene materials and contemporary pornographic ones, which the courts and legal profession have yet to address for apparently one basic reason: the First Amendment.

The most controversial of all the legal (as opposed to etymological and historical) debates over pornrotica at the present time is whether the proposed definition of pornography in the antipornography ordinances, discussed below by Lauren Robel, is constitutional given First Amendment free speech guarantees. But the adjudication of antipornography ordinances has not removed the issue from the confining boundaries of legal liberalism and traditional discourses about sexuality. Instead, it has resulted in a typical legal stalemate over conflicting civil liberties on the question of whether pornography is advocacy (free speech under the First Amendment) or action (a violation of women's civil rights).[14] While this disagreement between feminists and civil libertarians is most dramatic, it is the least solvable from a juridical point of view, because the division between speech and conduct is not only "strained and artificial" but also "wholly unresponsive to the very problem of harm against women" that these antipornography ordinances address (Klausner, 1984–85, 753 [quotations]; Tribe, 1978; West, 1987; Elmer, 1987–88).

One aspect of the current legal disagreement over conflicting civil liberties can be understood only in light of the Foucauldian assertion that the promotion of sexually explicit materials serves the interests of the patriarchal state because it is a vehicle for preserving, not protesting, the status quo. In other words, the deadlocked debate is both more complex and more significant than it sometimes appears on the surface. The present juridical stalemate has erroneously placed radical feminists on the side of fundamentalists in advocating the banning of such material through antipornography ordinances. At the same time, many reformist and socialist feminists appear to have allied themselves with the purveyors of pornrotica, arguing that such material is protected by the First Amendment and that, in addition, consenting adults have the sexual right to engage in all intimate sadomasochistic acts short of murder (Soble, 1986; A. Russo, 1987).

The dichotomous breakdown of these four groups is misleading for a variety of reasons, the most important being that only one of the four is attempting to "desexualize" society by banning or severely regulating the production and distribution of pornography, namely, the radical feminists. The other three groups—members of the radical right, the producers and distributors of pornrotica, and the reformist feminists—are all advocating a "resexualizing" of society through the promotion of pornography behind the banner of the First Amendment and sexual rights based on subjective and increasingly obsolete legal definitions of obscenity. They are, in a word, trying to reinforce, albeit with some minor modifications, the idea that basically male-dominated views about sexuality should continue to determine private identity. This is particularly true of heterosexual and homosexual sadomasochists, for whom the First Amendment is very personal, allowing them physically to harm or be harmed by "consenting adults." Since resexualizing represents nothing more or less than an extension of the nineteenth-century construct of sexuality, it cannot liberate women or men. Only desexualization can do that. As Michel Foucault pointed out over twenty years ago,[15] hope for desexualizing society lay with the Second Women's Movement because feminist deconstructive methodology held out the best possibility for analyzing sexuality outside the usual discourses conducted within the traditional masculine boundaries (Martin, 1982).

For all of these reasons, I can no longer accept the standard liberal defense of contemporary pornrotica in the name of freedom of expression, which does not consider its potential harm to women. Despite all the claims of the proponents of the liberal erotization of modern society (D'Emilio and Freedman, 1988), most U.S. women continue to operate from a cultural and institutional base of inequality when it comes to matters of "fully" consensual sex and continue to be exploited and silenced through a civil libertarian defense of pornography as protected speech (West, 1987). Therefore, I must sadly concur with Kathleen Lahey that, "in the form of violent pornography, . . . the liberal ideal has achieved a moment of perfection" (Lahey, 1984–85, 661). Therefore, I do not agree with the assertions of the Feminist Anti-Censorship Taskforce that women will be sexually liberated by more pornrotica. In terms of the difference between resexualizing or desexualizing society, the exact opposite is true.

FACT's pornographic publication *Caught Looking* is no better or worse than the liberal male standards of individuality and sexuality that it imitates so well. Most important, it does not encourage the type of honest dialogue that is necessary about the "quality of women's internal lives" (West, 1987, 144). The book's random assortment of "genital engagements" from homosexual, heterosexual, and autoerotic perspectives is really a pictorial throwback to the "money shots" of early pornographic films described below by Linda Williams. The articles interspersed among the genitalia contain false equality arguments (i.e., sexual liberation of women through more pornography), ignoring, as do the graphics, the overwhelming amount of pornographic materials that are now designed to keep women in their "proper places" through violent object lessons.

As long as this slick publication is touted as an example of "feminist" pornography, what chance do women have of breaking the barrier of historical and legal indifference to the negative and potentially harmful aspects of contemporary pornrotica? What are their chances of creating and asserting a renascent female grotesque (or erotica) that will not further reinforce the connection between sex and violence? (West, 1987; Myers, 1987). The likelihood of doing either is not promising, for two reasons. First, since the 1970s, as a result of modern distribution techniques, several generations of young women and men have internalized models for pornrotica that are dominated by male violence against females. Consequently, there is little demand for any other kind of pornography, and demand (or awareness) drives the industry. Second, because women, in particular, have internalized male versions of their sexuality for so long, it is difficult for them even to begin to articulate the nature of their suffering from pornography, let alone how their perceptions of their own sexuality differ from male proscriptions about it.

The silencing aspects of pornography itself, analyzed below by Richard Miller, simply reinforce women's societally and legally imposed silence about the very nature of their pain and pleasure in life. Neither type of silence is automatically alleviated by speaking out against male pornography or by producing "feminist" pornography, because "women have not learned to speak the truth," especially about when they do and do not "consent" to or enjoy sexual acts. "It is now commonplace," according to Robin West, "that women 'don't feel at home' with male language—but this is no wonder, when what we've mainly learned to do with it is lie . . . about the quality of our internal lives" (West, 1987, 144; MacKinnon, 1987).

At best, *Caught Looking* represents the type of male-identified feminism that further silences the suffering of women on this issue because it stigmatizes all those who do speak out against pornrotica as sexually inhibited. It is also typical of the dangerously shallow and uncritical liberal response to the increase in actual violence against women and children in contemporary society, and to the increasing association between violence and sex in the mass media (A. Russo, 1987; *Humanities in Society,* 1984; Hollyday, 1984; and Soley, 1984). The "more-is-better" approach of FACT and the ACLU to the mass phenomenon that pornrotica has become should be viewed as a form of hysterical liberalism stemming from the *fear of not being liberal in a conservative era.*

"More is better" also represents an exceedingly elitist position. Statistics indicate that "legal leaders" (and *both* conservative and liberal Supreme Court Justices) are far "ahead" of mass opinion and more influential than average citizens in determining public policy on this highly controversial sexual issue (Grossman, 1985). Yet on almost all other social problems, the legal profession traditionally follows rather than leads public opinion. Why this discrepancy regarding pornrotica? Privileged male views that cut across political and class lines on sexuality offer the best explanation for the fact that conservative and liberal men (and their male-oriented female supporters) seem so comfortable with one another in hiding behind an ahistorical interpretation of the First Amendment to prevent serious consideration of the relationship in our time between degradation, violence, sex, and technology. Understanding and resolving the significance of the interconnectedness of these issues for the quality of American female life for the remainder of this century will not be achieved by further legal debates among such liberals or conservatives within the legal profession. As long as both sides continue to ignore the sexist history and discriminatory function of pornography, conservatives will continue to pay lip service to regulating it and liberals will continue to claim that *more* pornrotica is the answer to the problems created *by* pornrotica. (If this were true, then sex crimes in the United States should have decreased since the 1970s) (Grossman, 1985; Dworkin, 1987; Klausner, 1984–85; and Diamond, 1980).

Approximately one hundred years after the original invention of sexuality, with all its hypocritical and repressive elements, the most conservative and most liberal factions in U.S. society are unwittingly in a sexual alliance, despite their different intentions and goals. The radical right wants to ban pornography in order to resexualize society by returning to a nineteenth-century version of repressive sexuality along the lines that Margaret Atwood carries to their logical and frightening extreme in *The Handmaid's Tale*. The pornography industry wants to resexualize society simply by flooding the market with pornrotica, to keep the profits flowing. And FACT, along with the ACLU, wants to resexualize society in the name of the First Amendment, because more of the same is easier than rethinking liberal legal premises or their own sexuality. Thus the least emancipated areas in America will remain the millions of bedrooms across the country, regardless of sexual preference. Only a handful of radical feminists are attempting to desexualize society by exposing standard legal and cultural debates over sexuality for what they really are: sexist social-control tactics, disguised as sexual liberation, that are harming women.

It is a mistake to view the current debate as a question of heterosexual versus homosexual preferences; it is also not a question of sexual liberation versus sexual inhibition. It is a question of desexualizing society (and thereby endorsing nonviolent sex, which does not subordinate and objectify women as unequal partners) or resexualizing society (with all of its violent, degrading, and harmful elements) at the end of the twentieth century.

Uniquely American patterns of censorship have also contributed to the dramatic change in pornography in the last two decades (Hoff-Wilson, 1984). Because censorship in the last half of the nineteenth century focused so exclusively on repressing representations of sexuality, varied forms of popular media developed in the twentieth century include more violence than sex in order to attract public attention while at the same time avoiding laws designed to enforce moral purity. This can easily be documented by looking at the increase in expressions of violence in movies just before, during, and after World War II. The same is true of television from the 1950s forward. Then, beginning in the 1960s, with the legal liberalization of sexually explicit material, sex and violence became more integrated—first in print and then in visual media—although the tendency remains for violence to prevail over sex in order to avoid X-ratings except in uncut videocassette versions. This unregulated practice allows R-rated films to revert to their original X-rated combination of material that clearly links sex with violence and to be rented or sold to many who cannot legally attend an X-rated film.

While historians and lawyers continue to disagree over the meaning and legal status of pornrotica, some social-science and literary studies have suggested that it is rapidly becoming the new opiate of the masses. Thus, the "raptures and bliss of the cosmic fuck" are replacing both religion and science as ways to attain heaven on earth in our sex-and-violence obsessed era (Rushdoony, 1974, 33). Other studies are now maintaining that pornography has always been a frontier literature, presaging or predicting future sexual relationships (Leach, 1975, 17–26). Indeed, behavior depicted in early sexually explicit representations is now largely accepted as normal among consenting adults.

While this frontier function of pornography appears to be a valid generalization about the past, it may not be for the present. It is possible that today's pornrotica has a demographic profile. By the end of the twentieth century, it may not be as prevalent or as much in demand as the population significantly ages. The current AIDS epidemic constitutes another reason why pornography may not continue to live up to its previous reputation as a self-fulfilling sexual prophecy. Until a cure or prevention for AIDS is found, unrestricted and indiscriminate sexual relations may temporarily become a thing of the past. Demography and disease may ultimately be the determining factors in the battle over whether to resexualize or desexualize society on the eve of the twenty-first century. This is another reason why Atwood's book about a fascistic future, in which impotent male leaders pervert feminist principles beyond recognition in order to control the reproductive capacities of women, should be read carefully by all concerned about the potential impact of pornrotica on U.S. society.

In any case, until pornography receives adequate historical and legal gender analysis from which society can draw lessons and new paradigms for the future, rather than the past, I can only agree with David Holbrook, who has said that "Our failure to discriminate against pornography . . . marks a deep failure in our intellectual life" (Holbrook, 1975, 2). Even more important, as long as pornography continues not to have a history, its negative importance will continue to be denied, and the variety of its acceptably sexist and violently grotesque disguises will increase. We know this to be true of rape. By denying its historical gender implications, men have long regarded rape not "as a physical and mental attack on the body and soul of another human being, but rather as a crime against property. . . ." (Semiotica, 1985, 39).

Without histories, people, events, and issues involving personal suffering are taken less seriously than would otherwise be the case. For example, "an injury uniquely sustained by a disempowered group will lack a name, a history, and in general a linguistic reality," and thus the pain or harm is often transformed by both the victim and the perpetrator into "something else" (West, 1987, 85). So until pornography has a written history, those who would resexualize U.S. society can use its ahistorical status and outmoded legal interpretations about obscenity under the First Amendment to serve their own disparate private and public interests with impunity. But most important, without a history, contemporary pornrotica will continue to silence women when it comes to thinking and speaking the truth about the meaning of their own sexual lives.

NOTES

I want to thank Kathleen Barry, Elizabeth Defeis, Susanne Kappeler, Marjorie Lightman, and Christie Farnham and her daughter Lucetta Pope for their comments on a much longer version of this essay. Questions and suggestions by participants in a 1987 Hunter College Women's Studies seminar directed by Dorothy O. Helly also helped me recast several segments of an earlier draft.

1. For a review of the deficiencies in the latest histories of sexuality in the United States, see D'Emilio and Freedman (1988), xi–xx, quotation at xiii.

2. American women's history and American legal history continue to be dominated by the broadest kind of political and theoretical liberalism reflecting binary and adversarial views of reality. The most familiar dualisms include traditional Lockean power relationships: between public and private spheres; between the authority of the state and individual freedom; and between individual equality and group rights. Unless the remaining conservative and sexist constraints of legal and historical liberalism are recognized through deconstructive techniques, it will be impossible to transcend either the male language or male standards by which the historical and legal status of women continues to be judged.

Increasingly, most major examples of differences between liberal historians, lawyers, and radical feminists in the 1980s have, like pornography, *related to sexuality,* such as prostitution, abortion, surrogate motherhood, and evidence admissible in rape trials. This should not come as a surprise because feminism did not simply begin, as civil libertarians like to assert, "as a traditional civil liberties quest for constitutional and legislative equality." While feminism may have historically overlapped on occasion with the goals of liberal legalism, its most radical and comprehensive forms since the mid-nineteenth century have always gone beyond civil libertarianism in its quest to transform society's attitudes and treatment of women. In the twentieth century more and more of these transformational issues dividing mainstream liberal and radical feminists focus on sexuality—an issue that, in its many complex manifestations, does not easily lend itself to traditional case-law solutions. See *New York Times,* Nov. 8, 1987, p. A27, Op-Ed piece by New York University (NYU) law professor Stephen Gillers and board member of New York ACLU; and *New York Times,* Nov. 24, 1987, p. A22, letter to editor commenting on Gillers's Op-Ed piece by Laura Anne Silverstein, NYU Law Women Steering Committee. For more details about legal liberalism, see Joan Hoff, *Too Little—Too Late: Changing Legal Status of U.S. Women from the American Revolution to the Present* (Bloomington, Ind.: Indiana University Press, forthcoming), chap. 1.

3. The best theoretical review of the critical-theory interpretation of U.S. law can be found in Roberto Mangabeira Unger, *The Critical Legal Studies Movement* (Cambridge, Mass.: Harvard University Press, 1986). For individual examples of the work of this New Left school of thought, see David Kairys, ed., *The Politics of Law* (New York: Pantheon Books, 1982), Introduction, pp. 1–7, 281–309; and a special double issue of the *Stanford Law Review* 36 (1984): 1–674. The critical legal theory movement contains four basic elements: (1) a rejection of the notion that an idealized juridical model exists from which only "bad" decisions deviate; (2) a recognition that democracy in the United States seldom exists for most people outside of the public sphere and that the public/private debate often masks control of the society by corporate or other powerful, but not popularly (or democratically) based, interests; (3) a denial that the law is neutral or objective and disconnected from socioeconomic, cultural, and political forces; and (4) an insistence that the basic function of the law is to serve and rationalize the dominant ideology and political economy. Except for those who have been influenced by the critical legal studies movement, few legal historians have systematically analyzed the implications for women of a legal system that supports not only capitalism but also sexism.

4. Some feminists have also been aided in their opposition to pornography by Foucault's multicausal interpretation of power and resistance to it over the centuries. He has provided clues for understanding the complex process whereby the invention of sexuality became the basis for power in the modern state and at the same time the source for illusory resistance to it. According to Foucault, both power and resistance are made up of unequal sexual relationships interacting on social "fields of force." In the nineteenth century these "polymorphous techniques of power" were not successfully catalogued in a "great archive of the pleasures of sex." For centuries, the courts and churches had tried to institutionalize Christian confession rites along these same multifaceted lines of power.

Juridical and religious confessional procedures had always been highly individualized forms of self-sexual analysis since the prime topic of this unequal interaction between confessor, judge, or torturer and the potential penitent was, of course, his or her secret sex life. But it was not until the nineteenth century, with the "medicalization of the effects of confession," that the "sexual domain was no longer accounted for simply by the notions of error or sin, excess or transgression, but was placed under the rule of the normal and the pathological" (Foucault, 1980b, 11, 63, 67, 92–102).

Using Foucault's breathtaking poststructuralist critique of contemporary society, radical feminists have been able to demystify the variety and value of women's roles more successfully than was heretofore possible with the theories of either Marx or Freud. Building upon Foucault's ideas about power and resistance, others in different disciplines have begun to provide the basis of a radical feminist analysis for deconstructing traditional views of power and the institutionalization of heterosexuality. Not all of these studies agree with one another or completely with Foucault, but in general they credit him with having not only exposed the most repressive aspects of the monocausation theories of Marx and Freud, but also stripped the last vestiges of validity from essentialist sexual liberation arguments from Reich to Marcuse (Baudrillard, 1977; Faust, 1981; Ariès & Béjin, 1985; Semiotica, 1985, 1–266; Capland, 1987; Martin, 1982; Scott, 1986; Myers, 1987).

Foucault's works, especially the last two volumes of his trilogy on The History of Sexuality, emphasize the arbitrarily ascribed gender roles of women more than those of either Marx or Freud, primarily because of his conviction that middle-class women were the first to be "sexualized," that is, invested with sexuality and "assigned a new destiny charged with conjugal and parental obligations," in order to be of value in the new bourgeois order of things (Foucault, 1980b, 121).

5. Interestingly, Kendrick has discovered that the word pornography did not appear in Samuel Johnson's 1755 Dictionary. For approximately one hundred years, therefore, it lay dormant, to emerge in the mid-1800s with a quite different connotation from that of its Grecian origins. During that same century, the word began to be used to describe very private musuem collections and appeared in guidebooks for world travelers that included references to artifacts excavated from the buried city of Pompeii, accidentally discovered in 1710. By the 1750s rumors abounded among the aristocratic art world about the "lascivious" frescoes and a particularly sensuous marble statue of a satyr copulating with a goat—which King Charles promptly locked away in a room at the Royal Museum of Protici, ordering "that no one should be allowed access to it" (Kendrick, 1987, 6).

Royal edicts notwithstanding, "gentlemen with appropriate demeanor (and ready cash for the custodian)" readily gained admission not only to this "locked chamber" but also to the on-site "secret museum" at the Pompeii digging that contained an expanding section including the brothel areas. Nonetheless, in 1824 the first guide to the city in English did not mention the special collection. Not until 1875 did an English guide circumspectly mention "this resort of Pagan immorality . . . [open] to those who may wish to see it." In 1830 a French guidebook tersely referred to the restricted area as a "chamber . . . devoted to licentious scenes." By 1879 French travelers learned about "coarse paintings . . . indicat[ing] that it was intended for the most shameful debaucheries" (Kendrick, 1987, 5, 7).

Systematic archeological work at Pompeii did not begin until the 1860s. Unlike other artifacts that offended or titillated the sensibilities of eighteenth- and nineteenth-century European high society, those in and around the city of Pompeii were preserved rather than destroyed. Such preservation posed a linguistic problem for art historians. In 1850 the German C. O. Muller coined the word "pornographers" to describe those who had produced such sensual works of art after finding the Greek word in a second-century source by the chronicler Athenaeus. The French bibliophile Paul Lacroix also used the word in the early 1850s in his six-volume history of prostitution—again relying on Athenaeus (Kendrick, 1987. 11–12).

6. From the first edition of *Webster's Dictionary* in 1828 through the 1860 edition, the word pornography did not appear. Then, beginning in 1864, *Webster's* gave the first definition of pornography as "a treatment of, or a treatise on, the subject of prostitutes or prostitution." The second definition, however, referred to pornography as "licentious painting employed to decorate the walls of rooms sacred to bacchanalian orgies, examples of which exist in Pompeii." This reference to Pompeii did not survive into the twentieth century.

By 1917 the first definition in *Webster's* remained the same, but the second had been shortened to read simply: "obscene or licentious writing, painting, or the like." A pornographer in these editions was listed simply as "a writer on prostitutes, prostitution, or obscene or licentious subjects." Except for the addition of the adjective "pornorastic," from the Greek for harlot and hence meaning "unchaste" or "licentious," and the nouns "pornograph," to describe "pornographic writing; picture or the like," and "pornocracy," meaning "government by profligate women [or harlots]," the first and second definitions remained essentially the same until the 1961 *Webster's Third New International Dictionary* appeared.

Although the first definition in 1961 again referred to the original Greek usage, it contained no reference to a scientific or other type of treatise. Instead it read: "a description of prostitutes or prostitution." The second definition became: "a depiction in writing or painting of licentiousness or lewdness; *a portrayal of erotic behavior designed to cause sexual excitement*—compare EROTICA" (emphasis added). The adjective and adverb, "pornographic" and "pornographically," were also added in 1961 with the meaning "of or relating to licentious art or literature; pandering to base appetite or desire; descriptive or suggestive of lewdness; OBSCENE." Included in this section was a usage by Aldous Huxley: ". . . merely gross, a scatological rather than a pornographic impropriety."

These definitions prevailed through the 1970s editions of *Webster's Third New International Dictionary* until the 1976 6,000 *Words* supplement. Pornography's first definition now became "material (as a book) that is pornographic," and the second stated: "the depiction or portrayal of acts in a sensational manner so as to arouse (as by lurid details) a quick intense emotional reaction" as in "the *pornography of violence*." The words "porn," "porno," and "porny" also appeared for the first time in this 1976 supplement, with one usage referring to "sex offenders possessing *porn*," and another denying that "*porno* incites the viewer to anything but erotic feelings and expressions."

In the course of the twentieth century, *Webster's* definitions of variations of the word pornography closely parallel the original 1909 and subsequent editions of the *OED*. By 1982, however, the column length devoted in the *OED* to pornography had, in keeping with its mythopoeic phallic nature, grown from 7½ inches in 1909 to 20½. Moreover, the second definition now contained a significant addition, namely, the qualification "*hard* or *soft*." It also distinguished "between erotic art (or soft pornography) and hard pornography, which by connecting sex with violence, hatred, pain, and humiliation, stimulated gratification of sexual desire in deviate ways."

7. According to Foucault, the terms "erotic" and "erotica" appear to have been misappropriated from ancient Greece, where "erotics" was but one of the four distinct types of stylized ethics that focused on the subject of boys, specifically on mores associated with the well-known Greek practice of "boy loving" (Foucault, 1986, 36, *passim*). If Foucault and Paul Veyne are correct that the early Greeks (and later Romans) conferred less desirable or inferior aspects of Eros on female/male relationships, then the term erotics originally described boy loving, not woman loving—that is, male standards of beauty based on free choice, self-mastery, and equality (Veyne, 1987, in Ariès and Bejin). As the following dictionary analysis demonstrates, we have been unaware of, and hence content with, a twentieth-century corruption of the original meaning of erotics.

A dictionary search of Eros, erotic, and erotica surprisingly reveals that none of the nineteenth-century editions of *Webster's* contained the word Eros. Less than a column inch of text was devoted to "erotic, erotical, and erotomany" in 1860. By 1897 the *New English Dictionary* devoted four column inches to variations of erotic, but it also did not refer to Eros as a separate word. By 1917 *Webster's* had picked up Eros; but only in the 1940s and 1950s did it temporarily indicate that in art Eros was often represented as "a winged youth or boy." All later references simply equate Eros with Cupid without gender identification. Although *The Imperial Dictionary of the English Language* had identified Eros as simply the "Greek equivalent of Cupid" in 1883, the *OED* waited until its 1972 supplement to present a 6½-column-inch definition and literary references for Eros as the god of love "or a representation of him: = cupid." The *OED*'s primary, contemporary definition, therefore, retains a gendered meaning more in keeping with Foucault's interpretation of Eros and erotics.

In editions that appeared in the 1970s, however, both dictionaries gave secondary definitions referring to Freud's use of the term as sexual pleasure whose energy was derived from the libido. (In fact, *Webster's* had included the Freudian psychological definition in the 1960s, and the single word psychoanalysis in the 1940s and 1950s, but without any accompanying explanation.) Before the 1970s, however, the only definition of Eros or erotic that referred to a specific mental state was associated with the word "erotomania," meaning a form of melancholy, madness, or insanity "arising from passionate love" or "marked by morbid affection for persons of the opposite sex" (*OED*, 1897; *Webster's*, 1917).

While these dictionary definitions are important because they indicate that it took over half a century for Freudian terminology to permeate the etymological world, they are also significant as indices of how much more quickly literary figures were able to convince word experts that there should be a distinction between the erotic and the pornographic, regardless of historical or linquistic merit. Unfortunately, most modern feminists also accept this questionable dichotomy. The first definitions of erotic contained but one reference to any kind of literature: amorous or amatory poems (*OED*, 1897, 1933; *Webster's*, 1848, 1860, 1909, 1917, 1922). *Not until the 1940s does the word "erotica" appear in standard English dictionaries.* In 1948, for example, *Webster's Second New International Dictionary* defined the word as "literary or artistic items of erotic theme."

Again, as with the word pornography, a significant etymological change occurred in the 1960s and 1970s with respect to erotica. In 1963, *Webster's Third New International Dictionary* added this phrase to its 1948 definition: "books treating sexual love in a sensuous or voluptuous manner—compare pornography." In that same edition the column inches devoted to variations of the word erotic jumped from one column inch in its first edition, to two in the second, to four in the third. It was not further elaborated upon in the 1976 supplement, *6,000 Words*. Less spectacular in terms of space, but more so in terms of changing meaning is the presentation in the 1972 *OED* supplement. While erotic and eroticism were unchanged, erotica was introduced as "matters of love; erotic literature or art (freq. as a heading in catalogues)," accompanied by over a column inch of literary usages dating from 1854 to 1967. In addition, such words as eroticize, erotize, erotogenic, and erogenous were included in the *OED* litany. Interestingly, erotomaniacs were no longer described as mad; instead, references were cited using the term to describe everything from a sexually idiosyncratic individual like Oscar Wilde to the "erotomaniac gleam at the top of the phallic cigar [of Groucho Marx]" (*OED*, 1972). Somewhat along the same lines, erotomania in *Webster's Third* was no longer a form of insanity, but simply a "symptom of mental disorder" stemming from "excessive sexual desire" (*Webster's*, 1971).

8. Kathy Myers argues (not entirely convincingly) for the creation of feminist erotica by saying that Foucault's concept of power "gives us the tools to analyse the patriarchal order (not as a monolithic system of oppression, but as a specific socio-historic articulation of power relations) and also provides the ammunition for change (a re-organization of power relations). It shifts feminism from the site of oppositional practice (a defense against the bastions of patriarchal power) to that of a positive practice working to deploy power." It is

on these grounds that she contends that rather than "dismissing the power of the [pornographic] imagination and fantasy as politically undesirable," as the radical feminists do, or extolling it as socially unacceptable and therefore subversive and liberating, as the proponents of pornography do, women should create their own erotica by restructuring "the systems of language, association and meaning which organise [their] consciousness" (Myers, 1987, 14–15). The postscript to Susanne Kappeler's book contains a more convincing argument for overcoming the "subject-object relation [which] . . . is at the core . . . of inequality, domination and power." Rejecting pornographic representations, she bases her argument on a feminist critique that "must evolve forms of communication that are neither ego-trips nor solid objects, but forms of exchange [which] . . . will negotiate the relationships of the individual with the collective, the subject with sociality, not with an objectified other. The personal is political, because the personal is the minimal social unit. . . . feminist critique will envisage intersubjectivity: revolution, not *coup d'etat*" (Kappeler, 1986, 212, 219).

9. Even *A Feminist Dictionary*, edited by C. Kramarae and P. Treichler, for example, quickly establishes positive meanings for "erotic," "erotica," and "eroticism" in three short entries and then devotes 4½ pages to negative connotations of variations of the words "pornography" and "pornographic." The most often quoted feminist distinction between pornography and erotica is Gloria Steinem's: "[Erotica] contains the idea of love, positive choice, and the yearning for a particular person. Unlike pornography's reference to a harlot or prostitute, *erotica* leaves entirely open the question of gender." The article in which Steinem unfortunately promoted this ahistorical distinction can be found in Lederer, 1980, 35–39.

10. For over a century—from the broad Queen's Bench meaning of obscenity in *Regina v. Hicklin* (1868) LR 3 QB 360, to *Pope v. Illinois*, 107 S. Ct. 1918 (1987)—its legal definition gradually narrowed in both English and American common law (Kendrick, 1987; Copp and Wendell, 1983). The *Hicklin* test (like the Comstock Law) had been intended to apply not only to *sexually* explicit materials but also to any "immoral influence" that would corrupt the vulnerable minds of youth—particularly young men (AGCP, 1986, 1:247; Klausner, 1984–85). Thus, legal obscenity under *Hicklin* focused on acts or writings that violated prevailing standards of propriety. But this definition proved too broad and imprecise after the invention of sexuality and the resurrection of the word pornography. In the course of the next hundred years, attempts to diminish the scope of similar decisions and legislation prevailed in the United States until, by the 1960s, "the range of permissible regulation [of obscene materials] could properly be described as 'minimal' " (AGCP, 1986, 1:253–54).

The success in narrowing the definition of obscenity was the result in no small measure of the influence of lawyers who, relying on the private literary definitions, made sexually explicit pictures, words, and films subject to protection under the First Amendment. A few famous cases involving major literary works and films were won in the 1930s and 1940s, but the major U.S. case law precedents (until *Pope*) occurred in the 1950s and 1970s. In *Roth v. United States*, 354 U.S. 476 (1957), the Supreme Court declared that only obscene material "utterly without redeeming social importance" fell outside the jurisdiction of the First Amendment. This decision ultimately meant that most ideas, however hateful and controversial, were protected if they demonstrated "even the slightest redeeming social importance" (MacKinnon, 1987; Grossman, 1985; Klausner, 1984–85, 731; and *Harvard Law Review*, 1984). Anything deemed legally obscene is not, therefore, considered to be "speech" under the First Amendment. The catch in all of this legalese was how to define what constituted obscene material.

In 1973 the Justices came as close as they ever have to a comprehensive definition. *Miller v. California*, 413 U.S. 15 (1973) set three conditions for determining whether visual or printed material is obscene. This tripartite definition held that obscenity exists when (1) an average person using "contemporary community standards" concludes that the work in its entirety appeals to "prurient interest" in sex; (2) the work is "patently offensive" as defined by state or federal laws; and (3) when the entire work "lacks serious literary, artistic, political, or scientific value." The third point constituted the so-called LAPS test. While Supreme Court decisions between 1973 and 1987 paid lip service to "community standards," actual prosecutions of obscenity declined. In any case, as Catharine MacKinnon noted, this definition turns obscenity into a "moral idea" based on the application of good and bad literary standards while pornography remains a "political practice" (MacKinnon, 1985, 21).

Then, in *Pope v. Illinois,* the Supreme Court further narrowed the definition of obscenity by negating entirely the idea that the value of any particular work could "vary from community to community based on the degree of local acceptance it has won." Throwing out the "average person" reference in *Miller,* the Justices ruled that the "LAPS test" could only be determined by a "reasonable person," not an "ordinary person" (107 S. Ct. 1921 [1987]). This decision appears to have eliminated community standards for determining legal obscenity, thus rendering the remaining portions of the *Miller* definition even less applicable to the undefinable: pornography. Ironically, as the depiction of sexual violence has proliferated beyond all reason, a "reasonable" and presumably gender-neutral person is now sought to determine the overall value of material alleged to be obscene.

11. Using gender analysis, feminists in the Second Women's Movement began to question not only the sexist assumptions of existing legal definitions of obscene materials but also the implicitly and explicitly harmful societal effects of mass-distributed pornography on women. Now more women are writing about sexually explicit material, in part because of the mindless violence and mass distribution of pornography that have revolutionized this underground industry in the last twenty years. Modern audio-video technology, like the innovations in printing a century earlier, has basically transformed the content and accessibility of sexually explicit material and has prompted some feminists to speak out on a subject they continue to have little to do with producing except as exploited victims (Barry, 1979; Dworkin, 1981; Faust, 1981; MacKinnon, 1987; Tong, 1984; Kappeler, 1986; A. Russo, 1987). In particular, radical feminists are concerned with the variety of pornographic representations of women that, in sexually subordinating and objectifying them misleadingly by projecting false images of women, imply that women enjoy being abused sexually (Klausner, 1984–85, 733–35).

12. Although the U.S. Supreme Court summarily distinguished obscenity from pornography in *Miller,* the Justices did not abide by that distinction. In addition to the Supreme Court's unfortunate interchangeable use of the words "obscene," "pornographic," and "erotic," also see Dworkin, 1985, 335–70; Grossman, 1985, 1–15 (corrected version); and Klausner, 1984–85: 734, n. 102.

13. For a review of both sides, see West, 1987, 134–39; Bessmer, 1982; A. Russo, 1987, 103–12; *Caught Looking,* 1986; *Humanities in Society,* 1984, 1–101; Snitow et al., 1983; and Barry, 1979.

14. For details, see Hoff, 1989, chap. 9.

15. Foucault noted in the early 1970s that

the real strength of the women's liberation movement is not that of having laid claim to the specificity of their sexuality and the rights pertaining to it, but that they have actually departed from the discourse conducted within the apparatuses of sexuality. Ultimately, it is a veritable movement of desexualization, a displacement effected in relation to the sexual centering of the problem, formulating the demand for forms of culture, discourse, language and so on which are no longer part of that rigid assignation and pin-down to their sex which they had initially in some sense been politically obliged to accept in order to make themselves heard. (Foucault, 1980, 219–20)

REFERENCES

Ariès, Philippe, & Béjin, André (1985). *Western Sexuality: Practice and Precept in Past and Present Times*. New York: Basil Blackwell, Inc.

Attorney General's Commission on Pornography (1986). *Final Report [Meese Report]*. 2 vols. Washington, D.C.: Government Printing Office.

Bakhtin, Mikhail (1984). *Rabelais and His World*. Bloomington, Ind.: Indiana University Press. (Original work published 1965.)

Barry, Kathleen (1979). *Female Sexual Slavery*. Englewood Cliffs, N.J.: Prentice-Hall, Inc.

Baudrillard, Jean (1977). *Oublier Foucault*. Paris: Éditions Galilée.

Bessmer, Sue (1982). "Antiobscenity: A Comparison of the Legal and the Feminist Perspectives." In *Women, Power and Policy*, ed. Ellen Boneparth. Elmsford, N.Y.: Pergamon Press.

Brennan, Teresa, & Pateman, Carole (1979). "Mere Auxiliaries to the Commonwealth: Women and the Origins of Liberalism." *Political Studies* 27, no. 2: 183–200.

Brusendorff, Ove, & Henningsen, Poul (1983). *The Complete History of Eroticism*. Secaucus, N.J.: Castle. (Originally published in six volumes between 1961 and 1963.)

Butler, Melissa (1978). "Early Liberal Roots of Feminism: John Locke and the Attack on Patriarchy." *American Political Science Review* 72, no. 1: 135–50.

Califia, Pat (1981). "Feminism and Sadomasochism." *Heresies: A Feminist Publication on Arts and Politics* 3, no. 4 (issue 12): 30–34.

Capland, Pat, ed. (1987). *The Cultural Construction of Sexuality*. London: Tavistock Publications.

Clarke, Lorenne M. G. (1979). "Women and Locke: Who Owns the Apple in the Garden of Eden." In *The Sexism of Social and Political Theory*, ed. Clark and Lynda Lange. Toronto: University of Toronto Press, 16–40.

Copp, David, & Wendell, Susan, eds. (1983). *Pornography and Censorship*. New York: Prometheus Books.

Cotham, Perry C. (1973). *Obscenity, Pornography, and Censorship: A Christian Perspective*. Grand Rapids, Mich.: Baker Book House.

Davis, Natalie Zemon (1965). *Society and Culture in Early Modern France*. Stanford: Stanford University Press.

D'Emilio, John, and Freedman, Estella B. (1988). *Intimate Matters: A History of Sexuality in America*. New York: Harper & Row.

Diamond, Irene (1980). "Pornography and Repression: A Reconsideration of "Who" and "What." In *Take Back the Night*, ed. Laura Lederer. New York: William Morrow, 1980, 187–203.

Dorsen, Norman and Gora, Joel (1985). "The Burger Court and the Freedom of Speech." In *The Burger Court: The Counterrevolution That Wasn't*, ed. Vincent Blasi. New Haven: Yale University Press.

Dworkin, Andrea (1981). *Pornography: Men Possessing Women*. New York: Perigee.
——— (1987). *Intercourse*. New York: The Free Press.

Dworkin, Ronald (1985). *A Matter of Principle*. Cambridge: Harvard University Press.

Ellis, Kate; Hunter, Nan D.; Jaker, Beth; O'Dair, Barbara; & Tallmer, Abby (1986). *Caught Looking: Feminism, Pornography & Censorship*. New York: Feminist Anti-Censorship Taskforce (FACT) Book Committee.

Elmer, Jonathan (1987–88). "The Exciting Conflict: The Rhetoric of Pornography and Antipornography." *Cultural Critique*, no. 8: 45–78.

Faust, Beatrice (1981). *Women, Sex & Pornography*. New York: Penguin Books.

Fiedler, Leslie (1978). *Freaks: Myths and Images of the Secret Self*. New York: Simon and Schuster.

Foucault, Michel (1980a). *Power/Knowledge: Selected Interviews and Other Writings, 1972–1977.* Ed. Colin Gordon. New York: Pantheon Books.
——— (1980b). *The History of Sexuality.* Vol. 1: *An Introduction.* New York: Vintage Books. (Original work published in 1976.)
——— (1986a). *The History of Sexuality.* Vol. 2: *The Use of Pleasure.* New York: Vintage Books. (Original work published in 1984.)
——— (1986b). *The History of Sexuality.* Vol. 3: *The Care of the Self.* New York: Pantheon Books. (Original work published in 1984.)
Garry, Ann (1984). "Pornography and Censorship." In *Philosophy and Sex,* ed. Robert Baker & Frederick Elliston. Buffalo, N.Y.: Prometheus.
Gillette, Paul J. (1965). *An Uncensored History of Pornography.* Los Angeles: Holloway House Publishing Co.
Gordon, Robert W. (1982). "New Developments in Legal Theory." In *The Politics of Law: A Progressive Critique,* ed. David Kairys. New York: Pantheon Books.
Gould, Carol C., ed. (1983). *Beyond Domination: New Perspectives on Women and Philosophy.* Totowa, N.J.: Rowman & Allanheld Publishers.
Grossman, Joel B. (1985). "The First Amendment and the New Anti-Pornography Statutes." American Political Science Association (APSA) *News for Teachers of Political Science,* no. 45 (Spring): 16–21.
Harvard Law Review (1984). "Note: Anti-Pornography Laws and First Amendment Values." 98:460–81.
Hoff, Joan (1989). *Too Little—Too Late: Changing Legal Status of U.S. Women from the Colonial Period to the Present.* Bloomington, Ind.: Indiana University Press.
Hoff-Wilson, Joan (1984). "The Pluralistic Society." In The New York Public Library, *Censorship: 500 Years of Conflict.* New York: Oxford University Press.
Holbrook, David (1975). *The Case Against Pornography.* La Salle, Ill.: Library Press.
Hollyday, Joyce (1984). "An Epidemic of Violence: Manifestations of violence against women." *Sojourners Magazine* 13, no. 10: 10–12.
Hughes, Douglas A., ed. (1970). *Perspectives on Pornography.* New York: St. Martin's Press.
Humanities in Society (1984). Special issue on Sexuality, Violence, and Pornography. 7, nos. 1 & 2: 1–101.
Hyde, H. Montgomery (1964). *A History of Pornography.* New York: Farrar, Straus & Giroux.
Kairys, David, ed. (1982). *The Politics of Law.* New York: Pantheon Books.
Kappeler, Susanne (1986). *The Pornography of Representation.* Minneapolis: University of Minnesota Press.
Kendrick, Walter (1985). "Exorcising Pornography." *New Boston Review* 10, no. 5 (November 1985): 9–10.
——— (1987). *The Secret Museum: Pornography in Modern Culture.* New York: Viking.
Klausner, Marian Leslie (1984–85). "Redefining Pornography as Sex Discrimination: An Innovative Civil Rights Approach." *New England Law Review* 20, no. 4: 721–57.
Kramarae, Cheris, & Treichler, Paula A. (1985). *A Feminist Dictionary.* Boston: Pandora Press.
Lahey, Kathleen A. (1984–85). "The Canadian Charter of Rights and Pornography." *New England Law Review* 20, no. 4: 649–85.
Leach, Michael (1975). *I Know It When I See It.* Philadelphia: Westminster Press.
Lederer, Laura, ed. (1980). *Take Back the Night: Women on Pornography.* New York: William Morrow, 187–258.
Lo Duca, J. M. (1966). *A History of Eroticism.* Covina, Cal.: Collectors Publications.
Lorde, Audre (1981). "The Master's Tools Will Never Dismantle the Master's House." In *This Bridge Called My Back: Writings by Radical Women of Color,* ed. Cherrie Moraga and Gloria Anzaldua. New York: Kitchen Table, Women of Color Press.

MacKinnon, Catharine A. (1984). "Not a Moral Issue." *Yale Law & Policy Review* 11, no. 2: 321–45.

——— (1985). "Pornography, Civil Rights, and Speech." *Harvard Civil Rights–Civil Liberties Law Review* 20, no. 1: 1–70.

——— (1987). *Feminism Unmodified: Discourses on Life and Law*. Cambridge: Harvard University Press.

Marcus, Isabel. "Feminist Strategies: The Shoe That Never Fits." Paper presented at Sixth Berkshire Conference on the History of Women, June 3, 1984, Smith College. Quoted with permission of author.

Martin, Biddy (1982). "Feminism, Criticism, and Foucault." *New German Critique* 27, no. 3: 3–30.

Michelson, Peter (1971). *The Aesthetics of Pornography*. New York: Herder and Herder.

Myers, Kathy (1987). "Towards a Feminist Erotica." In *Visibly Female: Feminism and Art: An Anthology*, ed. Hillary Robinson. London: Camden Press.

Nicholson, Linda J. (1983). "Feminist Theory: The Private and the Public." In *Beyond Domination: New Perspectives on Women and Philosophy*, ed. Carol C. Gould. Totowa, N.J.: Rowman & Allanheld Publishers.

——— (1986). *Gender and History: The Limits of Social Theory in the Age of the Family*. New York: Columbia University Press, 1986.

Okin, Susan Moller (1979). *Woman in Western Political Thought*. Princeton, N.J.: Princeton University Press.

Rushdoony, Rousas J. (1974). *The Politics of Pornography*. New Rochelle, N.Y.: Arlington House Publishers.

Russo, Ann (1987). "Conflicts and Contradictions Among Feminists Over Issues of Pornography and Sexual Freedom." *Women's Studies International Forum* 10, no. 2: 103–12.

Russo, Mary (1986). "Female Grotesque: Carnival and Theory." In *Feminist Studies/ Critical Studies*, ed. Teresa de Lauretis. Bloomington, Ind.: Indiana University Press.

Scott, Joan C. (1986). "Gender: A Useful Category of Historical Analysis." *American Historical Review* 91, no. 5: 1053–75.

Seldes, George, compl. 1985. *The Great Thoughts*. New York: Ballantine Books.

Semiotica (1985). Special Issue: The Rhetoric of Violence. 54, nos. 1–2: 1–266.

Simon, Anne E. (1985). "The Politics of Law: A Progressive Critique." *Women's Rights Law Reporter* 8, no. 3: 199–204.

Smith-Rosenberg, Carroll (1985). *Disorderly Conduct: Visions of Gender in Victorian America*. New York: Knopf.

Snitow, Ann; Stansell, Christine; & Thompson, Sharon, eds. (1983). *Powers of Desire: The Politics of Sexuality*. New York: Monthly Review Press.

Soble, Alan (1986). *Pornography: Marxism, Feminism, and the Future of Sexuality*. New Haven: Yale University Press.

Soley, Ginny (1984). "Our Lives at Stake: The cultural roots of sexual violence." *Sojourners Magazine* 13, no. 10: 13–15.

Stanford Law Review (1984). Special Double Issue: Critical Legal Studies. 36: 1–674.

Stone, Lawrence (1985). "Sex In The West." *The New Republic*, July 8, 1985, 25–37.

Theodoracopulos, Taki (1981). "Ugly Women: A Treatise on Ugliness." *The American Spectator*, March 1981, 16–17.

Thompson, Roger (1979). *Unfit for Modest Ears: A Study of Pornographic, Obscene and Bawdy Works Written or Published in England in the Second Half of the Seventeenth Century*. London: The Macmillan Press, Ltd.

Tong, Rosemarie (1984). *Women, Sex, and the Law*. Totowa, N.J.: Rowman & Allanheld, Publishers.

Tribe, Lawrence H. (1976). *American Constitutional Law*. Mineola, N.Y.: Foundation Press, supplement 1979.

——— (1985). *Constitutional Choices*. Cambridge: Harvard University Press.

Veyne, Paul, ed. (1987). *From Pagan Rome to Byzantium*. Vol. 1 in Philippe Ariès and Georges Duby, gen. eds., *A History of Private Life*. Cambridge: Harvard University Press.

West, Robin (1987). "The Difference in Women's Hedonic Lives: A Phenomenological Critique of Feminist Legal Theory." *Wisconsin Women's Law Journal* 3:81–146.

2

Representing Pornography

Feminism, Criticism, and Depictions of Female Violation

SUSAN GUBAR

It is hardly necessary to rent *I Spit On Your Grave* or *Tool Box Murders* for your VCR in order to find images of sexuality contaminated by depersonalization or violence. As far back as Rabelais's *Gargantua,* for example, Panurge proposes to build a wall around Paris out of "the pleasure-twats of women [which] are much cheaper than stones": "the largest . . . in front" would be followed by "the medium-sized, and last of all, the least and smallest," all interlaced with "many horney joy-dinguses" so the fortification would be impregnable, except for the "ordure and excretions" of the flies it would doubtlessly attract.[1] Two centuries later, one of Rabelais's compatriots, the Marquis de Sade, described the rage of a sexually initiated daughter against a woman who refuses to consider her "pleasure-twat" "cheaper than stones." The Sadeian heroine first sodomizes her puritanical mother with an artificial penis, then has her infected with syphilis, and finally performs infibulation to prevent the infected semen from leaking out: "Quickly, quickly, fetch me needle and thread! . . . Spread your thighs, Mama, so I can stitch you together[.]"[2]

One century later in England, the author of *My Secret Life* explained that, when in a state of sexual excitement, "he is ready to fuck anything, from his sister to his grandmother, from a ten-year-old, to a woman of sixty, for a standing prick has no conscience." To this credo, he adds the admonition, "—Woe be to the female whom he gets a chance at, if she does not want *him,* for he will have *her* if he can" (p. 361). The sexually aroused man in the contemporary American film *Looking for Mr. Goodbar* curses the woman who does not want him as much as she wants a room of her own and the freedom to choose a succession of male lovers. After he resentfully determines to have her when he gets the chance ("All you got to do is lay there. Guy's got to do all the work"), he

'y knifes her to death, exclaiming, "That's what you want,
vhat you want."

...dividual works are labeled, such passages remind us of the
pornography, a gender-specific genre produced primarily by and
out focused obsessively on the female figure. In their depictions of
...ale sexuality, narratives from *Gargantua* to *La Philosophie dans le boudoir,
My Secret Life,* and *Looking for Mr. Goodbar* explain why definitions of the
pornographic have recently moved away from "obscenity," a term that generally
refers to the sexually stimulating effects of a picture, a novel, or a film on the
male reader/observer, and toward "dehumanization," a word that is used to
evoke the objectification of women. As Irene Diamond has demonstrated, during
the past decade the generally held assumption that pornography is about male
sexuality has been qualified by those who argue that "the 'what' of pornography
is not sex but power and violence, and the 'who' of concern are no longer male
consumers and artists but women" (Diamond, 1980, 132).

While feminists aligning themselves with civil libertarians continue to argue
for women's sexual freedom by questioning the credibility of any kind of
censorship ("What turns me on is erotic; what turns you on is pornographic"),
those other feminists who have drafted antipornography ordinances view pornography itself as an infringement on women's freedom, for, as they see
it, "pornography is the theory, and rape the practice."[3] Diametrically opposed,
both groups are nevertheless implicitly invoking theories of representation,
as the *Oxford English Dictionary* suggests they must if they are to deal with
what the lexicographers tellingly define as a "description of the life, manners, etc. of prostitutes or their patrons." Whether it is pictorial or linguistic,
pornography is a description—if not of "prostitutes," then of sexually active
women; if not of "patrons," then of male consumers—and it therefore can be
used to explore not only the politics of representation but the politics of theories of representation.

Even within the circumscribed area that is the subject matter of this debate
between libertarian and pro-ordinance feminists, both of whom exclude
homosexual pornography in order to focus explicitly on women dehumanized as
sexual objects or degraded as the victims of physical abuse, the judgment we
make about pornography as a social phenomenon will be based on aesthetic
criteria. It will depend on whether we define "pornography" and "art" as
mutually exclusive, comparable, or identical terms. Recent theorists deem a
work pornographic not for its "obscenity," which stimulates "prurient" reactions
that presumably could be measured by social psychologists, but for, in the words
of Andrea Dworkin and Catharine MacKinnon's Minneapolis Ordinance, the
work's "sexually explicit subordination of women, graphically depicted, whether
in pictures or in words."[4] But in this new context, too, historians and theorists of
pornography must juxtapose it with presumably legitimate forms of sexually
explicit painting, literature, or film. The controversies over the impact of pornography on men's and women's lives therefore illuminate a number of crucial
issues currently facing feminist criticism, most especially the relationship be-

tween gender and genre on the one hand and between ideology and evaluation on the other hand. Does a genre produced primarily by and for men necessarily demean women and alienate or exclude the female spectator/reader? Does an explicitly misogynist image invariably result in a misogynist ideology, and will it inexorably produce non-art or bad art? And what do our answers to these questions tell us about the aesthetic history we have inherited or about the future tasks of feminist criticism?

Le Viol / **The Rape**

If we turn to the emergence of sexually explicit pictorial representations of women tied up or fragmented into body parts, as such art historians as Whitney Chadwick and Mary Ann Caws have, it would be hard to evade the significance of the surrealists in general and of René Magritte in particular.[5] For, while literary works by Rabelais and Sade may function as remote models, contemporary photographs and drawings of mutilated but submissive and desirous females resemble more vividly the naked, caged, mute mannequins produced after 1919, the year that Marcel Duchamp drew a moustache on a reproduction of the *Mona Lisa* and entitled it *L.H.O.O.Q. (Elle a chaud au cul* [She has hot pants]). Indeed, it is possible to speculate that *Hustler* could market a cover picture of a woman being fed into a meat grinder (so that only her bare buttocks and toppled legs are left to become grist for the mill) because the surrealists had previously produced stools composed of women's legs (fig. 1, Kurt Seligmann's *Ultra-Furniture* [1938]) and scenic tableaux in which male dummies sit at a table on which a woman lies with her body covered over with food (fig. 2, Meret Oppenheim's *Cannibal Feast* [1959]).

Similarly, so-called snuff films and split beaver shots, in which women are presented as dismembered or disassembled, hark back to surrealist paintings in which women's bodies are stuffed into bottles (fig. 3, Magritte's *La Bouteille* [The bottle, n.d.]) or where the woman's figure is literally cut up and framed into five segments that divide her face, her breasts, her belly and genitals, her knees, and her feet (fig. 4, Magritte's *L'Evidence eternelle* [The eternal evidence, 1930]). Women fetishized as nothing but "tits" or "cunts" in the *Taskmaster* or *Leather Bound* magazines shelved at Doc Johnson's Marital Aids Bookshop resemble the breasts and toes that grow out of a nightgown and shoes, the feminine costume placed on display in Magritte's tribute to Sade, *La Philosophie dans le boudoir* (fig. 5, Philosophy in the boudoir, 1947). Precisely because Magritte produced so many images that adumbrate what Annette Kuhn calls the "bits and pieces" of contemporary pornographic photography (Kuhn, 1985, 35–37), his disturbing work dramatizes the contradictory ways in which sexually explicit representations can be and have been defined as antonyms, synecdoches, or synonyms of art.

Perhaps none of Magritte's portraits more shockingly fragments the female by turning her into a sexual body than *Le Viol* (fig. 6, The rape, 1947). Like his paintings of bottled, divided, and incomplete women—which depend on princi-

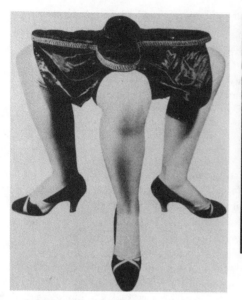

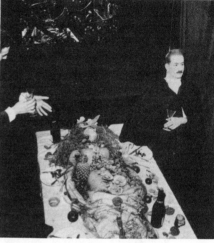

Fig. 2. Meret Oppenheim,
Cannibal Feast, 1959.
("Exposition Internationale du
Surréalisme [EROS]," Galerie
Daniel Cordier, Paris, 1959–60.)

Fig. 1. Kurt Seligmann,
Ultra-Furniture, 1938.
("Exposition Internationale du
Surréalisme," Galerie des
Beaux-Arts, Paris.)

ples of association (the woman as first source of fluids), anatomical tricks (the female assistant sawed into parts), and the animation of the inanimate (shoes with toes and dresses with breasts)[6]—*Le Viol* exploits these sorts of techniques with results that could well be disturbing to the female spectator. Endowed with blind nipples replacing eyes, a belly button where her nose should be, and a vulva for a mouth, the female face is erased by the female torso imposed upon it, as if Magritte were suggesting that anatomy is bound to be her destiny. That the face associated with the body is sightless, senseless, and dumb implies, too, that Magritte may be subscribing to the view of one of William Faulkner's fictional surrogates, a man who celebrates the feminine ideal as "a virgin with no legs to leave me, no arms to hold me, no head to talk to me," and who therefore goes on to define woman generically as "merely [an] articulated genital organ" (Faulkner, 1927, 26).

While an anatomical surprise turns the female into a bearded lady, the articulation of the woman as genital organ makes her inarticulate, closing down all of the openings that ordinarily let the world enter the self, so that Magritte's subject seems monstrously impenetrable or horrifyingly solipsistic. Paradoxically, even as it fetishizes female sexuality, *Le Viol* denies the existence of female genitalia, for the vulva-mouth here is only a hairy indentation. In this reading of

Fig. 3 *(right)*. René Magritte, *La Bouteille*, n.d. (Collection Dr. Joseph Moldaver, New York.)

Fig. 4 *(below left)*. René Magritte, *L'Evidence eternelle*, 1930

Fig. 5 *(below right)*. René Magritte, *La Philosophie dans le boudoir*, 1947. (Thomas Claburn Jones collection, New York.)

Fig. 6. René Magritte, *Le Viol,*
1947. (Menil Foundation, Houston.)

the painting's title, the represented figure—robbed of subjectivity and placed on
display like a freak—deserves to be raped: this is the only consummation that
will penetrate her self-enclosure, and, given the humiliation of her fleshiness, it
is all she is good for. When the female is simultaneously decapitated and
recapitated by her sexual organs, the face that was supposed to be a window to
the soul embodies a sexuality that is less related to pleasure and more to
dominance over the woman who is "nothing but" a body. Because such an image
of mindless physicality justifies rape and thereby perpetuates an ideology of
submission that can be understood as a clear-and-present danger to women, it
might be viewed by some observers as an example of precisely the sort of
pornography that should be censored as not only unartistic but anti-artistic: from
this perspective, the painting itself rapes the female spectator by objectifying her
as her sexual parts and thereby robbing her of her humanity.

Yet a sketch of *Le Viol* appeared earlier on the cover of André Breton's
Qu'est-ce que le Surréalisme? (1934), and its subject reappears modified in
many of Magritte's other paintings. These recurrences dramatize its centrality in
the public movement of surrealism and in the private development of Magritte's
oeuvre. Quite different interpretations of the painting, which take these two facts
into account, tend to share a focus on disruptive strategies that, whether sub-
versively comic or tragic in intent, clarify and justify the aesthetic status of the
painting. In opposition to the approach that labels *Le Viol* inadequate as art, such
readings emphasize the fact that Breton's contemporaries repeatedly employed
absurd, provocative, and fantastic symbols to defamiliarize conventional ways of
seeing both art and reality. For, in their exploitation of erotic and perverse
images, of many different art forms and media, and of unconscious material

manifested in dreams or madness, the surrealists mocked the hypocrisies of bourgeois morality as the origins of repression and alienation.

In this context, *Le Viol* flaunts the mind-body split at the center of Western culture, taunts the prudery that teaches us to cover the body and not the face, and jokes that love is blind. The face of the beloved *is* her body and vice versa, for we have wrapped ourselves up in false values that have robbed us of our appreciation of the hilarious and inexorable materiality our flesh is heir to. And, if the female face represented as a body means the female's body could be a face, the movability of her parts allows us to imagine the same "impossible freedom" John Berger finds elsewhere in Magritte's work, which meditates on "the notion of a self that has left its own skin" (Berger, 1980, 159). In addition, the painting's title, with its allusions to veiling and unveiling and to the image of a violin,[7] asks us to consider why we live in a world of such sexual analogies as, for example, that of the face and the body or the female and the musical instrument. As an instrument of pleasure, moreover, the woman appears ludicrously inadequate because by erasing the difference between face and body, the sexual imagination of men is destined to be self-subverting. In this reading, the title contains Magritte's admission that the male artist, superimposing his image of the female body on the face of his model, rapes the woman whose portrait he paints.

Although *Le Viol,* as a sample of surrealist rhetoric, satirizes conventional portraiture as a crude form of sexual reification, within the biographical background of Magritte's development it expresses grief turned into vindictive mockery, or so Martha Wolfenstein has argued (Spitz, 1985, 83). Specifically dealing with Magritte's adolescent vision of his drowned mother's body, Wolfenstein interprets the image of *Le Viol* as a "pretended mistake." For instead of seeing his mother's face (which was covered by her nightgown after her suicidal leap into a river), the thirteen-year-old boy saw only the body of the recovered corpse. Horrified by his haunting glimpse of the exposed body and the concealed face, he retaliated by painting the face as the body, just as elsewhere he reimagined his mother as a strangely reversed mermaid whose face and upper body are those of a fish and whose lower torso and legs are human and female (Spitz, 1985). With respect to *Le Viol,* the surrealists' penchant for transforming (or superimposing) one image into (or onto) another serves as a screen for Magritte's defense against bereavement, as he revenges himself against the mother he was not supposed to see by viewing her as deprived not only of her eroticism but also of *his* sight, smell, and taste. He had been seduced and abandoned, the title suggests now, and, committed to an aesthetic strategy that seeks "to make the most familiar objects howl,"[8] he must rape the most familiar of all objects, the first object of his desire.

Whether Magritte's painting is considered gloomily private or gleefully public in its experimentation, both of these approaches, stressing his interrogation of the difference between the imaginary and the real, defend the work against the charge that it is pornographic or demeaning to women, for it becomes almost quintessentially liberating in its subversive untying of the major human knots of love and death, the mind and the body, and the relationship not only between parents and children but also between male and female. In terms of the large issues surrounding the definitions of art and pornography, we shall see that such a claim could lead the critic beyond the implicit assumption that art may be pornographic to the even more radical claim that pornography is actually a vanguard form of artistry. Paradoxically, as we shall also see, the antithetical view that *Le Viol* is offensive in its dehumanization of women leads the theorist to a similar identification of pornography and art through the argument that all art is (or has historically been) pornographic in its defamation or domination of women. To the extent that extreme exponents of these diametrically opposed views agree, however, their perspectives will help us answer the questions about gender and genre, ideology and evaluation with which we began. In any case, these divergent attitudes toward *Le Viol* serve as a miniature or microcosm of the dialogue in which numerous critics of pornographic fiction have engaged.

Literary Critics of Pornography

Although visual and print media construct their images quite differently, address dissimilar audiences, and function in disparate ways as commodities in the pornography industry, both the formal and the thematic questions raised by Magritte's *Le Viol* reappear in the analyses of pornographic literature produced by feminist and nonfeminist critics alike. Examining the asymmetrical effects of pornography on male and female readers, its indebtedness to the conventions of primal dreams and private fantasies, and the psychological motivations of its authors, such theorists also deal with precisely the themes that emerge in Magritte's work: the son's revenge against the mother, the sexualization and resulting reification of the female figure, and the issue raised so vividly in *Le Viol* of violation or transgression. As in our discussion of Magritte's painting, moreover, there is a striking correlation between the final judgment on pornography's status and the theorists' critical approach: those who emphasize the effect of the work on the spectator, consumer, reader, or society tend to condemn pornography as unartistic; however, those who focus on the verbal strategies and historical conventions of the work itself or on authorial motivations and intentions generally view pornography as a kind of artistry. Yet in spite of their antithetical approaches and evaluations, and for dramatically different reasons, both sides—when taken to their logical extremes—assert that art and pornography are so closely linked that we cannot distinguish between the two.

First, thinkers from D. H. Lawrence to Steven Marcus, George Steiner, and Susan Griffin have claimed that the term "artistic pornography" is oxymoronic. Writing in 1928 to protest a police raid on his paintings, Lawrence condemned pornography because it leads to "secrecy" and "self-abuse," which, he believed, are always "pernicious" (Lawrence, 1956, 41). In contrast to the "obscene," which redirects the individual through the shock of sexual stimulation, pornography—according to Lawrence—should be censored. Not all of the contemporary theorists who condemn pornography as the antithesis of art agree with him about obscenity or censorship, but all share his emphasis on the "pernicious" effects pornography has. Though he is opposed to censorship, for example, Steven Marcus nevertheless believes that a text like *My Secret Life* encourages the reader to regress, for it is "nothing more than a representation of the fantasies of infantile sexual life, as those fantasies are edited and reorganized in the masturbatory daydreams of adolescence" (Marcus, 1964, 289). In *The Other Victorians,* Marcus coins the word "pornotopia" (p. 269) to emphasize the similarities of pornography and utopian fantasy: in the nowhere of pornotopia, time is always bedtime; space is always the supine, female body; man is an enormous, erect penis inhabiting a "pornocopia" of inexhaustible sexual plenitude that masks anxiety and deprivation.

Marcus's view that "inside of every pornographer there is an infant screaming for the breast from which he has been torn" (p. 277) informs the critiques of Steiner and Griffin, both of whom interpret pornographic representation as a mirror of an immature mind that traps the reader in an arrested universe. In "Night Words," Steiner speculates that "there may be deeper affinities than we as yet understand between the 'total freedom' of the uncensored erotic imagination and the total freedom of the sadist" (Holbrook, 1972, 234). Steiner, explaining how "easily blurred" the line between Swinburne's *Lesbia Brandon* and, say, *Sweet Lash* is, simply rejects "the inescapable monotony of pornographic writing" (pp. 228–29). According to Griffin's *Pornography and Silence,* too, the predictable, programmatic sadism in pornography eroticizes domination with tragic consequences, for through the "transformation from image to act and act to image, we become imprisoned in a world of mirrors" that teaches us to see women as the willing, desirous, and deserving slaves of punitive masters (p. 110). Like Marcus, Griffin believes that "in [his] rejection of his mother, [the budding pornographer] has rejected a part of himself" (p. 66), and so, mourning the effects on the female of the pornographer's war against nature and maternal nature, she argues that "it is by the false images of ourselves, expressed and given a life by pornography, that we are enslaved" (p. 77). Like Steiner's, her emphasis on the detrimental effects of such works leads to the view that "the pornographic mind and the racist mind are really identical" (p. 158), a claim that is related to Kathleen Barry's point that pornographic texts and pictures, which stimulate male masturbation accompanied by conscious fantasies of "cultural sadism," function as "handbooks or blueprints for sadistic violence, mutilation, and even gynocide," defamatory material that society would not tolerate against any group other than women (Barry, 1984, 174).

In contrast to writers from Lawrence to Barry, a second group of critics, who claim that pornography can be artistic, generally approach their material from the perspective of the history of censorship. If such works as Radclyffe Hall's *The Well of Loneliness* and James Joyce's *Ulysses* could be banned as pornographic, literary historians like David Foxon, H. Montomery Hyde, David Loth, and Maurice Charney explain, we must remain wary of the cultural relativism that necessarily shapes definitions of the obscene, a warning that is relevant even when we shift our criterion of the unacceptable from obscenity to depersonalizing or violent representations of sexuality. Beginning with Ovid's textbook on seduction, the *Ars Amatoria,* and the flagellation scenes in the saints' lives included in *Acta Sanctorum,* many of these books trace the evolution from the scandalous fabliaux of Boccaccio and the scurrilous jokes of Rabelais to later narratives like *Fanny Hill, La Philosophie dans le boudoir,* and *My Secret Life.*

Often, too, composed before the emergence of feminist criticism, such histories of "pornographic art" speculate either that the shift from the bawdy to the obscene may be part of "the revolt against authority [which] first took the form of heresy, then politics, and finally sexual licence" or that, given the Obscene Publications Act in England (1857) and the Comstock Act in America (1873), the commercial success of pornography in the second half of the nineteenth century correlates with (and, indeed, may be caused by) legislative efforts at censorship.[9] Whether they attribute the rise of pornography to scientific empiricism, the Enlightenment, the development of the novel form with its middle-class readers, or a Judeo-Christian mythology that segregates sexuality from the rest of life, these accounts emphasize the generic, stylistic, and tonal differences to be found in texts that frequently exploit strategies of transgression to satirize the prevailing respectabilities of the culture that produced them.

From this perspective—that pornography is simply one kind of literature— other critics argue that it is anarchic and therefore aesthetically privileged. Peter Michelson in *The Aesthetics of Pornography,* for example, points to the flamboyantly irreverent novels and poems of William Burroughs and Allen Ginsberg to claim that "the pornographic genre, precisely because of its moral anarchy, has provided a touchstone for a modern imagination disgusted with the blind and mechanical (or electronic) optimism of rich and powerful societies" (Michelson, 1971, 18). In France, the literary counterpart to, say, the cult of Lenny Bruce is the mythologizing of the Marquis de Sade, who has been pronounced a nihilistic, anti-Enlightenment philosopher by prominent intellectuals like Simone de Beauvoir, Roland Barthes, and Georges Bataille.[10] The most influential representative of this stance in America is Susan Sontag, who argues that neither the purported aim nor the effect of books that excite the reader sexually is a defect in a genre that strives for psychic disorientation. Examining contemporary novels like *Story of O, The Image,* and *Histoire de l'oeil,* Sontag claims that the "pornographic imagination" turns the artist into "a freelance explorer of spiritual dangers" who advances "one step further in the dialectic of outrage" (Sontag, 1969, 45) so as to speak about the forbidden, the extinction of the self, whether associated with physical death, with mystical attempts to transcend the personal, or with rebellious efforts to transgress the boundaries of conventional consciousness.

Sontag's view, informed by her fascination with modernist (and especially French) modes of experimentation, has surfaced perhaps most unpredictably in the feminist writings of the English artist Angela Carter, who "would like to think" that Sade "put pornography in the service of women" (Carter, 1978, 37). Defining pornography with admirable brevity as "propaganda for fucking," in *The Sadeian Woman* Carter speculates that the "pornographer as terrorist" is always women's "unconscious ally" (p. 22), for violent pornography diagnoses male political dominance as a symptom of tyrannical sexual relations in an unfree society. What Carter effectively demonstrates through her analysis of the life and work of Sade, then, is that pornography is not only art but art of special significance to the female reader. Although her book implicitly opposes all forms of censorship and therefore represents a shift in feminism, which could also be charted through such explicitly libertarian-feminist studies as *Women Against Censorship*, edited by Varda Burstyn, and *Magic Mammas, Trembling Sisters, Puritans and Perverts* by Joanna Russ, a number of the feminists who seek legislative controls over pornography also blur the distinction between pornography and literature, not to defend pornography as a form of art but to critique art as a form of pornography.

Indeed, Kate Millett's *Sexual Politics*—one of the touchstone texts of feminist criticism—examines the fiction of D. H. Lawrence, Henry Miller, and Norman Mailer to prove "how contemporary literature has absorbed not only the truthful explicitness of pornography, but its anti-social character as well" (Millett, 1969, 72). Millett demonstrates that the sexual antagonism of men is not limited in its representation to a special group of texts labeled "pornographic," but that, on the contrary, it is at the heart of Western civilization. Like Leslie Fiedler, who argues in a quotation cited by Carter that "All the idealizations of the female from the earliest days of courtly love have been in fact devices to deprive her of freedom and self-determination" (Carter, 1978, 38), Millett implies that the most sexually abusive passages in works like "The Woman Who Rode Away," *Sexus,* and *An American Dream* bring to the surface a script which is not only flagrantly dramatized in hard-core pornography but which is also embedded in other so-called legitimate and seemingly romantic forms of writing about women. When Griffin refers to "the pornographic writer Juvenal" (p. 34), or when she lists the story of Samson and Delilah and *Native Son* as instances of the myth that "a man's *life* depends on the death of a woman" (p. 91), she makes a comparable point.

"Throughout history," according to Susan Brownmiller, "no theme grips the masculine imagination with greater constancy and less honor than the myth of the heroic rapist" (Brownmiller, 1975, 289). From Katharine Rogers and Andrea Dworkin to Florence Rush, feminist historians of misogyny have emphasized its pervasiveness in both "high" and "low" cultural forms, with Rush arguing about child pornography that the frequent use of child sexuality by nineteenth-century photographers and authors like Lewis Carroll and Dostoyevsky "contributed to the real use, abuse and sexual manipulation of children" and that, therefore, "the progression from the erotization of children in art and humor to pornography is short" (Lederer, 1980, 76). Most recently, claiming that a "feminist critique of pornography" should consist of "the exposition of the pervasive presence of sexism and pornographic structures throughout our culture," Susanne Kappeler identifies "the pornographic structure of representation" itself as "a common place of art and literature," for painter and spectator or writer and reader "bond in the exercise of usurping female subjectivity and experience"; thus "the pornographer only reproduces, on a less elevated level and within a less exclusive circulation, what the artist does in the esoteric fields of high culture; and he derives from it more profit in return for reduced prestige" (Kappeler, 1986, 25–26, 103, 102). Different as this condemnation of art as pornography is from Sontag's and Carter's celebration of pornography as art, both views remind us that, because feminist criticism figures prominently on both sides of the argument, feminist critics—like other feminists—must come to terms not just with diverse perspectives but with disagreements.

Pornartgraphy

Because, as we have seen in the range of interpretive stances toward pornographic fiction (and toward Magritte's *Le Viol*), debates about pornography replicate debates about representation, can it be that the terms art and pornography cannot be fixed in any stable equation? Both those who condemn art as pornography and those who celebrate pornography as art agree on the inextricable entanglement of these two terms. This suggests that any monolithic idea of what constitutes "art" or "the aesthetic experience" must be radically qualified, a point that has been amply demonstrated through numerous analyses of folk tales, slave narratives, gothic romances, and science fiction.[11] Just as important, the slippage or reciprocity in the terms "art" and "pornography" implies that, whether literature is demoted to the pornographic or pornography is promoted to the literary, evaluation is enmeshed in the ideological values of the critic. Regardless of the generic or ideological bases of these debates, clearly pornography has been shot out of the canon we call literary history by those theorists who claim it produces an unaesthetic response through a set of conventions that are considered "immature" or "deviant."

If we take seriously the antithetical arguments of, say, Carter and Millett, however, such ghettoizing of pornography throws out the baby with the bathwater. For as the most sexually liberating form of art or as the epitome of the sexual oppression reinscribed by art, pornography is crucial for understanding our cultural past. From the combined perspective of the opposing approaches of Carter and Millett, moreover, we would also be bound to conclude about our initial questions that, yes, a genre produced predominantly by and for men probably has represented and will represent women as degraded sexual objects, but that, no, an explicitly misogynist representation cannot be equated with a sexist ideology and does not inexorably produce non-art or bad art. Such answers place the ideological significance of the text at the center of the critic's concern even as they attempt to dislodge such an ideological analysis from the evaluative process.

To begin with the subject of genre, it might be useful to explore how Millett and Carter can agree that pornography represents male domination and disagree about whether it should therefore be termed "misogynist" or "feminist." Does the scene of a woman's sexual degradation promulgate or prevent violence to women? Is it symptomatic or diagnostic in status? The recent controversy over *Swept Away*, exacerbated by its director's female signature, depends on whether one views the film as a record that reinscribes the inexorability of male dominance or as a satire that decries it. Significantly, though, the pornographic genre frequently produces this ambiguity itself through narrative devices meant to frame and justify sexual (and frequently violent) scenes in terms that vary from the scientific and medical to the moral. Even feminism has been exploited as such a frame in a spate of recent movies like *I Spit On Your Grave,* in which the heroine is first gang-raped and then revenges herself through a series of sexual crimes that include seductions culminating in castration and hanging. We are being shown, we are told, what we need to know: in the case of *I Spit On Your Grave,* we are presumably being instructed on how even independent women are vulnerable to sexual attack and how this abuse only breeds further violence. To accept such narrative devices as legitimizing is to promulgate as naïve a theory of representation as is produced by discounting them altogether.

Only when we understand how these narrative, framing devices function both in pornography and in so-called legitimate forms of representation throughout several literary periods and in alternative national and racial contexts will we be able to identify and distinguish between various kinds of misogyny, in much the same way we have been able to differentiate, for example, nineteenth-century American domestic feminism from the British suffrage movement or from contemporary lesbian separatism. What has inhibited this type of analysis in the case of conventional pornography is a traditional division of labor in feminist criticism that, on the one hand, deals with the creative process of the female writer but that, on the other hand, generally ignores the male writer to explore the female reader's response to male-authored literature, a critical convention that means we have not yet fully come to terms with the authorial motivations, historical contexts, and aesthetic conventions of genres composed by and for men.

When we turn to the issue of evaluation and ideology in terms of our frequently common experience that a brilliant text, say *King Lear* or *The Rape of the Lock,* can contain misogynist passages or that a progressive text in its time, say Olive Schreiner's *The Story of an African Farm* or Margaret Fuller's *Woman in the Nineteenth Century,* may include confused, incoherent, or insipid sections, it is hardly surprising that ideology and aesthetic success cannot be identified. Yet, that *Looking for Mr. Goodbar* is more effective and ambitious than *Tool Box Murders* (which contains similar scenes of rape and murder) actually makes the former film more, rather than less, disturbing. Indeed, the violence against women we find in so much pornographic art dramatizes the potentially unnerving contradiction between a purportedly neutral formal achievement and a malevolent world view that could harm people, much as do racist and fascist films like D. W. Griffith's *Birth of a Nation* or Leni Riefenstahl's *Triumph of the Will.*

Yet the black or Jewish studies scholar will often find her best insights into the social structures sustaining racism or fascism precisely through her interpretations of such material. Similarly, the feminist scholar who follows Betty Friedan's recent advice to ignore pornography as a trivial form of oppression will neglect those texts that are crucial documents of or about women's subordination (Friedan, 1985). Perhaps, then, the paintings, novels, poems, and films that endure and demand repeated interpretive engagements are not those that are ideologically congruent with our own values but rather those whose form and content effectively express the ideological tensions and contradictions of the culture from which they originated and to which they refer. In any case, the disjunction between assessments of aesthetic and ethical values ought to lead to a fuller consideration of what kind of art is produced from an ideology that feminists might find disturbing.

A Return to the Scene of the Crime

In the context of this general discussion, the traditional feminist reading of *Le Viol* can be extended by taking into account those interpretations that are based on art and personal history. The shock Magritte's portrait administers through a typically surrealist juxtaposition of realistic details with fantastic central images depends on incongruity, and it therefore might lead us to focus on those aspects of the figure where our expectations about the female face or body are undercut. Certainly there is an odd masculine cast to the face composed of a female torso and an equally strange allusion to the male torso in the bulge around the belly button, where the female form would have an indented waist, as well as in the long neck that sinuously stretches upward to penetrate the hair at the top of the figure and in the way the pubic hair functions like a mustache or beard. What could the significance of this almost hermaphroditic iconography be?

Given Magritte's fascination with Freud, we might view the painting as an image of Medusa, the woman whose face Freud associated with female genitalia, the sight of which petrify (horrify and arouse) men. Arguing that the growing boy relinquishes his belief in the mother's penis when he discovers the female is "castrated," Freud identified castration with precisely the decapitation Magritte's figure emblematizes in *Le Viol*. Also, Magritte's erect female figure resembles Freud's Medusa, who not only "repels sexual desires" and "displays the terrifying genitals of the Mother" but whose snakey locks "replace the penis, the absence of which is the cause of the horror" (Freud, "Medusa's Head," 1922, 105). Because what triggers loathing (female genitals presumed to be castrated) also mitigates that loathing (the erection that reassures the man of his difference), Sarah Kofman's analysis of Freud's theory—specifically his belief that "Woman's genital organs arouse an inseparable blend of horror and pleasure" (Kofman, 1985, 85)—can help explain the mixture of revulsion and desire associated with the inspection of female body parts both in Magritte's painting and in so much surrealist art.

The self-enclosed autonomy and erect unicity of Magritte's central figure, however, also recall "the woman's (mother's) phallus which the little boy once believed in and does not wish to forego" because its absence demonstrates that "his own penis is in danger" (Freud, "Fetishism," 1927, 199). But what Freud actually demonstrates in his writing about the phallic mother is that disbelief in the woman's phallus eventually proves to the little boy that his own penis is not in danger. Like Medusa, the omnipotent mother *must* be (defined as) castrated by

Freud as well as by Magritte precisely because she is *not,* and thus the painting provides evidence for Susan Lurie's speculation that penis envy is a fantasy constructed to solve the terrifying problem that "women possess the whole range of individual powers that the male identifies with his penis and yet have 'no penis'" (Lederer, 1980, 166). Unveiling the body of the phallic mother, Magritte dephallicizes it, as if to demonstrate that his representation of her castration reduces the threat of his own vulnerability or subjugation. In a discussion of his belief in a pictorial effort that "puts the real world on trial" (Magritte, 1938, 160), Magritte explained that "woman was responsible for *Le Viol,*" and he thereby indicts woman for causing *The Rape.* Magritte's personal reasons for resenting his mother's autonomy only highlight his contemporaries' obsession with female reproduction: the Paris *Exposition Internationale du Surréalisme* (1938), for example, originally contained in its central hall twenty mannequins, one of which had a glass globe with a goldfish installed at stomach level (Finkelstein, 1979, 72).

But the masculinity of the central figure in *Le Viol* also suggests that the male has been castrated, robbed of the phallus the female now incarnates. Such a view is borne out by the numerous paintings Magritte produced of effaced, absent men composed only of empty suits, with apples where their heads should be (fig. 7, Magritte's *L'Idée* [The idea, 1966]), or of faces obliterated by leaves or birds (fig. 8, Magritte's *L'Homme au chapeau melon* [The man in the bowler hat, 1964]), or of figures emptied of corporality except for their ghostly facial features (fig. 9, Magritte's *Paysage de Baucis* [Landscape of Baucis, 1966]). If the phallicism of the female denies women's difference in *Le Viol,* Magritte's personal dilemma has psychocultural implications. For it corroborates many critics' belief that sexually explicit representations perpetuate reciprocal, interdependent images of men and women and that the anxieties of men are displaced onto their female doubles: the man without the phallus sees the woman as phallus; the man without a body sees the woman as body; the man without the mother sees the mother as himself. As an inverted self-portrait, *Le Viol* resembles the lampoons reproduced in the magazine *Minotaure,* one of which composes the male profile (complete with wart, mustache, and receding hairline) out of four erotically posed nudes (see fig. 10, 1934).

Robert Stoller's two points about pornography—that its essential dynamic is hostility and that its moment of greatest thrill can be traced back to the moment of greatest trauma in the author's or reader's life (Holbrook, 1971, 120, 125)— take on special significance not only in light of Magritte's adolescent tragedy but also in terms of the needs of all boys to establish their sexual identities by separating from the source of their identities. As Marcus and Griffin show in their discussions of the motivations of pornographers, and as Nancy Chodorow and Walter Ong have theorized in their analyses of psychosexual development, masculine self-definition evolves through a process of agonistic differentiation from the mother. If we read pornography this way, we would interpret female characters and their fates in the narrative or their attributes in the visual frame as portraits of the male artist's fears about himself, fears over which the work seeks

Fig. 7. René Magritte, *L'Idée*, 1966.
(Location unknown.)

Fig. 8. René Magritte, *L'Homme au chapeau melon*, 1964. (Collection Simone Withers Swan, New York.)

Fig. 9. René Magritte, *Paysage de Baucis*, 1966. (Private collection, courtesy of Timothy Baum, New York.)

Fig. 10. Anonymous Erotica from *Minotaure*, no. 3–4, 1934. (Courtauld Institute, London.)

to triumph. By recreating in his own image the woman who created him, by repossessing through fantasy the woman who had to be relinquished, by punishing the woman whose separateness was itself experienced as a punishment, and by eroticizing the woman whose eroticism was taboo, the pornographer converts his greatest trauma into his greatest thrill, a fact that explains why the perusal of pulp magazines and the communal showings of stag films have functioned like *rites de passage* for so many adolescent boys.

Given our recognition that sexuality is culturally constructed, moreover, we could move from a psychoanalytic to a historical framework by establishing the socially shaped anxieties that attend masculinity in a given period. Recently, a number of feminist thinkers have begun to speculate that the proliferation of violent pornography since 1970 is part of a male backlash against the women's liberation movement (Russell, 1977, 12). It may be, as Alan Soble has claimed, that pornography is less a matter of retaliation and more "an attempt to recoup in the domain of sexual fantasy what is denied to men in production and politics" (Soble, 1986, 81). But even as what Soble calls "a compensation for sexual powerlessness," its long history has to be contextualized in terms of the history of the relationship between the sexes.

Such contextualization would probably demonstrate about surrealism that its intensified hostility toward women can be linked to a modernist crisis in masculinity which Sandra M. Gilbert has analyzed in terms of the Great War (Gilbert, 1983) and which both of us have traced back to early twentieth-century redefinitions of female sexuality (in psychoanalysis) and autonomy (in the suffrage movement), to the so-called death of God, and to the breakdown of a number of (imperialist and capitalist) myths of heroic individualism (Gilbert and Gubar, 1988). Magritte's paintings illustrate how the dread inspired by male images of corporeal absence is often balanced against revulsion at female bodily presence, as male anxiety about the instability of subjectivity spills over to male disgust with the female subject. Breton's famous characterization of the technical breakthrough of surrealism as "an unprecedented *will to objectification*" (Breton, 1936, 53 [italics his]) more often than not results in the objectification of the female through staged events like Dali's "The Object as Revealed in Surrealist Experiment," where the revelatory action consists of luring a little old woman to come along on an adventure and then extracting one of her teeth (Finkelstein, 1979, 74). That the experimental strategies of surrealism are so enmeshed in violence against women means that formal (as well as content-oriented) elements may function as framing devices that simultaneously justify and perpetuate female degradation.

As this discussion of Magritte and his contemporaries is meant to demonstrate, a number of consequences for literary scholars would attend the study of "pornartgraphy," consequences for feminist research into pornography in particular and for feminist criticism in general. To take the latter first, such an approach implies that we need to pay more attention to male literary traditions in terms of their production of images of male and female sexuality. While we should retain our initial concern over the effects of representations on women, we could extend our analyses to their functions for men. As crucially important as excavations of the female literary tradition are, recent attempts to substitute a feminist canon for the masculinist one we inherited are in danger of replicating the past by substituting one ideologically defined book list for another.[12] Not only do such efforts ignore texts by women that do not "fit" into a feminist mould, they also prevent us from interpreting the aesthetic interactions between the sexes in literary history as an index of the relationship between the sexes in history.

In terms of research on "pornartgraphy," women's studies scholars could begin interpreting the history of pornography, the records of which still, for the most part, remain shelved in rare book and rare art collections or in that corner of the video rental shop least frequented by feminists. Besides providing studies of the responses of men and women to sexually explicit representations in given historical periods, including the present time, feminist critics could begin to examine the significance of pornographic texts like *Sodom or the Quintessence of Debauchery, The Sod's Opera,* and *1601* in the respective *oeuvres* of the Earl of Rochester, Gilbert and Sullivan, and Mark Twain because our understanding of so-called mainstream literary figures has been distorted by the ghettoization of pornography. The relationship between "legitimate" works (Richardson's *Clarissa,* Nabokov's *Lolita*) and "pornographic" spin-offs (Sade's *Justine,* Louis Malle's *Pretty Baby*) would be further illuminated through an investigation of national, religious, and racial conventions.

For the most part, the functions of particular fantasies (the man dressed up as a girl or the domineering woman) have not yet been studied either in visual or in written works, although Stoller and Gilbert have begun this analysis with, respectively, transvestite magazines and canonized poems and novels (Holbrook, 1972; Gilbert, 1982). In addition, recent efforts to emphasize the female figure in pornographic representations have virtually erased a long and important tradition of (male) homosexual pornography. Just as ignored are the significance of the female pseudonym and the feminine fictional perspective in pornography, as well as the obscene fiction produced by women from Marguerite de Navarre to Edith Wharton, Anaïs Nin, Ayn Rand, and Gael Greene. Is our understanding of, say, *Cannibal Feast* or *Looking for Mr. Goodbar* changed when we interpret them as the products of the female imagination? What we know about the relationship between hostility and sexual desire is almost entirely limited to our knowledge of male-authored texts, a fact that has led not only to nostalgic reconstructions of the Victorian stereotype of female passionlessness but also to the unexamined assumption that there is no such thing as female voyeurism or fetishism.[13]

Finally, it seems pointless to defend *I Spit On Your Grave* or *Tool Box Murders* as aesthetic constructs. The crudity and cruelty of their images, as well as the punitive formulas of their plots, do not enlarge or deepen our sense of what it means to be human. My twelve-year-old daughter (from whom I hide the pictorial illustrations included here) tells me about pornography, "It's stupid, sexist, and violent," asking about my work on this essay, "What else is there to say?" For her sake, I wish that nothing more had to be said. Yet, although the women's studies scholar may be afflicted with an uncomfortable intimation of her dependency on the very documents that she finds most troubling, she needs to counter simple efforts to legislate against pornography with the historically based evidence that, as we have seen, in many instances art and pornography are indistinguishable.

Given the cultural history we have inherited from Rabelais to Sade to Magritte, it would be foolhardy to think we can dismiss, segregate, or eliminate dehumanizing or violent constructions of male and female sexuality. Furthermore, given the contemporary scene we inhabit—that is, a society in which a rape occurs every three minutes—it is clearly important that we understand the dynamics of a genre that has been viewed as both the diagnosis and the symptom, both the cause and the effect, of sexual violence. If, as Alain Robbe-Grillet has claimed, "Pornography is the eroticism of others" (Charney, 1981, 1), it is primarily the eroticism of the female as other which has produced a series of sometimes brilliant, sometimes banal, but always unsettling representations that have evolved as pertinaciously as has patriarchal culture itself.

NOTES

This essay originally appeared in *Critical Inquiry* 13, no. 4 (Summer 1987), published by The University of Chicago Press.
I am indebted to the participants in the 1985–86 multidisciplinary faculty seminar on pornography at Indiana University, especially David Rogers, as well as to the students in my graduate seminar on Feminist Criticism, especially Susan Andrati. As always, my thinking has been shaped by Sandra M. Gilbert, whose speculations on gender and genre and on ideology and evaluation helped me make sense of our work on the *Norton Anthology of Literature by Women* and stimulated my approach to pornography in this essay. Finally, Shehira Davezac, Donald Gray, and Edward Gubar provided useful suggestions while I was working on this essay.

1. I am using the translation by Jacques LeClercq (1936) because it is employed in Hélène Iswolsky's translation of Mikhail Bakhtin's *Rabelais and His World* (1984). With no analysis of gender, Bakhtin's exclusive focus on the grotesque wipes out the significance of Rabelais's sexual imagery.

2. A brilliant reading of this text appears in Carter, 1978, 120–36.

3. The first saying, by Ellen Willis, appears in *Powers of Desire*, ed. Anne Snitow, Christine Stansell, and Sharon Tompson (New York: Monthly Review, 1983), p. 463; the second was coined by Robin Morgan, *Going Too Far* (New York: Random House, 1977), p. 169.

4. In the 1983 Minneapolis Ordinance drafted by Andrea Dworkin and Catharine MacKinnon, this definition is supplemented and qualified by the list of nine oppressive presentations, one of which must also appear to characterize a work as pornography. Some of these are fairly general—"(i) women are presented as dehumanized sexual objects, things or commodities"—while others are more specific—"(viii) women are presented being penetrated by objects or animals." The ordinance is reprinted in Appendix II of *Women Against Censorship*, ed. Varda Burstyn (Vancouver & Toronto: Douglas & McIntyre, 1985).

5. Linda Nochlin's *Woman as Sex Object* (New York: Newsweek, 1972) is the essential background text on the visual presentation of women. Especially useful, too, are Chadwick, 1985, and Caws, 1986.

6. Although Sarane Alexandrian's *Surrealist Art* (1969) does not deal specifically with these paintings, it provides the critical vocabulary I am employing here: p. 120.

7. Jack J. Spector, 1972, also traces the painting's title back to *Violette Nozieres* (Brussels, 1933), a book produced by several surrealists (including Magritte) about a young criminal heroine who, "presumably tormented by an incestuous attachment to her father, murdered both her parents": p. 174.

8. Wolfenstein quotes Magritte in an unpublished manuscript summarized by Ellen Handler Spitz, 1985, 86.

9. Foxon, 1965, 50. Marcus meditates on the relationship between the evolution of Victorian pornography and the growth of a middle-class ideology.

10. Perhaps the best example of this work is Roland Barthes, *Sade/Fourier/Loyola*, for Barthes claims that "Debauchery is imaginative; under its impulsion, Sade invented" (1976, 151).

11. A glance at the essays in Elaine Showalter's anthology, *The New Feminist Literary Criticism* (New York: Pantheon, 1985), will suffice to illustrate how feminist critics have established this point about, say, sentimental fiction composed by nineteenth-century American women (the essay by Nina Baym, pp. 63–80), lesbian literature (the essay by Bonnie Zimmerman, pp. 200–24), and black literature (the essay by Barbara Smith, pp. 168–85). For an overview of the impact of race, class, and gender on canonization, see Lillian S. Robinson's essay "Treason Our Text," pp. 105–22.

12. Although the recovery of women writers and the revisionary reading of their works continue to remain an important part of the feminist critical enterprise, I am referring here to some of the valorizing gestures made in order to include into the canon an excluded work of art. These issues are taken up in "The Mirror and the Vamp: Reflections on Feminist Criticism," an essay that Sandra Gilbert and I have completed for a forthcoming volume, to be entitled *Critical Projections*, edited by Ralph Cohen.

13. Judith Walkowitz discusses the myth of female passionlessness in the first wave of the women's movement (1980, 145–57). For a recent discussion on "Is the gaze male?" see Ann Kaplan, *Women and Film: Both Sides of the Camera* (New York: Methuen, 1983).

REFERENCES

Alexandrian, Sarane (1985). *Surrealist Art*. New York: Thames and Hudson. (Originally published 1969.)

Anonymous (1966). *My Secret Life*. New York: Grove. (Originally published c. 1894.)

Bakhtin, Mikhail. (1984). *Rabelais and His World*. Trans. Hélène Iswolsky. Bloomington: Indiana University Press. (Originally published 1968.)

Barry, Kathleen (1984). *Female Sexual Slavery*. Englewood Cliffs, N.J.: Prentice-Hall.

Barthes, Roland (1976). *Sade/Fourier/Loyola*. Trans. Richard Miller. New York: Hill and Wang. (Originally published 1971.)

Beauvoir, Simone de (1972). "Must We Burn Sade?" In *The Marquis de Sade*. London: New English Library.

Berger, John (1980). *About Looking*. New York: Pantheon.

Breton, André (1970). "Crisis of the Object." In *Surrealists on Art*, ed. Lucy R. Lippard. Englewood Cliffs, N.J.: Prentice-Hall, pp. 51–55.

Brownmiller, Susan (1975). *Against Our Will: Men, Women and Rape*. New York: Simon and Schuster.

Carter, Angela (1978). *The Sadeian Woman and the Ideology of Pornography*. New York: Pantheon.

Caws, Mary Ann (1986). "Ladies Shot and Painted: Female Embodiment in Surrealist Art." In *The Female Body in Western Culture*, ed. Susan Rubin Suleiman. Cambridge, Mass.: Harvard University Press, pp. 262–87.

Chadwick, Whitney (1985). *Women Artists and Surrealism*. Boston: Little, Brown and Company.

Charney, Maurice (1981). *Sexual Fiction*. London and New York: Methuen.

Chodorow, Nancy (1978). *The Reproduction of Mothering*. Berkeley: University of California Press.

Diamond, Irene (1980). "Pornography and Repression: A Reconsideration." In *Women: Sex and Sexuality*, ed. Catharine R. Stimpson and Ethel Spector Person. Chicago: University of Chicago Press, pp. 129–44.

Dworkin, Andrea (1981). *Pornography: Men Possessing Women*. New York: Putnam.

Faulkner, William (1927). *Mosquitoes*. New York: Liveright.

Finkelstein, Heim (1979). *Surrealism and the Crisis of the Object*. Ann Arbor: UMI Research Press.

Foxon, David (1965). *Libertine Literature in England 1660–1745*. New Hyde Park, N.Y.: University Books.

Freud, Sigmund (1950). "Medusa's Head" and "Fetishism." In *Collected Papers*, Vol. V, ed. James Strachey. London: The Hogarth Press, pp. 105–06, 198–204.

Friedan, Betty (1985). "How to Get the Women's Movement Moving Again." *New York Times Magazine*, November 3, 1985.

Gilbert, Sandra M. (1982). "Costumes of the Mind." In *Writing and Sexual Difference*, ed. Elizabeth Abel. Chicago: University of Chicago Press, 1982, pp. 193–219.

———. (1983). "Soldier's Heart: Literary Men, Literary Women, and the Great War." *Signs* 8, no. 3 (Spring 1983): 422–50.

Gilbert, Sandra M., and Susan Gubar (1988). "Tradition and the Female Talent." In *The War of the Words*. New Haven: Yale University Press, pp. 125–64.

———. "Sexual Linguistics: Gender, Language, Sexuality." In *The War of the Words*, pp. 227–71.

Griffin, Susan (1981). *Pornography and Silence: Culture's Revenge Against Nature*. New York: Harper Colophon.

Holbrook, David, ed. (1972). *The Case Against Pornography*. London: Tom Stacey.

Hyde, H. Montgomery (1964). *A History of Pornography*. London: Heinemann.

Kofman, Sarah (1985). *The Enigma of Woman: Woman in Freud's Writings*. Trans. Catherine Porter. Ithaca: Cornell University Press. (Originally published 1980.)

Kuhn, Annette (1985). *The Power of the Image: Essays on Representation and Sexuality*. London: Routledge & Kegan Paul.

Lawrence, D. H. (1956). "Pornography and Obscenity." In *Selected Literary Criticism*, ed. Anthony Beal. New York: The Viking Press.

Lederer, Laura, ed. (1980). *Take Back the Night*. New York: William Morrow.

Loth, David (1961). *The Erotic in Literature: A Historical Survey of Pornography as Delightful as it is Discreet*. London: Secker & Warburg.

Magritte, René (1970). "Lifeline" (1938). Trans. Felix Giovanelli. In *Surrealists on Art*, ed. Lucy R. Lippard. Englewood Cliffs, N.J.: Prentice-Hall, pp. 157–61.

Millett, Kate (1969). *Sexual Politics*. New York: Avon.

Marcus, Steven (1964). *The Other Victorians*. New York: Basic.

Michelson, Peter (1971). *The Aesthetics of Pornography*. New York: Herder and Herder.

Ong, Walter (1981). *Fighting for Life*. Ithaca: Cornell University Press.

Rabelais, François (1964). *Gargantua and Pantagruel*. Trans. Jacques LeClercq. New York: New Heritage Press. (Originally published 1936.)

Rogers, Katharine (1966). *The Troublesome Helpmate: A History of Misogyny in Literature*. Seattle: University of Washington Press.

Russell, Diana (1977). "On Pornography." *Chrysalis* 4: 12.

Soble, Alan (1986.) *Pornography: Marxism, Feminism, and the Future of Sexuality*. New Haven: Yale University Press.

Sontag, Susan (1978). "The Pornographic Imagination." In *Styles of Radical Will*. New York: Delta. (Originally published 1966.)

Spector, Jack J. (1972). *The Aesthetics of Freud*. New York: Praeger.

Spitz, Ellen Handler (1985). *Art and Psyche: A Study in Psychoanalysis and Aesthetics*. New Haven: Yale University Press.

Walkowitz, Judith (1980). "The Politics of Prostitution." In *Women: Sex and Sexuality*, ed. Catharine R. Stimpson and Ethel Spector Person. Chicago: University of Chicago Press, pp. 145–57.

3

Pornography and the Religious Imagination

MARY JO WEAVER

One of the more perverse images in the current debate about pornography pictures antipornography feminists and right-wing evangelicals joining hands to defeat a common enemy. In this scenario Susan Griffin, say, or Andrea Dworkin forms a chorus with Jerry Falwell or Jimmy Swaggart to raise their voices against those entrepreneurs whose fortunes are built on the debasement and dismemberment of women. While this imaginal coalition has been criticized by Beatrice Faust as politically dangerous, because "people who are conservative about porn are usually conservative about lesbianism, abortion, health education and rape crisis centers" (1980, p. 19), it has not been analyzed for its religious incongruities.

An alliance between an antipornography feminist like Susan Griffin and a right-wing evangelical Christian like Jimmy Swaggart is unwise on the basis of irreconcilable theological assumptions.[1] A pact between Andrea Dworkin and Jerry Falwell is impossible because of their profound disagreements about the nature of pornography itself. Although I will use Susan Griffin and Jimmy Swaggart to concentrate on some theological issues raised by the pornography debate, I want to note a crucial distinction between militant feminists and fundamentalists that touches upon the vexing question of defining pornography.

Whatever problems one might have with, for example, Dworkin's overstatements—as, for example, throughout *Woman Hating* (1974) or *Intercourse* (1987)—or with her legal strategies, it is still possible to praise her contributions to the definition of pornography. Her work has helped to change the terms of the debate so that pornography is now an issue of power rather than an index of purity. And since her arguments are political rather than moral, her work makes some clear definitional distinctions between antipornography feminists and antipornography religious conservatives. To Jerry Falwell, for example, pornography means dirty movies, whereas to Dworkin (1979) it means representations of sexually explicit violent attacks upon women by men. As Alexander Bloom has said, "trying to define pornography is like peeling an onion . . . [but] what is at issue for the Right is not what is at issue for the feminists. It is, in fact, more likely that their notions of what is and is not pornographic are widely divergent" (1987). In fact, because religious conservatives imagine God as a dominating sovereign who demands human submission, they fail to criticize what anti-pornography feminists perceive as the root of pornography, power used to render others sexually docile.

Both Griffin and Swaggart make connections between religion (or the lack thereof) and pornography that are predicated on traditional Christianity. On the one hand, according to Susan Griffin (1981), Christianity is the foundation of the pornographic imagination because it legitimizes patterns of domination and submission, patterns that are hyperbolized in pornographic enactments. When she warns that "we cannot choose to have both eros and pornography" (p. 249), she means in part that we must choose between Christianity and eros, between the bondage and discipline of traditional Christianity and the biophilic freedom of erotic nature. Jimmy Swaggart, on the other hand, links pornography with the failure of Americans to follow fundamentalist Christian teachings. For him, a strong religious commitment is the only means of saving American culture from the "demons of pornography." When he warns, as he often does on his televised revivals, that we must choose between pornography and religion, he means that a return to that "old-time religion" is the only defense against the perverse panderings of the pornography industry.[2]

By connecting pornography and traditional Christianity, Griffin appears to be antireligious. At the same time, by calling people to return to traditional Christian values in order to overcome pornography, Swaggart appears to be deeply religious. But in the context of a contemporary theological movement—indebted to process thought—that is critical of traditional Christianity, it is possible to suggest, paradoxically, that Griffin's viewpoint is more profoundly religious and Swaggart's more deeply pornographic than either appears at first glance.

When writers like Susan Griffin, Steven Marcus (1964), Sara Harris (1969), Milton Rugoff (1971), and Bernard I. Murstein (1964) criticize Christianity, they often focus on Christian sexual ethics in order to show the links between sexual repression and pornography. Furthermore, by attaching sexual repression to Christianity, historians like Barbara Walker (1983, pp. 910–20) assume that other religions are sufficiently free sexually that one need not look to them for the roots of the pornographic imagination. Finally, by basing their antireligious argument solely on traditional Christianity, antipornography feminists like Andrea Dworkin (1974, p. 73) fail to allow for the possibility that new directions in contemporary theology might allow them to argue against pornography and religious conservatives at the same time without dismissing Christianity itself.

I will argue that the elective affinity between Christianity and pornography does not rest with Christian teachings about sex but with traditional Christian teaching about women as inherently inferior. Although such teaching is not peculiar to Christianity—it can be shown that the patterns of domination and submission found in Christianity are based on an ancient male fear of women found in virtually all religions—the Christian tradition appropriated ideas about female inferiority and combined them with a tendency to spiritualize erotic language in its mystical tradition.

Traditional Christianity and Pornography

To both antipornography feminists and antipornography religious conservatives,[3] Christianity is an institutionalization of divine/human interaction based on a dualistic system in which the divine is understood to be transcendent, superior, and dominant, whereas humanity is considered immanent, inferior, and submissive. This revealed order of things, as found in the Bible and in the Christian tradition, is presumed to be replicated in human relations so that the male inherits the lordly qualities of God the Father, while the female is enjoined to be submissive to God's rule as it is enacted by the male (father, husband, brother, bishop). But if critics like Griffin and preachers like Swaggart both accept this traditional version of Christianity as normative, they disagree about how to interpret it.

Antipornography feminists condemn traditional Christianity because it provides a religious justification for the pornographic imagination. According to them, its teachings about the inferiority of the body and the identification of the body with the female support the humiliation and degradation of women that is the emotional and theoretical foundation for pornography. Feminist theologians like Rosemary Ruether (1975) and Mary Daly (1968), as well as critics like Susan Griffin (1981), condemn traditional Christianity both for its treatment of women and for its teachings about sex. From the very beginning, they say, Christianity has taught us how to debase women and hate sex. And, indeed, even a casual reading of the "Fathers" of the church (Tavard, 1973) shows that the Christian tradition is full of scorn for women, scorn that overflows into canon law (Henning, 1974) and medieval theology (McLaughlin, 1974). The notion of women as inherently lustful, an opinion of "the Fathers," is reflected in clerical attitudes toward women and in the witchcraft mania (Russell, 1972).

If the Gospel is "good news" about salvation, it is bad news about sex. Ancient warnings against the allurements of "the world, the flesh and the devil" were most easily imagined in terms of the flesh, and although one could easily make a case, as Rosemary Ruether has done (1974),[4] that the explicitness of patriarchal warnings against sexual expression constituted a way for agitated celibates to discharge some of their sexual energy, the fact remains that the teachings of traditional Christianity are built upon a hatred of women and a profound abhorrence of sex. Nietzsche's chilling comment—"Christianity gave Eros poison to drink; he did not die of it, but degenerated into a vice" (cited in Sadock, Kaplan and Freedman, 1976, 32)—seems no more than a commonsense interpretation of a flawed tradition. When Christian crimes against women are castigated, especially in the context of the witchcraft mania, Christian teaching about sex is often cited as bearing the burden of those crimes. R. E. L. Masters says simply, "Almost the entire blame for the hideous nightmare that was the witch mania, and the greatest part of the blame for poisoning the sex life of the West, rests squarely on the Roman Catholic church" (1962, xxvi). To overcome pornography, therefore, it appears as if one must reject Christianity, with its dominating God and its double standard of sexual relations as substantiated in Christian sexual ethics.

Antipornography religious conservatives, on the other hand, find in traditional Christianity the basis for a well-ordered, divinely inspired plan for human conduct. Gene Getz (1974), a conservative Christian author, uses texts about bishops from the pastoral epistles to show that God intended men to be gentle, temperate, sensible, and in command of their households. In this view, wives are enjoined to support, love, and understand their husbands so that all can grow in Christ. From the very beginning, say religious conservatives, Christianity has taught us how to honor women and to regulate sex so that it can be enjoyed. "Sex was given to us for pure pleasure," according to Jack and Carole Mayhall (1978), and Rusty and Linda Raney Wright (1981) tell their readers that they can get the most out of sex by placing it within a context of communication and commitment. Christianity, therefore, provides believers with those parameters that insure stable family life. Religious conservatives like Tim and Beverly LaHaye have used statistical data to prove that "Christians are considerably more satisfied with their love life than non Christians" (1976, p. 206), and the Christian philosopher Neil Gallagher argues that "if husbands and wives gave each other the robust sex God intended, there'd be very little market for porno" (1981, p. 207). The "eternal woman" whose vocation was surrender, described by Gertrude von le Fort (1934), a religious writer and convert to Catholicism, has been appropriated and transformed by Marabel Morgan (1973) into "the total woman," whose "surrender" ought to be to seduce her husband every day for a week. "The Creator of sex intended for His creatures to enjoy it," she chirps (p. 131); "sex is as clean and pure as eating cottage cheese" (p. 141).

Conservative Christians find in their tradition a consistent honoring of womanhood and an elevation of female status. Dr. James C. Dobson's *Straight Talk to Men and Their Wives* is clear in its assertion that those ordained by God to be bearers and nurturers of new life have an exalted place within Christianity: they are protected and revered, saved from the hostile interactions of the workaday world and assured of stability and love. The relations between the sexes are based on a divinely ordained complementarity that involves human beings in covenant relationships with one another for the good of all. The divine scheme of the relations between the sexes enhances virtue and leads to happiness. If sex has been disparaged by Catholics, who subordinate the ideal of marriage to the ideal of virginity, Protestants extol marriage as a blessed vocation and fundamentalists have taken pains in the last few years to relate sex to the life of the spirit.[5] Josh McDowell, a traveling evangelist for Campus Crusade for Christ, talks about sex and prayer as two dimensions of the same experience, and Peter Gardella, a scholar who examined conservative Christian sexual ethics in *Innocent Ecstasy* (1985), argues that Christianity gave America an ethic of sexual pleasure. According to religious conservatives, the wholesome sexuality advocated by Christianity is antithetical to the presumably perverse eroticism fostered by the pornographic imagination. In order to overcome pornography, therefore, it appears as if one must accept fundamentalist Christianity.

Christian Sexual Ethics and Pornography

When we examine attitudes toward Christian sexual ethics, we find two distinct lines of thought. The first, relating to the perception that Christianity is detrimental to a happy sex life, tends to indict Christian sexual ethics as hopelessly repressive and to suggest that Christianity, more than any other religion, bears the blame for the linkage between sex and pornography. The second, based on biblical celebrations of marriage and family, praises Christianity for making a healthy sex life possible.

Those who perceive Christian sexual teachings as repressive argue in effect that sex was an acceptable and healthy pastime until Christian sexual ethics made it into a guilt-ridden, barely tolerated duty limited to the begetting of children (Walker, 1983, 910–20). By describing sex in purely functional terms, they argue, Christians have separated sex from pleasure and made it into a forbidden, evil, dangerous activity. Growing out of this attitude is the view that pornography is a reaction to such a distorted view of sex or an extension of its images to perverse intensifications. Pornography, therefore, can be laid at the doorstep of Christian sexual ethics, which perpetuates negative teachings about sexual interaction. "The worship of virginity must be posited as a real sexual perversion," says Dworkin; "the dualism of good and evil, virgin and whore . . . inherent in Christianity finds its logical expression in the rituals of sadomasochism" (1974, 73).

In opposition to these views, one can find a positive evaluation of Christian sexual ethics by religious conservatives who understand Christianity as enhancing human sexual life by regulating it with the virtue of chastity. Since unbridled sex, according to them, is destructive of virtue, and since virtue helps to integrate sex into a stable and loving pattern of human life, pornography thrives on the denial of Christianity, not on its affirmation. Christianity defeats pornography by drawing men and women into God's plan for human relationships and future happiness in heaven. Erotic sexuality is healthy within marriage and, for Catholics, perfectly acceptable within its procreative and unitive context.

AMBIGUITIES IN CHRISTIAN SEXUAL ETHICS

Christianity contains statements about sex that have had a deleterious effect on sexual pleasure. As Ruether has shown, the "lack of any development of the sex relationship as a personal love relationship . . . committed patristic thought to a puritan-prurient ambivalence toward sex as either 'dirty' or objectively instrumental" (1974, 166). The hagiographical tradition, as Donald Weinstein and

Rudolph Bell have shown, exalted virginity in such a way that it made "women's place in society [something] that can only be described as dismal" (1982, 97). Stories of female saints who debased or punished themselves to prove their love for God reveal, claims Marina Warner, "the psychological obsession of the religion with sexual sin, and the tortures that pile up one upon another with pornographic repetitiousness underline the identification of the female with the perils of sexual contact" (1976, 71).

At the same time, however, Christian teachings about sex reflect an inherited tradition that in some ways, celebrated sex. The biblical injunction to "increase and multiply" gives divine sanction to sexual activity within marriage. In addition, the blessings of children and the joys and special pleasure attached to sexual intercourse on the Sabbath testify to the inherent goodness of sexual activity. And, of course, one of the most erotic poems in ancient literature is found in the Bible. The Song of Solomon celebrates the joys of sexual love: the lovers in the poem long for one another's touches and smells as they anticipate the pleasures of sexual intercourse. The uninhibited celebration of the body as the male rapturously describes his beloved's lips, breasts, and belly is a canonical endorsement of sexual pleasure. Contemporary fundamentalists, who look to scriptural texts as a warrant for their behavior, have taken a verse from this book—"Oh that his left hand were under my head and his right hand embraced me"—as a divine approval for clitoral stimulation (Ehrenreich, Hess, and Jacobs, 1986, 50). New translations of this biblical text, notably the one by S. Craig Glickman (1976), are meant to show Christians what God intended romantic love to be.

Finally, it is not altogether clear that Roman Catholic teaching about sex is universally repressive or, as Boswell has shown (1980), that it has been universally consistent. While it is true that Catholic teaching about marriage is based on natural law theory, which makes procreation the primary end of marriage with sexual pleasure clearly secondary, Peter Gardella perceives in Catholic sexual ethics a fundamental sensuality. According to him, the first American writer to prescribe orgasm for women was the Catholic bishop of Philadelphia, Francis Patrick Kenrick, who said, among other things, that women have the right to experience orgasm by touches after intercourse if they have not achieved orgasm during intercourse (p. 9). Orgasm is also a growing concern for conservative fundamentalists. Jack and Carole Mayhall (1978) tell their readers that sex is good and that God's command to increase and multiply means "do not cheat each other of normal sexual intercourse . . . a wife who never has an orgasm is being cheated" (p. 216).

EXCURSUS: WORLD RELIGIONS AND WOMEN'S PLACE

When critics blame Christianity for teaching us how to hate women, they indict Christianity for not overcoming an ancient male fear of women that predates the birth of Christ (Lederer, 1968). Even granting the negative impact Christianity has had on women, however, one must be careful to examine other religious traditions as well so that Christianity does not assume more blame for its treatment of women than other groups.[6] Christians are sometimes perceived as bringing a cold shower of repression to a relatively uninhibited sexual world, a perception that must be tested against the roles and opportunities for women afforded by other traditions. Phyllis Bird has shown (1974), for example, that women in Judaism were treated as chattel, as son-makers, and as legal nonpersons whose chief glory lay in making time and space for men to study Torah.[7]

Similarly, in recalling Plato's fond relationship with Eros, it must be remembered that he was talking not about his sex life but about his ability to perceive contemplation as a lusty experience. As Susan Moller Okin (1979) has shown, women in ancient Greece were defined and treated functionally, made to serve men's needs and those of the state. If the Hindu pantheon has a representation of goddesses, there is no reason to believe that women's social, economic, or political status in India was enhanced by their religious system. The Buddhist canon contains several revealing stories about the Buddha's abhorrence of women: once when someone offered him a woman, the Buddha replied, "Why try to tempt me with that thing? It is a bag full of shit and piss. I wouldn't touch it with my foot" (*Sutanipata: The Group of Discourses* IV.9, Magandiya #835). Scanty sources make it hard to evaluate pagan religions. Judith Ochshorn (1981) has argued that ancient polytheistic religions were good for women until monotheistic Yahwism, led by misogynist priests, destroyed women's possibilities in the ancient Near Eastern world. But her argument has been criticized by scholars like Carol P. Christ (1984) and Sarah Pomeroy (1982). Indeed, Joan O'Brien (1982) has concluded that Ochshorn's work is "flawed by her failure to see the pervasive effects of patriarchy, whether in a polytheistic or a monotheistic setting" (p. 744).

Some feminists want us to believe that societies dominated by goddesses were matriarchal (Stone, 1976, 1979), but it is not clear that such was the case (Binford, 1982). Carol P. Christ argues persuasively that women need to reclaim the power of Goddess religion (1985), but that does not necessarily mean that life was any better in societies that honored the Goddess. If Christianity is bad for women, therefore, it is one part of a complex pattern of male fear of women that has pervaded virtually every religion. As Jill Raitt (1980) has shown, stories about vaginas with teeth—found in almost every society we know about—symbolize male fear of castrating females and make the *vagina dentata* a particularly useful symbol to interrogate the neutralization of the female threat by religious authorities. Raitt's collection of examples shows the universality of male fear of women and leads us to expect a male need to tame women in virtually every canon of folklore and religion in the world.

CHRISTIAN SEXUAL ETHICS NOT TOTALLY AT FAULT

Ironically, I would suggest that Christian sexual ethics are bad for women not because of Christian teachings about the life of the body, but because of religious beliefs about the life of the soul. The Christian roots of the pornographic imagination, as described by Griffin and others, are to be found not in moral handbooks about sexual conduct, but in the textbooks of theology and the spiritual life, both ancient and modern. Theology, the study of God's nature and of the relationships between the divine and human realities, is based on a dualistic understanding of the spiritual and material worlds, a distinction upheld by the belief that God is a radically transcendent and dominating being. In Western Christian spirituality, especially in Roman Catholicism, virginity, as "an ideal that derived ultimately from pre-Christian sources in Hellenistic dualism, pervaded every segment of medieval society" (Weinstein and Bell, 1982, 99).

Blaming Christian sexual teachings, themselves, for the pornographic imagination, therefore, is untenable; it will be more productive to look for the foundations of the pornographic imagination in the patterns of domination and submission that are found primarily in Christian beliefs about women as inferior creatures, and in the tendency of the Christian tradition to separate procreative sex from erotic pleasure, or in the teachings that place eroticism within a context of female submission.

Spiritual Life and the Inferiority of Women

Traditional Christian theology is based on a belief in the radical transcendence of God and a consequent division of all reality into higher and lower realms. In this system, everything is divided according to a pattern of heavenly (spiritual) existence and earthly (bodily) life. In the creation story in the Bible, for example, the maker is divided from the thing made in such a way that the creator is inherently superior to the created order and stands in a relationship of mastery over it. According to traditional Christology, the redeemer, though "truly man," has a divine nature and so is divided from those redeemed by virtue of his status as the preexistent son of God. In human relations, the "degrading idea that 'man is the beginning and end of woman' is reinforced by the parallel man: woman; God: creature," as Mary Daly reminded us (1968, 51). In religious life, the spiritual realm is divided from earthly life on the assumption that bodily life is inherently inferior to the life of the soul.

Christian sexual teaching and Christian spirituality both follow these divisions. Using Aristotelian biological categories, medieval Catholics were able to define sex in purely functional terms and argue that women were passive vessels of the male life force. Pleasure was subordinated to procreation in such a way that sexual intercourse could be assessed solely in terms of its childbearing functions, and since those functions were considered to be the result of the divine curse placed on Eve, women who were wives and mothers were not considered worthy of spiritual advancement. The spiritual life, as Ruether (1986) has shown, was based on the misogynist belief that only males were made in the image of God. Since sex was designed for procreation, and women made to be used for the propagation of the species, both sex and women were assigned to the lower realms of existence, believed to be necessary evils, and perceived as highly dangerous to the life of the spirit.

The mystical life was the heroically attainable goal of those who could abstain from the allurements of the body and channel their energies into spiritual pursuits. Abstinence from sex was part of a program that enjoined devotees to fast from food and sleep, mortify their flesh, ward off demons of self-involvement and self-abuse, and spend long hours in prayer and contemplation. This system is not peculiar to Christianity: mystics with an ascetic agenda can be found in most of the world's religions. In the Christian tradition, only virgins (those who had never had sex, or who had renounced it) could attempt to pursue the higher calling of mystical life, because virginity allowed devotees to transcend the body in order to ascend, spiritually, into heaven. Women who hoped for mystical union with God could do so only by denying their sexuality in vows of perpetual virginity, a heroic renunciation that, according to Weinstein and Bell "was virtually assured of failure not only because the flesh was weak, but because the world demanded marriage and motherhood" (1982, 98). Furthermore, whereas "men could be sanctimonious about their ability to resist sexual assaults, women, considered the lustful and morally weak sex, had great difficulty in establishing their credibility in the face of gossip and male ridicule" (p. 88).

Paradoxically, therefore, it is in the spiritual tradition, where, rhetorically at least, all souls are equal before God, that some of the most virulent misogynist language can be found. The theological understanding of a radically transcendent God whose qualities were appropriated by males to the disparagement of women and bodily life is the basis for the double standard identified by antipornography feminists as the foundation of the pornographic imagination. Stories of medieval sanctity, as Weinstein and Bell have shown, were full of tales of heroic men beset by the devilish power of women: "heroic resistance to blatant, sexual seduction could never be repeated often enough" (p. 81). In the lives of male saints, women were portrayed as sexual predators and allies of the devil, but female saints "who described their own sexual problems did not often allow themselves the luxury of blaming them on the devil, perhaps being too deeply instilled with the prevalent notion that women were the lustful sex to think of shifting their responsibility to outside forces" (p. 87). This tendency to associate women with sex and its powers, and the belief that mystical experience was most properly reserved for men constitute common religious themes, giving further substance to the view that male hatred for and "fear of women lies deep in the mythic consciousness of men" (Russell, 1972, 283).

In traditional Roman Catholicism and conservative fundamentalism, women must be ruled by a father and then by a husband (or, in the case of nuns, by a bishop). The medieval adage—*aut maritus, aut murus,* either a husband or an enclosure wall (Suenens, 1963, 46)—presented women with their only options. Furthermore, the doctrine of complementarity—a form of sex-role discrimination that relegates men and women to specific roles on the basis of their supposed divinely assigned natures—continues to tell Christian women that God designed them for subservient roles. Since this traditional vision operates on a model in which women are necessarily subservient, antipornography feminists rightly suggest that it must be rejected, and antipornography religious conservatives wrongly link the defeat of pornography to the Christian vision. It is not far-fetched to say that pornography is an intensification of the gender differences in traditional Christianity. "Good Christian businessmen" who spend their lunch hours in "adult" bookstores live not in two worlds but in one, single universe in which men dominate women. Pornography, therefore, does not grow at the expense of traditional Christianity but as a further distortion of the already distorted social roles embodied in its own religious vision.

Jimmy Swaggart's recent fall from grace, resulting from his kinky sexual practices with a prostitute, underscores my point. It is revealing that Swaggart did not have sexual intercourse with the "fallen woman" he accompanied to motel rooms but "used her" for autoerotic stimulation and fellatio. In his tearful public confession he admitted to weakness and "shameful conduct" but was able to assure his congregation that he had not "committed adultery" with her, thereby ensuring that his own personal pillar of a good Christian society—the sanctity of his marriage and family—remained solid. Religious traditions that tend to be overly agitated about sexual misconduct often define legitimate sexual activity in narrow ways so that "proper" sexual expression is limited to "the missionary position." As long as a man does not assume this position, he has not had "sexual intercourse." Swaggart's conduct may not be typical, but his theological beliefs are shared by a majority of religious conservatives who inhabit a world where God dominates men and men dominate women.

Spiritualization of Erotic Language

Although the functional definition of women and sex supported the Neoplatonic desire for a disembodied spiritual life, spiritual communion was often articulated in highly erotic language. Those women who had taken vows of virginity in order to seek spiritual union with God gave up sex but did not necessarily forego erotic pleasure. In fact, when looking for highly erotic passages in the Christian tradition, I find it instructive to read the mystics. Teresa of Avila's sixteenth-century experience of God as a lover marks the apex of her spiritual quest and, at the same time, is astonishingly erotic:

> The Lord wanted me while in this state to see sometimes the following vision: I saw close to me toward my left side an angel in bodily form. . . . I saw in his hands a large golden dart and at the end of the iron tip there appeared to be a little fire. It seemed to me this angel plunged the dart several times into my heart and that it reached deep within me. When he drew it out, I thought he was carrying off with him the deepest part of me; and he left me all on fire with great love of God. The pain was so great that it made me moan, and the sweetness this greatest pain caused me was so superabundant that there is no desire capable of taking it away. (1976, 193.)

Such erotic descriptions of spiritual union were not confined to women. Indeed, John of the Cross, probably the most consistently erotic spiritual writer in the Christian tradition, describes his own spiritual experience with passion. Addressing God, he says, "You dwell alone, not only as in Your house, nor only as in

Your bed, but also as in my own heart, intimately and closely united to it. And how delicately You capitivate me and arouse my affections toward you" (1979, 644). The theme of spiritual betrothal to God was a mainstay of religious life. The "Office of St. Agnes," recited before a woman took her vows of perpetual virginity, makes a romantic connection between the candidate for religious life and God: "For Him alone I keep my troth; to Him I surrender . . . with His ring my Lord Jesus Christ has betrothed me" (*The Hours of the Divine Office in English and Latin*, 1963, vol 1, 1702, 1708).

The use of erotic language to describe relations with an asexual deity upheld a dangerous separation between sexuality and eroticism in the Christian tradition. By pairing sex exclusively with procreation, the Roman Catholic church's teachings never allowed for sex as a pastime, a pleasure, or a means of intimate communication between spouses. This limited understanding of sex may account for the fact that one finds little on eroticism, sexual perversion, or pornography in Catholic moral theology textbooks. Because any extramarital activity was mortally sinful, celibate moralists were not as interested in proscribing perverse sex as they were in speculating about the various kinds of questions that arose within the confines of procreational, married sex. Moral theology textbooks usually have significant sections on married sexual activity: when to have intercourse, in what position, after what kinds of foreplay, with what kinds of intentions, with what kinds of fantasies, under what conditions (Ford and Kelly, 1963, vol. 2, 208–34). Perversions of erotic pleasure are relatively absent in moral texts—with, perhaps, the exception of Alfonso de Liguori (1821, 298–337), who discusses various "unnatural sexual practices"—because the erotic impulse had been effectively removed from sexual life. Erotic language was kept alive in celibate longing for God.

This tendency to spiritualize erotic feelings, embedded deeply in the Christian tradition, is not confined to Catholics. Nineteenth-century American Methodists regularly produced ecstatic testimonies (Merritt and King, 1843); Pentecostal Aimee Semple McPherson "taught that fulfillment came through ecstatic experience and showed how such experience looked and felt" (Gardella, p. 83); and the pious Phoebe Palmer, who waited for God in "thrilling anticipation," assured her readers that her own "insatiable desires" had been filled by God, and that her Savior was even now "wooing [her six-year-old daughter] to the embrace of his love" (1871, 36, 258).

Nor was erotic spirituality a one-sided affair. Bernard of Clairvaux, a twelfth-century spiritual writer, puzzled over the annunciation story in the New Testament. Since the angel says to Mary, "Hail, the Lord is with you," it appeared to Bernard that the Lord was already there (with Mary) before asking her permission. Little wonder, exclaimed Bernard, since "the virgin's ointment yielded its sweet odour; its fragrance came up to His glorious presence and found favor in His sight." God, "borne upon the wings of His exceeding longing, . . . reached the Virgin whom he loved, whom He had chosen for Himself, whose beauty He desired" (1954, 128). John of the Cross repeatedly praised virginity for its power to attract the divine lover.

Eroticism, therefore, is a central part of the Christian tradition, but in a spiritualized form. When Griffin bids her readers to choose eroticism, she opposes it to traditional Christianity without making the distinction between Christian literature about female inferiority and spiritual treatises about erotic relationships between the soul and God. Christianity contains a possibility for the erotic that can be appreciated even though the traditional teachings about women as inferior and subservient, in need of male mastery, must be rejected. On the other hand, when conservative fundamentalists link the erotic impulses of sex to traditional Christianity without questioning its sexual double standards, they fail to see that the vision they endorse is inherently pornographic because it is based on patterns of domination and submission.

Virtually all of the books by conservative Christian writers about marriage assume that proper sexual pleasure can be found only in marital relationships where the man is clearly the head of the family. Writing collaboratively, Jack and Carole Mayhall, in *Marriage Takes More than Love* (1978), describe marital "Responsibilities." Interestingly, Jack wrote the chapters "Choosing to Lead," "Choosing to Solve Problems," "Choosing Headship," "Choosing to Encourage," and "Choosing Responsibility," whereas Carole wrote the chapter entitled "Choosing to Submit." She did not want to submit to her husband, she says, but was finally led to the profound truth that "to obey God meant obeying Jack" (p. 189). She was rewarded for her decision by Jack's behavior: "when I chose to obey," she assures her readers, "Jack became less demanding and . . . we grew closer" (p. 189).

The conservative Christian vision, therefore, is predicated on a pattern of dominance and submission, and the erotic possibilities of Christian spirituality are linked with a reading of the tradition that upholds male mastery. If an alternative theological vision were explored, however, it might be possible to argue against pornography and traditional Christianity without relinquishing the spiritually satisfying parts of the religion.

An Alternative Christian Vision and Erotic Life

With its double standard of sexual relations, Christian dualism postulates a theological system in which God is utterly transcendent, totally Other, the Lord and Master of the universe. Since that system has been criticized by feminist theologians of many different theological persuasions, it is not surprising that alternatives to it are diverse and often controversial. Some feminist interpreters reject religion altogether, whereas others abandon Judaism or Christianity in favor of Goddess religion (Christ, 1987; Starhawk, 1979). Many of those who reject Christianity to embrace some form of neo-paganism claim to be searching for a religion of immanence that cannot be found within the Christian tradition (Spretnak, 1982).

Although I understand the attraction of an immanent deity as found in Goddess religion, I do not agree that it is totally absent from the Christian tradition. Undoubtedly divine transcendence has been the predominant theme in

Christianity, but not the only one, and it is worth examining an alternative offered by process thought to see whether it, too, upholds the pornographic imagination. In *Beyond God the Father* (1973), Mary Daly flirted with a process alternative but was so repulsed by official Christianity that she did not pursue "God the Verb" beyond that book either as an argument or as a spiritual possibility for women.

Classical Western spirituality has been based on a system of mastery believed to replicate God's relationship with the world: the Creator masters the primal chaos to create the world, and men master the flesh to attain the life of the spirit. In poetic terms, mystics look at the material universe and say, "This, neither, is Thou": nothing that can be seen, felt, experienced, or touched is genuinely divine, and those attempting spiritual union with the deity are enjoined to put a "cloud of unknowing" between themselves and everything else in order to make room for God. Known as the *via negativa,* or the way of negation, this form of spiritual life is based on a denial of human experience, a denial of what Griffin refers to as eros, that is to say, the child in us, the experience of falling in love, the exquisite joys of bodily life, and the experience of vulnerability and suffering. Given a God who is uninvolved in changing patterns of existence, whose relationship to humanity is one of omnipotent mastery, a spirituality attempting union with God encourages qualities that replicate the divine personality. Traditional Catholic spirituality and contemporary fundamentalist spirituality both follow this pattern. Although neither group continues to argue that women are naturally *inferior,* both continue to believe that women have a divinely ordained place within the universe that requires the direction and control of men.

Yet a minor and radically different theme in the Christian tradition is that of the divine immanence. One modern expression can be found in process theology, a system based on the work of Alfred North Whitehead (1929). Process thought has adumbrations in biblical stories of divine immanence, in the Christian doctrine of the Incarnation, and in those poets of the spiritual life who look at the created order and say, "This also is Thou." Dante's cosmic drama of salvation is upheld by his experience of having fallen in love with Beatrice,[8] and Meister Eckhart's creation-centered spirituality is based on the belief that what can be experienced, felt, touched, and known in this world is, very often, of the divine order.[9] Known, if at all, as the "way of affirmation," this kind of spirituality celebrates those experiences Griffin identifies with eros and conceptualizes the relationship with God as one of partnership and mutual vulnerability.

Process thought is a modern appropriation of these spiritual insights coupled with a sense of the dynamism of nature, the reality of time, and the possibility of novelty. Process theology has been nurtured by the revolution in the scientific world view—Darwin's evolutionary work and Einstein's theory of relativity— and the scientific respect for mystery as found in the work of subatomic physicists like Fritjof Capra (1975, 1982).

Because process theology develops the partnership and communicative elements of the divine/human interaction, it can break the tradition of religious tyranny and make way for a theology that can displace the dominance of men over women with genuinely mutual patterns of relationship. In the classical theology of traditional Christianity, although the creative center of the universe, God is the supreme exception to human experience and has no necessary relationship with the world. God, in other words, appears not to need the world at all and is said to sustain its life as an act of supreme goodness and generosity. For process theologians, however, God does need the world and the bustle of choices that make up human and subhuman existence. For Whitehead, God is the supreme exemplification of all metaphysical and human categories, not their exception. Far from being unrelated to this world, the process God is that being who is conditioned and affected by everything that happens here and understand-able only in terms of relationships. God is absolute not in the traditional sense of being final, total, unlimited, and unchangeable, but by being encompassing in influence, related to and suffering with all entities, and being the ultimate and highest destiny of each.[10]

In process philosophy, God's power lies in the lure of beauty, in the tenderness of compassionate persuasion, not in force or domination or mastery. If experience has claimed that human beings relate to God in strength, love, vulnerability, and weakness, process thought has made the same claims for God. God relates to humanity in strength because of the visions present in what Whitehead calls the divine primordial nature; in love because of a desire for more extensive and intensive relationships; in vulnerability because the divine destiny is tied to human destiny; and in weakness because God needs what human beings can give. Since the divine concrete experience depends on what human beings are able to give, God lures humanity on so that human beings—all life, really—will experience more and so have more to give to the process. Process thought assumes that God is related, persuasive, and involved with the world and that religion is a relationship with the deity that enriches both partners beyond their ability to achieve alone.

According to process theologians, human beings emulating this God are open to possibility, involved with the whole created order, aware of their choices and their own development, and unwilling to define the universe or themselves in dualistic terms. In process theology there is no double standard for males and females, or for animate and inanimate life; there are no gender differences to exploit, no mastery images to uphold, no need to control the passions, the body, or, by extension, women. For Whitehead, what used to be perceived as op-positions are now merely contrasts: "It is as true to say that God is one and the World many, as that the World is one and God many . . . as true to say that God creates the World, as that the World creates God" (1929, 530). For Charles Hartshorne, Whitehead's chief interpreter, God is like a teacher who is enriched by his or her sympathetic involvement in the pupil's learning experience (1967).

Although it may be hard to imagine that such a theology could be born out of a sexist culture, or, more to the point, that it could change centuries of traditional belief and behavior that encourage mastery, domination, and submission, the utopian possibilities offered by process thought have been articulated by a growing number of philosophers and theologians and have found some resonance in feminist theology (Davaney, 1981). If the hierarchical model of Christianity found in traditional Catholicism and contemporary fundamentalism upholds the pornographic imagination by encouraging believers to emulate a dominant God who requires submission from believers, then the very possibility for an alternative theological vision holds some promise for another order of divine-human interaction that can alter patterns of human interaction. In the process model, mutuality does not depend upon a hierarchical arrangement but encourages vulnerability and mutual openness.

Conclusion

Process theology opens a new dimension of the religious imagination. As Marjorie Suchocki says, "the process concept of God provides a metaphysical grounding to the values of openness and mutuality so essential to the feminist program" (1981, 65). Process theology enables one to imagine a Christianity that is not a source of and foundation for the pornographic imagination and makes it possible for antipornography feminists to retrieve those parts of the Christian vision which some of them may find life enhancing. What Griffin associates with eros—celebration of life, falling in love, poetry, mutuality, change, vulnerability, and beauty—are the very elements that a process system recognizes as most clearly embodying the divine reality. In this system, the God of mastery is replaced by a God whose only power over humanity is in the lure of beauty. While one must choose between eros and pornography, therefore, one does not necessarily have to choose between Christianity and eros.

For religious conservatives, however, whatever joy they may find in sex, the choice remains fixed between religion and eros precisely because religion is conceptualized in the traditional terms of domination and submission. There can be no real relationship between Christianity and eros in a religious system that insists on subservience from women and is built upon the double standards derived from the God of mastery. Religion as defined by conservatives is not antithetical to pornography but supportive of it, and an appropriation of the "old-time religion" is an affirmation of the very framework upon which perverse extensions of dominating masculinity are constructed. The antipornographic views of religious conservatives that purport to be deeply religious, are, therefore, profoundly pornographic, whereas the antipornographic views of feminist critics that appear to be antireligious are open to the designs of a new theological vision. Because the theological assumptions of conservative religionists and feminists are so clearly antithetical to one another, there can be no fruitful alliance between them. It is not possible to imagine traditional religion and eros, nor is it possible to argue that conservative religion can save the world from pornography. It is possible, however, to have a newly imagined religion that welcomes eros, a religion based on process thought, which not only undermines pornography but also undermines the old, tyrannizing tradition of conservative Christianity.

NOTES

I wish to thank Susan Gubar and Richard Miller for their careful readings of this text in several versions.

1. I realize that my coalition is more imaginary than real, and that Susan Griffin, herself, is not part of any such group. Because her writings are so lucid about the incompatibility of eros and Christianity, however, she makes a perfect foil for religious conservatives and allows me to raise some intriguing theological questions. The possibility of a real coalition between conservative Christians and some antipornography feminists has frightened more than one interpreter (see Bloom, 1987, and Faust, 1980).

2. Readers may be frustrated by the lack of *textual* support for the opinions of Swaggart and Falwell. I find it maddening, myself, since their predilection for preaching over writing has forced me to watch more hours of television evangelism than is healthy. Falwell's book, *Listen, America!* (1980) is only vaguely useful and Swaggart's *Rape of a Nation* (1985) is, like his preaching, a series of condemnations against the evils of the modern world. Both men are powerful preachers and hold common cause against illicit sex, drugs, pornography, the women's movement, homosexuality, welfare, and other American "vices." Swaggart has recently been caught in a sexual scandal, and it is not yet clear what the facts are in the case. According to Debbie Murphree (*Penthouse*, 1988), the television evangelist engaged her in a series of perverse sexual practices.

3. I am using "religious conservatives" as a catch-all phrase including right-wing Roman Catholics, Evangelical Christians, and mainline Protestants. I have chosen Swaggart as a representative of that view because he preaches it so forcefully and because he has an enormous television outreach. His current moral disgrace does not change my point that the theological presuppositions of conservative Christians make any alliance between them and antipornography feminists impossible.

4. Indeed, Ruether continues to criticize traditional Christianity and to refine her arguments. This particular contention is not only an early example of her thinking, but one of the most explicit on this particular issue.

5. Some of the conservative Christian impetus toward a more sensual Christianity can be found in Gardella, 1985. A review of some of the literature and ideas of fundamentalists about sex can be found in Ehrenreich et al., 1986.

6. Indeed, not all people who study pre-Christian periods are as hard on Christianity as feminist interpreters. Michel Foucault (1980), for example, sees some positive aspects to early Christian views on women in terms of the erotic aspects of heterosexual relations.

7. Since I am trying to demonstrate that there are multiple intellectual strands in Christianity, I do not want to reduce other religious traditions to one, dispiriting theme. I recognize that women in Judaism were also revered as mothers, sometimes praised for bravery, and celebrated for insight. On the whole, however, Bird's interpretation gives me a way to say that Christianity is not the only religion where women's lives were dismal in a religiously sanctioned way.

8. Although it is anachronistic to make a clear connection between Dante and process thought, the fact that Dante's work is an exercise in the "way of affirmation of the images" makes him a historical forerunner. Dorothy L. Sayers has been most explicit on Dante's connections with the way of affirmation. See her *Introductory Papers on Dante* (1954) and her introduction to her translation of *The Divine Comedy* (1949, 1955). In some ways Sayers popularized the interpretation of Dante made by her friend Charles Williams. See his posthumously published *The Figure of Beatrice* (1961).

9. Eckhart, a German Dominican (1260–1337), was a famous preacher and spiritual director who taught at the University of Paris but is primarily remembered for his sermons, which are replete with references to feminine dimensions of the divine and which were preached primarily to the Beguines, a late medieval independent sisterhood

persecuted and suppressed for their refusal to capitulate to the cloister model of religious life. For a modern reading of Eckhart, see Matthew Fox, *Breakthrough: Meister Eckhart's Creation Spirituality in a New Translation* (1980).

10. Process thought has its own vocabulary and cannot be easily reduced to simple explanations as I have tried to do here. My intention, however, was not to provide a full-blown explanation of process thought—for that, see Cobb, 1976; Cousins, 1971; Suchocki, 1986; and Williams, 1981—but simply to suggest that the Christian tradition may not be as bankrupt as some antipornography feminists claim it is, and that Christianity cannot be reduced to the "traditional" dualistic interpretations that bolster the conservative viewpoint.

REFERENCES

Bernard of Clairvaux (1954). *Super Missus Est,* Homily III. In *Saint Bernard On the Christian Year: Selections from his Sermons.* London: A. R. Mobray. Original work written in twelfth century and can be found in *Sancti Bernardi Opera Omnia,* vol. 1, Part 1, p. 1686. Paris: Apud Gaume Fratres, 1839.

Binford, Sally R. (1982). "Are Goddesses and Matriarchies Merely Figments of Feminist Imagination?" *The Politics of Women's Spirituality,* ed. Charlene Spretnak. New York: Doubleday, pp. 541–49.

Bird, Phyllis (1974). "Images of Women in the Old Testament." In *Religion and Sexism,* ed. Rosemary Ruether. New York: Simon and Schuster, pp. 41–89.

Bloom, Alexander (1987). "Peeling the Pornographic Onion." *The World and I* 2 (February 1987): 424–31.

Boswell, John (1980). *Christianity, Social Tolerance and Homosexuality.* Chicago: University of Chicago Press.

Capra, Fritjof (1975). *The Tao of Physics.* New York: Bantam Books.

———(1982). *The Turning Point.* New York: Simon and Schuster.

Christ, Carol P. (1984). "The Female Experience and the Nature of the Divine [Review]." *Journal of the American Academy of Religion* 52:786–88.

———(1985). "Symbols of Goddess and God in Feminist Theology." *The Book of the Goddess Past and Present,* ed. Carl Olson. New York: Crossroad, pp. 231–51.

———(1987). *The Laughter of Aphrodite: Reflections on a Journey to the Goddess.* San Francisco: Harper and Row.

Cobb, John B. (1976). *Process Theology: An Introductory Exposition.* Philadelphia: Westminster Press.

Cousins, Ewert H., ed. (1971). *Process Theology: Basic Writings by the Key Thinkers of a Major Modern Movement.* New York: Newman Press.

Daly, Mary (1968). *The Church and the Second Sex.* New York: Harper and Row.

———(1973). *Beyond God the Father.* Boston: Beacon Press.

Davaney, Sheila Greeve, ed. (1981). *Feminism and Process Thought.* Lewiston, N.Y.: Edward Mellen Press.

De Beauvoir, Simone (1952). *The Second Sex.* New York: Alfred A. Knopf.

Dobson, James C. (1980). *Straight Talk to Men and their Wives.* Waco, Tex.: Proven Word.

Dworkin, Andrea (1974). *Woman Hating.* New York: E. P. Dutton & Co.

———(1979). *Pornography: Men Possessing Women.* New York: Putnam Perigree.

———(1987). *Intercourse.* New York: The Free Press.

Ehrenreich, Barbara; Hess, Elizabeth; & Jacobs, Gloria (1986). "Unbuckling the Bible Belt." *Mother Jones,* July/August 1986, pp. 46–51, 78–85.

Falwell, Jerry (1980). *Listen, America!* New York: Doubleday.

Faust, Beatrice (1980). *Women, Sex and Pornography.* New York: Macmillan.

Ford, John C., and Kelly, Gerald (1963). *Contemporary Moral Theology.* Westminster, Md.: The Newman Press.

Foucault, Michel (1980). *History of Sexuality,* vol. 1. New York: Vintage Books.

Fox, Matthew (1980). *Breakthrough: Meister Eckhart's Creation Spirituality in a New Translation.* New York: Doubleday.

Gallagher, Neil (1981). *The Porno Plague.* Minneapolis: Bethany House Publishers.

Gardella, Peter (1985). *Innocent Ecstasy: How Christianity Gave America an Ethic of Sexual Pleasure.* New York: Oxford University Press.

Getz, Gene A. (1974). *The Measure of a Man.* Ventura, Cal: Regal Books.

Glickman, S. Craig (1976). *A Song for Lovers.* Downers Grove, Ill.: Varsity Press.

Griffin, Susan (1981). *Pornography and Silence.* New York: Harper Colophon.

Harris, Art, and Berry, Jason (1988). "Jimmy Swaggart's Secret Sex Life." *Penthouse,* July 1988, p. 104.

Harris, Sara (1969). *The Puritan Jungle.* New York: G. P. Putnam's Sons.

Hartshorne, Charles (1967). *A Natural Theology for Our Time.* Lasalle, Ill.: Open Court.

Henning, Clara (1974). "Canon Law and the Battle of the Sexes." In *Religion and Sexism,* ed. Rosemary Ruether. New York: Simon and Schuster, pp. 267–91.

The Hours of the Divine Office in English and Latin (1963). Translated by the Staff of Liturgical Press. Collegeville, Minn.: Liturgical Press.

John of the Cross (1979). "The Spiritual Canticle." In *The Collected Works of St. John of the Cross.* Trans. Kieran Kavanaugh. Washington, D.C.: Institute of Carmelite Studies, pp. 394–565. (Original work written c. 1582.)

LaHaye, Tim and Beverly (1976). *The Act of Marriage.* New York: Bantam Books.

Lederer, Wolfgang (1968). *The Fear of Women.* New York: Harcourt Brace Jovanovich.

Liguori, Alfonso Maria de (1821). *Theologia Moralis,* Tomus Secundus, pp. 316–37. Antwerp: Janssens and van Merlen. (Originally written 1763.)

McLaughlin, Eleanor (1974). "Equality of Souls, Inequality of Sexes: Woman in Medieval Theology." In *Religion and Sexism,* ed. Rosemary Ruether. New York: Simon and Schuster, pp. 213–66.

Marcus, Steven (1964). *The Other Victorians.* New York: Basic Books.

Masters, R. E. L. (1962). *Eros and Evil.* New York: Julian Press.

Mayhall, Jack and Carole (1978). *Marriage Takes More Than Love.* Colorado Springs, Colo.: NavPress.

Merritt, Timothy, and King, D. S. (1843). *The Guide to Christian Perfection.* Boston: Merritt and King.

Morgan, Marabel (1973). *The Total Woman.* Old Tappan, N.J.: Fleming H. Revell Company.

Murstein, Bernard I. (1974). *Love, Sex and Marriage through the Ages.* New York: Springer.

O'Brien, Joan (1982). "The Female Experience and the Nature of the Divine [Review]." *Theological Studies* 43:742–44.

Ochshorn, Judith (1981). *The Female Experience and the Nature of the Divine.* Bloomington: Indiana University Press.

Okin, Susan Moller (1979). *Women in Western Political Thought.* Princeton: Princeton University Press.

Palmer, Phoebe (1871). *The Way of Holiness, with Notes By the Way.* 51st ed. New York: W. C. Palmer, Jr. (Originally written in 1854).

Penthouse (1988). "Debbie Does Swaggart." *Penthouse,* July 1988, pp. 107–22.

Pomeroy, Sarah B. (1982). "The Female Experience and the Nature of the Divine [Review]." *American Historical Review* 87:1367–68.

Raitt, Jill (1980). "The *Vagina Dentata* and the *Immaculatus Uterus Divini Fontis.*" *Journal of the American Academy of Religion* 48:415–31.

Ruether, Rosemary (1974). "Misogynism and Virginal Feminism in the Fathers of the Church." In *Religion and Sexism,* ed. Rosemary Ruether. New York: Simon and Schuster, pp. 150–84.

———(1975). *New Woman, New Earth.* New York: Seabury Press.

———(1986). *Sexism and God-Talk.* Boston: Beacon Press.

Rugoff, Milton (1971). *Prudery and Passion.* New York: G. P. Putnam's Sons.

Russell, Jeffrey Burton (1972). *Witchcraft in the Middle Ages.* Ithaca: Cornell University Press.

Sadock, B. J.; Kaplan, H. I.; & Freedman, A. M. (1976). *The Sexual Experience.* Baltimore: Williams and Wilkins.

Sayers, Dorothy L. (1954). *Introductory Papers on Dante.* London: Methuen.

———(1949, 1955). *The Divine Comedy.* London: Penguin Books.

Spretnak, Charlene, ed. (1982). *The Politics of Women's Spirituality: Essays on the Rise of Spiritual Power within the Feminist Movement.* New York: Doubleday.

Starhawk (1979). *The Spiral Dance.* San Francisco: Harper and Row.

Stone, Merlin (1976). *When God Was a Woman.* New York: Harcourt Brace Jovanovich.

———(1979). *Ancient Mirrors of Womanhood.* Boston: Beacon Press.

Suchocki, Marjorie (1981). "Openness and Mutuality in Process Thought and Feminist Action." In *Feminism and Process Thought,* ed. Sheila Greeve Davaney. Lewiston, N.Y.: Edward Mellen Press, pp. 62–82.

———(1986). *God, Christ, Church.* New York: Crossroad.

Suenens, Leon Josef Cardinal (1963). *The Nun in the World.* Westminster, Md.: Newman Press.

Swaggart, Jimmy (1985). *Rape of a Nation.* Baton Rouge: Jimmy Swaggart Ministries.

Tavard, George (1973). *Woman in Christian Tradition.* Notre Dame: University of Notre Dame Press.

Teresa of Avila (1976). *The Book of Her Life.* In *The Collected Works of St. Teresa of Avila,* vol. 1, pp. 1–308. Trans. Kieran Kavanaugh. Washington, D.C.: Institute of Carmelite Studies. (Original Work written c. 1568).

Von le Fort, Gertrude (1934). *The Eternal Woman.* (English trans. 1962.) Milwaukee: Bruce Publishing Co.

Walker, Barbara G. (1983). *The Woman's Encyclopedia of Myths and Secrets.* San Francisco: Harper and Row.

Warner, Marina (1976). *Alone of All Her Sex.* New York: Alfred A. Knopf.

Weinstein, Donald, & Bell, Rudolph M. (1982). *Saints and Society.* Chicago: University of Chicago Press.

Whitehead, Alfred North (1929). *Process and Reality: An Essay of Cosmology.* New York: Macmillan.

Williams, Charles (1961). *The Figure of Beatrice.* London: Noonday Press.

Williams, Daniel Day (1981). *The Spirit and the Forms of Love.* Lanham, Md.: University Press of America reprint. (Original work published 1968).

Wright, Rusty and Linda Raney (1981). *Love, Sex, and Marriage.* Westwood, N.J.: Barbour Books.

4

Social Science and Public Policy

Looking at the 1986 Commission on Pornography

EDNA F. EINSIEDEL

Social science research has often been harnessed in the service of public-policy responses to social problems. Such a process is fraught with difficulty when the policy issue under consideration is highly controversial. Such problems as racial balance in the schools or the relation between television violence and antisocial behavior are only two examples of issues surrounded by controversy that has been generated not just by the research itself but also by the use of the research for policy ends.

The 1986 Attorney General's Commission on Pornography recently completed another official examination of the pornography issue sixteen years after the first pornography commission published its report. The hue and cry over the 1986 report is another reminder that policy making on issues that have seen the involvement of vocal and visible interest groups, that demand the balancing of important and competing societal interests, where battle lines are drawn on political, ideological, moral, economic, and constitutional levels, is no task for the fainthearted or thin-skinned. The debate over the conclusions and recommendations of this commission will rage on—this is to be expected. It is instructive, however, to examine the process of policy making, particularly from the point of view of its intersection with social science research, if only to better understand the nature of this interaction process and to contribute in some small way to the growing interest in public-policy analysis.

Because of the confusion generated by the dissimilar findings of the 1970 and the 1986 commissions, we might start our examination of this interaction with a look back to 1970.

In examining the pornography issue in 1970, the Commission on Obscenity and Pornography found that there were hardly any studies available on the issue (Cairns, Paul, and Wishner, 1970), making the origination of studies mandatory.

Fueled by a $2 million budget, the commission sponsored much of the fundamental research on the effects of exposure to sexually explicit materials. The impetus for further research that these early studies provided was in itself one of the significant contributions of the commission. As its Effects Panel noted, "One of the contributions of the work of the Panel has been to place the dimensions of human sexual behavior on the agenda for continuing inquiry. By providing resources in terms of funds and technical guidelines, the Panel has helped to legitimate systematic inquiry into an area that heretofore has either been ignored or feared" (Report of the 1970 Commission on Obscenity and Pornography, p. 171).

The role that social science findings were to play for the 1970 Commission was a pivotal one. This was reflected in the structure of the commission staff, which was headed by a behavioral scientist; the hiring of staff members with behavioral science training; the allocation of the bulk of the commission budget to social science studies; and the ultimate decision to base much of its recommendations on the social science findings.

The use of social science research by the 1986 Commission was entirely different. To begin with, the context had changed significantly from 1970. Compared to the budget of the 1970 Commission, that of the 1985 Commission was a pittance, a mere half a million dollars. The commission's mandate specifically precluded sponsorship of original research, for reasons we can only speculate on. Certainly, one could argue that the volume of research completed in the last fifteen years was more than what was available to the 1970 Commission. On the other hand, it was rather ironic that while the Office of Legal Policy within the Justice Department was disbursing $400,000 for the commission, the Office of Juvenile Justice within the same department had also funded a content analysis of *Playboy, Penthouse,* and *Hustler* magazines for some $750,000 (see *Washington Post,* June 18, 1985).

Given that the 1986 Commission was also a creation of the attorney general's office, it was inevitable that a law-enforcement approach was to predominate. This orientation was particularly evident in the composition of the professional staff, which consisted of four lawyers and four law-enforcement investigators. As the only staff social scientist, I was left with the sole responsibility of organizing, evaluating, and summarizing the research from the last sixteen or so years.

While the 1970 Commission put all its eggs in the social science basket, with the recommendations of its working panels based primarily on the research findings of the studies commissioned, the 1986 Commission's format of choice was the public hearing, which featured testimony from a variety of sources. There are arguably strengths and weaknesses in this device as a tool for information gathering. It was useful in that it allowed a diversity of *political* viewpoints among social scientists to be heard. Thus, social scientists advocating sexual freedom were heard from as well as those warning of potential harms from exposure to pornography. Some were selected for feminist leanings, others for their role in the 1970 research efforts, still others for their championing of academic freedom of inquiry.

On balance, the social science hearing accomplished goals that had little to do with understanding what the research was saying, and indeed, the welter of conflicting opinions only served to confuse rather than enlighten most of the commissioners. While this is not to dismiss entirely the importance of public hearings, and while it was of some importance that the various research and political viewpoints of social scientists were heard by the commission, public hearings in the end are a form of theater. They are also a way of representing viewpoints and special interests, which in a democracy is obviously critical, as well as a way of manipulating public opinion. By themselves, however, hearings are less useful as a means of educating the public and policy makers alike about the issue at hand and about social science research in particular.

Research Conclusions of the 1970 and 1986 Commissions

The conclusions drawn from the research by the 1970 and 1986 commissions could not have been more diametrically opposed. The 1970 Commission concluded that "empirical research designed to clarify the question has found no reliable evidence to date that exposure to explicit sexual materials plays a significant role in the causation of delinquent or criminal sexual behavior among youth and adults" (p. 169). The commission thus concluded that "greater latitude can safely be given to adults in deciding for themselves what they will or will not read or view" (p. 171). The 1986 Commission, on the other hand, concluded that exposure to sexually violent material as well as to nonviolent but degrading sexually explicit material led to the perpetuation of attitudes that condoned sexual violence and, more importantly led to the commission of acts of sexual violence against women. In attempting to understand the divergence in these conclusions, it might help to put these research findings in perspective.

The Socio-Political Context

There are four factors that differentiate the settings within which the 1970 and the 1986 commissions operated, all of which had direct or indirect impacts on the research.

First, the nature and amount of pornography had changed. The 1970 Report described adult men's magazines as substantially depicting partially nude females with breast and buttock exposure and "a self-imposed taboo against the depiction of female genitalia [that was] rigidly observed," a description that sounds almost archaic today. In 1970, *Playboy* was the only widely circulated magazine of this genre at that time. By 1975, there were eight other titles competing for a somewhat larger audience, and by 1985, there were some fourteen titles dominated by *Playboy, Penthouse,* and *Hustler.*[1] By this time, the distribution of sexually explicit materials had also expanded in concert with the development of new technologies (AGCP, 1986).

The availability and type of material on the market had a direct bearing on the stimulus materials used in the research. In 1970, many of the experimental studies utilized sexually explicit materials from sex research institutes (the Kinsey Institute in Bloomington, Indiana, and its counterpart in Hamburg, West Germany) because of the difficulty of obtaining materials from the open market. One study had to rely on confiscated items from the Bureau of Customs collection while another had to use materials created by the researcher himself—a film of "a female sensuously disrobing" (Tannenbaum, 1970). It is as much an indication of changing times that subsequent researchers used material that commonly depicted oral sex, group sex, in some cases bestiality, and anal intercourse, in addition to garden-variety heterosexual intercourse. Many of these materials were easily obtainable from the local video outlet or the corner periodical outlet (see, for example, descriptions of stimulus materials in Linz, 1985; Zillmann and Bryant, 1984; Donnerstein, 1980).

Public tolerance was also much in evidence in opinion polls, with increasing numbers reporting exposure to sexually explicit materials. Gallup poll figures from 1985 showed that it was a small minority—about one in ten—that had not seen or read *Playboy* or *Penthouse*.[2] Alongside greater exposure, however, appeared to be greater public concern, especially among women, who expressed greater willingness to ban outright materials featuring sexual violence.[3]

The political climate had also changed significantly. A conservative administration was at the helm with a Department of Justice that was particularly noted for its lack of support for civil rights. Fueled by a constituency from the right that had consistently attempted to push pornography onto the public agenda, the public debate was now taking on a new twist with a segment of the feminist movement sharing a similar objective of restraints on pornography. While these factions were often portrayed as bedfellows, the gulf between their rationales of harm versus morality and family values was wide and deep.

The feminist assumptions that causally implicated pornography in sexual violence had an important impact on research efforts; indeed, they provided some rationale for testing hypotheses linking pornography to sexual violence. For example, Baron and Straus's work (1984, 1985) on the relationship between circulation rates of adult men's magazines and rape rates posited a theory of rape that drew on four aspects of social culture: the proliferation of pornography, sexual inequality, culturally legitimate violence, and social disorganization. Malamuth and Billings (1986) compared research on pornography in the context of the sexual-communication model (i.e., pornography is communication about sexuality with no untoward effects and some beneficial ones) and the feminist model, suggesting pornography as reflective of male subjugation of women. Noting limitations in the former, they recommended greater research attention to the feminist model.

Finally, there were important differences in the research strategies employed in the early studies compared to subsequent ones. While 1970 findings suggested that no significant behavioral changes, other than slight increases in behaviors already within one's repertoire, occurred as a result of exposure to sexually explicit materials, subsequent research was demonstrating effects on attitudes, perceptions, and behaviors, particularly for certain classes of materials. How did the research strategies differ? Four factors emerged as differentiating earlier research from subsequent studies.

First, most of the 1970 studies involved one-time exposures to the stimulus materials. Subsequent studies had subjects exposed to materials over several weeks' duration, with subjects exhibiting significant changes in perceptions and attitudes.

Second, the 1970 studies examined sexually explicit materials as one class and did not evaluate differences in classes of stimuli. Significantly missing was an examination of sexually violent materials. This oversight was subsequently rectified in later studies, particularly those done by Neal Malamuth, which investigated in programmatic fashion the effects of exposure to sexual violence.

Third, the catharsis model (suggesting inhibition of aggressive tendencies after viewing violence), which provided the framework for some of the 1970 research studies (see, for example, Kutchinsky, 1973), had by the time of the later studies become obsolete as an explanatory model for media effects (Geen and Quanty, 1977; NIMH, 1982; Comstock, 1987). The majority of studies succeeding the 1970 Commission Report, on the other hand, tended to be grounded on models that *did* predict some type of effect from the media. One example of such a model was the social learning model, which implies that predominant behavioral portrayals in the media (1) increase perceptions of behaviors as normative and culturally acceptable; (2) reinforce such perceptions by portraying the consequences of these behaviors; (3) suggest attribution of responsibility; and (4) demonstrate the performance of such behaviors (Bandura, 1977, 1986). Such a model, it should be noted, has applicability to the learning of both positive and negative behaviors. Its primary proponent, for instance, has demonstrated its applicability to the learning of aggressive behavior as well as the acquisition of new behaviors in therapeutic settings (Bandura, 1986).

Fourth, subsequent studies were characterized by a more diverse array of dependent variable measures, or measures of effects. Studies included attitudinal measures of rape-myth acceptance and acceptance of sexual violence (see Burt, 1980), which had the added advantage of being tested for reliability and validity across a variety of studies. Measures of perceptual changes were also employed (for example, commonly investigated were perceptions of both victim and assailant in a mock rape situation). Included here were refinements in physiological measures of arousal, diminishing some of the earlier validity problems inherent in self-reports and improving diagnostic and treatment procedures for sex offenders. Such measures were also finding utility in laboratory experiments on nonoffender populations.

A diversity of behavioral-change measures was also utilized, including the typical aggression paradigm involving delivery of "shocks" as well as aversive noise, other retaliatory behaviors, jury verdicts in mock rape trials, and choice and viewing of sexually explicit fare. To a large extent, these measures as well as their theoretical orientations seemed to be influenced by the same models utilized in the TV-violence-and-antisocial-behavior research stream, which received considerable attention in the sixties and seventies.

These changes simply illustrate that social context, time, research paradigms, methodological changes, and the natural cumulation of the research process itself have significant impacts on research findings.

The Research Findings

The concerted attention focused on violent pornography produced results that offered some convergent validation for social scientists wary of weaknesses inherent in individual measurement approaches or single populations. These findings can be summarized as follows:

• Exposure to a sexually violent depiction in the laboratory has resulted in more aggressive sexual fantasies among those exposed.

• Rapists are aroused by depictions of both forced and nonforced sex. College males tend to be more aroused by the latter than by the former.

• When the depictions of forced sex show the victim as having an orgasm or not exhibiting pain or disgust, college males have also exhibited arousal under such conditions.

• Depictions of sexual violence among college males have been shown to result in significant increases in the acceptance of rape myths and sexual violence toward woman.

• Such depictions have also been shown to affect perceptions: victims of rape tend to be seen as more worthless, more responsible for the assault, while perpetrators tend to be absolved of responsibility and to be viewed less negatively.

• Sexually violent depictions have been found to lead to laboratory aggression against women.

• Such laboratory aggression toward woman has also been found to significantly correlate with self-reported sexually aggressive behaviors.

Other than the data on rapists (see Quinsey, 1984; Abel, Barlow, Blanchard and Guild, 1977; Abel, Rouleau and Cunningham-Rathner, 1985), the evidence for this set of materials comes primarily from laboratory experimental research (see summaries by Malamuth, 1984, 1985).

The policy conclusion based on these findings was that exposure to sexually violent materials increased the likelihood of sexual aggression. While missing the caveats and qualifiers endemic to the jargon of social scientists, was it a totally unreasonable conclusion? We could indeed argue that laboratory behaviors are one thing and that their measurement immediately after exposure simply enhances their performance; we could also maintain that attitudes do not necessarily predict behaviors and that the causal pathways remain an open question.[4] But measurement problems and other ethical constraints also ensure that certain questions can hardly be definitively answered. In a subsequent meeting of social scientists under the sponsorship of the surgeon general's office,[5] these conclusions about the negative effects of sexually violent material received general concurrence. For instance, the workshop "consensus statements" held that: (1) prolonged use of pornography increases beliefs that less common sexual practices are more common; (2) pornography that portrays sexual aggression as pleasurable for the victim increases the acceptance of the use of coercion in sexual relations; (3) acceptance of coercive sexuality appears to be related to sexual aggression; (4) in laboratory studies measuring short-term effects, exposure to violent pornography increases punitive behavior toward women (Mulvey and Haugaard, 1986).

For nonviolent pornography (the second major category used by a number of researchers), the research findings did not meld in the same neat way. The 1970 studies, as mentioned earlier, demonstrated essentially no negative effects. Whatever changes were observed or reported were slight increases in masturbatory or coital behaviors, depending on availability of a partner, behaviors already established in an individual's repertoire. Subsequent experimental studies, however, showed contradictory results. A few studies showed no changes in aggression post-exposure; others demonstrated that aggression toward female targets increased, particularly under conditions of provocation and highly arousing stimuli; still others exhibited perceptual and attitudinal changes akin to those obtained for sexually violent material.

How were these contradictions reconciled by the researchers? Donnerstein suggested that when restraints against aggression were lifted and when the subjects were provoked and exposed to highly arousing material, aggressive behavior was likely to occur (Donnerstein and Barrett, 1978; Donnerstein and Hallam, 1978). In a similar vein, Zillmann and Sapolsky (1978) also suggested that arousal levels, combined with "hedonic valence," or how pleasing or displeasing the material was to the viewer, likely accounted for the varying results.

On the correlational level, one study stood out as particularly intriguing (if not potentially controversial). This was an aggregate analysis of rape rates in the fifty states in the U.S. and their correlation with aggregate circulation rates of the top ten adult men's magazines. The carefully conducted analysis controlled for potentially confounding third factors, such as likelihood to report rape, law-enforcement capacities to deal with violent crime, the proportion of total males as well as single males in the population, and such sociological variables as "social disorganization" that promote an environment for violent crime. Despite these controls, a correlation coefficient of .64 was obtained, indicating the robustness of the original relationship. The authors, however, strenuously maintained that the observed relationship was an artifact of some other third factor (see Baron and Straus, 1986). While the lack of complementary confirmation on the experimental side prompted caution about the results of this study, it was nonetheless difficult to dismiss out of hand.[6]

On the whole, a number of unresolved problems remained with studies on nonviolent pornography that precluded conclusions that were more definitive. For example, there was the lack of consistency in the types of materials utilized. For the experimental studies, stimulus materials generally included a wide range, from nudity to a variety of sexual activity ranging from masturbation to heterosexual and homosexual intercourse, anal and oral intercourse, group sex, and so forth. Somewhere in this welter of sexual activities could be interspersed a variety of themes, including unequal power status (Malamuth, 1984; Sherif, 1980), differential contexts, or, in the words of some feminists, "degradation, subordination, humiliation." In social science terms, different message attributes might have confounded some of the experimental findings.

With the exception of two studies done in Canada (Check, 1985 and Senn, 1985), no other study attempted to examine the effects of themes of sexually explicit materials, an approach that might increase our understanding of whether in fact all nonviolent pornography is created equal.

In addition, others have maintained that some sexually explicit material can be beneficial (Wilson, 1978) or therapeutic (Heiby and Becker, 1980; Heiman, LoPiccolo, and LoPiccolo, 1976). This variation in the findings does not necessarily indicate a contradiction and, as pointed out earlier, one can draw on the social learning framework to explain both positive and negative effects.

The Policy Output

The leitmotif of the commission's *Report* became clear in a chapter entitled "Harms." It is here that the commission suggests that there can be *harmful* effects from exposure to different classes of pornography. Several aspects about this section are striking:

First, there was a recognition that not all sexually explicit materials are alike in their effects. Like the Fraser Commission in Canada (Report of the Special Committee on Pornography and Prostitution, 1985), the U.S. commission categorized sexually explicit materials into classes or tiers. These categories included violent sexually explicit materials, nonviolent but degrading sexually explicit materials, nonviolent and nondegrading sexually explicit materials, and nudity.

Second, the discussion of effects, particularly for the first two categories, was based on the notion of harm. It was a notion that was clearly akin to that promoted by feminist antipornography supporters.

Third, the findings of harm turned on the idea of either explicit sexual aggression or the images of degradation. The *Report* maintained that there was no evidence of harm for simple sexual explicitness or nudity.[7]

How did the social science evidence stack up? In terms of the evidence on sexually violent material, the convergence of a variety of findings is difficult to quarrel with. The research of Neal Malamuth stands out as particularly significant because of the programmatic approach of his research efforts to examine effects from a variety of angles: he compared responses of "normal" males with offender populations; he correlated laboratory measures with measures of "naturalistic aggression"; he varied content cues; he used physiological measures of arousal; and finally, he investigated correlations between arousal patterns and attitudinal as well as behavioral indicators (see reviews in Malamuth, 1984; Malamuth, in press; and Check and Malamuth, 1985). The only study that examined longer-term effects (exposure over several weeks) did not find such effects (Ceniti and Malamuth, 1986). Further investigation is clearly called for on longitudinal effects, particularly since such effects have been found to occur in the area of televised violence (Huesmann et al., 1983).

The data for nonviolent pornography, on the other hand, did not offer the same kind of "neat" convergent validation. There were only two studies at the time of the review that manipulated classes of materials into three distinct categories: violent pornography, nonviolent and degrading pornography, and nonviolent nondegrading materials, or "erotica." Only the first study attempted to measure effects on sexual aggression, and, in this instance, the data were not as clear-cut. The second study examined female subjects only.

There was thus a problem in terms of attempting to explain an apparent contradiction in the data, and, while there was much speculation that the stimulus materials for those studies finding negative effects in fact employed highly degrading images of women, and those with null effects were simply sexually explicit,[8] it remained speculation. In this instance, while the research review suggested that the data were hardly conclusive, the commission, on the other hand, suggested that attitudinal changes among those exposed to material considered degrading to women could also promote sexual violence:

> Because the causal link is less the subject of experimental studies, we have been required to think more carefully here about the assumptions necessary to causally connect increased acceptance of rape myths and other attitudinal changes with increased sexual aggression and sexual violence. And on the basis of all the evidence we have considered, from all sources, and on the basis of our own insights and experiences, we believe we are justified in drawing the following conclusion: over a large enough sample a population that believes that many women like to be raped, that believes that sexual violence or sexual coercion is often desired or appropriate, and that believes that sex offenders are less responsible for their acts, will commit more acts of sexual violence or sexual coercion than would a population holding these beliefs to a lesser extent. (AGCP, 1986, 333)

Based on the four classes of materials and its conclusions, the commission recommended more vigorous prosecution of obscenity laws, particularly for sexually violent material. A major problem with this approach was that current obscenity law is based on sexual explicitness (of the prurient variety); the notion of pornography as harm as outlined by the commission, on the other hand, suggests that certain sexually violent materials would fall outside the rubric of the "obscene," a point that the commission conceded (p. 394). Recognizing that not all materials considered "pornographic," especially vis-à-vis the first two classes, might be legally obscene, it was nevertheless argued that obscenity laws were sufficient instruments to deal with the classes of materials that raised the greatest amount of concern.

The Interaction between Social Science and Public Policy

The proper "fit" between social science findings and the making of public policy is always difficult to establish. In discussing this interphase, there are two assumptions that we make:

First, social science evidence can make a significant contribution to policy making, but it is not the sole foundation of policy making. To make such an assumption is to have a limited, if not naïve, perspective of the policy-making process. Schooled in the rational processes of the scientific method, such an admission is at best grudgingly made by social scientists—myself included—who have high expectations that the policy-making process will be similarly structured. As many analysts of public policy have observed, policy making is as much an expression of values, of the aggregation of interests, of intuition, as it is an interpretation of social science (see Weiss, 1977; Horowitz, 1971; Cater and Strickland, 1975).

Second, if policy making is as much a value-laden enterprise as it is a process that could be "rational," i.e., based on empirical procedures, so is social science research. The kinds of questions we consider, the way we frame those questions, the variables we select for examination—or those that we ignore for that matter—the interpretations we give to our findings, reflect our interests, the influence of our peers, and our normative preferences. To view the social science research process as an objective, value-free enterprise is also a distorted view of social science itself.

Having said that, what can be gleaned from the use of social science research by the 1986 Commission? We will limit our discussion to three areas: defining the social problem, the process of interpreting social science findings, and the policy recommendations that might flow directly from the social science evidence.

Three vital contributions of social science research to policy making lie in the areas of conceptualization and problem definition, the obtaining of systematic data, and the recommendation of alternative strategies that stem directly from the data. How did social science fare on each of these levels?

DEFINING THE PROBLEM: PORNOGRAPHY AS A VARIABLE OF INTEREST

Clearly, the social issue at hand is the potential effects from exposure to pornography. For the policy maker, the focus on a specific explanatory variable, pornography in this instance (the "independent variable"), is as much politically derived as it is reality based. The variable may be placed on the public agenda by special-interest groups and made an issue for consideration by the government in a number of ways, the appointment of a commission being one of them. That pornography is chosen for examination, however, does not alter the fact that it is simply one of a number of explanatory factors of certain social consequences, a point the *Report* took pains to recognize (pp. 309–12).

This focus on pornography has also been complemented on the social science side by researchers' increased attention to the issue in the last decade and a half for theoretical—and practical—reasons. The fact that in our attempt to explain potential sexual behaviors we choose to focus on pornography—in much the same way we have zeroed in on television to help explain antisocial behaviors—as a factor that might be theoretically implicated suggests the attribution of some significance to its capacity to explain the behaviors or social problems of interest. It also suggests that social values or political assumptions, such as the harm or harmlessness of certain material, are worthy of testing.

That commissions or social scientists have chosen to focus on pornography, however, hardly means there is consensus on the problem definition. Whether pornography is even a proper focus of inquiry is as much a subject of public debate, and the disagreement within the feminist community attests to this fact.[9] Furthermore, when research efforts focus on variables that are equally the subject of political analyses, they wind up being judged by the same criteria used to judge political studies (Becker and Horowitz, 1972). The upshot is that social scientists may sometimes find themselves in the curious position of devaluating the very variables whose supposed explanatory power or parsimony was theorized as significant to begin with.

CONCEPTUALIZING THE PROBLEM
In her analysis of the influence of social science on policy, Weiss (1982) has argued that social science plays an important role in affecting the shape and content of policy discourse: "Because research provides powerful labels for previously inchoate and unorganized experience, it helps to mould officials' thinking into categories derived from social science" (p. 291). She maintains that the ideas derived from research provide "organizing perspectives" that help to make sense of information and experience, or frameworks to help interpret problems and suggest policy alternatives.

In looking to social science for such a perspective, the 1986 Commission found current research wanting. Dissatisfied with the violent-nonviolent classes commonly found in the literature, the commission noted:

> We have unanimously agreed that looking at all sexually explicit materials, or even all pornographic materials, as one undifferentiated whole is unjustified by common sense, unwarranted on the evidence, and an altogether oversimplifying way of looking at a complex phenomenon. In many respects we consider this one of our most important conclusions. Our subdivisions are not intended to be definitive, and particularly with respect to the subdivision between non-violent but degrading, we recognize that some researchers have usually employed broader or different groupings. Further research or thinking, or just changes in the world, may suggest finer or different divisions. To us, it is embarking on the process of subdivision that is most important,

and we strongly urge that further research and thinking about the question of pornography recognize initially the way in which different varieties of material may produce different consequences. (pp. 320–21)

Thus we have its proposal for the four classes of sexually explicit material outlined earlier.

From a policy perspective, this categorization was an amalgam of logic, social science, values, and politics. Logic because it was based on the presence or absence of certain attributes—violence and degradation, for instance; social science because there was a partial meshing with the two classes used by a number of researchers (violent and nonviolent pornography); values because it appeared to have "bought into" the feminist separation between erotica and pornography; and politics because the separation between the degrading versus the merely sexually explicit allowed some terrain for compromise. For liberals, it was important not to condemn the sexually explicit, and for conservatives, if most pornography could be called "degrading," then the sexually explicit was an elusive class that might encompass sex-education materials but no more.

Beyond such considerations, the argument for "subdivisions" was not that far afield from what common sense—or theory—would suggest, regardless of whether one agreed or disagreed with the commission's categorization scheme: that different attributes in the stimulus material might have different effects. This proposition raises the issue of whether the research findings supported the policy conclusions drawn.

The answer, from a strictly social science standpoint, is no. As we pointed out earlier, there are some contradictions in the research findings on nonviolent pornography that have not been satisfactorily resolved, and the Check study (1985), which specifically examined the effects of three instead of two classes of pornography, did not come up with definitive or clear-cut findings. The commission's *Report* did recognize this inconclusive status in the research but took the position that absence of evidence on behavioral effects did not preclude that negative effects could occur. Relying more on "experience" and "common sense," the commission argued that "degrading materials" could also result in attitudinal changes supportive of the acceptance of sexual coercion.

While it is tempting to join the chorus of outrage from the social science quarter that greeted the commission conclusions (see *New York Times,* 1986; MacNeil-Lehrer Report, 1986), it is doubtful that the research questions on nonviolent pornography will be resolved in the context of the normal strictures of the disciplinary process.

For many of us, the class of nonviolent pornography represents that nightmarish terrain where specific media are implicated, where visions abound of trigger-happy prosecutors unleashed to do duty for vocal minorities, and where findings of negative effects elicit images of Victorian prudery. For some researchers well versed in the horrors of seeing research misinterpreted and misused, it is hardly surprising that the nonviolent class evokes an arm's length reaction.

THE INTERPRETATION OF DATA

Unfortunately, it is quite often the case that social science research fails to produce clear-cut findings. These findings must be interpreted by both social scientists and policy makers, and interpretation is as much politics as it is logic—"a value-laden process where truth is partially a matter of whose priorities are being reviewed," observed some policy analysts (Patton et al., 1982).

For the social scientist, the task is fraught with the possibility that certain interpretations might be misunderstood, misused, or, worse still, taken as the basis of undesirable (from the social scientist's point of view) policy alternatives. His or her language is cautious, full of caveats, emphasized limitations, and a call for further research; the policy maker or layman, on the other hand, is impatient with qualifiers and requires more definitive statements and conclusive generalizations—requirements that do not have the luxury of the extended time frame of the disciplinary process.

From the point of view of the policy maker, the question becomes what the researcher says at this point in time with regard to the policy question at hand and what is sufficient evidence to justify particular policy alternatives.

Herein lies the dilemma for social scientist and policy maker alike. It is a dilemma that plagues any interpretation of media effects that has inevitable implications for competing societal interests. McLeod and Reeves (1981) suggested two apt metaphorical labels for the two extremes among those who interpret social science findings:

> Type One worriers fear the possibility of making too strong inferences and, consequently, tend to accept a position of no media effects. The evidence they cite tends to be from field studies of persuasion using gross measures of both media exposure and attitude change. The lack of major change and the apparent stability are attributed to selective exposure and selective perception, and the major impact is thought to be reinforcement of preexisting attitudes. . . .
>
> Type Two worriers hold a diametrically opposing set of concerns in making research inferences. They worry most about overlooking any media effect and frequently cite the difficulties that beset attempts to find even "obvious" effects. . . . They worry less about the proportion of effect that media variables account for, noting that even a small effect—say, 2 percent in an election campaign—can make a very great difference.
>
> Type Two worriers note, too, that communication variables tend to be less reliably measured . . . and hence that correlation coefficients understate considerably their "true" predictive power. They are not likely to hesitate counting as effects the media acting as mere conduits of public events. . . . Finally, they seem to assume that the public spends so much time with television and other media that there must be some kind of effect in at least some segment or subpopulation of the audience.

Among the commissioners, these two viewpoints were much in evidence. In his personal statement on the issue of pornography, one commissioner argued:

> It appears extremely naïve to assume that the river of obscenity which has inundated the American landscape has not invaded the world of children. This seven billion

dollar industry pervades every dimension of our lives. There are more stores selling pornographic videos than there are McDonald hamburger stands. . . . It is my belief that the behavior of an entire generation of teenagers is being adversely affected by the current emphasis on premarital sexuality and general eroticism seen nightly on television, in movies, and other sources of pornography. (Dobson, 1986)

Beyond the polemic, this statement was a classic argument of assuming effects from pervasiveness of certain media content.

Extrapolating from the research, another commissioner suggested: "The simple capacity of nonviolent material to produce strong arousal in both offenders and the general population may, in and of itself, produce higher levels of sexual violence. Of equal importance, 'standard' commercial pornography may, over time and with significant exposure, work to undermine learned inhibitions against sexual violence" (Ritter, 1986).

On the other side of the continuum, two commissioners argued:

> First, it is essential to state that the social science research has not been designed to evaluate the relationship between exposure to pornography and the commission of sex crimes; therefore, efforts to tease the current data into proof of a causal link between these acts simply cannot be accepted. Furthermore, social science does not speak to harm. . . . (rather) it speaks to a relationship among variables or effects that can be positive or negative.
>
> In a laboratory setting, exposure to sexually violent stimuli has a negative effect on research subjects as measured by acceptance of rape myths and aggression and callousness toward women. We do not know, however, how long this attitudinal change is sustained without further stimulation; more importantly, we do not know whether and why such an attitudinal change might transfer into a behavioral change.
>
> . . . Human behavior is complex and multi-causal. To say that exposure to pornography in and of itself causes an individual to commit a sexual crime is simplistic, not supported by the social science data, and overlooks many of the other variables that may be contributing causes. (Levine and Becker, 1986)

That the same body of data generates such widely divergent conclusions among policy makers is hardly unexpected.

Given our traditional liberal sympathies, not surprisingly, the Type One view predominates among us social scientists.[10] This view is exemplified among those who deemphasize the role of the media as a significant contributing causal factor and emphasize instead the multicausal influences on sexual aggression (see Malamuth, 1985; 1988). On a correlational level, some social scientists might disavow an observed relationship as spurious or possibly caused by some as yet unidentified third factor (see Baron and Straus, 1985, 1986). On an experimental level, it might be an objective to attribute results to one dimension of the stimulus material as opposed to another. It has been maintained, for instance, that it is violence and not sex that brings about certain effects (see Donnerstein, 1985).

It was the Canadian pornography commission (Report of the Special Committee on Pornography and Prostitution, 1985) that quite astutely observed:

Those who see freedom of speech as the highest value argue that the data must demonstrate that concrete harm *to individuals* [emphasis added] is caused by pornography in order to support controls on it. They reject the idea that controls can be justified by a showing of some generalized harm, or by showing (or arguing) that pornography impairs the realization of other social values. Thus they reject the contention of the conservatives that controls can be justified because pornography fosters disintegration of the moral values of society, the place of the family, and the sanctity of marital sexual relations. They also reject the contention of feminists that controls on pornography can be justified because pornography impedes the realization of equality for women and diminishes their humanity. . . .

Those who choose the equality guarantee as their point of departure approach the question of what the data should show to justify legislative intervention in quite a different way than do those who reason from the freedom of speech premise. . . .

The proponents of the equality approach are, of course, more tolerant of existing shortcomings of empirical research about the actual harms to individuals of pornographic material. They point out that the momentum of such research is in the direction of being able to show harms. . . .

The differences between these two approaches are quite striking. The egalitarian approach does not require that the whole burden of justifying legislation should fall upon the research data; the libertarian approach does. Moreover, the libertarian approach imposes, in effect, a very high burden of proof before the data will be taken . . . demonstrably to justify incursions on freedom of expression. (P. 98)

A Look Back and to the Future

The current debate among social scientists and between social scientists and policy makers on the issue of pornography is one that, interestingly enough, is not unique to the present situation. Sixteen years ago, the same conundrum was recognized by some social scientists and policy analysts alike.

In 1970, the issue was the contradiction in the findings between the President's Commission on the Causes and Prevention of Violence and the Commission on Obscenity and Pornography. While the former reported undesirable effects from the portrayal of violence on TV, the latter maintained short-lived effects, none of them worrisome ("behaviors already in one's repertoire"). A prominent social psychologist asked then: "Can it be that these seemingly different conclusions were affected to some extent at least by a prevailing liberal ideology and its attitudes toward aggression and sex?" (Berkowitz, 1971). A policy analyst similarly observed that the difference in recommendations was the result "not of different empirical findings, but of different judgments about similar findings" (Wilson, 1971, 47).

Some sixteen years later, we find ourselves in the same dilemma, only worsened by the fact that (a) the parallel violence research has become more rigorous and more definitive (see NIMH, 1982); (b) the violence research has been instrumental in making inoperative the catharsis hypothesis, which had provided a convenient rationale for the notion of pornography as "safety valve";[11] (c) the research has been coming up with "negative effects" that do not conform with 1970 findings; and (d) the policy effort has been spearheaded by an administration whose politics we love to hate.

It is not at all clear how we resolve this dilemma, particularly in the context of an issue that arouses such extreme passions. The larger questions are ones of politics and values for which social science is not the sole, or perhaps even the most important, arbiter. In the larger scheme of things, we as a polity have to address the question of how much importance to attach to pornography as a social problem. There is further the additional issue of what to do if indeed it is defined as a major problem.

Many may indeed be justifiably strongly opposed to this commission's solution of more vigorous obscenity prosecution—a recommendation that hardly makes sense to those who argue that obscenity laws are based on morality and sexual explicitness and not on the proposition of harm. Others may accept the notion of harm but argue that an arsenal of laws already exists to deal with the outcomes or injuries. Within the cacophony of "best solutions," social scientists, like any interest group, must raise their voices to be heard.

Many of us hold dear the proposition that knowledge is power, and hence we advocate the educational approach (see Malamuth, 1984; Mulvey and Haugaard, 1986). There is indeed much to be said for this approach. Results from debriefing procedures employed in various studies have demonstrated the efficacy of educational programs designed to mitigate the effects of exposure to pornography. The success of such procedures has prompted some to suggest that participation in such experiments can be beneficial because of what subjects can learn (or unlearn) about rape myths, sexual violence, and other related issues (Check and Malamuth, 1985).

One of the tragedies of this commission unfortunately was its refusal or inability to deal with sex education as a viable alternative. This option offers itself as a strategy that has distinct roots in the principles of social learning, the same theoretical paradigm that some social scientists have relied on for explaining pornography effects. Just as some argue that television can teach prosocial as well as antisocial messages, one could also make the argument that the media can fruitfully be used to teach healthier messages about sexuality. Individuals can also be taught coping strategies in much the same way that some have argued for educating parents and children on intelligent television use. Purely from a social science perspective, this is one strategy that "makes sense." But our vested interest in this approach must be recognized as such, because it is as much a reflection of our opposition to other alternative approaches.

In terms of the social science–public policy relationship, there is much to be learned from this particular case. For policy makers, having social science data hardly guarantees their use, much less their "proper" use. From the research point of view, the probabilistic nature of research findings sometimes leads to a range of interpretations, with choices made just as often on the basis of our ideological preferences as on the nature of the data themselves. Perhaps in the end, the lessons learned result as much from having raised these issues.

NOTES

1. The combined circulation rates of all three magazines have gone from 10.1 million in 1975 to 11.3 million in 1980 to 8.8 million in 1985 (Audit Bureau of Circulation, 1986). But it is difficult to interpret this as a drop in interest in sexually explicit material, as (a) more magazines have cropped up in the same period of time, and (b) more dissemination channels have developed.

2. In 1970, 20 percent of adults surveyed by the 1970 Commission said they had seen or read a magazine which they "regarded as pornographic." Asked what these magazines were, titles mentioned then included such magazines as *Esquire, Cosmopolitan,* and even *Good Housekeeping.* See Abelson et al., 1970.

3. A *Washington Post*–ABC News survey conducted in February 1986 showed four in ten males indicating that "laws against pornography in this country are not strict enough"; seven in ten women expressed the same opinion.

4. The question of the relationship between attitudes and behaviors and how predictive the former are of the latter has been raised elsewhere (see Vance, 1985). While recognizing that attitude-behavior inconsistencies can and do occur, the weight of the research evidence suggests support for a positive relationship between the two (see, for example, Ajzen and Fishbein, 1977, and Zanna and Fazio, 1982). For a discussion on the relationship between attitudes and behavior in the context of exposure to sexual violence and sexual aggression, see Malamuth (in press).

5. In testimony before the Attorney General's Commission on Pornography, the surgeon general offered his office's assistance to the commission. The surgeon general's office had no funds, however, and nothing was done until preliminary social science drafts were produced which appear to have outraged certain special interest groups. A six-page letter written by Eagle Forum head Phyllis Schlafly to the attorney general attacking particularly the social science findings of certain types of sexually explicit materials having positive effects and urging another review of the social science material appeared to have been effective in loosening the Justice Department pursestrings further. Money was suddenly found to fund a pornography workshop attended by selected prominent social scientists under the auspices of the surgeon general's office (Letter from P. Schlafly to the Attorney General, 1986).

6. In their various analyses of rape rates using a multivariate model, Baron and Straus examined the effects of four major variable classes: social disorganization, sexual inequality, "legitimate violence" (or the degree of acceptability of the use of violence in society such as the use of corporal punishment in schools), and sex magazine circulation rates. In addition, they controlled for the following variables: percent of the urban population, percent of the black population, percent of the young adult population (ages eighteen to twenty-four), percent males between fifteen and twenty-four (demographic groups charged with highest rape rates), the Gini Index of economic inequality, percent single males fifteen and older, and percent of the population unemployed. What is surprising about their results is the model's ability to explain 83 percent of the state-to-state rape variance. In summarizing their findings, they concluded: "Our attempts to discover spurious relationships have not been very successful despite approaching the issue from several perspectives and with a variety of measures" (Baron and Straus, 1985). In the same paper and during their testimony, they argued strongly against censorship and cited the 1970 Commission findings of no effects for nonviolent pornography. A few months later, in a book by *Penthouse* writers, Baron and Straus maintained that the commission had disregarded "our recent demonstration that when appropriate statistical controls are introduced, the correlation between sex-magazine-readership rates and rape rates no longer holds" (Baron and Straus 1986, 352).

7. There was considerable disagreement among commissioners as to the effects of the third category of sexually explicit materials. They threw up their hands on this category and decided to write individual statements.

8. The difference in opinion on nonviolent pornography is most evident between Dolf Zillmann and Edward Donnerstein. Donnerstein has publicly maintained that nonviolent pornography has no effects because it is the violence, not the sex, that causes negative effects (see *Penthouse*, July 1985; Colloquy, 1988). Zillmann suggested before the commission that Donnerstein had data on negative effects that he had elected not to publish (Zillmann, 1985). Donnerstein responded that he has on numerous occasions failed to replicate these findings.

9. See, for example, the difference between Robin Morgan (1980), who wrote that "pornography is the theory; rape is the practice," and Betty Friedan (1986), who argued that the pornography debate is "a dangerous diversion of feminism. . . . Porn doesn't really hurt anybody." Groups such as Women Against Pornography are countered on the other side by the Feminist Anti-Censorship Taskforce within the American Civil Liberties Union.

10. A Carnegie study of some 60,000 faculty members in colleges and universities found sociologists, anthropologists, political scientists, and psychologists to score highest on a liberalism-conservatism scale. While 41 percent of all faculty scored liberal to very liberal, 72 percent of sociologists, 64 percent of anthropologists, 62 percent of psychologists, 61 percent of political scientists, and 57 percent of economists did so. (Cited in Weiss, 1977).

11. In 1970, the cathartic or safety-valve effects were suggested by studies examining Danish data showing reductions in sexual offenses with liberalization of pornography laws (see Kutchinsky, 1970). In 1985, a "substitution hypothesis" was advocated as the explanation for these results, suggesting that decreases in child molesting in Denmark and West Germany, for instance, have occurred because the greater availability of pornography (due to removal of restrictions) presumably allows potential sex offenders to substitute masturbatory behaviors for sex crimes.

REFERENCES

Abel, G.; Barlow, D.; Blanchard, E.; and Guild, D. (1977). "The Components of Rapists' Sexual Arousal." *Archives of General Psychiatry* 34:895–903.

Abel, G.; Rouleau, J., and Cunningham-Rathner, J. (1985). "Sexually Aggressive Behavior." In *Modern Legal Psychiatry and Psychology*, ed. W. Curran, A. McGarry and S. Shah. Philadelphia: F. A. Davis.

Abelson, H.; Cohen, R.; Heaton, E.; and Suder, C. (1970). "National Survey of Public Attitudes toward and Experience with Erotic Materials." In *Technical Report of the Commission on Obscenity and Pornography*, vol. 6, pp. 1–255. Washington, D.C.: Government Printing Office.

Attorney General's Commission on Pornography (1986). *Final Report*. Washington, D.C.: U.S. Government Printing Office.

Audit Bureau of Circulation (1986). Circulation Summary for Adult Men's Magazines Provided to the Attorney General's Commission on Pornography.

Ajzen, I., and Fishbein, M. (1977). "Attitude-Behavior Relations: A Theoretical Analysis and Review of Empirical Research." *Psychological Bulletin* 84:888–918.

Bandura, A. (1977). *Social Learning Theory*. Englewood Cliffs, N.J.: Prentice-Hall.

——— (1986). *Social Foundations of Thought and Action*. Englewood Cliffs, N.J.: Prentice-Hall.

Baron, L., and Straus, M. (1984). "Sexual Stratification, Pornography, and Rape in the United States." In *Pornography and Sexual Aggression*, ed. N. Malamuth and E. Donnerstein. Orlando, Fla.: Academic Press.

——— (1985). Testimony before the Attorney General's Commission on Pornography, Houston, Texas, September 13.

———— (1986). "Two False Principles." In *The United States of America versus Sex: How the Meese Commission Lied about Pornography*, ed. P. Nobile and E. Nadler. New York: Minotaur Press.

Becker, H., and Horowitz, I. L. (1972). "Radical Politics and Sociological Research." *American Journal of Sociology* 78:1, July.

Berkowitz, L. (1971). "Sex and Violence: We Can't Have It Both Ways." *Psychology Today*, December, 17–23.

Burt, M. (1980). "Cultural Myths and Support for Rape." *Journal of Personality and Social Psychology* 38:217–30.

Cairns, P.; Paul, J.; and Wishner, J. (1970). "Psychological Assumptions in Sex Censorship: An Evaluation Review of Recent Research." In *Technical Report of the Commission on Obscenity and Pornography*, vol. 1. Washington, D.C.: U.S. Gov't. Printing Office.

Cater, D., and Strickland, S. (1975). *TV Violence and the Child*. New York: Russell Sage Foundation.

Ceniti, J., and Malamuth, N. (1985). "Effects of Repeated Exposure to Sexually Violent or Sexually Nonviolent Stimuli on Sexual Arousal to Rape and Nonrape Depictions." *Behavior Research and Therapy* 35.

Check, J.V.P. (1985). "The Effects of Violent and Nonviolent Pornography." Report to the Dept. of Justice, Ottawa, Canada.

Check, J.V.P., and Malamuth, N. (1985). "Pornography and Sexual Aggression: A Social Learning Theory Analysis." In *Communication Yearbook*, vol. 9, ed. M. L. McLaughlin. Beverly Hills, Ca.: Sage Publications.

Colloquy (1988). "The Methods and Merits of Pornography Research: Critique by D. Linz and E. Donnerstein and Response by D. Zillmann and J. Bryant." *Journal of Communication* 38, 2 (Spring):180–92.

Comstock, G. C. (1987). "Violence." In *The International Encyclopedia of Communications*, ed. E. Barnouw. New York: Oxford University Press.

———— (in press). "Television and Film Violence." In *Youth Violence: Programs and Prospects*, ed. S. J. Apter and A. P. Goldstein. New York: Pergamon Press.

Dobson, J. (1986). Personal Statement. In AGCP, *Final Report*. Washington, D.C.: U.S. Gov't. Printing Office.

Donnerstein, E. (1980). "Aggressive Erotica and Violence against Women." *Journal of Personality and Social Psychology* 39:269–77.

———— (1985). Speech before the Association for Education in Journalism convention, Memphis, Tennessee, August 1985.

Donnerstein, E., and Barrett, G. (1978). "The Effects of Erotic Stimuli on Male Aggression towards Females." *Journal of Personality and Social Psychology* 36:180–88.

Donnerstein, E., and Hallam, J. (1978). "The Facilitating Effects of Erotica on Aggression toward Females." *Journal of Personality and Social Psychology* 36:1270–77.

Friedan, B. (1986). "A Feminist Diversion." In *The United States of America vs. Sex*, ed. P. Nobile and E. Nadler. New York: Minotaur Press.

Geen, R., and Quanty, M. B. (1977). "The Catharsis of Aggression: An Evaluation of a Hypothesis." In *Advances in Experimental Social Psychology*, vol. 10, ed. L. Berkowitz. New York: Academic Press.

Heiby, E., and Becker, J. D. (1980). "Effect of Filmed Modeling on the Self-Reported Frequency of Masturbation." *Archives of Sexual Behavior* 9:115–21.

Heiman, J.; LoPiccolo, L.; and LoPiccolo, J. (1976). *Becoming Orgasmic: A Sexual Growth Program for Women*. Englewood Cliffs, N.J.: Prentice-Hall.

Huesmann, L.; Eron, L.; Klein, R.; Brice, P.; and Fischer, P. (1983). "Mitigating the Imitation of Aggressive Behaviors by Changing Children's Attitudes about Media Violence." *Journal of Personality and Social Psychology* 44:899–910.

Kutchinsky, B. (1970). "Towards an Exploration of the Decrease in Registered Sex

Crimes in Copenhagen." In *Technical Report of the Commission on Obscenity and Pornography*, vol. 7. Washington, D.C.: Government Printing Office.

——— (1973). "The Effect of Easy Availability of Pornography on the Incidence of Sex Crimes: The Danish Experience." *Journal of Social Issues* 29, 3:163–81.

Levine, E., and Becker, J. (1986). Personal Statement. AGCP, *Final Report*. Washington, D.C.: U.S. Gov't. Printing Office.

Linz, D. (1985). "Sexual Violence in the Mass Media: Effects on Male Viewers and Implications for Society." Ph.D. diss., University of Wisconsin.

MacNeil-Lehrer Report, PBS, July 8, 1986.

Malamuth, N. (1984). "Aggression against Women: Cultural and Individual Causes." In *Pornography and Sexual Aggression*, ed. N. Malamuth and E. Donnerstein. Orlando, Fla.: Academic Press.

——— (1985). "The Mass Media and Aggression against Women: Research Findings and Prevention." In *Handbook of Research on Pornography and Sexual Assault*, ed. A. Burgess. New York: Garland Press.

——— (1988). "Do Sexually Violent Media Indirectly Contribute to Antisocial Behavior?" In *Public Communication and Behavior*, vol. 2, ed. G. Comstock. New York: Academic Press.

Malamuth, N., and Billings, V. (1986). "The Functions and Effects of Pornography: Sexual Communication versus the Feminist Models in Light of Research Findings." In *Perspectives on Media Effects*, ed. J. Bryant and D. Zillmann. Hillsdale, N.J.: Lawrence Erlbaum.

McLeod, J., and Reeves, B. (1981). "On the Nature of Mass Media Effects." In *Mass Communications Yearbook*, ed. G.C. Wilhoit and H. DeBock. Beverly Hills, Ca.: Sage Publications.

Morgan, R. (1980). "Theory and Practice: Pornography and Rape." In *Take Back the Night: Women on Pornography*, ed. L. Lederer. New York: William Morrow.

Mulvey, E., and Haugaard, J. (1986). *Pornography and Public Health*. Washington, D.C.: U.S. Surgeon General's Office.

National Institute of Mental Health (1982). *Television and Behavior: Ten Years of Scientific Progress and Implications for the Eighties*. Baltimore, Md.: U.S. Dept. of Public Health.

New York Times, May 17, 1986.

Patton, M.; Grimes, P.; Guthrie, K.; Brennan, N.; French, B.; and Blyth, D. (1977). "In Search of Impact: An Analysis of the Utilization of Federal Health Evaluation Research." In *Using Social Research in Public Policy Making*, ed. C. Weiss. Lexington, Mass.: Lexington Books.

Penthouse (1985). "Dr. Edward Donnerstein: *Penthouse* Interview." July 1985, pp. 165–68, 180–81.

Quinsey, V. L. (1984). "Sexual Aggression: Studies of Offenders against Women." In *Law and Mental Health: International Perspectives*, vol. 1, ed. D. Weisstub. New York: Pergamon Press.

Report of the 1970 Commission on Obscenity and Pornography (1970). New York: Bantam Books.

Report of the Special Committee on Pornography and Prostitution (1985). Ottawa: Minister of Supply and Services.

Ritter, Fr. Bruce (1986). Personal Statement. AGCP, *Final Report*. Washington, D.C.: U.S. Gov't. Printing Office.

Schlafly, P. (1986). Letter to Attorney General Edwin Meese, January 15.

Senn, C. H. (1985). "A Comparison of Women's Reactions to Nonviolent Pornography, Violent Pornography, and Erotica." Master's thesis, University of Calgary.

Sherif, C. W. (1980). "Comment on Ethical Issues in Malamuth, Heim and Feshbach's 'Sexual Responsiveness of College Students to Rape Depictions: Inhibitory and Disinhibitory Effects.'" *Journal of Personality and Social Psychology* 38:409–12.

Surgeon-General's Workshop Report (1986). *Pornography and Public Health*. Washington, D.C.: U.S. Surgeon-General's Office.

Tannenbaum, P. H. (1970). "Emotional Arousal as a Mediator of Erotic Communication Effects." In *Technical Report of the Commission on Obscenity and Pornography*, vol. 8, pp. 326–56. Washington, D.C.: Government Printing Office.

Vance, C. (1985). "What Does the Research Prove?" *Ms.*, April 1985, p. 40.

Weiss, C. (1977). *Using Social Research in Public Policy Making*. Lexington, Mass.: D.C. Heath.

——— (1982). "Policy Research in the Context of Diffuse Decision-Making." *Journal of Higher Education* 53:6 (November).

Wilson, J. (1971). "Violence, Pornography, and Social Science." *The Public Interest* 22 (Winter): 45–61.

Wilson, W. C. (1978). "Can Pornography Contribute to the Prevention of Sexual Problems?" In *The Prevention of Sexual Disorders: Issues and Approaches*, ed. C. Qualls, J. Wincze, and D. Barlow. New York: Plenum Press.

Zanna, M., and Fazio, R. (1982). "The Attitude-Behavior Relation: Moving toward a Third Generation of Research." In *Consistency in Social Behavior*, ed. M. Zanna, E. Higgins, and C. Herman. Hillsdale, N.J.: Lawrence Erlbaum.

Zillmann, D., and Bryant, J. (1984). "Effects of Massive Exposure to Pornography." In *Pornography and Sexual Aggression*, ed. N. Malamuth and E. Donnerstein. Orlando, Fla.: Academic Press.

Zillmann, D., and Sapolsky, B. (1977). "What Mediates the Effects of Erotica on Annoyance and Hostile Behavior in Males?" *Journal of Personality and Social Psychology* 35:587–96.

5

Pornography as a Legal Text

Comments from a Legal Perspective

ROBIN WEST

During the last decade, women have begun to describe their experiences of pornography. Many of those descriptions have been harrowing tales of victimization. First in public hearings in Minneapolis and later in front of the Meese Commission on Pornography, women who had grievously suffered from pornography found a voice and a forum, and broke their silence. What they have told us is disturbing and unsettling and transformative—if we listen, it will change forever what we see when we see pornography. From their testimony, it seems clear that many women—who knows how many—have been badly damaged, injured, and oppressed by pornography, either by the violence in its production, by the sexual violence it depicts, or by the acts of sexual violence it can inspire.[1] If we listen to these stories, we will learn something important: pornography causes real women real harm, and the harm is brutal.

But not all women who have broken silence on the issue of pornography have told stories of victimization. Women's voices have not spoken in unison. Some women who have described their experiences of pornography for the first time have very different stories to tell. Those stories are also disturbing and unsettling and, I believe, transformative, but in a different way. From their testimony, it seems clear that some women—perhaps many women—have felt pleased, amused, thrilled, aroused, and even liberated by pornography (see, e.g., Vance, 1984; Snitow, 1983). If we listen hard to these stories, we can no longer think of pornography as simply an instrument of patriarchal terror. If we listen to these stories, we will also learn something important: pornography can be and has been helpful to some women. For some women, pornography is a rebellious attack on the repressive institutions of family, marriage, and monogamous and compulsory heterosexuality, and for some women it is for that reason alone an important source of pleasure and liberation.

I have no reason to doubt the sincerity or truth of either sort of testimony, for I have had both experiences, and I suspect that I am not unique. Surely we can posit the existence of a third class of women—perhaps larger than the first two—who have on occasion been liberated by pornography, and on other occasions been damaged, brutalized, or more generally simply oppressed by it. We might summarize the testimony of the last ten years in this way: according to *our own* accounts, women's experiences of pornography have been more than just diverse, they have been profoundly contradictory. For the third group in particular, women's experience of pornography might be described as an "experience of contradiction." This experience of contradiction, I believe, demands explanation.

The feminist community—itself deeply divided over the meaning, content, and importance of pornography—has provided two explanations of the contradictory nature of women's experience of pornography. Both proffered accounts, I believe, are wrong, and dangerously so. First, Catharine MacKinnon, feminist lawyer, scholar, and primary spokesperson for the feminist antipornography movement, argues forcefully that the pleasure some women allegedly derive from pornography (and from submission, and from sexual masochism) is simply false: the pleasure itself is a product of pornographic manipulation, and, far from being a meaningful counterexample to a sweeping denunciation of pornographic texts, women's enjoyment of pornography constitutes proof positive of pornography's evil (MacKinnon, 1984, 1985). On the other side of the debate, FACT feminists (Feminist Anti-Censorship Taskforce—a coalition of feminist lawyers, writers, and academics opposing feminist as well as conservative antipornography initiatives) strongly imply that at least some of these stories of oppression, damage, and injury are false. According to FACT, women who claim they've been damaged, injured, oppressed, discriminated against, or coerced by pornographic texts—which are, after all, merely "words and pictures"—may suffer, but what they suffer from is an unhealthy tendency to falsely characterize themselves as infantilized victims. Words and images, after all, can't hurt us. It's sticks and stones that cause bruises (Amicus Curiae Brief, 1984).

We should be wary of both of these explanations. The contradictory experience of oppression and liberation that pornography engenders in women should not be dissolved by a precipitate dismissal of either experience as false. The testimony of those women who have derived pleasure from pornography texts doesn't *sound* false; nor does the testimony of those women who have found pornography to be oppressive. For those of us who have had both experiences, the charge that one or the other experience is a function of false consciousness sounds even more dubious. But we should be wary of these explanations for another reason as well. Subjective feelings of contradiction can be invaluable aids to radical analysis, both feminist and otherwise. An experience of contradiction is often a sign that the objective event is itself riddled with contradiction and tension. Feminists should not just acknowledge, but *insist* upon, women's contradictory experiences of pornography (and of sexual submission, and of sexual masochism), rather than deny them, or condemn the half that leaves us uncomfortable as "false." For it may be that women have contradictory experiences of pornography because of contradictions in the pornographic texts themselves, and it may be that the contradictions in those texts in turn reflect contradictions in the patriarchy that produced them. If so, then explorations of these felt contradictions should be central, not peripheral, to feminist analyses of patriarchal domination. Exploration of the "experience of contradiction" may be the beginning of an exploration of the contradictions of patriarchy. It need not be an admission of any inadequacy in ourselves.

In this essay, I will attempt to advance our understanding of pornography by providing a different sort of explanation of the experience of contradiction. My explanation will draw on yet a third experience I have had of pornography, which again I suspect I share with many women. I have experienced pornography as an *authority* in my life, in much the same way I experienced the authority of my parents as a child, or the authority of legal texts as an adult. I have received pornography as I have received these other authorities: as an imperative description of some aspect of the world from which I was to infer some aspect of my own identity. In the case of pornographic authority the aspect of the world described was of the "true" nature of female sexuality and sexual relations, from which I inferred a definition of my own sexuality. I will argue, based on this third experience of pornography-as-authority, for a particular metaphoric way of thinking about pornography. I will argue that we should think of pornography as the authoritative "legal text"—the Constitution, so to speak—of patriarchy. The recent increase in the amount of pornography and its change in content, I will claim, represent the transition of patriarchy from a political hierarchy enforced through brute superior strength—boots and fists—to a political hierarchy enforced instead through the legalistic mechanisms of authoritative texts—legitimation, mystification, and abstraction. This third experience of pornography can help us understand the contradictory feelings of liberation and oppression that pornography engenders in women. Pornography engenders these contradictory feelings, I will suggest, not because women suffer from false consciousness, and not because our sexual feelings are hopelessly chaotic, but rather because pornography functions as a "legal text," and *all* legal texts engender contradictory feelings of oppression and liberation in the class they help to subordinate. If we focus on pornography's role as an authority in our lives, we will better understand our contradictory experiences of pornography and hence our ambivalence toward its regulation, control, or censorship.

My argument will ultimately be a pragmatic one: I will propose that this way of thinking about pornography is highly functional. First, when we think of pornography as a particular type of text, namely a *legal* text, much of the intra-feminist debate regarding the content, importance, meaning, and value of pornography appears in a new and less disabling light. Women's contradictory experience of pornography reveals, ultimately, the contradictory, unstable, indeterminate content of the patriarchal ordering to which it gives voice. And, as is true of all legal texts, the indeterminacy provides an opportunity for feminist transformation, not just of the pornographic text, but also of the patriarchal hierarchy that underlies it.

Pornography as Legal Text

Let me give content to my working hypothesis about pornography—that pornography is the legal text of patriarchy—by expanding on the two key terms of the definition: "patriarchy" and "legal text."

By the word "patriarchy," I mean something quite specific. Women, by virtue of their sex, live under the rule of two political sovereigns—the state and men—rather than one. Patriarchy is the political rule women inhabit by virtue of their sex. The expropriation of women's sexuality is the "point" of patriarchal politics: men are sovereign, and women are subjects (Hart, 1961). Let me try to make this claim more concrete, and thereby more convincing. Think for a moment about a simple assault—a verbal threat that puts another in fear. In every American jurisdiction, assaults are tortious, meaning they are compensable private harms. If accompanied by an uninvited touching, they are criminal—they are punishable by the state. Someone who threatens another verbally is a tortfeasor, and someone who puts another in fear through a nonconsensual touching is a criminal. Yet women suffer unpunished and uncompensated sexual assaults continually. Women who live in urban areas and walk rather than drive or take taxis endure tortious or criminal sexual assaults *daily*. Although we have a trivializing phrase for these encounters—"street hassling"—these assaults are not at all trivial. They are frightening and threatening whispered messages of power and subjection. They are, in short, assaults. Yet, men who harass women on the street are not apprehended, they are not punished, the victims are not compensated, and no damages are paid. The entire transaction is entirely invisible to the state.

Now the sexual assaulter on the street—who is not punished for the criminal assault, who is not liable for the tortious assault, and who has no expectation whatsoever of being either punished or held liable—is not a criminal and he is not a tortfeasor; rather, he is a sovereign. He is not a thug, he is boss. Unchecked, threatening exercises of power that will not even be seen much less stopped by the state may be crimes and torts definitionally, but they are not "crimes" and "torts" experientially. They are instances of political sovereignty. The woman who is sexually assaulted on the street—continually, daily—with no expectation that she will be compensated for her injury and with no expectation that the assaulter will be held accountable for the assault, does not experience the assault as a criminal or tortious assault. She does not experience it as a compensable injury, or as a punishable crime. She does not experience herself as a potential litigant with an enforceable right, or as a potential prosecutrix who will be heard by the community. Rather, she experiences herself as the subject of unchecked power, and she experiences the assault as an exercise of unchecked power. She experiences it as another lesson in her subjection to—her subordination to—the whims of a superior political power, namely the sexual man. She experiences the sexual assault not as a tort, and not as a crime, but as a lesson in politics. She reacts not as a coequal citizen who has been wronged, but rather as a political subject. She absorbs the assault rather than resists it.

The same is true for more damaging and injurious forms of sexual violence. Definitionally, battery, rape, and incest are all criminal and tortious acts—as are assaults. But when a man has forcible intercourse with a woman without her consent, and does so knowing—correctly—that the act will not be punished, he does not view himself as a criminal; he views himself as a political sovereign, and he is right: he is one. The woman's point of view is correlative. When a woman endures a rape or beatings with no expectation of compensation or punishment, she does not view herself as a victim with a victim's entitlements. She views herself as a political subject, and she is right: she is one. When a child endures the sexual abuse of the molester without even the knowledge that this conduct is wrong, she does not experience the abuse as a violation of her rights. She experiences it as constitutive of her identity—her political reality—and she is right: it is constitutive of her reality of being under the thumb of a sexually abusive man.

What is so hard for many people to see or understand is that so long as male sexual violence against women and girls is unseen and unpunished, women will continue to live under two political sovereigns—the state and men—rather than one. Sexual violence against women and girls is presently unpunished for a variety of reasons. In many instances it is legal (marital rape). Where illegal, it is often perceived as trivial (sexual assault on the street). Where illegal and nontrivial, it is often invisible (domestic violence in the home). In many cases it is tolerated as natural or inevitable (date and acquaintance rape). But whatever the reason, so long as male sexual violence against women is unchecked, the sexually violent man is a political sovereign, and the woman or girl is politically subordinate. This sphere of political sovereignty is what I mean by the word "patriarchy." Control over female sexuality is the purpose for which this political sphere exists, and unchecked, random, male sexual violence—in the home, workplace, and street—is the mechanism by which its hierarchical structure is enforced.

I will argue in a moment that the words and images we call "pornographic" constitute the "legal texts" of this political state. First, though, I want to explain in some detail what I mean by the phrase "legal text." The phrase "legal text" is itself controversial; legal theorists disagree over its meaning. "Legal positivists" argue that a "legal text" is simply a text that communicates a positive, posited command from a political superior to a political inferior. People with power tell people with less power what to do, and the "legal text" is the mode of communicating the order (Dworkin, 1986). "Interpretivists," by contrast, argue that "legal texts" do more than simply convey a political sovereign's command. A "legal text," according to the interpretivist, communicates not just the positive and posited command of the political sovereign but also the shared societal principles that the command presupposes and either explicitly or implicitly endorses. These shared societal principles are the background presuppositions regarding the world, without which the legal text literally read simply would not make sense. But we must be more specific about what it means to "make sense." For a legal text to "make sense" to both parties—the sovereign as well as the subordinate—it must be more than simply coherent. A legal text is a normative text—it tells the subordinate party what that party must do, should do, and will do. For a legal text to "make sense," it must make *normative* sense: it must fit into our common "sense" of what we should do, and of what we should be told to do, and why and when it is all right for us to be told what to do. Put differently, a legal text only "makes sense" when both the command and the political hierarchy that produced that command appear to be just—when they accord with our sense of justice. The "legal text," then, in the interpretive tradition, communicates not only the positive command of the political sovereign but also the background beliefs necessary to maintain the social consensus that both the command itself and the hierarchy that generates it are just.

Now, politically, positivism and interpretivism are both relatively neutral theories of law; they reflect neither a right, left, nor center political orientation. However, both positivism and interpretivism have analogues in left-wing legal scholarship. Left-wing legal scholars are attuned to a *source* of sovereignty to which mainstream scholars are blind, and that is economic sovereignty, and hence economic hierarchy. This shared sensitivity to economic power and its implications for law and legal theory lends common ground to all left-wing legal scholarship. That shared commitment, though, has radically different jurisprudential implications, depending upon whether it is combined with a positive or interpretive theory of the nature of legal texts. First, the left-wing legal scholar who is committed to a positivist view of law tends to see legal texts as the means by which the commands of the economically empowered—the capitalist class—are communicated to the economically subordinate—the working class. This kind of left-wing legal positivist position is often called "instrumentalism."[2] The jurisprudential claim of instrumentalism is that legal texts in our society are instruments of economic power. Alternatively, the left-wing scholar who is drawn to an "interpretivist" view of legal texts sees legal texts as performing a more complex, "legitimating" task. The legal text is not simply the mechanism for communicating the commands of the economically empowered. Rather, it performs the more complex and subtle role of "legitimating" that economic hierarchy. This left-wing interpretivist view might be called "critical interpretivism."[3] The jurisprudential claim of critical interpretivism is that the legal text "legitimates" underlying economic hierarchies. This is the commitment that unifies the otherwise diverse views of the new "Critical Legal Studies" (CLS) movement in left-wing legal scholarship. I will argue in subsequent sections that the intra-feminist debate about pornography is a mirror reflection of the intra-left "instrumentalist vs. critical interpretivist" debate regarding legal texts. In fact, I will claim, since pornography is the legal text of patriarchy, it is precisely the same fight. But before turning to pornography, let me illustrate the difference between instrumental and critical accounts of law by focusing on the operation of legal texts in a familiar context.

Think about the relationship between our economic system and our "legal texts" of contract and property law (hereinafter, "liberal legal texts"). The material, concrete reality of severe imbalances of economic wealth creates "political hierarchies": people with great material resources have considerably more power than people who lack material wealth. The wealthy, by virtue of their greater power, can expropriate the labor of the less wealthy: the wealthy can exploit the poor for profit, because the poor depend on the wealthy for survival. To positivist instrumentalist legal scholars, contract law and property law, instrumentally understood, consist of that class of legislative and judicial pronouncements that dictate the terms of the private economic relationships between these economically empowered and disempowered groups. In this view, the "legal texts" of property law and contract law positivistically convey the imperative commands of the dominant economic party—the wealthy— to the subordinate party—the working class. Thus, the appellation "instrumentalist": the legal text is simply the instrumental tool of the economically empowered class.

The major contribution of the CLS movement to left-wing and progressive legal scholarship has been to put this instrumental view of the relationship of liberal legal texts to economic class into question. According to the critical scholars, contract and property law embody much more than simply the commands of the economically empowered, and liberal legal texts of contract and property *do* much more than simply communicate those commands. At a minimum, the texts of contract and property law include not just economic commands but also the beliefs necessary to render those commands acceptable. So viewed, the most crucial function of liberal legal texts is not to communicate the economically stronger party's threat to use the organized force of the state to back up his position of privilege—although it does serve that purpose. Rather, the major function of contract law is that it legitimates that privilege through the creation of neutral-sounding apolitical "rights." Thus, the legal texts of corporate liberalism, read interpretively and critically, do the work of ensuring that the severe material imbalances reflected in our contractual relations are perceived as natural and fair. That is its legitimating role. In this view, law controls our behavior not so much through coercion and the threat of coercion, but rather by legitimating imbalances of power (Kairys, 1982).

The most important way in which liberal legal texts legitimate economic hierarchy is by articulating what critical scholar Robert Gordon calls the "utopian promises" of legitimation (1982, 286). "Utopian promises" are the implied or express ideals that the legal text suggests the economic hierarchy will deliver. We can see two such promises in the liberal legal texts of contract and property law. The first utopian promise is *equality*. The imbalance of power—the inequality—between a capitalist and a worker is "masked" or "obfuscated" in the legal description of their relationship as a contract between formally equal contracting parties. Economically and politically unequal, capitalist and laborer become, in their formal, legal definitions, perfectly equal, even interchangeable parties: they are "A" and "B," "promisor" and "promisee," "offeror" and "offeree." The capitalist and the worker that emerge from this legal description are not a "capitalist" and a "worker"—the former dependent upon the latter for profit, and the latter dependent upon the former for survival—but instead highly abstract legal actors. They are perfectly equal, "in the eyes of the law." Contract law promises legal equality.

The second "utopian promise" of contract and property texts is freedom. Once the "capitalist" and the "worker" are redefined as "promisor" and "promisee," the relationship between them is not only formally equal but also formally *consensual*. The worker was not *coerced* into his labor contract by virtue of economic scarcity; rather the promisee "consented" to the contract. If one has consented to one's position, then the position is freely chosen, not coerced. Thus, contract law promises freedom: contracts are products of freedom, not of economic duress or material coercion (Gabel and Feinman, 1982, 172).

However, legal texts must do more than simply make promises—without more (much more), no one would believe them. To render economic hierarchy acceptable, liberal legal texts must also, in some way, make plausible the claim that those promises have been fulfilled. One way that legal texts do so is by generating an authoritative world view—an image of reality—and an authoritative account of the "person" that fits that reality. If these authoritative images come to be believed, then the utopian promises of the texts become virtually self-fulfilling. Critical scholars call these images "belief clusters." Thus, to return to our example, the authoritative description of the human being communicated by contract law is that of an atomistic individual who achieves her highest potential by choosing between alternatives provided by a given social and material world. The distinction between "choices" driven by economic necessity and "choices" derived from voluntarily adopted preferences simply disappears when the individual and the material world are described in these abstract terms. Economic coercion becomes contractual freedom. Professor Gordon describes the process in this way:

> Law, like religion and television images, is one of these clusters of belief . . . that convince people that all the many hierarchical relations in which they live and work are natural and necessary. A small business is staffed with people who carry around in their heads mixed clusters of this kind: "I can tell these people what to do and fire them if they're not very polite to me and quick to do it, because (a) I own the business, (b) they have no right to anything but the minimum wage, (c) I went to college and they didn't, (d) they would not work as hard or as efficiently if I didn't keep after them . . . , (e) if they don't like it they can leave," etc.—and the employees, though with less smugness and enthusiasm, believe it as well. Take the ownership claim: the employees are not likely to think they can challenge that because to do so would jeopardize their sense of the rights of ownership, which they them-

selves exercise in other aspects of life ("I own this house, so I can tell my brother-in-law to get the hell out of it"); they are locked into a belief-cluster that abstracts and generalizes the ownership claim. (Gordon, 1982, 287)

Given the authoritative account of the human being and of the world that the legal text provides, the legal relationship between capitalist and worker becomes one of formally equal and formally free contracting parties—both parties are equally capable of the one act that the legal text has authoritatively depicted as the essence of personhood. Both are equally capable of freely consenting to the contract that joins them. To the extent that these depictions are believed, the "equality" and the "consent" that characterize unequal, coercive, hierarchical relationships "in the eyes of the law" also come to characterize those relationships in the eyes and self-images of the subordinate. To both the weak and strong alike, the hierarchies that subordinate become something to celebrate instead of something to condemn:

Recall the example given earlier of the person who works in small business for the owner of the business. It is true that the owner's position is backed up by the ultimate threat of force—if she does not like the way people behave on her property she can summon armed helpers from the state to eject them—but she also has on her side the powerful ideological magic of a structure that gives her the rights of an employer and owner, and the worker the duties of an employee and invitee of the owner's property. The worker feels he cannot challenge the owner's rights to eject him from her property if she does not like the way he behaves, in part . . . because he accepts her claim as legitimate; he respects individual rights of ownership because the power such rights confer seems necessary to his own power and freedom. . . . But the analogy he makes is possible only because of his acquiescence in a belief structure that abstracts particular relationships between real people . . . into relations between entirely abstract categories of individuals playing the abstract social role of owner, employee, etc. (Gordon, 1982, 288–89)

The end result of this process is that the political hierarchy the text legitimates will appear to be not only free and equal, but inevitable as well. The belief clusters that bolster the promises come to be experienced not as one possible way to organize society among alternatives but rather as an authoritative, correct description of a natural, objective world (Gordon, 1982, 288). When a text operates in this way, its power derives not from the direct coercive control it exerts over our behavior but rather from its capacity to determine, almost inalterably, the way we view ourselves. It legitimates by grasping hold of our imagination. Gordon explains:

[T]he main constraints upon making social life more bearable are these terrible, constricting limits upon imagination . . . these structures are as obdurate as they are because they are collectively constructed and maintained—we have to use them to think about the world at all, because the world makes no sense apart from our systems of shared meaning. (Gordon, 1982, 291)

With that introduction to what I mean by "legal text," let me return to my claim that pornography is the legal text of patriarchy. If we take seriously the feminist claim that women live within a separate political hierarchy, the purpose of which is the control and expropriation of female sexuality, and the enforcement mechanism of which is male sexual violence, and if we take seriously the critical insight that a legal text consists of not just the sovereign's posited commands but the belief structures and utopian promises that legitimate the hierarchy, then pornography emerges as the legal text of patriarchy. And, like all legal texts, pornography can be viewed either instrumentally or critically. Viewed instrumentally, pornography conveys posited commands backed by force, which occasionally affect the subordinate's behavior directly—the commands to which pornography gives voice are sometimes enforced through male violence. Just as the law occasionally "causes" instances of state violence through court judgments, so pornography, systematically if only occasionally, provokes instances of male sexual violence. Viewed critically, however, pornography, the legal text of patriarchy, does more. Like liberal legal texts, pornographic texts legitimate as well as coerce. Just as liberal legal texts depict economic hierarchies in a way that makes them appear both rational and just, so pornographic texts depict patriarchal hierarchy as both rational and just. Like legal texts, pornography controls us by threatening us, but like legal texts, it also controls us by laying claim to our imagination.

Thus, my claim is that pornography governs our behavior in patriarchy in a way that parallels the manner in which legal texts govern our behavior in liberal society. Both in patriarchy under pornography and in liberal society under law, hierarchy is maintained not just by brute force and threat of brute force, and not even primarily by brute force, *but also* by the legitimating power of promises and authoritative definitions of reality and selfhood. In patriarchy under pornography, women are controlled by the word and the picture *as well as* by the boot and the fist, just as in liberal legalism, workers are controlled by the images of freedom and abstract equality *as well as* by the threat of economic deprivation. Both in patriarchy under pornography and in liberalism under law, hierarchy is depicted in a way that makes it appear desirable and inevitable, rather than simply threatening. The extent to which women accept the descriptions of themselves and of the world generated by pornography is the extent to which they will believe that the "utopian promises" of patriarchy have been met. To that extent, patriarchy appears to be both just and good—to that extent, women accept and endorse it. Coercion is not required to secure compliance. Law replaces brute force. The pornographic text replaces the boot and the fist.

The purpose of patriarchy, however, is quite different from (and perhaps at odds with) the purpose of liberal legalism. The purpose of liberal legalism (or at least one purpose of liberal legalism) is the *commodification* of our productive life, toward the end of its marketable exchange, and the redefinition of the self so as to accommodate that *exchange*. The purpose of patriarchy, by contrast, is not commodification and exchange of female sexuality. Rather, the purpose of patriarchy is the *ownership* of female sexuality, and the redefinition of the female so as to accommodate its ownership (not its exchange). In both systems, the individual is "objectified." In liberalism, however, the individual (and his labor) is objectified so as to facilitate exchange. In patriarchy, the individual (and her sexuality) is objectified so as to facilitate ownership.

As a result of this difference, the legitimating utopian promises of pornographic texts differ dramatically from and even conflict with the legitimating utopian promises of liberal legal texts, both in their content and in their intended audience. Patriarchy neither promises nor accords the realm of individual determination that legal liberalism promises (and to some degree delivers). The legitimating utopian promises of pornography are emphatically not legalism's promises of freedom and equality—pornography depicts *everything but* free and equal sexual exchanges.[4] Indeed, for many consumers, pornography may provide a refuge from liberalism's promises of freedom and equality (Benjamin, 1985). The utopian promises of pornographic texts are diametrically opposed to liberalism's. The utopian promises of pornography are that women will take pleasure in, be fulfilled by, and are made better off by the forced, unfree, unequal, unbargained-for expropriation and ownership of our sexuality by men, and that this is true regardless of women's "expressed preferences" and regardless of women's felt desires. Thus, the utopian promises of pornography are the hedonistic, private promises of pleasure and subjective well-being. Male ownership of female sexuality is just and good, pornography promises, for *women as well as men,* not because such a relationship is free and equal but rather because this unfree, unequal, nonconsensual, unbargained-for status is pleasurable to women and increases women's well-being. The central message of modern pornography is that women want, take pleasure in, and are made better off by forced sex. Pleasure and well-being, not consent and equality, are the utopian promises of pornography.

The *audience* of pornography is also different from the audience of liberal legal texts, at least at first blush. Liberal legal texts convey their promises directly to the subordinate classes. Pornographic promises, by contrast, although *about* women, are rarely directed *to* women. While liberal legal texts control behavior by defining a conception of the subordinate *for the subordinate,* pornography controls behavior by defining a conception of women *for men.* This distinction, however, may be more apparent than real. What men think *of* women becomes what women think of women; in a system of total dominance, what men think of women becomes what women are.

In all other respects, however, pornography operates in a way that parallels the function of liberal legal texts. As shown above, the authoritative descriptions of the world and of the human being found in liberal legal texts help to make liberalism's promises of freedom and equality appear to be met. Similarly, the authoritative descriptions of the world and of female sexuality found in pornography help to make patriarchy's promises—that the expropriation of female sexuality will be both pleasurable and beneficial to women—appear to be met. Liberal legal texts make credible liberalism's promises of freedom and equality by authoritatively defining the world as one of scarce resources, and the human being as a contractually competent, rational individual, abstracted away from particular material needs and the hierarchy to which those needs give rise. Pornography makes credible patriarchy's promises by defining the world— men—as inevitably sexually charged and dangerous, and defining women as sexually willing, pliant, passive, obedient, and accessible. If the liberal legal text's conception of the world and of the individual were right, then liberalism would indeed be the guarantor of freedom and equality. Similarly, if the pornographic conception of the world—of male sexuality—were right, then expropriation of women's sexuality would be inevitable, and if the definition of female sexuality were right, then the expropriation of our sexuality would indeed be pleasurable: even the *forced* expropriation would be pleasurable. If the descriptions were true, then patriarchal expropriation would be acceptable—it would be both necessary for female security, and thus for female well-being, and conducive to female pleasure. Critical scholars have shown us how liberal legal texts confine the worker by curtailing his imaginative capacity to envision himself and his economic relations in a radically different way from those mandated by corporate capitalism. In a parallel way, pornography confines women by filling both men's and women's minds and bodies with a particular sexual image and by limiting our ability to imagine ourselves otherwise: namely, as in full sovereign possession of our sexuality.

Legal Texts and the Pornography Debate

The pornography debate has badly divided the feminist legal community for one simple reason: pornography is radically indeterminate. It is radically indeterminate in a multitude of senses. First, and perhaps most obviously, it is notoriously difficult to define. We don't know what it is, and it is increasingly obvious that we don't know it when we see it either. It has some causal connection to violence, or maybe it has none at all: it indirectly affects "dispositions," but, on the other hand, it is "merely words and images." Its control is absolutely central to feminist progress, or maybe it is absolutely irrelevant; banning pornography would transform patriarchy, or perhaps it would further entrench it. Its meaning is radically indeterminate: most of it is "violent pornography" (whatever that is), or almost none of it is; it depicts rape and other acts of felonious assaults, or it depicts nothing but harmless and purely voluntary, consensual sadomasochistic images. The violence is staged, or the violence is real. The pleasure some women take in pornography is a function of false consciousness, or the pleasure women derive from pornography reflects a rebellious and even a radical impulse.

To be more precise, feminists presently divide on four key questions regarding pornography: (1) the nature and extent of a causal relationship, if any, between pornography and male sexual violence; (2) the importance of pornography to patriarchy, and hence of its control to feminist progress; (3) the meaning of pornographic texts and, more specifically, the extent to which they portray scenes of violence and rape, as opposed to scenes of consensual sadomasochism (as opposed to violence), and consensual play-acted fantasies of "capture" (as opposed to rape); and (4) the significance of what I have called the "experience of contradiction." Antipornography feminists argue that (1) pornography causes violence against women both directly and indirectly; (2) banning pornography is central to feminist progress; (3) pornography almost always depicts sexualized violence and rape; and (4) women's enjoyment of pornography is a function of false consciousness, and never an expression of "authentic" female sexuality. On the other side, "Anti-Censorship" feminists argue that (1) pornography consists of words and images and that while words and images may affect attitudes, they rarely if ever "cause" violence; (2) the fight against pornography is peripheral at most to feminist struggle, and pornography's total disappearance would have no impact upon the transformation of patriarchy; (3) pornographic texts rarely depict violence, although they frequently employ consensual, voluntary sadomasochistic imagery and themes; and (4) women's enjoyment of some pornography can be consistent with authentic female sexuality and may even evidence a radical and feminist impulse. Both sides claim the feminist banner. Both characterize their position as derived from feminist tenets and both characterize the opposing position as in an important sense antifeminist, patriarchal, misogynist, or pornographic. If either side is right, then an awful lot of women who think of themselves as feminists are wrong. From the literature, it would appear that the pornography issue has caused a dangerous dissolution of feminist theory, practice, and commitment. From the literature on pornography, it would appear that feminism is in trouble.

In this section, I will not try to resolve any of these issues. I will, however, insist that we recharacterize the debate. I will argue that the intra-feminist pornography debate is not about feminism at all, but rather it is about legalism and the nature, function, meaning, and importance of legal texts. More specifically, I will argue that feminists divide over pornography because of ambiguities and contradictions in pornography itself. Those contradictions are shared by *all* legal texts; they are not unique to pornography. *All* legal texts are contradictory and ambiguous, and in precisely the ways pornography is contradictory and ambiguous. Intra-feminist debates over the nature, meaning, importance, and possibilities of pornography find their parallel, and perhaps their resolution, not in debates within feminism, but in debates within left-wing legal scholarship on the nature, meaning, importance, and possibilities of legal texts. The feminist debate over pornography does not reflect a fatal contradiction within feminism. Feminists who disagree on this issue are all feminists; the claim of each side that the other side is antifeminist is just wrong. This is true not because pornography is "peripheral" to feminism. Rather, it is because the pornography debate is not, ultimately, *about* feminist commitments or feminist theory. The pornography debate is what it is because of the legalistic nature of pornographic texts. To the extent that it is about anything at all, it is about the nature, meaning, importance, and possibilities of legal texts, and hence the nature of the law.

THE VIOLENCE PORNOGRAPHY CAUSES

First, it is not surprising that feminists can't agree on the nature of the causal connection between pornography and violence, or on the importance of pornography to feminist struggle. This debate has nothing to do with feminism and everything to do with legalism. The ambiguous causal relationship between pornography and violence finds its perfect correlate in the ambiguous causal relationship between any legal text and the state violence it legitimates, and the intra-feminist debate over the importance of pornography to patriarchy finds its perfect correlate in the intra-left "instrumental vs. critical" debate over the importance of legal texts to liberalism. A legal text occasionally "causes" an act of state violence, and it always threatens to do so: contract law occasionally "causes" a sheriff to attach a judgment debtor's assets; property law occasionally "causes" a tenant's forced eviction; criminal law occasionally "causes" a criminal to be forcibly confined.[5] The "mere words and images" that constitute property, contract, and criminal law do occasionally but emphatically combine with state power in such a way as to cause violence against the subordinated class (Gordon, 1982, 288). Similarly, pornography occasionally but persistently "causes" identifiable acts of male violence. The "mere words and images" that constitute pornographic texts occasionally but emphatically combine with patriarchal power to direct sanctioned violence against women. Of course it is true that pornography does not *always* have such a direct causal connection to patriarchal violence, and that patriarchal violence is not always caused by pornography: this is true of all legal texts. But it does not follow that pornography is unrelated to violence against women, any more than that legal texts are unrelated to lock-ups, evictions, and wage scales.

Most contractual relationships never wind up in court, but it is nevertheless the case that those that do have a powerful determining effect on those that don't. Contract law—legal texts about contract rights—is the communicative means by which the lesson of "what happens to you if you breach" is conveyed to the rest of the contracting world. Similarly, most heterosexual relationships do not end in the violent expropriation of the woman's sexuality. Nevertheless some do, and those that do have a powerful, determining effect on those that do not. Violent pornography may be the communicative means by which the authoritative lesson of "what happens to you if you resist the giving of your sexuality" is conveyed to the rest of the sexual world.

IMPORTANCE

Second, disagreement among feminists over the importance of pornography to women's struggle against patriarchy does not reveal a state of confusion within feminist theory. Disagreement over the importance of pornography is perfectly mirrored in left-wing disagreement over the importance of legal texts. On the one hand, legal texts seem to be "mere words and images"—and how can words and images "do" or cause anything? Time spent addressing legal texts would better be spent addressing the political reality they mask, transform, and legitimate. The "mere words and images" debate over pornography is on par. Pornographic images are indeed merely words and images. Yet pornographic words and images, like the legal texts of liberalism, have an intimate connection with the political sphere they reflect, and with the violence that sphere sanctions. We ignore that relationship at our peril.

It is both the intimacy of the text with the coercive force behind it and the ambiguity of that connection that to my mind gives pornography its legalistic character and that distinguishes pornography from other legitimating texts of patriarchy, such as advertising or romance novels. To be more specific: the intimate connection between pornographic "words and images" and violent patriarchal force has three aspects, all of which have parallels in the intimate connection between the "words and images" of liberal legal texts and economic coercion. First, the pornographic text *itself* is often a *product of patriarchal force*. Romance novels, by contrast, are not. Just as contract and property law are the outcome of economic and political struggle (in a way that other legitimating texts of capitalism are not), so a pornographic text is itself often the product of a violent, sexual struggle, or a threatened violent struggle: the real-life kidnapping and coercion behind the apparent consent of Linda Marchiano in *Deep Throat* (Lovelace and McGrady, 1980), the underage and drugged teenagers and children used in videos (AGCP, 1986, 405). Second, pornographic texts *depict* violence against women as a major theme (AGCP, 1986, 323). Again, romance novels do not. Pornography conveys the threat of coercion, violence, and injury *at the same time that it conveys the patently contradictory legitimating promises of pleasure and well-being*. Legal texts do likewise—the promise of freedom and equality goes hand in hand with the patently contradictory threats of material deprivation. And third, pornographic texts, unlike romance novels and advertising, consistently, if only occasionally, "cause" patriarchal violence (AGCP, 299–353, 901–1037). The legal texts of contract and property similarly lead to state-sanctioned violence. Other legitimating texts of capitalism do not. In terms of its content, pornography is indeed much like romance novels and advertising. But in terms of their intimacy with violence, pornographic texts are most unlike romance novels or advertising, and most like legal texts of contract and property law.

However, this intimate connection between command and state violence is ambiguous: violence is not the only way and not even the primary way that the legal texts of contract and property law affect our behavior, and similarly the intimate relationship between violent pornography and male sexual violence is not the only way that pornographic texts affect our sexual behavior. What the critical legal studies movement has successfully shown is that many of the words and images of contract law are indeed "mere words and images" and function as such: many of those words are neither depictions of violence, products of violence, nor direct or indirect threats of violence. The same is true of pornography. Pornographic texts, like liberal legal texts, control us by threatening us, but, also like those texts, they also control us by conveying authoritative *descriptions* (not threats) of our social world. Descriptions control us by convincing us of their truth, not by threatening us. The antidote to the paralyzing effect of these *descriptions*—these "mere words and images"—with which pornography legitimates patriarchy—does indeed seem to be "more speech." Thus, pornography is both like other legitimating aspects of patriarchal culture (such as advertising and romance novels) in its reliance on words and images, and at the same time unlike them in the intimacy of its tie to the violence of the political realm it reflects. Precisely the same ambiguity characterizes all legal texts. They are both like other legitimating aspects of the political hierarchy they reflect in their reliance on descriptive words and images, and they are most unlike those other legitimating forces in their intimate connection with the violence sanctioned by that political world. It is therefore not surprising that feminists are divided over the importance of pornography or the strategy with which we should address it. This is a function of the legalistic nature of pornography, not of a breakdown in feminist theory. The same ambiguity surrounds all legal texts. It is truly hard to tell whether the law's "words and images" are all or nothing.

MEANING

Third, feminists are divided over what pornography depicts and hence what it "means." Think, for example, about this central, even paradigmatic, pornographic plot: a woman is "captured," then "raped," then comes to enjoy the intercourse, and finally to "beg for more." The meaning of this recurrent plot line is patently ambiguous. Was the woman really *raped,* or did she consent at the outset to being overcome? Is the film a depiction of a violent sexual assault that the victim ultimately enjoys, or is it a depiction of consensual, albeit masochistic, submission? The answer to that question seems to matter a great deal: is it *violent rape* that this plot legitimates, or is it simply one sort of sexual pleasure, a minority pleasure to be sure, but nevertheless a pleasure? Is the promise of this plot that women enjoy *violent rape,* or is the promise that we will enjoy "capture" fantasies in the nonthreatening realm of consensual sexuality? One would think that we would be able to answer these simple questions regarding plot by viewing the pornography: surely anyone can tell the difference between the depiction of a "capture fantasy" and the depiction of a violent rape. What is most bewildering (initially) about the intra-feminist pornography debate is that apparently we can't. Feminists who know all there is to know about these stories—who've watched as many of these films as anyone would ever want to see—report drastically conflicting interpretations of films that employ this plot line as well as others. Feminists can't agree on what these films are even nominally about.[6]

If pornography is the legal text of patriarchy, however, it is not so surprising that feminists are divided over what pornography depicts, and hence what it "means." The radical ambiguity of pornography's meaning—its indeterminacy—like the ambiguous causality between pornography and violence, is a factor of the legalistic function pornography serves. Like any legal text, the distinguishing feature of a pornographic text is that it communicates *both* a threat and a promise, *and that it does so simultaneously.* Like all legal texts, the meaning of a pornographic text depends in large part upon who is looking at it, and for what purpose: the meaning of the text can be located either in its promise of deliverance, transcendence, pleasure, and well-being or in its threat of coercion, expropriation, and violence. It is the function of pornography to communicate both. It is the function of pornography to be ambiguous in precisely this way. But it is not *only* pornography that is ambiguous in this way. It is the function of all legal texts to be ambiguous in precisely this way.

Of course the meaning of all texts—literary as well as legal—is somewhat indeterminate. But it is legal texts, not literary texts, that are indeterminate *in precisely the way in which pornography is indeterminate*.[7] Legal texts *always* merge threat with promise: contract law, for example, at one and the same time conveys a threat of material deprivation while promising that from the very system that threatens material deprivation will come freedom and equality. The promise of liberation and equality is at direct odds with the underlying threat of deprivation, and both promise and contradictory threat are communicated simultaneously. That simultaneity is the cause of the indeterminacy of the text's meaning. In the same way, the promise of pornography is in direct contradiction with its underlying threat. The promise is of pleasure and well-being. The *threat,* though, is of physical violence. When a threat of violence accompanies a promise of pleasure, the result is going to be incoherence, no less than when a threat of material deprivation accompanies a promise of freedom and equality. The indeterminacy of meaning revealed by conflicting feminist interpretations of pornographic texts is a function of the legitimating role of those texts. It does not reflect a fundamental contradiction in feminist theory. Even less does it reflect ambivalence over feminist commitments.

THE EXPERIENCE OF CONTRADICTION

Finally, it is not surprising that some women have experienced pornography as profoundly liberating and others have experienced pornography as profoundly oppressive. This too is a function of the legalistic nature of pornography. Subordinate classes *always* have an ambiguous experiential relationship to the legal texts that reflect the hierarchy that oppresses them—this is part of the nature of a legal text. Legal texts reinforce political hierarchies that are *contingent, not necessary,* orderings of the social world. Those hierarchies can be dismantled and changed, and one method of changing them is through changing the content as well as the dominant interpretations of the legal texts they generate. Thus, one way of challenging the economic ordering enforced by liberal legal texts is by insisting upon expansive rather than restrictive readings of the legitimating promises contained in them. If the promises of "freedom and equality" contained in contract law, for example, can be read to mean *material* equality and *substantive* or affirmative freedom, rather than formal equality and market freedom, then the legal text can itself become a means of radically transforming the economic order that produced it. Once an expansive reading of a legal promise is even articulated, the hierarchy must at least confront, if not deliver on, a strong version of its legitimating promises. The subordinate party who sees in the legal text this transformative and political opportunity might subjectively experience that text as liberating rather than as oppressive. That experience is not necessarily one of false consciousness. It may simply be politic.

For this reason, the "experiences" of liberal legal texts by subordinate parties are almost always profoundly contradictory—the same text will be felt by some members of the subordinate class as oppressive and by others as liberating. To take an example from another area of law: is the Fourteenth Amendment a legitimating and oppressive racist text, or is it a liberating and transcendental promise of a racially just society? What is its promise? Does it promise only a narrow and formal version of "equal opportunity" that will in practice do nothing but reaffirm existing racial privilege, or does it promise true racial equality? The answer depends in large part upon the orientation and power of the interpreter. When the text is being used as a tool of legitimation, then the promise of "equal opportunity" becomes a cynical assurance that the legal system will adopt a deaf and "color-blind" stance to the material reality of subordination and dis-advantage. But this narrow interpretation is hardly mandatory. In the hands of a skillful and progressive advocate, the promise of "equal opportunity" can mean something radically different. "Equal opportunity" can mean that black people in this society are entitled to real opportunity and substantive equality—and that whites are obligated to ensure that those opportunities exist and that equality is made meaningful. The racially subordinated person who experiences the Four-teenth Amendment as a tool of legitimation will "experience" that text as oppressive. But the subordinate who sees in the Fourteenth Amendment a political opportunity to transform that legitimating promise into a promise of transcendence will experience the same text as liberating. The same experiential ambiguity characterizes virtually every legal text. Depending upon its interpreta-tion, the legal text can be a window through which we glimpse a new political ordering, or a cynical legitimating promise of existing privilege; the same text can be either a tool with which the underlying privilege is attacked or a weapon with which existing privilege is maintained. It is not surprising that such texts are experientially indeterminate.

To return to pornography, let me end this section with a perhaps banal reminder. As long as people are both sexual and communicative, there will be texts describing sexual relationships. Patriarchy, however, is neither necessary, inevitable, natural, nor eternal. Consequently, textual depictions of sexuality are only contingently, not necessarily, pornographic. If patriarchy changes, texts depicting sexual relationships should change as well. While there will always be texts depicting sexual relationships, those texts need not always be pornog-raphic—they need not always be legitimating texts *of patriarchy*. The "pornog-raphy" we sometimes experience as liberating may simply be those depictions of sexuality which are concededly products of patriarchy but that have within them interpretive suggestions of a nonpatriarchal future, rather than legitimation of the patriarchal present. To insist upon nonpatriarchal interpretations of ambiguous pornography that will further this society toward a nonpatriarchal future is not necessarily an act of false consciousness. Again, it may simply be politic. Legal texts do not just reflect the underlying privilege that produces them; they carry within them legitimating promises that, if read expansively, can be turned against the privilege that produced them, carrying us closer to the utopian world beyond the privilege. When we experience pornography as liberating rather than oppressive, we may be experiencing that potential.

Patriarchy under Pornography: Opportunity and Risk

If, as I have argued, pornography is the legal text of patriarchy, then the rise of pornography constitutes not just an obstacle to feminist progress but also an opportunity. A legal text does not simply convey the commands or whims of whatever powerful group has generated the text. If the legal text is to serve its legitimating purpose, it must do more: it must also describe the world in such a way as to make its utopian promises at least minimally plausible. The meaning a legal text "has" at any particular time depends upon the interpreter. By seizing upon the utopian promise in a legal text, a progressive interpreter can "turn the text against the privilege" that generated it. It is for this reason that the interpretation of legal texts in an advanced legal society becomes an arena of struggle and not simply the repository of the wishes and world view of the powerful. One problem with instrumental accounts of the nature of law is that they deny this opportunity (Gordon, 1982, 285–86). Similarly, I believe, there are deep problems with the "instrumentalist" feminist view of pornography that, in Andrea Dworkin's words, the pornographer is the policeman in a police state, and pornography, his command (Dworkin, 1985, 13). Pornography is no more simply the command of the patriarchal ruling class than is liberal legalism simply the whim of the capitalist class. Rather, pornographic texts, like liberal legal texts, contain as well deep utopian promises for the subordinate: if they did not, they could not so successfully fulfill their legitimating role. Two strategic consequences follow.

First, if pornography has a legalistic relationship to patriarchy, then we may be able to transform patriarchy not by abolishing its text but by rewriting and reinterpreting that text so that it speaks to the future, not the present, and hence furthers that future instead of retarding it. When we have the power to do so, we should rewrite and reinterpret pornography so that it reflects not patriarchy but the world that will supplant it, just as we should rewrite the Fourteenth Amendment so that it reflects not racist privilege but the world that will follow racism. We can undertake both projects in spite of the fact that sexual politics are still patriarchal and that racism is still rampant. We can urge, in short, that pornography actually deliver on its utopian promises: that "sexually explicit texts" depict what is truly pleasurable, and what is truly beneficial to women. We can demand that pornography—the text of patriarchy—depict and *help deliver* a nonpatriarchal sexual world, just as we can demand that the Fourteenth Amendment—a legitimating legal text of racism—depict and *help deliver* a racially just society. Legal texts always present this opportunity: one way to dismantle hierarchies is by reinterpreting their legal texts in such a way as to force compliance with their legitimating promises. That is the opportunity of legalism. If pornography has become the legal text of patriarchy, then one way to dismantle the patriarchy may be by seizing interpretive power over its legal texts. The interpretation of pornography could and should become an "arena of sexual struggle," just as the interpretation of legal texts has become an arena of class struggle. I view projects such as *Pleasure and Danger* (Vance, 1982) and *Powers of Desire* (Snitow, 1983) as part of this reinterpretive task, and I applaud them for their feminist, not just their libertarian, value.

However, these sorts of interpretive victories are necessarily ambiguous, even when they succeed. As Gordon explains, "Hard-won struggles to achieve new legal rights for the oppressed begin to look like ambiguous victories. These real gains may have deepened the legitimacy of the system as a whole" (Gordon, 1982, 286). Similarly, the gains for women that occur within the interpretive arena of pornographic legal texts carry a danger: they may relegitimate instead of dismantling the overriding framework of patriarchy. By insisting upon actual benefit and real pleasure, feminists working to rewrite pornographic texts rather than abolish them may be reinforcing the overriding framework in which the promise of benefit and pleasure simply legitimates patriarchal privilege. Progressive, incremental movement within pornography, like progressive, incremental victories within law, may be both genuine and truly dangerous at the same time.

However, it may be a risk worth taking. To draw one analogy: the United States Constitution, prior to *Brown* v. *Board of Education,* was, in the eyes of many black and civil rights lawyers, a thoroughly racist document, in both intent and execution. The civil rights movement transformed that thoroughly racist legal text into a document of liberation, and it did so, in part, by reinterpreting its words and images in a manner that forced it to deliver on its legitimating promise. This legal, transformative, ideational victory could not have been achieved without the material and political struggle that accompanied it. But nevertheless, the legal victory *was* in large part an ideational and interpretive victory. The meaning of the text was fundamentally reinterpreted, and by virtue of that transformative act, a group's self-identity and sense of self-worth was radically transformed. The text that had theretofore been interpreted as legitimating segregation and a two-tiered racist society suddenly could be read as condemning it, and, as a result, a group's self-identity, which had theretofore been defined in such a way as to legitimate its own subordination, suddenly was redefined in such a way as to render subordination intolerable. In part because of an interpretive legal victory, people of color came to see themselves as rights bearers rather than as subordinates, and as worthy rather than as worthless. Legal victories are often overstated, but they should not be understated: *Brown* changed the dominant interpretation of a racist text and thereby changed a nation's consciousness.

If pornography is the constitution of patriarchy, we may be able to achieve similar transformations of consciousness through interpretive and reinterpretive transformations of pornography. Pornography's primary importance in women's lives, I have argued, is its legitimating power—through its words and images, it legitimates the violent structure that is patriarchy and defines a female self and a vision of female sexuality that legitimate that violence as pleasurable, beneficial, natural, and necessary. But if patriarchy has now developed a constitution— pornography—then the fight against patriarchy can now proceed in a new sphere: the quasi-legalistic sphere of pornography, where the tools of power are the ideational weapons of words, images, mystification, reification, and legitimation, rather than the political weapons of boots, fists, assaults, batteries, and threats. If the emergence of pornography means that patriarchy has become legalistic, and hence ideational and interpretive, then the fight for control over women's sexuality has become at least in part a fight for the interpretive power of self-definition.

The rise of pornography suggests a second opportunity for feminism as well. If pornography is patriarchy's legal text, then whether or not we can transform it, we can surely trash it. Legal texts confine us by grasping hold of our imagination, and pornography is no exception: it confines us by laying claim to our imaginative capacity for self-definition. Before we can define ourselves to ourselves for ourselves, we need to shake loose of the definitions of selfhood imposed upon us pornographically.

Gordon explains the danger of underestimating the importance of trashing legal texts this way:

> Perhaps a promising tactic . . . of trying to struggle against being demobilized by our own conventional beliefs is to try to use the ordinary rational tools of intellectual inquiry to expose belief-structures that claim that things must necessarily be the way they are. The . . . point is to unfreeze the world as it appears to common sense as a bunch of more or less objectively determined social relations. . . . Things seem to change in history when people break out of their accustomed way of responding to domination, by acting as if the constraints on their improving their lives were not real and that they could change things; and sometimes they can, . . . but they never knew they could change them at all until they tried. (Gordon, 1982, 289–92)

It would surely be a mistake to overemphasize the idealistic component of the current struggle between feminism and patriarchy. That struggle is still primarily over boots and fists—over male sexual violence, pure and simple. But it would also be a mistake to *underestimate* the extent to which that struggle has been idealistic and ideational, and an even bigger mistake to underestimate the struggle involved—the sheer effort—in conceiving of oneself in terms other than those provided by the dominant legal culture. It is difficult to conceive of our sexuality and of sexual relationships in terms other than those provided by pornographic ideology. One thing the modern explosion of pornography might mean is that the biggest threat to patriarchy, right now, is that women will succeed in this struggle: we will find the voice to commence the process of redefinition and reconceptualization.

As the civil rights movement came to power, civil rights lawyers began to glimpse alternative interpretations of that racist document the United States

Constitution and to construct alternative conceptions of racial identity, racial value, and race relations. One obstacle, whether or not the greatest obstacle, to this ideational process, was the confining, constraining impact of the dominant legal ideology on imagination. In the case of pornography, one obstacle, if not the greatest obstacle, to women's reconceptualization of female sexuality as belonging to women instead of to men is the censorial power of pornographic ideology itself. Pornography constrains us by silencing our inner voice, by making it impossible to hear ourselves, much less possess ourselves, by making it difficult to envision sexual alternatives to its authoritative image. But even stating this obstacle reveals the opportunity it presents, for one way that pornography silences us is by simply dominating the field. One way to struggle against patriarchy is by fighting the image of us that pornography promulgates, but another way is by fighting the dominance of the pornographic imagination. We do the latter by ending our own silence. We fight the dominance of the pornographic imagination in the same way we fight the dominance of other forms of legal ideology—by understanding its content, its history, its source, and its contingency in our lives, and then by exercising our censored, suppressed, silenced imagination, by generating our own sexual imagery, by becoming our own sexual authority, and by thereby repossessing our own sexual world.

NOTES

1. See Lovelace and McGrady, 1980. Two public forums have proven especially important to women who have been victimized by pornography: the Public Hearings before the Minneapolis City Council in December of 1983, and the 1986 Attorney General's Commission on Pornography. See Brest and Vandenberg, 1987, for a summary of the testimony presented in the Public Hearings Before the Minneapolis City Council, Session II (Dec. 1983), and the Attorney General's Commission on Pornography, 1986, "Victimization" chapter, pp. 767–837 [hereinafter Meese Report].

2. For a slightly different view of the relationship between legal positivism and Marxist instrumentalism, see Gordon, 1982, 284–86.

3. Liberal interpretivism regards the societal principles communicated in legal texts as *moral* principles, while critical interpretivism tends to regard those principles as politically contingent. Contrast Dworkin, 1986 (liberal interpretivism) with Unger, 1986 (critical interpretivism).

4. For a sampling of plot summaries, see The Meese Report, 1499–1803.

5. Gabel and Feinman make a similar point (1982, 181).

6. The Meese Report has further confused the issue rather than clarified it by lumping together "violent pornography" with sadomasochistic depictions. The Report *defines* violent pornography as including sadomasochistic imagery. This definitional strategy is extremely unfortunate. In my view, it renders much of the Report incoherent. It is literally impossible to determine whether the Report is condemning the legitimation of a minority sexual preference or condemning the depiction of sexualized violence. Meese Report, 323–53, 901–1037.

The antipornography feminist theorists follow the same strategy. See MacKinnon, 1987 and Sunstein, 1986.

7. The literature on the indeterminacy of legal texts is vast. For an introduction, see the essays collected in Kairys, 1982.

REFERENCES

Amicus Curiae Brief of the Feminist Anti-Censorship Taskforce, *American Booksellers Association v. Hudnut*, 771 F.2d 323 (7th Cir. 1984). Written by Nan Hunter and Sylvia Law.

Attorney General's Commission on Pornography (1986). *Final Report.*

Benjamin, Jessica (1985). "The Bonds of Love: Rational Violence and Erotic Domination." In *The Future of Difference*, ed. Hester Eisenstein & Alice Jardine. Boston: G. K. Hall.

Brest, P., and Vandenberg, A. (1987). "Politics, Feminism, and the Constitution: The Antipornography Movement in Minneapolis." *Stanford Law Review* 39:607–61.

Dworkin, Andrea (1985). "Against the Male Flood." *Harvard Women's Law Journal* 8:1.

Dworkin, Ronald (1986). *Law's Empire.* Cambridge: Belknap Press.

Gabel, Peter, and Feinman, Jay (1982). "Contract Law as Ideology." In *The Politics of Law: A Progressive Critique*, ed. David Kairys. New York: Pantheon Books.

Gordon, Robert (1982). "New Developments in Legal Theory." In *The Politics of Law: A Progressive Critique*, ed. David Kairys. New York: Pantheon Books.

Hart, H. L. A. (1961). *The Concept of Law.* Oxford: Clarendon Press.

Kairys, David, ed. (1982). *The Politics of Law: A Progressive Critique.* New York: Pantheon Books.

Lovelace, L., and McGrady, M. (1980). *Ordeal.* Secaucas, N.J.: Citadel Press.

MacKinnon, Catharine (1984). "Not a Moral Issue." *Yale Law and Policy Review* 2:321.

——— (1985). "Pornography, Civil Rights, and Speech." *Harvard Civil Rights–Civil Liberties Law Review* 20:1.

——— (1987). *Feminism Unmodified: Discourses on Life and Law.* Cambridge: Harvard University Press.

Snitow, Ann; Stansell, Christine; and Thompson, Sharon, eds. (1983). *Powers of Desire: The Politics of Sexuality.* New York: Monthly Review Press.

Sunstein, Cass (1986). "Pornography and the First Amendment." *Duke Law Journal* 1986:589.

Unger, Roberto M. (1986). *The Critical Legal Studies Movement.* Cambridge: Harvard University Press.

Vance, Carol, ed. (1984). *Pleasure and Danger: Exploring Female Sexuality.* Boston: Routledge & Kegan Paul.

PART TWO

FOR ADULT USERS ONLY

Contemporary Ramifications

6

Public Opinion and Pornography Policy

DORIS-JEAN BURTON

The focus of this chapter is an analysis of contemporary public opinion on the role of pornography in society, broad policy preferences, and the prospects for policy change. The analysis is particularly concerned with any gender differences as well as any differences between women who work full time outside the home and housewives. The results of this analysis are discussed in terms of the relationships between public opinion, policy preferences of the public, and actions by public officials. These actions could range from Supreme Court decisions to enacting or amending federal statutes, enforcing local obscenity ordinances, enacting local zoning ordinances, or enacting the antipornography statutes proposed by feminists.

Public opinion is particularly important in the area of obscenity and pornography because of the community-standards rule established in *Miller v. California* (1973). In *Smith v. United States* (1977) the Supreme Court had ruled that appeal to prurient interest and patent offensiveness are objective facts for a jury to determine using community standards. The decision in *Pope v. Morrison* (1987) emphasized that community standards apply only to whether the material appeals to prurient interest and whether it is patently offensive. Community standards do not govern the literary, artistic, political, or scientific value of the work. (See chapters 5 and 9 of the present volume for a more complete discussion of the legal aspects of pornography.)

The Gender Gap and Attitudes toward Pornography

Usually the results of public opinion polls are analyzed according to such categories as gender, race, income, educational level, political party, political ideology, and region of country. Until the "gender gap" appeared in the 1980 presidential election, relatively little attention was focused on women's political attitudes and policy preferences. Often gender differences were small, leading analysts to conclude that they were unimportant. The conventional wisdom had been that men and women had similar voting patterns, although women were less politically active and less interested in politics.

The General Social Survey (GSS) conducted by the National Opinion Research Center has asked questions about pornography since 1973. GSS defines pornography as materials "that show or describe sex activities." This definition makes it impossible to examine a range of public offensiveness. This is not unusual, however, for only two polls have been more specific ("The War on Pornography," 1985, and Glassman, 1978). Polls conducted by Gallup (March 1977, December 1981); CBS News/*New York Times* (January 1978, November 18, 1980); NBC News/Associated Press (February 1981); ABC News/*Washington Post* (May 1981); *Time* (May 1981, September 1981, June 1981); *Los Angeles Times* (October 1981); Roper (July 1981); and *Newsweek* (March 1985) indicate that the public thinks something should be done about pornography, but the public is not sure what should be done. The responses also indicate that wording the questions differently will result in different levels of public support for laws that regulate pornography (Burton, 1986).

The GSS questions reflect theories about the role of pornography in society and ask whether pornography provides information about sex, whether sexual materials damage morals, whether sexual materials cause rape, whether sexual materials provide sex outlets, whether the respondent has attended an X-rated movie recently, and finally whether pornography should be totally banned, banned for those under eighteen, or unregulated. In 1984 the poll also began asking respondents how firm their opinion was and how important this issue was to them. Data from 1973, 1978, and 1984 (see Table 1) are analyzed. A 6 percentage point change overall (Page and Shapiro, 1983) and a 10 percentage point change within subgroups (Shapiro and Mahajan, 1986) are interpreted to be statistically and substantively significant.

A majority of men and women believe sex materials provide information on sex, but by 1984 nearly 6 percent fewer overall believe this is true. A majority of men and women also agree pornography serves as a sexual outlet, and significantly more men and women believe this in 1984, but there is no gender gap as the percentages of men and women who believe this statement increase in tandem over time. There is a significant trend over time for the public to believe sexual materials damage morals, moving from 56 percent agreement in 1973 to 65 percent agreement in 1984. By 1984, 6 percent more men and 10 percent more women agree with this statement than in 1973. The gender gap has widened from 15 percent to 19 percent, with nearly three-fourths of the women compared to slightly over half the men agreeing that sexual materials damage morals. There has not been a significant increase overall in the percentage of people who believe sexual materials lead people to commit rape, but there is a large gender gap here, which has remained basically unchanged since 1973. By 1984, two-thirds of all women believe sexual materials lead to rape, compared to slightly

TABLE 1

The Gender Gap in Attitudes toward Pornography
(Percentage who agree)

	1973			1978			1984		
	All (1504)	*Men* (701)	*Women* (803)	*All* (1532)	*Men* (643)	*Women* (889)	*All* (1473)	*Men* (598)	*Women* (875)
BELIEF									
Sex materials provide info. on sex	65.5	66.2	64.9	65.3	67.5	63.8	60.6	61.6	59.9
Sex materials damage morals	56.1	48.1	63.0*	60.0	54.1	64.3*	65.1	54.1	73.0*
Sex materials cause rape	53.8	46.1	60.7*	61.2	53.0	67.5*	59.6	49.3	67.3*
Sex materials provide a sexual outlet	60.8	60.2	61.4	66.9	65.8	67.8	69.0	68.1	69.6
POLICY PREFERENCE									
Illegal to all	42.6	35.9	48.5*	43.6	34.1	50.6*	41.1	30.0	48.9*
Illegal under 18	48.0	53.7	43.0*	49.0	55.6	44.3*	54.6	63.4	48.5
Legal	9.4	10.4	8.5	7.3	10.4	5.1*	4.2	6.6	2.6*
SEEN X MOVIE	25.4	31.4	20.1	15.0	20.3	11.1*	23.6	30.0	19.1*
IMPORTANCE OF ISSUE									
One of most important							11.2	8.1	13.3*
Important							33.4	26.0	38.5
Not very important							40.0	48.0	34.5
Not important at all							15.5	17.0	13.8
FIRMNESS OF OPINION									
Very likely to change							2.6	2.6	2.6*
Somewhat likely to change							14.4	16.2	13.1
Somewhat unlikely to change							29.3	32.9	26.8
Very unlikely to change							53.7	48.4	57.5

*p = .0001
Responses of "don't know" and "no answer" are not included in the percentages.

less than half of all men. Thus the gender gaps on the issue of morals and rape are approximately the same. Men have been the traditional market for pornographic materials. Thus it comes as no surprise that men are one and one-half times more likely to have seen an X-rated movie than women. This has remained fairly stable over time.

Over half (51.8 percent) of all women say pornography is an important or highly important issue, compared to around one-third (34.1 percent) of all men. Both men and women have firmly made up their minds on the pornography issue, with 81.3 percent of the men and 84.3 percent of the women reporting they are somewhat or very unlikely to change their minds on this issue.

The survey offers only three policy preference choices: (1) laws against the distribution of pornography to anyone, whatever the age, (2) laws against distribution to persons under eighteen (the current status), and (3) no laws forbidding the distribution of pornography. Since 1973, there has been no change in the total percentage of people who prefer to ban pornography. There has been a significant trend in favor of the status quo, accompanied by a decrease in the percentage of people who think there should be no laws regulating pornography distribution. Nearly half of the women have consistently preferred to ban the distribution of all pornography. There is a widening gender gap from 12.6 percent in 1973 to 18.9 percent in 1984 as men increasingly preferred the status quo. A shrinking percentage of both men and women prefer an "absolutist" view of the First Amendment with no restrictions on the distribution of pornography.

Pornography Attitudes and Age and Education

Previous research (Levine, 1973; Sprafkin, Silverman, and Rubinstein, 1980) has indicated that both education and age influence attitudes toward pornography. The data in Table 2 indicate that persons with less education were more likely to want to make pornography illegal, as were older persons. Even with age and education controlled, however, the gender gap remained. For example, women under thirty were nearly twice as likely as men to prefer to make pornography illegal. Only at age seventy or over was there no gender gap on the basis of age. With more education the gender gap narrowed for those preferring to make pornography illegal, but even for those with graduate degrees, a 7.8 percent difference remained between men's and women's preferences to ban pornography. While 10.4 percent of the men with graduate degrees preferred to remove all restrictions, only 3.6 percent of the graduate women preferred this policy.

The importance of the pornography issue is also related to age and educational background. Importance rises generally as age rises, with only 6 percent of women and 4.1 percent of men under thirty indicating that this is one of the most important issues, compared to 16 percent of women and 15.6 percent of men over seventy. The more education one has, the less important the pornography issue is. While 16.9 percent of women with less than a high-school education think pornography is one of the most important issues, only 7.4 percent of women with graduate degrees feel pornography is one of the most important issues.

The firmness of one's opinion on pornography is also affected by age and education. The older one gets, the less likely one is to change one's mind on this issue, even if one has very little information available. On the other hand, the more education one has, the less sure one is of one's opinion. As education level rises, liberal attitudes and tolerance also rise, but in this instance these values

TABLE 2

Attitudes toward Pornography by Age and Education (1984)

POLICY PREFERENCE	LT 30	30–39	40–49	AGE 50–59	60–69	70+	Total
Illegal to all							
M (178)	15.2	15.3	29.5	47.4	50.0	67.4	30.0
W (413)	27.7	39.0	48.8	67.0	73.6	68.9	48.6
Illegal under 18							
M (376)	78.9	76.3	65.3	46.1	39.2	32.6	63.4
W (414)	67.7	58.5	51.2	27.7	26.4	29.2	48.8
Legal							
M (39)	5.8	8.4	5.3	6.6	20.8	—	6.6
W (22)	4.5	2.5	—	5.3	—	1.9	2.6
IMPORTANCE OF ISSUE							
One of most important							
M (48)	4.1	6.1	11.6	12.0	8.1	15.6	8.1
W (113)	6.0	11.6	16.1	22.3	18.3	16.0	13.4
Important							
M (154)	17.0	30.3	26.3	37.3	29.7	22.2	26.0
W (325)	33.9	35.7	45.2	47.9	42.3	33.0	38.5
Not Very							
M (284)	55.0	50.8	50.5	36.0	40.5	40.0	48.0
W (292)	45.9	41.7	27.4	20.2	24.0	29.2	34.6
Not at all important							
M (106)	24.0	12.9	11.6	14.7	21.6	22.2	17.9
W (115)	14.2	11.1	11.3	9.6	15.4	21.7	13.6
FIRMNESS OF OPINION							
Very likely to change							
M (15)	4.2	4.6	—	—	2.7	—	2.6
W (22)	5.1	3.6	.8	3.2	—	—	2.6
Somewhat likely to change							
M (95)	21.6	16.8	17.9	13.3	10.8	4.4	16.2
W (110)	22.7	14.7	13.0	5.4	5.8	5.0	13.2
Somewhat unlikely to change							
M (193)	37.1	35.9	35.8	33.3	18.9	24.4	32.9
W (224)	33.3	34.5	23.6	14.0	21.2	19.8	26.9
Very unlikely to change							
M (284)	37.1	42.7	46.3	53.3	67.6	71.1	48.4
W (478)	38.9	47.2	62.6	77.4	73.1	75.2	57.3

TABLE 2 *(Continued)*

POLICY PREFERENCE	EDUCATION					
	LT H.S.	*H.S.*	*J.C.*	*B.A.*	*Grad.*	*Total*
Illegal to all						
M (177)	41.5	27.6	33.3	20.0	20.8	29.9
W (416)	59.9	48.2	33.3	37.6	28.6	48.8
Illegal under 18						
M (376)	52.6	67.2	60.0	71.3	68.8	63.5
W (414)	37.0	49.2	61.5	62.4	67.9	48.6
Legal						
M (39)	6.9	5.2	6.7	8.8	10.4	6.6
W (22)	3.1	2.6	5.1	—	3.6	2.6
IMPORTANCE OF ISSUE						
One of Most						
M (48)	10.2	9.0	6.7	3.8	4.1	8.1
W (113)	16.9	22.5	7.7	12.9	7.4	13.3
Important						
M (154)	31.2	26.2	26.7	18.8	20.4	26.1
W (326)	29.8	41.5	46.2	43.0	29.6	38.4
Not very important						
M (284)	36.3	47.6	47.7	63.8	63.3	48.1
W (293)	28.4	35.1	41.0	36.6	59.3	34.5
Not important at all						
M (105)	22.3	17.2	20.0	13.8	12.2	17.8
W (117)	24.9	11.0	5.1	7.5	3.7	13.8
FIRMNESS OF OPINION						
Very likely to change						
M (15)	2.5	2.8	6.7	2.3	2.1	2.6
W (22)	4.2	1.7	2.6	2.2	7.1	2.6
Somewhat likely to change						
M (95)	16.6	16.4	26.7	15.0	12.5	16.2
W (110)	8.3	25.8	7.9	14.3	10.7	13.2
Somewhat unlikely to change						
M (193)	18.5	36.4	20.0	46.3	41.7	32.9
W (224)	28.5	24.8	47.4	42.9	42.9	26.8
Very unlikely to change						
M (383)	62.4	44.4	46.7	37.5	43.8	48.3
W (480)	69.0	57.7	42.1	40.7	39.3	54.4

conflict with other beliefs regarding the harm of pornography and how this harm can be regulated. Men and women with less than a high-school education have their minds firmly made up.

Pornography Attitudes and Religion

Traditionally, foes of pornography have had religious backgrounds (Brownmiller 1975; Sprafkin, Silverman, and Rubinstein, 1980) and have based their arguments against pornography on morality. Religion continues to play an important role in attitudes, but religious preference is not nearly as important as frequency of church attendance and the strength of religion. As shown in Table 3, between 1973 and 1984, 6 percent fewer men preferred to make pornography illegal, while women hovered around 49 percent during this time period. Men and women who attend church at least once a week (about one-third of those polled) were about equally likely to want to ban pornography in 1978, but by 1984 a 15.8 percent gender gap had developed in this group. Among people who attend church less often, much higher percentages of women than men in all categories would ban pornography.

Those with strong religious beliefs are more likely to prefer banning pornography, but there is a significant difference between men and women at all levels—around 16 percent. Note, however, that the percentage of both men and women with strong religious beliefs who would prefer to ban pornography declined from 1978 to 1984. By 1984 less than half of the men with strong religious beliefs would ban pornography for everyone. The gender gap has narrowed from 1978 to 1984 for those who prefer no restrictions on pornography. But in all these instances, the within-sex differences from one extreme of the responses to the other are greater than any of the between-sex differences.

Data not shown in Table 3 indicate that religious factors also influence whether people think pornography is an important issue. Men who attend church every week are twice as likely as all men to think pornography is one of the most important issues, and women in this category are one and one-half times as likely to think pornography is an important issue. The same relationship is also true for those with strong religious beliefs, but it is not quite as pronounced. Frequent church attendance and strong religious beliefs also strengthen the firmness of one's opinion.

Attitudes on Pornography Policy and Women's Role

In 1978 the GSS included five questions pertaining to women's role in society and the saliency of women's rights. These questions asked (1) whether the respondent agreed or disagreed that women should take care of running their homes and leave running the country up to men; (2) whether the respondent approved or disapproved of a married woman earning money in business or industry if she had a husband capable of supporting her; (3) whether or not the respondent would vote for a qualified woman for president; and (4) whether or not the respondent agreed that most men are better suited emotionally for politics than most women. In 1973, 1978, and 1984, questions were asked about whether a pregnant woman should be able to obtain a legal abortion if she was married

TABLE 3

Religious Factors and Policy Preferences

| | CHURCH ATTENDANCE | | | | |
POLICY PREFERENCES	Less than once a year	Sev. times a year	2 – 3 times a month	Ev. week or more	Total
Illegal to all					
1973 M	—	—	—	—	35.9
1978 M	35.1	26.1	26.2	61.3	34.1
1984 M	19.1	26.4	31.0	49.6	29.8
1973 W	—	—	—	—	48.5
1978 W	37.8	43.9	53.1	65.1	50.6
1984 W	35.0	32.2	46.4	65.4	48.9
Illegal under 18					
1973 M	—	—	—	—	53.7
1978 M	61.1	62.2	66.7	32.4	55.6
1984 M	73.2	66.7	62.9	45.4	63.6
1973 W	—	—	—	—	43.0
1978 W	54.0	51.0	44.5	30.9	44.3
1984 W	61.4	62.6	51.4	33.4	48.5
Legal					
1973 M	—	—	—	—	10.4
1978 M	12.5	11.8	7.1	6.3	10.4
1984 M	7.7	6.9	6.0	5.0	6.6
1973 W	—	—	—	—	8.5
1978 W	8.3	5.1	1.8	4.0	5.1
1984 W	3.6	5.2	2.2	1.2	2.6

| | STRENGTH OF RELIGIOUS BELIEF | | |
POLICY PREFERENCES	Strong	Not very strong	Somewhat strong	Total
Illegal to all				
1973 M	—	—	—	35.9
1978 M	54.1	26.6	34.1	34.1
1984 M	46.0	22.8	26.0	32.2
1973 W	—	—	—	48.5
1978 W	66.2	40.8	50.0	50.6
1984 W	60.9	35.3	41.0	49.9

TABLE 3 *(Continued)*

Illegal under 18				
1973 M	—	—	—	50.7
1978 M	36.8	62.9	58.5	55.6
1984 M	48.5	70.0	74.0	61.9
1973 W	—	—	—	43.6
1978 W	30.4	54.7	44.1	44.3
1984 W	37.3	60.7	57.4	47.5
Legal				
1973 M	—	—	—	10.4
1978 M	9.2	10.5	7.3	10.4
1984 M	5.4	7.2	—	5.8
1973 W	—	—	—	8.5
1978 W	3.4	4.6	5.9	5.1
1984 W	1.8	4.1	1.6	2.6

and wanted no more children or if the family was poor and couldn't afford any more children. As indicated in Table 4, earning women had more feminist attitudes and were more pro-choice than housewives. They were also 10 percent less likely to want to ban pornography. Nearly 46 percent of the housewives felt women should stay home, compared to 19 percent of the earning women and 29 percent of the men. There is a 26.4 percent gap between the opinion of housewives and earning women. While 75 percent of the housewives would vote for a woman for president, 56 percent of them still felt men were better suited emotionally to run the country. Earning women were the group most likely to vote for a woman, but there was no significant difference between them and earning men. Nor was there a significant difference between earning men and women regarding women's emotional ability to run the country. The gap is between the housewives and everyone else.

The attitudes shown in Table 4 are similar to the findings by Poole and Zeigler (1985) and Andersen and Cook (1985). Generally, earning women are more pro-choice and feminist than housewives. Attitudes about pornography are more mixed. In 1973 housewives and earning women's opinions differed more from men's opinions than from each other. By 1978, the gap between earning women's opinions and housewives' opinions was beginning to widen with respect to their beliefs about pornography and morals, their beliefs about pornography and rape, and their pornography policy preference. Housewives were the group who most wanted to make pornography illegal, and they did not support feminist positions on abortion or women's role in society. When the educational level of the earning women and housewives is controlled, significant differences remain for beliefs about whether or not pornography leads to rape and for policy preferences. High-school graduates who are housewives prefer to ban pornography by a 3 to 2 margin over their earning peers.

When one compares only married housewives and married women who work

TABLE 4

Opinions of Earning Men, Earning Women, and Housewives

	Men	Earning Women	Housewives
ABORTION, NO MORE KIDS			
1973	53.6	47.3	39.2
1978	43.6	46.4	31.1
1984	48.4	48.5	30.4
ABORTION IF POOR			
1973	57.3	54.4	46.9
1978	50.8	54.4	38.1
1984	50.5	53.8	32.3
WOMEN STAY HOME*	28.9	19.2	45.6
WOMEN EARN*	76.1	83.5	65.6
VOTE FOR A WOMAN FOR PRESIDENT*	86.0	87.6	75.4
WOMEN TOO EMOTIONAL*	40.5	35.5	55.9
PORN DAMAGES MORALS			
1973	44.8	60.7	64.4
1978	50.7	56.8	70.7
1984	51.1	66.5	77.1
PORN LEADS TO RAPE			
1973	42.5	55.6	63.9
1978	49.0	58.4	76.5
1984	48.7	58.1	77.7
POLICY PREFERENCES			
Illegal to all			
1973	32.4	47.1	49.3
1978	31.8	44.9	54.7
1984	24.1	39.4	57.7
Legal			
1973	9.7	10.3	6.6
1978	9.0	6.1	4.9
1984	6.4	2.1	2.5
IMPORTANCE OF PORN ISSUE†			
Most imp.	7.5	10.8	16.5
Somewhat imp.	27.3	40.1	35.6

*1978 data
†1984 data

full time outside the home (thereby eliminating widows and older women), significant differences remain regarding attitudes toward abortion, beliefs about pornography and rape, the firmness of opinion on pornography, and policy preferences for pornography. Age, the presence of children, education, and frequency of church attendance are also significantly different. Church attendance for earning women and housewives was the same in 1973, but in 1978 and 1984 housewives attended church more often than earning women. There was no difference in the other religious factors, so frequent church attendance may simply indicate that housewives have more available time than women who work outside the home.

Discussion

Between 1973 and 1984 opinions on the role of pornography in society changed somewhat, but opinions on its regulation changed very little. By 1978 more men agreed that pornography was harmful to morals and led to rape, but this belief had no impact on their policy preferences. By 1984 the GSS indicated that 62 percent of all respondents felt sexual materials damaged morals (a gain of 9 percent since 1973), and 55 percent believed sexual materials caused rape (a gain of 5 percent since 1973). Smith (1987) also argues that this is a significant change, particularly with respect to the negative impact of pornography on morals and rape.

If the public is asked whether they favor or oppose tougher laws dealing with pornography, as many as three-fourths of the respondents may reply affirmatively (Gallup, 1985). But the GSS data from 1973 to 1984 indicate little change in policy preferences, with 41 percent wanting to ban pornography and 54 percent wanting to have laws against distribution of pornography to those under eighteen. Only 4 percent wanted no restrictions on the distribution of pornography, which Smith (1987) claims is a significant linear decline. He further argues that if the Attorney General's Commission on Pornography had consulted the appropriate polls, it could have concluded that support for government regulation rose from the mid-seventies to the mid-eighties.

Research indicates that public officials, whether elected or appointed, local or national, pay attention to public opinion. Kuklinski and McCrone (1980, 329) argue that the extent of officials' attention to and behavior in accord with public opinion is related to the cost involved. Officeholders do not take the initiative to search out public sentiment, but clear and precise communication of public opinion reduces this cost and thus encourages representative behavior, regardless of whether or not the officials fear electoral defeat. The problem with the pornography issue is that opinion is mixed. While a majority may want tougher laws dealing with pornography, they are split on their views on current community standards, with 43 percent saying standards should be stricter and 48 percent saying standards should remain the same. Thus the results of the polls do not provide crystal-clear indicators to policy makers, and there is also a gender gap, the implications of which are not clear cut.

Shapiro and Mahajan (1986) argue that gender differences may become more important because of women's rising level of political participation (see also Poole and Zeigler, 1985, 121), because women form a large pool of eligible voters, and because women pay greater attention to some issues and government policies than men do. Men and women who have similar preferences on the ERA and other women's rights issues may have different candidate choices because women consider these policy preferences in their choice of candidates, whereas men do not (Klein, 1984). This would indicate that women might weight a candidate's stand on pornography more heavily than men do. However, the saliency of an issue is another important factor influencing voter behavior. The pornography issue is viewed as one of the most important issues by only a small percentage of voters. Thus this issue is unlikely to be one that is crucial to voters' choice of candidates. Antipornography feminists have widespread support from nonfeminist housewives on the issue of pornography, but housewives have a lower voting rate than employed women or men (Poole and Zeigler, 1985, 43) and also do not try to persuade others of their political views as much as working women do (Andersen and Cook, 1985, 619). However, Poole and Zeigler argue that the gender gap is not so great as the gap that exists between employed women and housewives.

The 1984 GSS data indicate that feminists have an uphill battle to change the public's policy preferences on pornography. Bessmer (1981, 153) argued, "Feminists face the awesome task of redefining the terms of public debate on a long-standing and highly emotional issue. Traditionalist opponents of obscenity must be converted to a new and more liberal philosophy while traditionalist defenders of it must be brought to recognize distinctions between benign and progressive explicit sexual materials and violent, misogynist ones." Monroe (1981) indicates that when the public favors the status quo, it has a greater chance of its governmental representative fulfilling its wishes; but when the public wants change, it is successful only 60 percent of the time. Issues of less salience to the public also have a lesser chance of leading to policies that reflect the public's preference. Noncrisis issues, even those for which the public has a clearly preferred policy, may get trapped in the political process and simply be forgotten.

On a brighter note, the results of the *Newsweek* poll (1985) indicate that the public is beginning to accept feminist claims that pornography is harmful to women and would support more regulation of pornography that combines sex and violence. For antipornography feminists, the most encouraging part of the *Newsweek* poll is that 73 percent of the respondents would ban magazines that show sexual violence, 68 percent would bar theaters from showing movies that depict sexual violence, and 63 percent would bar the sale or rental of videocassettes featuring sexual violence. However, these attitudes are not clearly compatible with those expressed about current community standards in the same poll. We do not know the characteristics of those who now support these feminist views in the *Newsweek* poll, i.e., whether it is traditionalist opponents or traditionalist defenders of pornography who are changing their minds. This is an important fact for feminists to know if they want to control the legislative action on this topic. It would be easy for antifeminists to take over this debate and maneuver legislative action in directions contrary to what the antipornography feminists have in mind.

Another indication of the uphill battle feminists face is the fact that only 17 percent of those polled by the GSS were at all likely to change their minds about pornography, and 53 percent were very unlikely to change, despite the fact that 26 percent of the respondents indicated that they did not have all the information they needed to make up their minds. It is thus not at all clear that a feminist campaign to educate the public on the harmful effects of pornography would necessarily win more supporters to its point of view. Feminists will also have an uphill battle with policy makers since they are attempting to achieve change rather than maintain the status quo. It will be especially difficult since nearly two-thirds of all men support the status quo and women are about evenly split between the status quo and banning all pornography.

The low salience of the pornography issue is an another problem. This issue was very salient to only 11 percent of those polled in 1984 (GSS). The anti-pornography battle is being waged by two elites—feminist antipornography activists allied with moral conservatives versus legal absolutists—with the mass of men and women relatively uninvolved. Even before the Indianapolis anti-pornography statute was declared unconstitutional by the Seventh Circuit (Gross-man, 1985) and ultimately by the Supreme Court, there was little legislative activity. Only Indianapolis, of all the cities where a campaign was mounted for such legislation, actually passed the legislation and had it signed by the mayor. One can argue that this was because of the radical nature of the antipornography ordinance itself, but it is just as likely that there has not been enough public concern and interest-group activity to make any progress on the regulation of pornography. The Meese Report and its attendant publicity may create increased saliency, which may then lead to further action.

The decision by the Circuit Court of Appeals affirmed by the Supreme Court isn't surprising either. Even though the courts know the public wants something done, the courts are far more concerned with the underlying First Amendment right (McClosky and Brill, 1983, 59–63) than is the public. The overbreadth of the Indianapolis statute and its failure to exempt even works of serious literary, artistic, or scientific value meant it was destined to fail.

In conclusion, the pornography battle is one that does not seem a likely candidate for a clear-cut political victory by either side. While public officials have a great deal of data available on public attitudes, and while the public seems to want something done, just what it wants done is less clear. This, too, indicates that the prospects for legislative action are low (Kuklinski and McCrone, 1981). A total ban on pornography, as nearly half the women want, is not likely to occur, not only because of First Amendment concerns but also because 70 percent of all men oppose this solution. A compromise approach that expands the definition of obscenity specifically to include materials that combine sex and violence may be more politically feasible. This solution may be particularly attractive since the ad hoc coalition of moral conservatives and feminists may make it politically expedient. Legislatures could take action to redefine pornog-raphy and then pass the buck to the courts to decide whether the expanded definition was consitutional.

References

Andersen, Kristi, and Cook, Elizabeth A. (1985). "Women, Work, and Political Attitudes." *American Journal of Political Science* 29 (3):606–25.

Attorney General's Commission on Pornography (1986). *Final Report.* Washington, D.C.: Government Printing Office (The Meese Report).

Bessmer, Sue (1981). "Anti-Obscenity: A Comparison of the Legal and the Feminist Perspectives." *Western Political Quarterly* 34, (1):143–55.

Brownmiller, Susan (1975). *Against our Will: Men, Women and Rape.* New York: Simon and Schuster.

Burton, Doris-Jean (1986). *"Women, Public Opinion, and Pornography."* Paper presented at the annual meeting of the Midwest Political Science Association, Chicago, Ill., April 1986.

Glassman, Marc B. (1978). "Community Standards of Patent Offensiveness: Public Opinion Data and Obscenity Law." *Public Opinion Quarterly* 42:161–70.

Grossman, Joel B. (1985). "The First Amendment and the New Anti-Pornography Statutes." *News for Teachers of Political Science* 45 (Spring):16–21.

Klein, Ethel (1984). *Gender Politics.* Cambridge, Mass.: Harvard University Press.

Kuklinski, James H., and McCrone, Donald J. (1981). "Electoral Accountability as a Source of Policy Representation," in *Public Opinion and Public Policy: Models of Political Linkage,* ed. Norman Luttbeg. 3d ed. Itasca, Ill.: F. E. Peacock Publishers, Inc., 320–41.

Levine, James P. (1973). "Constitutional Law and Obscene Literature: An Investigation of Bookseller Practices." In *The Impact of Supreme Court Decisions,* ed. Theodore L. Becker and Malcolm M. Feeley. 2d ed. New York: Oxford University Press, 119–38.

McClosky, Herbert, and Brill, Alida (1983). *Dimensions of Tolerance: What Americans Believe About Civil Liberties.* New York: Russell Sage Foundation.

Miller v. California (1973). 413 U.S. 15.

Monroe, Alan D. (1981). "Consistency between Public Policy Preference and National Policy Decision." In *Public Opinion and Public Policy: Models of Political Linkage,* ed. Norman Luttbeg. 3d ed. Itasca, Ill.: F. E. Peacock Publishers, Inc., 400–409.

Page, Benjamin I., and Shapiro, Robert Y. (1983). "Effects of Public Opinion on Policy." *American Political Science Review* 77:175–90.

Poole, Keith T., and Zeigler, L. Harmon (1985). *Women, Public Opinion and Politics.* New York: Longman, Inc.

Pope v. Morrison (1987). 55 L.W. 4595.

Shapiro, Robert V., and Mahajan, Harpreet (1986). "Gender Differences in Policy Preferences: A Summary of Trends from the 1960s to the 1980s." *Public Opinion Quarterly* 50:41–61.

Smith, Tom W. (1987). "The Polls—A Review—The Use of Public Opinion Data by the Attorney General's Commission on Pornography." *Public Opinion Quarterly* 51:249–67.

Smith v. United States (1977). 431 U.S. 291.

Sprafkin, Joyce N.; Silverman, Theresa; and Rubinstein, Eli A. (1980). "Reactions to Sex on Television: An Exploratory Study." *Public Opinion Quarterly* 44:303–15.

"The War on Pornography" (1985). *Newsweek,* March 18, 1985, 58–67.

7

Violent Pornography

Mimetic Nihilism and the Eclipse of Differences

RICHARD B. MILLER

I

Since at least the time of Plato, social theorists have debated the effect of the arts on the moral fiber of community. While Plato's proposal to censor some forms of art in the *polis* finds little sympathy in Western countries today, the debate has been intensified in the United States, Europe, and Japan by the proliferation of violent pornography. The issue is complicated because violent pornography is difficult to distinguish from obscenity, from nonviolent erotica, and from other forms of art. Some examples drawn from recent sources may enable us to define such materials:

An issue of *Sheik* shows a woman stabbing her vagina with a large butcher knife. She is also cutting her labia with a pair of scissors. She is smiling.

The cover of the magazine *Rope* depicts two Asian women, naked from the waist up, gagged and tied with an elaborate system of knots and cords. The ropes are arranged on the torsos to accentuate their breasts.

One photograph shows the legs and vagina of a woman spread up from the floor. Over her stands the figure of a man (no face), dressed in an undershirt and jeans. He is forcing a jack-hammer into her vagina. In the corner the caption reads, "A Simple Cure for Frigidity."

A *Penthouse* photo essay, "Bound for Glory," depicts the abduction, bondage, and potential rape and murder of women as a glamorous exercise.[1]

In one popular film, *Super Vixens,* an off-duty policeman beats his female "one night stand" into a "bloody pulp," throws her into a bathtub, electrocutes her with an electric heater while he screams obscenities at her, and finally destroys her body by burning down the house (Jacobs, 1984, 14).

In the film *I Spit on Your Grave,* a woman is gang-raped. Later she carries out her revenge by enticing one of the rapists into a bubble bath, at which point she castrates him. She seduces another rapist, and, as he is about to have an orgasm, she hangs him.

One copy of the magazine *Bondage and Discipline Quarterly,* includes a ten-page section in which "Cathy" ties, handcuffs, and strips "David" and puts him on a leash. The last picture shows her, semiclad, riding him, his face covered with a leather muzzle. One caption in the section reads, "Bound with ropes and hung from the rafters, her cat stings his flesh. Screams for mercy go un-heeded." This issue of the magazine sells for six dollars.

As these examples show, pornography often, but not always, includes the display of exposed genitalia or sexual exchanges. In this essay I will define the materials under consideration here—violent pornography—to be images of people, usually but not always women, humiliated, bound, beaten, raped, tortured, or murdered for entertainment or profit. My definition is designed so as not to carry the burden of sexuality; thus, judgments about legitimate or illegitimate *sexual* practices are not implied. This is not to suggest, however, that there is no difference between violent pornography and other depictions of violence, but that this distinction can be made with more general conditions that need not carry the burden of defining "the sexual" and distinguishing sexual pleasure from other forms of pleasure. The distinction between violent pornography and other depictions of violence lies in the fact that violent pornography suggests that the willful and deliberate brutalization of another can be the source of entertainment, condoning for viewing amusement the gratuitous, willful victimization of others, who are usually portrayed in a highly vulnerable condition.

II

Efforts to assess materials like those mentioned above are beset by several vexations, which cluster into three groups. The first and most basic cluster concerns the *aesthetic and hermeneutical ambiguity* of pornographic materials. Is pornography best understood as a visual medium whose proper domain for analysis is aesthetics? If violent pornography is an aesthetic medium, should we confine our analysis to the consideration of its phenomenal properties, its use of figures and forms, the relation between surface and depth, and the structural configuration of parts within a totality of a bounded perceptual field? Should we focus on texture, balance, unity, and theme in order to appreciate critically the work of pornography? Or is pornography best conceived as a mode of discourse, a speech-act in which certain forms of behavior are suggested if not implicitly commanded?[2] If pornography is a mode of discourse, then is the proper domain for analysis hermeneutics rather than aesthetics? What tools are most appropriate for deciphering the signs and structures of pornographic works, when construed as modes of discourse? Or is the distinction between aesthetics and hermeneutics implied in these questions untenable given this curious phenomenon under consideration? Is the first real vexation of pornography the fact that it defies the commonplace distinction between aesthetics and hermeneutics?[3]

An affirmative answer to these last two questions seems to suggest itself. Pornography blurs the distinction between aesthetics and hermeneutics because pornography recommends certain forms of human behavior (a discursive act) by means of suggestive symbols and images within a bounded perceptual field from which the observer is to derive enjoyment or sensual pleasure (an aesthetic act). Pornographic media use suggestive images that appeal to affections and sensual pleasures; they are also speech-acts in that they bid their patrons to assent to judgments demanded by the medium.

Yet if pornography is in part a discursive act, then it is not clear how we can classify its discursive strategies according to conventional terms or categories. Is pornography oral or written discourse? How can it be either? Efforts to think about the role of mass media (of which pornography is a part) in technological societies seem to furnish a clue to this problem. In his work on symbol systems in modern culture, Richard Stivers argues that mass media exhibit the same characteristics commonly attributed to oral discourse of myth and ritual in pre-technological or so-called primitive societies: like primitive oral cultures, mass media form a closed and separate system and repeat commonplaces and clichés in a highly stylized manner. The system remains closed and separate insofar as its viewers fail to submit its messages to reflective criticism, disbelief, or empirical checks. The subtle strategy of such media in contemporary society is to deny the viewer the freedom that is a condition for such criticism by creating an altogether different sense of freedom, that is, freedom understood as an abundance of choices. The strategy is not simply to construct a world of seemingly unending choices as an end in itself, however, but to entice the reader with the suggestion that such a world is the real world. The system remains closed and separate because its authority—like the authority of myth and ritual in pre-technological societies—does not rest on a "reality check." Rather, the converse holds: "reality" is measured by the images created in the media (Stivers 1982, 11–13).

Pornography, as an item of mass media, operates according to roughly the same strategies of closed and separate systems. Pornographic messages are not subject to a "reality check" but bid us to gauge or to imagine our own experience according to the images promoted in the medium. Pornographic images ask us to suspend critical reflection, and in the place of such reflection pornography substitutes a plethora of sexual choices: bodily shapes, settings, orifices, participants, contexts, ages, and moods. The "freedom of choice" extolled by the mass media is refined in sexual terms by pornographic media, but in either case such freedom is a necessary condition for keeping the system closed and separate. Following the lead set by Stivers, then, we may say that pornography does not substitute freedom for restraint, but one form of freedom (the fantasy of unfettered choice) for another (rational criticism and suspicion).

A second current operates in mass media in general, and pornography in particular, which runs contrary to the celebration of sexual freedom mentioned above. Clichés and stereotypes are manufactured by the media and refined in pornography, leaving the viewer with a strange sense of familiarity, perhaps déjà vu. Commenting on the highly repetitive and predictable patterns in pornography, George Steiner argues that the essence of pornography is boredom because such materials leave little leeway to the creative workings of the imagination (1975, 204–205). Differences between persons or situations are generally negligible in pornography; patterns have become fixed, the activity routinized. The system remains closed, then, not only because we must suspend our criticism, but also because the grist for fantasy has been reduced to highly conventionalized formulas. The sexual freedom associated with pornography coexists in an uneasy tension with predictable patterns, fixed settings, and pseudo-individuals. Insofar as pornographic models are objectified and stereotyped, differences of individual detail are effaced. This effacement of detail is particularly true of violent pornography, which seeks to efface differences not only between the models themselves, but also between models, animals, and other physical objects. In fact, the distinctive feature of recent pornography is not simply that violence has increased but also that, as a precondition of violence, *differences must be eliminated.*

Indeed, the elimination of differences, at least within this first cluster of considerations, seems to be what pornography is all about: pornography is both aesthetic and discursive; as a discursive act, it is both free and fixed; fixed patterns, especially within violent pornography, resist any distinction between victims themselves or victims and other objects; and pornography's freedom, in turn, eclipses freedom of another sort.

III

While the vexations of violent pornography exemplify many of the characteristics of mass media in general, the vexations peculiar to violent pornography can be intensified if we turn to a second cluster of problems, problems concerning the *social and ethical ambiguity* of widespread violent pornography. Two widely divergent models are frequently invoked to assess the effects of viewing pornog-

raphy on human character and conduct: the "purgative" and the "exemplar_
The former argues for the benign if not beneficial effects of viewing pornography. The claim is that such viewing generates an aesthetic distanciation
between text and viewer, a distanciation that in turn causes a discharge of sexual
or emotional tension. By directly appealing to the libidinous, pornography
purges the viewer of negative affections or transforms them into less harmful
passions. Implicit in this account, then, is the claim that pornography, however
graphic and otiose, is essentially a fictional mode of representation, creating
another world in which the viewer may privately and vicariously participate. Left
without such useful fictions, unable to be transported to the private world of
fantasy, viewers of pornography may seek more harmful outlets for their frustrations or anxieties.

By this account, society clearly benefits from the open sale of pornographic
materials; the social order remains relatively stable because of, not despite, the
transgressions vicariously enjoyed by viewers of pornography. Real transgressions are supplanted by imaginary ones, and pornography thus plays a positive
social function.

Something of the purgative model can be found in Joseph Slade's semi-
autobiographical depiction of sex-film regulars in New York City (1975, 119–
39). Although Slade recognizes the potentially damaging and dehumanizing
aspects of pornography, he finally embraces the notion that peep shows and stag
films are relatively benign, that they can be confined to the realm of private
fantasy even if the fantasy is perhaps adolescent. Pornographic fantasies may not
supplant real sex, but such fantasies have positive effects in that they "permit
mental adultery while preserving monogamy." Sex-film regulars, by and large,
are not psychotics but are "our own next door neighbors and not certifiably
insane." Moreover, the appeal of pornography is not only sexual; it also "caters
to the voyeurism inherent in most of us." Questions about morality, art, or taste
in pornography may be interesting, but they are exaggerated in importance.
Rather, the "patrons know that what they are watching is artifice and illusion,
that real sex involves responsibilities, respect for others, and emotional and
intellectual involvement. They have fled those bonds in coming to the theaters,
and they know that they will return to them" (1975, 136–39).

Slade's account was written in 1971, before the proliferation of the kinds of
violent pornography mentioned above. I cite his article because it exemplifies a
more general attitude, namely, that pornography is essentially a private, fictional, humorous medium whose dehumanizing suggestions are left behind once one
leaves the theater. In fact, Slade gives us no reason to believe that his humorous
account of pornography would not apply *a fortiori* to more violent forms. As
much is suggested when Slade takes up the issue of violent pornography. By his
account, "overt sadism, masochism and bestiality are rare. . . . This picture
could change, of course, contingent primarily on the ingenuity of the Califor-
nians" (1975, 135). If we follow Slade's treatment of the issue, the fitting
response to pornography, and to the advent of violent pornography, is not

disbelief or suspicion, but laughter. Concluding his discussion of pornographic theaters, Slade quotes a fellow patron who remarks, after watching two hours of predominantly long-haired performers in a stag film, "At least you can tell the boys from the girls" (1975, 139).

The exemplary model, in contrast, would hold that pornography depicts behavior that the viewer positively identifies as a paradigm for sexual activity. Pornography generates not aesthetic distanciation but behavioral approximation or identification between text and viewer. Pornography is not so much fictional and private as it is factual and public. Thus construed, pornography is promotional, not just imaginary; it bids the viewer to accede to judgments demanded by the text. The effect of such viewing is to intensify, not to purge, sexual tensions and to bring the viewer even closer to the need for a violent outlet. By this account, we distort the true nature of pornography if we confine it to a private, imaginary, and harmless realm. Rather, pornography has genuine effects within the wider narratives of people's lives. We must "plot" the story of pornography and its viewers within the wider narratives of social violence, and contemporary sociologists are clamoring with data to document such accounts (Donnerstein, 1984, 53–81).

Despite the seeming differences between the purgative and exemplary approaches, however, they actually share a fundamental point of contact. Each approach establishes or denies a moral justification for pornography on the basis of its social effects. Whether pornography permits "mental adultery while preserving monogamy" or intensifies sexual desires, social consequence is the ruling consideration. Hence, the differences between the purgative and the exemplary model are effaced by the fact that each is firmly rooted in the soil of consequentialism. And, however plausible either model may seem when compared with the other, both are subject to the limits commonly associated with consequentialist reasoning: How are social effects properly measured? Within what time frame? What other factors must be present (e.g., anger) in order for violent pornography to elicit an antisocial response? Is mere exposure to such pornography, considered apart from other contingencies, necessary *and* sufficient for generating violent responses? Does a growing tolerance of violence in the media contribute to or diminish the seeming ill effects of violent pornography? Although current research indicates a strong correlation between viewing pornography and sexual aggression, "proving" this conclusion remains subject to doubt and, in any event, places a moral verdict on the shifting sand of highly contingent data.

An alternative effort to weigh the moral issues surrounding pornography would focus on principles, rights, or moral laws, irrespective of social effects. One such approach, as developed by Harold Gardiner, S.J., attempts to define "the obscene" in order to determine a special class of materials whose content is intrinsically immoral (1975, 159–74). Invoking the authority of Thomas Aquinas, Gardiner defines the obscene as any material that certainly, or at least probably, "rouses to genital commotion." Media whose chief objective is to arouse "genital commotion" must fall under the censure of Canon Law and of reasoning believers. The argument here illustrates a conservative form of Roman Catholic moral theology, which defines the essence of an act by examining its ordination toward a *telos*. Acts ordered away from natural ends or inclinations run contrary to the natural law and are thus intrinsically immoral. Venereal pleasure enjoyed as an end in itself, divorced from the conjugal act in valid marriage, is unnatural and therefore immoral; such pleasure is ordered to improper ends (1975, 164). Materials that promote this form of pleasure fall under the same general condemnation.

Whether Gardiner's in-principled approach marks a genuine moral advance for critics of pornography is doubtful. The most problematic feature of his argument is that his appeal to principles proceeds without reference to those commonly depicted in pornographic literature—women. Like the pornography he wishes to assail, Gardiner's argument is pitched in the direction of a male audience, is cast in terms of male libidinous affections, and is ignorant of the status of the female as stereotyped and abused in the pornographic text.[4] Gardiner's analysis assumes that it is sufficient for moral evaluation to attend to the adverse effects of pornography on the male viewer; the boundaries of Gardiner's approach, like those of Slade's, are thus defined by the location and vantage point of the male in the pornographic speech-act. Rather than providing any critical moral distance on pornography, then, Gardiner's account actually falls prey to the seduction of the pornographic speech-act in that both define their speech-acts in terms of male attitudes and experience. The place of the male viewer is sufficient for Gardiner's moral evaluation; as such, Gardiner's argument shares more in common with pornography than his criticisms might initially suggest. Hence, and most important, the common ground between Gardiner and his adversaries leaves us with yet another pornographic vexation: again differences disappear, this time between text and conservative critic.

An in-principled alternative to Gardiner's approach might focus on the rights and dignity of women, the implications of which might be put in the form of a question: Is pornography not defamatory literature? Is it not kin to other forms of hate literature, such as racist or anti-Semitic materials? Do not such materials bid us to assent to false images and stereotypes?

Arguing that the answer to all of these questions is yes, Eva Feder Kittay invokes a "universal moral imperative" to censure violent pornography, and the acts depicted therein, as intrinsically immoral (1984, 145–74). The chief pillar of Kittay's argument is the Kantian imperative to treat persons as ends, never as means only—an imperative that holds regardless of the historical, social, or cultural relativities of any particular sex/gender system. One may not use other persons merely as means to one's own ends, but must respect others as equals, as ends in themselves. Implicit in this Kantian approach is the claim that each moral agent acts as an autonomous subject, an "end in itself," and to treat other moral agents merely as means to one's own end is to violate the claim that such agents have to being ends in themselves. To act for one's self-chosen ends, while treating other agents merely as means, is to commit a performative self-contradiction. It follows that to exploit, degrade, or abuse others is to trespass on their inviolable claims that derive from being ends in themselves. On purely moral grounds, then, Kittay argues that some violent sexual acts are illegitimate—"Illegitimate by virtue of the moral impermissibility of harming another person and particularly for the purpose of obtaining pleasure or other benefit from the harm another incurs" (1984, 151). Violent pornography, whose intent is to cause harm to innocent persons, is hate literature and should be morally censured as intrinsically illegitimate, regardless of the social benefits that might accrue. The inviolable moral rights of women are defaced by violent pornography insofar as such literature depicts women in degraded, humiliated roles.

But to focus exclusively on rights and principles, for Kittay, is to overlook a wider constellation of morally relevant aspects of widespread violent pornography. Accordingly, she insists that the harm of violent pornography extends well beyond individuals thus depicted, that "society as a whole is harmed in its moral fiber when the moral status of all its members is not considered of equal worth by all the members of the society." A healthy social order and the morality requisite for such order are clearly jeopardized by the proliferation of defamatory literature. Violent pornography represents "a brutalization which causes a breakdown in our moral imagination, the source of that imaginative possibility by which we can identify with others and hence form maxims of universal validity" (1984, 161).

To Kittay, then, it seems counterintuitive to suggest that the dignity of women can be disfigured without widespread social consequences. However benign it might seem, violent pornography nonetheless trades in the currency of domination and subordination. Those who justify pornography according to its purgative benefits fail to question the terms on which their understanding of social benefits depends; to say that the social organism remains relatively stable when pornography is allowed to flourish presupposes that the organism's conditions are essentially healthy. But this presumption is precisely what Kittay and other such critics of pornography want to question. At the heart of the social order is a structure of male domination and female subordination that is stabilized through various strategies, including images and impressions like those promoted in pornography.

In Kittay's mind, then, violent pornography not only "causes a breakdown in our moral imagination"; it is also *symptomatic* of wider patterns of social interaction and exchange (1984, 145–46, 171). The brutalization of women in violent pornography reflects more general social structures. Hence, violent pornography is as much a product as it is a cause of moral and social breakdown. One implication of Kittay's claims, although she does not draw it, is that such literature is circular and self-enclosed; as a cause of social breakdown, it feeds on the pathologies of which it is a product.

Kittay's argument is an important one, for beneath her trenchant criticisms we find another set of false dichotomies and an elimination of differences. Whether one begins with a study of the strategies of the media in society (Stivers) or with the social mechanisms that are reflected in the media (Kittay), it makes no difference: violent pornography is a self-enclosed and separate system.

Moreover, with Kittay the differences between symptoms and causes, and rights and consequences disappear. Unlike our previous authors, however, Kittay's appeal to rights and social effects places violent pornography under double jeopardy.

Indeed, the elimination of differences within this second cluster of considerations runs parallel to that within the first. Dichotomous forms of moral discourse are hardly dichotomous at all. Purgative and exemplary models both operate according to canons of consequentialist reasoning; an in-principled approach of one conservative critic operates within, not apart from, the masculine lure of the pornographic speech-act; and feminist analyses of rights bear directly upon considerations of social effects. The world of violent pornography seems to blur our conventional boundaries; it vexes our commonplace distinctions. It seems that the chief transgression performed by violent pornography is to violate such boundaries—not boundaries *within* our moral discourse, but those more fundamental boundaries which provide the conventional structures, the basic conditions, *for* our moral discourse. The transgressive act of violent pornography is not to violate our conventions, nor is it simply to ignore them; rather, it is to *annihilate* them.

IV

A third cluster of vexations concerns the *relation* between the first cluster of ideas (hermeneutics and aesthetics) and the second cluster of ideas (social and ethical) adduced above. The issues pertinent to each cluster seem to move without much reference to the other, as if they proceeded on divergent tracks, with no point of intersection or common ground. Although considerations of pornography tend to efface distinctions within each cluster, the division *between* clusters seems unbridgeable. There is the strange feeling that by bridging the gap between these two clusters we are taking pornography *too* seriously—and seriousness, as Slade suggests, is not what pornography is all about. Our seriousness fails to follow pornography's bid to suspend our preoccupations with the moral and the reflective and to enter into its separate and closed realm of the imaginary.

Violent pornography reinforces this division of labor between these two clusters—indeed, it depends on such a division—insofar as it operates within a closed and separate system where disbelief or suspicion cannot freely operate. Such suspicion means that we must gain entry into the pornographic world, an entry requisite for critical scrutiny and moral evaluation to begin. As a separate and closed system, pornography is designed to resist the invasion of considerations from seemingly foreign regions of thought. The student of violent pornography must reckon with the problem that the conditions necessary for criticism are *denied* as an essential condition of the pornographic speech-act, that one is doing violence to the violent pornographic text by submitting it to critical scrutiny. Thus, another set of vexations: if we assess violent pornography according to criteria of social thought and ethics, we fail to accomplish much because pornography is designed to subvert, or at least ridicule, conventional moral attitudes and assumptions. If we bridge the division between these two clusters, then, we either belabor the obvious or force pornography *as pornography* to disappear under the light of normative criteria, introduced from a foreign domain.

We might bridge this gap without forcing violent pornography to disappear under the light of moral and reflective seriousness if we begin with the notion that pornography, as an aesthetic and discursive phenomenon, is essentially a *mimetic* form of representation. While the term mimesis may seem obscure to modern readers, it has a long and checkered history in Western philosophy. Mimesis in the arts, while disparaged by Plato, finds its first positive expression in Aristotle's *Poetics*. Aristotle understood poetry, especially tragedy, as exercising a mimetic function, by which he meant a creative imitation or representation of a world of human actions that is already there.[5] A mimetic work is not a copy of reality—it is not simply a photographic duplication—but a poetic construction that is the product of creative genius. The success of a mimetic work lies in its ability to imitate the logical structure, the meaning, of events. For Aristotle, moreover, tragedy imitates not only by capturing the structure of human events but by making them appear better or more noble than they would be in the realm of human affairs. Amplifying Aristotle's ideas, Paul Ricoeur defines mimesis as a "disclosure of a world," a world that constitutes a creative possibility for the viewer (or reader) (Ricoeur, 1981, 291–93). As a creative imitation of action, mimesis designates what Ricoeur, following François Dagognet, calls an "iconic augmentation" of a world of human activity, a refiguring of events in which their meaning or essential structure is displayed (1981, 179–80).

One problem with violent pornography, however, is that it seems to lack an ennobling function, understood in a moral or valorizing sense. And, if such pornography lacks an ennobling function, it seems inappropriate to say that it includes an augmentation, especially an iconic augmentation. Two aspects of pornography alleviate this problem, however. Pornography is iconic because it uses images and symbols to disclose a world, or a possible world, in which patterns and structures of human activity are figured for the receptive viewer. Violent pornography includes an augmentative function not because it ennobles human activity in any heroic sense but because it depicts violence and degradation in a positive light, as a source of pleasure and entertainment. In this sense, then, we can speak of an "elevation" occurring in the mimesis of violent pornography and thus, following Ricoeur, we can speak of pornography as "disclosing a world."

Another problem concerns the subject matter that is iconically augmented, or the world that is disclosed, in the violent pornographic text. We might say that the subject matter of violent pornography is sexually suggestive images, images of domination and subordination, or subjects that have been reduced to brute and brutalized objects. But these candidates, and there could be several more, are deceptive because they presume that the terms on which this question of subject matter is based are sound. I will resist this presumption and at the same time offer a different candidate as the subject matter of violent pornography, namely, *nothing*. By this I do not mean that violent pornography's subject matter is indeterminate, or trivial, or beyond critical scrutiny. Rather, I mean to follow the lead implied by mimesis, where one is to look not at the acts that are imaged but at the meaning and structure of acts that are figured in the representation. The acts that are imaged may be acts of violence, but the structure of such acts is essentially nihilistic. Indeed, violent pornography is an iconic augmentation of nothingness, a celebration of the surd of death and destruction. Moreover—and this is crucial—the nihilism of violent pornography provides a clue, indeed *the* clue, to its vexing, transgressive nature.

Violent pornography is essentially nihilistic not simply because it suggests a flagrant violation of customary attitudes and practices. The Dionysian festival also celebrates moral and social anarchy, but the difference between the festival and the pornographic speech-act lies in the fact that the former, at its core, celebrates fertility, life, and perhaps even the pursuit of immortality, while the latter refigures structures of servility and death—fatality as an end in itself. This difference is not trivial and constitutes a difference in kind, not degree, between the Dionysian festival and the world of violent pornography. The former represents a furious violation of conventions within life, while the latter denies the conditions of life itself and thus denies the conditions for boundaries *and* their violation.[6]

The distinction between Dionysian anarchy and the nihilism of violent pornography also suggests a distinction within the genre of pornography itself. Violent pornography is thanatic, whereas nonviolent or erotic pornography more closely resembles the festive anarchy of the Dionysian orgy. As Rosemarie Tong argues, erotica depicts pleasure, enjoyment, and, on some occasions, intimations of love (Tong, 1982, 1–17). Sexual exchanges include self-respect and mutuality. Even though some pain may be depicted, it is not inflicted as an exercise of domination or proof of one's superiority over another. Thanatica, in contrast, "not only depicts but celebrates . . . and encourages either the callous frustration of one's own or someone else's preferences as a sexual being or, worse, the intentional violation of one's own or someone else's rights as a sexual being" (1982, 4). In its most extreme form, thanatica depicts the annihilation of others and "elevates" such nihilistic visions by suggesting that the death of another can be a source of amusement. Thus, thanatica must be distinguished from erotica because the death celebrated therein represents an annihilation of the conditions for enjoyment, pleasure, or intimations of love. The world of violent pornography is much more radical than the Dionysian festival or erotica; violent pornography is radically nihilistic because the death it celebrates denies the condition for a moral world in which boundaries are either affirmed or furiously defied.

Violent pornography as understood here thus discloses a nonworld, or an antiworld, a world in which conventions, boundaries, and distinctions become mute—not a utopian world of private fantasy, but a dystopia, a world designed to annihilate the conditions for utopian imaginings and fictive possibilities. Violent pornography assumes a surd-like quality; it establishes an antiworld of violence to which one's initial response is neither laughter nor vocal disdain, but silence. Indeed, the silence that follows the disclosure of violent pornography, even among its receptive viewers, is but a symptom of its nihilistic, surd-like character; such pornography denies the conditions in which speech, as either laughter or derision, is appropriate. Violent pornography resists the dominion of speech because its surd-like quality denies the conventions on which speech depends and to which speech contributes. Violent pornography, of course, has its vocal advocates, but that fact is not without some irony, for, when violent pornography's advocates come to its defense with the aid of speech, they deny the nihilistic premises on which such pornography stands.

The claim that violent pornography is a representation of nihilism can thus account for the several aesthetic and hermeneutical vexations of such pornography—puzzlements about commonplace categories, and the distinctions therein, of perception and promotion, kinds of freedom, and degrees of freedom experienced by the viewer. The symbolic speech-act of violent pornography is indeed antispeech, endeavoring to annihilate the premises according to which symbols and language can signify a world. Commonplace categories and distinctions are thus blurred within our first cluster of ideas, and insofar as discursive practices rely on verbal distinctions, the eclipse of differences wrought by violent pornography is not without dramatic implications for aesthetics and hermeneutics. But the eclipse of differences should come as no surprise once the nihilistic strategies of violent pornography are brought into view.

Much the same can be said about the eclipse of differences when we turn to social and ethical aspects of violent pornography, drawing upon commonplace categories, and the distinctions therein, of positive and negative consequences, essential acts, rights, and social structure. Here the question is not simply whether violent pornography is "moral" or "immoral." Rather, the question is more radical: it is whether a moral world, with its categories and distinctions, is possible at all. If the answer is no, then considerations of purgation, identification, social consequences, genital commotions, women's rights, and social structure are rendered not only trivial, but moot. If the answer is yes, then such distinctions become valid and, with the assistance provided by the notion of mimesis, we can relegate violent pornography to the objectional status ascribed to other surds, other nihilistic endeavors, other versions of thanatica, in human experience.

V

The relation between violence, nihilism, and distinctions lies at the heart of my analysis of violent pornography's many vexations, and it may be instructive to conclude by distinguishing my account from a seemingly similar treatment of violence, distinctions, and social order as developed by René Girard (Girard, 1977). Girard locates the eruption of violent acts in premodern myths and cultures in the eclipse of differences, differences that generally contribute to the internal structuring of society. For example, twins must be banished lest their patrilineal heritage be confused; Oedipus must be sacrificed because his fate has nullified the kinship distinctions between father, son, mother, and wife; incest must be prohibited because it obscures the distinction between parent and child. Each of these examples represents an eclipse of differences, the emergence of a "monstrous double" whose presence must be eliminated in some form. Sacrificial rites grow out of such cultural crises; in response to the eclipse of differences, a surrogate victim is ritually sacrificed. The community institutionalizes such ritual practices as a recurring effort to maintain and renew social distinctions, which are structurally essential to the health of the community. The threat of violence permeates the primitive community, and ritual practices function to restrain the force of violence, especially reciprocal violence, from destroying the community from within. Ritual practices are cultural mechanisms by which the community is able to channel the subterranean currents of violence.

The sacrifice of scapegoats, according to Girard, is the most effective mechanism by which the perpetual danger of communal violence is tamed and humanized. Scapegoats are commonly drawn from the margins of the community, e.g., slaves, children, and livestock (1977, 271). Distinctions are restored, or maintained, by sacrificing some facsimile (but not an exact replica) of that which originally wrought an eclipse of differences. By Girard's account, ritual practices are prompted by some past, historic crisis. However strange the practice may appear to later ethnographers, it has its source in some primal, catastrophic event (1977, 167, chapters 2, 4). Thus, there is a logic to the rite, however illogical or vexing it may appear to the modern interpreter (1977, 27, 33).

Girard's provocative argument, summarized all too briefly here, seems to provide an explanation for violent pornography in contemporary society. One might argue that the women's movement has reduced, or eclipsed, traditional patriarchal distinctions and that violent pornography is a response to the emergence of a new "monstrous double." Violent pornography provides surrogate victims whose sacrifice restores a clear differentiation of sex roles and a patriarchal ordering of male-female relations. Like the sacrificial rites of primitive society, violent pornography provides a cathartic outlet for tensions created by social change. Confirmation of this thesis lies in the fact that violent pornography has increased in direct proportion to the advance of the women's movement. Efforts to restore patriarchal distinctions can be correlated directly with growing equality.[7] The emergence of child pornography, the depiction of master-slave relations, and the reduction of women to animal-like status all parallel the use of "marginal" surrogates in primitive societies.

Although this extension of Girard's argument seems highly plausible, it nonetheless contains a flaw from which his theory itself suffers. That flaw is the notion that violence is logical and that violence lies, almost ontologically, within the deepest structures of the social order. Girard fails to consider violence as a possible surd because his argument is premised on the ontology of violence—a premise that, by definition, excludes nihilism and irrationality from consideration. Girard's presentation, and its extension here, insists that violence must have a rational explanation; his account fails to consider the possibility of wanton violence, violence that is expressed purely for its own sake, with unqualified sadistic delight, without reference to social disturbance or social change.

Furthermore, an extension of Girard's argument is unable to account for the emergence of *female* domination and *male* subordination in some versions of violent pornography (like those mentioned above), since the argument must confine itself to explaining why women are surrogate victims. If we explain the emergence of violent pornography as a backlash against women's equality, then this role reversal appears anomalous. Yet if we understand such pornography as nihilistic, then this role reversal can be seen as an eclipse of differences. Indeed, one can interpret this role reversal as a clear outcome of the mimetic nihilism of violent pornography because now the violent protagonists imitate each other. Accordingly, the role reversal is not anomalous; it is an eclipse of differences that finds its fruition in the subjugated male.

If the secret of nihilism enables us to account for the several vexations within our two clusters of ideas (aesthetic-hermeneutical, social-ethical), then perhaps it permits us to draw the two together without forcing violent pornography to disappear under the light of reflective scrutiny. Success in this task rests on our ability to recognize the nihilistic strategy of violent pornography. In assessing the aesthetic, hermeneutical, social, and ethical aspects of the violent pornographic world, and in attempting to build bridges between these clusters of ideas, we must recognize that the world disclosed by violent pornography is not a world, but an antiworld. Only under this light, or within this darkness, does violent pornography refuse to disappear. But such is only fitting for violent pornography, for it is in darkness that distinctions become indistinguishable.

NOTES

This essay is a revised version of an article that appeared in *Soundings* 69 (1986).

I would like to thank the Multidisciplinary Seminar on Violent Pornography at Indiana University, especially Joan Hoff, Susan Gubar, and Mary Jo Weaver, for responding to the initial draft of this paper. I would also like to thank Howard Eilberg-Schwartz, Ashton Nichols, Barbara Olson, Luke Johnson, Barbara Klinger, and William Schweiker for their critical comments.

1. The first six examples are taken from a slide presentation entitled "Abusive Images of Women in Mass Media and Pornography," produced in 1981 by Women Against Violence in Pornography and Media (WAVPAM), a now-defunct organization founded in San Francisco. I would like to thank Douglas Freeman, head of collections of the Kinsey Institute at Indiana University, for access to these materials.

2. It seems anomalous to call pornography a speech-act because it lacks a recognizable verbal component. Thus, pornography seems to lack what is called locutionary and illocutionary force; pornography is neither a verbal proposition or inscribable utterance

(locution) nor a verbal utterance that includes a performative element (illocution, e.g., "I promise," or "I apologize"). Seen as a form of bidding that effects various responses from the viewer, however, pornography best approximates what has been labeled a "perlocutionary" speech-act. According to Paul Ricoeur (1981, 200), perlocutionary discourse "is the discourse as stimulus. It acts, not by my interlocutor's recognition of my intention, but sort of energetically, by direct influence upon the emotions and affective dispositions."

3. I do not wish to suggest that aesthetics and hermeneutics are entirely separate domains of inquiry. Certainly literary works are enjoyed as works of art. The distinction lies in the fact that aesthetics commonly addresses art and sensory percepts whereas hermeneutics commonly analyzes meanings that derive from words. Words may suggest sensual images, for which reason words have been called ideo-percepts. See *The Encyclopedia of Philosophy,* s.v. "Aesthetics, Problems of," by John Hospers.

4. I am assuming for this criticism that when Gardiner fashioned his argument the audience of pornography was predominantly male. The trend toward a mixed audience is only very recent.

5. Aristotle, *Poetics,* 1448a, 24; 1448b, 4–24; 1450a, 15–20.

6. It might be objected that Dionysian rituals were nihilistic insofar as they often included sacrifice, including human sacrifice. However, the Dionysian sacrifice and the subsequent eating of raw flesh and drinking of blood were sacramental in nature, a ritual quest for unity with the deity. Such unity, in fact, was part of a larger quest for immortality. Moreover, such rituals were linked to vegetation-worship and nature-worship; the rituals were thus tied to the cycle of the life process. Death was located within the larger cycle of death and rebirth; fatality, thus construed, was not an end in itself. Indeed, the presence of death did not serve to annihilate distinctions between life and death, but to reaffirm them. For discussions of the Dionysia and Dionysian rituals, see W. K. C. Guthrie, *The Greeks and Their Gods* (London: Methuen and Co., 1950), pp. 178–82; Lewis Farnell, *The Cults of the Greek States,* vol. 5 (Oxford: Clarendon, 1909), pp. 180–85.

7. Such an argument is implied in Irene Diamond, "Pornography and Repression: A Reconsideration," in *Women: Sex and Sexuality,* ed. Catharine R. Stimpson and Ethel Spector Person (Chicago: University of Chicago Press, 1980), p. 142.

REFERENCES

Donnerstein, Edward (1984). "Pornography: Its Effect on Violence Against Women." In *Pornography and Sexual Aggression,* ed. Donnerstein and Neil M. Malamuth. Orlando, Fla.: Academic Press, pp. 53–81.

Gardiner, Harold J. (1975). "Moral Principles Toward a Definition of the Obscene." In *The Pornography Controversy: Changing Moral Standards in American Life,* ed. Ray C. Rist. New Brunswick, N.J.: Transaction Books, pp. 159–74.

Girard, René (1977). *Violence and the Sacred.* Trans. Patrick Gardiner. Baltimore, Md.: Johns Hopkins University Press.

Jacobs, Caryn (1984). "Patterns of Violence: A Feminist Perspective on the Regulation of Pornography." *Harvard Women's Law Journal* 7: 5–55.

Kittay, Eva Feder (1984). "Pornography and the Erotics of Domination." In *Beyond Domination: New Perspectives on Women and Philosophy,* ed. Carol Gould. Totowa, N.J.: Roman and Allanheld, pp. 145–74.

Ricoeur, Paul (1981). *Hermeneutics and the Human Sciences.* Trans., ed., with an introduction by John B. Thompson. Cambridge: Cambridge University Press.

Slade, Joseph (1975). "Pornographic Theaters Off Times Square." In Rist, ed., *The Pornography Controversy,* pp. 119–39.

Steiner, George (1975). "Night Words: High Pornography and Human Privacy." In Rist, ed., *The Pornography Controversy*, pp. 203–16.

Stivers, Richard (1982). *Evil in Modern Myth and Ritual*. Athens, Ga.: University of Georgia Press.

Tong, Rosemarie (1982). "Feminism, Pornography and Censorship." *Social Theory and Practice* 8: 1–17.

8

Beyond the Meese Commission Report

Understanding the Variable Nature of Pornography Regulation

DAVID PRITCHARD

This essay addresses pornography regulation in a behavioral context. Specifically, it discusses how differences in the intensity and style of pornography regulation in the United States are largely determined by variable cultural, social, and political factors. Formal law is not an important predictor of differences in pornography regulation because formal law with respect to pornography is fairly constant throughout the United States.

Of course, formal law with respect to expression generally is relatively uniform, largely because of the strong free-expression guarantees of the First Amendment to the United States Constitution. In other words, there is no doubt that cultural, social, and political variables influence the regulation of expression.

Pornography is a special case, however, because citizen opinion with respect to it is sharply split. Poll after poll over the past several decades has demonstrated that about 90 percent of Americans support the notion of freedom of expression, at least in the abstract (McClosky & Brill, 1983, 48–49, 58–63). Support for freedom of pornography, on the other hand, is far from unanimous. In fact, it is fairly clear that most Americans favor continued regulation of at least certain kinds of sexually explicit expression (Glassman, 1978; McClosky & Brill, 1983; Einsiedel, 1986). The *Final Report* of the Attorney General's Commission on Pornography (commonly known as the Meese Commission) reflected that preference. The commission not only urged vigorous enforcement of existing laws that apply to the production and distribution of pornography, but it also recommended additional legislation and encouraged citizens to agitate for reform (Attorney General's Commission on Pornography, 1986).

Of course, pornography is only one of the several categories of expression that have inspired censorial impulses in the United States over the years. Despite the ideals of individual liberty that served as the foundation for the American Revolution and despite the Constitution's prohibition against government interference in freedom of speech and press, efforts to restrict expression deemed as unsavory have been common in American history.

Extreme political views, for example, have often been the target of the censor, though the Supreme Court of the United States has interpreted the First Amendment as granting virtually absolute protection to political expression (e.g., *Near v. Minnesota*, 1931; *New York Times Co. v. Sullivan*, 1964; *Brandenburg v. Ohio*, 1969. See, generally, Meiklejohn, 1960; Emerson, 1970). The same is not necessarily true, however, of words and images designed to appeal to audience members who are seeking gratifications other than the stimulation of political thought. Concern over the influence of what one media sociologist has called "mass entertainment" (Wright, 1986) has been fairly constant in American history and has often been accompanied by calls for stricter regulation of media content. In recent decades, there have been outcries about the allegedly corrupting influences of movies (e.g., Blumler & Hauser, 1933; Charters, 1934), radio entertainment (Herzog, 1944), comic books (Wertham, 1954), television (Surgeon General's Scientific Advisory Committee, 1972; Pearl, Bouthilet, & Lazar, 1982), rock-and-roll lyrics (Lewis, 1986; AGCP, 1986), and pornography (Commission on Obscenity and Pornography, 1970; AGCP, 1986).

In this context, the Meese Commission's call for additional legal firepower to be used against pornography was not surprising. The struggle for control of the words and images disseminated to the populace is in many ways only part of a larger battle over control of social, political, and cultural resources (Edelman, 1964; Gusfield, 1967; Plato, 1974; Tuchman, 1978; Gitlin, 1980. With specific respect to pornography, see Kittay, 1984; MacKinnon, 1984; and AGCP, 1986).

If all that proponents of legal change sought were a symbolic affirmation of norms they hold dear, then the actual enforcement of laws might not be a matter of great importance to them (Gusfield, 1967). If, however, legal change is intended to influence the behavior of people who are considered to be deviant (in the case of pornography, those who are engaged in the production and/or distribution of pornographic material), then it is important to consider the nature of the relationship between law and behavior.

In theory, law's influence on behavior could be direct and immediate. For that to be the case, citizens would have to have knowledge of the relevant body of law and would have to obey that law without fail. Behavior would conform to law, and when the law changed, people would adjust their actions accordingly. There would be no need for a law-enforcement apparatus; people would simply obey the law because it was the law.

Law does not work that way in the real world, however, For better or worse, law's influence on behavior "tends to be indirect, subtle and ambiguous" (Macaulay, 1984, 155) rather than direct and immediate. The Meese Commission realized the limits of law as an agent of behavioral change:

To know what the law can do, we must appreciate what the law cannot do. We believe that in many respects the law can serve important controlling and symbolic purposes in restricting the proliferation of certain sexually explicit material that we believe harmful to individuals and to society. But we know as well that to rely entirely or excessively on law is simply a mistake. (AGCP, 1986, 428)

That is not to say that the Meese Commission believed that law has no effect on behavior. "If there are attitudes that need changing and behaviors that need restricting, then law has a role to play," the commission said. "But if we expect law to do too much, we will discover only too late that few of our problems have been solved" (1986, 428–429). In other words, the degree of law's impact on behavior can be situated somewhere between the condition of having no influence at all and the condition of having massive, direct, and immediate effects on human behavior.

Having concluded that law's relationship to behavior is neither all nor nothing, however, the Meese Commission did little to explore what that relationship *is*. The final report of the commission offers no theory of how laws regulating pornography influence the actual behavior in question—the production and/or distribution of sexually explicit materials. In fairness, it must be noted that the commission was not asked to take on such theoretical tasks. And, perhaps because it realized its limitations in this realm, the commission itself called for additional research into variable enforcement of laws that apply to pornography (1986, 367).

This essay, which examines factors that may help explain variance in the quantity and quality of pornography regulation, is in part a response to that call. A complete behavioral theory of pornography regulation would identify and examine the operation of variable factors that influence the quality and quantity of pornography regulation, and would be linked to a behavioral theory of media regulation generally.

Full development of such a theory is far beyond the scope of this essay. Nonetheless, further theoretical work is important. A well-developed behavioral theory of pornography regulation (and of media regulation generally) not only would be of interest to scholars but also could inform the efforts of legal officials (i.e., legislators, police, prosecutors, judges) who from time to time may attempt to influence the quantity or quality of pornography regulation.

Defining Terms

It is easy, in discussions of sexually explicit materials, to become bogged down in definitions. The Supreme Court of the United States has attempted several times to define obscenity, with notable lack of conceptual clarity. Former Justice Potter Stewart epitomized the high court's definitional difficulties with obscenity when he penned the infamous "I know it when I see it" statement in his concurring opinion in *Jacobellis v. Ohio* (1964, 197).

In terms of the law, "obscenity" is not the same as "pornography," though the two words are sometimes used interchangeably. That is not the case in this article, however. Here, the term "obscene" is reserved for materials that would be legally obscene under prevailing constitutional standards (*Miller v. California*, 1973). "Pornography," on the other hand, is defined as the Meese Commission defined it: material that is "predominantly sexually explicit and intended primarily for the purposes of arousal" (1986, 228–29).

Using these definitions, all obscenity is pornographic, because sexual explicitness and appeal to arousal (i.e., "prurient interest") are integral portions of the legal definition of obscenity. But not all pornography—nor even most of it—meets the legal definition of obscenity outlined in *Miller v. California*. For example, much sexually explicit material intended primarily for the purposes of arousal (i.e., pornography) is not legally obscene either because it has "serious literary, artistic, political, or scientific value" (*Miller v. California*, 1973, 24) or because it does not depict sexual conduct "in a patently offensive way" (*Miller v. California*, 1973, 24). Before a piece of pornography can be found to be legally obscene, current constitutional standards require a prosecutor to demonstrate not only that the work depicts sexual conduct in a patently offensive way but also that it lacks serious literary, artistic, political, or scientific value. Failure to make such demonstrations precludes a finding of obscenity. In short, all obscenity is pornography, but not all pornography is obscene. For example, although *Playboy* is pornographic because it is sexually explicit and intended for the purposes of arousal, no American court has ever found the magazine to be obscene.

The other problem with affixing the label "pornography" to a given work is that the definition is all too often mistaken for a conclusion about the worth of the work. To categorize something as "pornography" is seen by some as a condemnation. Whatever the intent of other authors, however, here "pornography" is used as nothing more than a word that describes a certain class of expressive materials.

Another term that needs to be defined is "regulation." This essay uses the word "regulation" in the same way that Donald Black (1976) uses the word "law." Borrowing Black's definition of law gives the following definition of "regulation": Regulation is "governmental social control. It is, in other words, the normative life of a state and its citizens, such as legislation, litigation, and adjudication" (Black, 1976, 2. Black's formulation is not without its critics. See, e.g., Greenberg, 1983).

It is important to note that "the normative life of a state and its citizens" comprises more than the formal law and legal procedures denoted by the words "legislation, litigation, and adjudication." Regulation of pornography may be formal, to be sure. Statutes can be used in attempts to control the production and/or distribution of sexually explicit material; court action may be brought against people suspected of violating those statutes. But a variety of relatively informal procedures operates to fashion consensual, compromise outcomes in many disputes that find their way into court. Most criminal cases, for example, are disposed of by plea bargaining, not by adversary trials (Eisenstein & Jacob, 1977; Heumann, 1978). Similarly, most civil cases are settled out of court

(Trubek et al., 1983). In addition, much (if not most) regulation takes place completely apart from the formal legal system epitomized by courts. Police officers have broad discretion over whether to arrest suspected wrongdoers; prosecutors have virtually unfettered discretion to decide which cases to pursue. The lack of formal action (arrests, prosecution) does not mean that no regulation has taken place. Police may deal with a dispute without making an arrest (Silberman, 1978; Worden & Pollitz, 1984; with respect to pornography, see Comment, 1954–55); prosecutors may enforce norms by threats to prosecute rather than by actual prosecution (with respect to pornography, see Pritchard, Dilts & Berkowitz, 1987). And in some cases, law-enforcement officials may regulate by threatening formal legal action if the targets of regulation fail to pay bribes (Smith & Zekman, 1979).

In other words, regulation can be formal or informal, adversarial or consensual, legal or illegal. It can also be governmental or private. Although this article does not discuss private social control, it is important to note that what Stewart Macaulay (1983) calls "private governments" can be powerful enforcers of norms. Macaulay writes:

> Much of what we would call governing is done by groups which are not part of the institutions established by federal and state constitutions. If governing involves making rules, interpreting them, applying them to specific cases, and sanctioning violations, some or all of this is done by such different clusters of people as the Mafia, the National Collegiate Athletic Association, the American Arbitration Association, those who run large shopping centers, neighborhood associations, and even the regulars at Smokey's tavern. It may be necessary to draw a sharp line between public and private governments such as these in order even to think about law, but in reality there is no such division. To the contrary, one finds instead interpenetration, overlapping jurisdictions, and opportunities both for harmony and conflict among public and private governments. (Macaulay, 1983, 1)

With respect to pornography, what Macaulay calls "governing" is conducted not only by legislators and law-enforcement officials but also by distributors of sexually oriented material (see, e.g., Levine, 1969), by established special-interest groups on all sides of the issue (e.g., the American Civil Liberties Union, the American Booksellers Association, and the Feminist Anti-Censorship Taskforce, all of which favor tolerance of sexually explicit expression; and Citizens for Decency Through Law, the National Federation of Decency, and the National Coalition Against Pornography, all of which favor heightened legal action against pornography), and by local groups that may form on an ad hoc basis to influence the resolution of pornography-related conflicts (Zurcher & Kirkpatrick, 1976).

The interests and capabilities of these kinds of "governments" differ from context to context, even if the formal laws that apply do not. And in fact, formal law with respect to pornography is remarkably consistent throughout the United States. Formal law does not vary significantly because the Supreme Court of the United States has limited the flexibility of units of government to pass laws regulating nonobscene pornography, as the Meese Commission realized. "To the extent that legislation restricts material beyond the legally obscene, that legislation must confront an array of First Amendment-inspired barriers that few if any statutes could meet," the commission noted (1986, 393).

The Supreme Court has permitted occasional restrictions on sexually oriented businesses. Zoning laws that restrict adult theaters and bookstores to certain parts of a community have been upheld (*Young v. American Mini Theatres, Inc.,* 1976; *Renton v. Playtime Theatres, Inc.,* 1986), as have nuisance laws as they apply to such establishments (*Arcara v. Cloud Books,* 1986). However, the Supreme Court has not allowed such business regulations to have the effect of totally prohibiting "adults-only" establishments from a municipality (*Schad v. Borough of Mt. Ephraim,* 1981).

The Supreme Court has also upheld the constitutionality of laws limiting the dissemination of nonobscene sexually oriented materials when children are involved. For example, government may restrict the distribution of nonobscene pornography to minors (*Ginsberg v. New York,* 1968), may ban the exhibition of nonobscene films depicting sexual conduct by children under sixteen years of age (*New York v. Ferber,* 1982), and may restrict the broadcasting of indecent but nonobscene language at times when children would be likely to be in the audience (*FCC v. Pacifica Foundation,* 1978).

Unless children are involved, however, the Supreme Court has not been sympathetic to attempts to restrict nonobscene sexually explicit expression on the basis of its content. It unanimously overturned an obscenity conviction involving the R-rated mainstream Hollywood movie *Carnal Knowledge* (*Jenkins v. Georgia,* 1974); it refused to allow a municipality to prohibit outdoor theaters from showing movies with nude scenes when the scenes could be viewed from public places such as highways (*Erznoznik v. City of Jacksonville,* 1975); it affirmed the Seventh Circuit Court of Appeals' ruling that legislation defining and punishing pornography as a violation of women's civil rights was unconstitutional (*Hudnut v. American Booksellers Association,* 1986); and it affirmed the Tenth Circuit Court of Appeals' ruling that a state law restricting indecent but not obscene material on cable television was unconsitutional (*Wilkinson v. Jones,* 1987).

In short, the constitutional standards in this area are so strict that nothing but the hardest-core pornography can be regulated by formal statute, as the Meese Commission acknowledged (1986, 260): "In the final analysis, the effect of *Miller, Jenkins,* and a large number of other Supreme Court and lower court cases is to limit obscenity prosecutions to 'hard core' material devoid of anything except the most explicit and offensive representations of sex."

People who have been directly harmed by pornography have a variety of legal remedies other than attempting to persuade law-enforcement officials to initiate an investigation into possible violations of obscenity laws (Jacobs, 1984; Linz, Turner, Hesse, & Penrod, 1984; Robel, this volume). However, as Robel notes, such remedies are likely to be ineffective, in large part because those who claim to be victims of pornography often lack credibility with police, prosecutors, judges, and juries (see also Bumiller, 1984).

But the key point is that the legal remedies already exist. The formal legal aspects of pornography regulation do not vary significantly from community to community in the United States. What does vary is context—cultural, social, and political. Robel's implicit hypothesis is that the success of legal remedies for victims of pornography will vary directly with how credible a victim is to legal officials. The hypothesis is empirically testable and is independent of any variance in formal law.

Because formal law with respect to pornography is remarkably constant in the United States, any explanation for variance in the behavior of pornography regulation must be sought elsewhere.

Behavioral Aspects of Pornography Regulation

What follows has been heavily influenced by works of scholarship that on their surfaces have nothing to do with pornography: the hypotheses about the relationship between law and social change that Frederick Wirt (1970) generated from his study of the federal government's attempts to reduce racial inequality in a rural Mississippi county; the sociological theory of law proposed by Donald Black (1976); and the set of empirically derived postulates about the relationship between law and society advanced by Stewart Macaulay (1984).

These scholars form a diverse group, and their approaches to the relationship between law and society are not always consistent. Wirt, for example, views attributes of statutory law ("qualities of the regulation" is his phrase) as important *independent* variables (1970, 283–88; see also Lempert & Sanders, 1986, 390–92) whose existence is to be noted and whose effects are to be examined. He writes:

> Suffrage, education, and economic rights laid along a continuum reveal that the nature of the law gradually diminishes in its specificity and, possibly more important, in its provision of powerful sanctions, in the order given. The long-run increment in the extension of freedom to southern blacks is therefore a function partly of the law authorizing the extension. (Wirt, 1970, 287)

Wirt's formulation, however, begs the question of why some regulations are more specific than others, why some provide for more powerful sanctions than others, and so on. Black, on the other hand, asserts that the characteristics of statutes (which are included in his term "the style of law"), like all other aspects of regulation, are *dependent* variables to be predicted and explained:

> Like the quantity of law in general, the style of law varies across time and space. It varies across the world and over the centuries, and from one society or community to another. It varies across relationships, from one legal setting to another, from court to court, and from case to case. It varies with the stratification of social life, its morphology, culture, organization, and social control. . . . And, just as it is possible to explain the quantity of law in general, it is possible to explain the quantity of each of these styles. (Black, 1976, 5–6)

Black does not claim that the style of law has *no* effect on behavior or outcomes. But for Black, different styles of law are not independent of the social factors outlined in the quote above. It is Black's contention that the social factors that predict the behavior of law in general also predict styles of law, which in turn may then have some influence on the behavior of law.

From a theoretical standpoint, whether formal law is considered to be an independent or a dependent variable is an important issue. However, in practical terms—at least with respect to pornography regulation—this central theoretical question is not terribly important. Whether to consider law as an independent variable (i.e., as a predictor of certain outcomes) or as a dependent variable (i.e., as something to be predicted) is a significant issue in practice only if law actually varies. And, as noted earlier, formal law as it applies to pornography does not vary greatly from community to community in the United States in the late 1980s.

However, the behavior of pornography regulation—government social control—does vary, depending upon a number of contextual factors, including cultural variables, social variables, and political variables. These factors may interact in complex ways in any given pornography-related dispute. And the nature of their interactions is itself a variable that differs from context to context. The complexity of the sets of variables suggests that measuring them would be a formidable task. But however difficult it might be to measure the quantity and quality of any or all of these variables, together they predict and explain the quantity and style of pornography regulation (cf. Black, 1976). As such, they merit the attention of those who conduct research in this area.

Cultural variables, for example, include conventionality (or cultural location) and history. Conventionality, which Black (1976) defines as proximity to the cultural mainstream, is a quantitative variable, and the more conventional a person, group, or society, the more regulation that person, group, or society uses. Regulation varies directly with conventionality (Black, 1976, 68). The less conventional person, group, or society is less likely to call upon governmental social control to resolve a dispute than is a more conventional person, group, or society, everything else being equal. In a patriarchal society, women are less conventional—farther away from the cultural center—than men. A producer of X-rated movies is less conventional than a producer of more mainstream fare.

Interestingly, though, when people who have significant control over the production and/or distribution of pornography are brought to trial on obscenity charges, the judge and jury often find that the defendant looks quite conventional, "nicely dressed, well-spoken, and (with) a residence in the suburbs" (AGCP, 1986, 368). And a considerable body of research shows that defendants with conventional characteristics fare better in the criminal justice system than do defendants with unconventional characteristics. For example, research has focused on conventionality in terms of socioeconomic status (Gleason & Harris, 1976), physical attractiveness (Reskin & Visher, 1986), and courtroom behavior (Pryor & Buchanan, 1984).

History is the experience of a person, group, or society; its content varies.

Women, for example, have greater experience than men with a gender-based victimization, at least some of which may be associated with pornography (Griffin, 1981; Jacobs, 1984; AGCP, 1986). And the greater the experience with gender-based victimization, the less likely a person, group, or society is to ask for governmental social control—the law—to resolve a gender-related dispute, everything else being equal. This is as true for victims of pornography as it is for victims of sex discrimination in the workplace. As Bumiller (1984, 33) notes, "victims are discouraged from the invocation of rights because the law engenders reactions that defeat its effective use." When a victim seeks the assistance of the law, not only is she in some sense admitting helplessness, in that she was unable to solve the problem herself, but she also loses a measure of control over the dispute. When law touches a dispute, the dispute is inevitably transformed—stripped of its social context so that it can be fitted into an appropriate legal category (Mather & Yngvesson, 1980–81).

The important point is that cultural factors can influence the nature of the public and legal response to a pornography-related dispute. For example, whether or not a distributor of pornography acts in a fashion deemed to be appropriate when such a dispute arises helps determine the severity of the public and legal response (Comment, 1954–55; Kirkpatrick, 1975). Similarly, how the news media report a dispute may affect not only the public's designation of the dispute but also the willingness of legal officials to take vigorous action (Pritchard, 1986; Pritchard, Dilts, & Berkowitz, 1987).

Social variables include wealth, organization, and prestige. Such variables do not exist on their own, however. Instead, they combine in several ways to form complex variables. For example, a group may have a high level of organization and a high level of prestige, a high level of organization but a low level of prestige, a low level of organization and a low level of prestige, or a low level of organization but a high level of prestige.

Typically, a person, group, or social system that ranks high on one social variable also has high levels of the others. That is not always the case, however. Sometimes an individual, group, or social system will rank high on one factor, but low on another. The result can be status inconsistency, which has attracted the attention of many sociologists in recent decades. Status inconsistents can be divided into two categories: "under-rewarded" and "over-rewarded." People who have high income but a low-status occupation, for example, are "over-rewarded" inconsistents. By contrast, people with high education (and thus high prestige) but low income are "under-rewarded" inconsistents (Zurcher & Kirkpatrick, 1976).

The distinction may be important in pornography regulation. Zurcher and Kirkpatrick (1976) suggest that under-rewarded status inconsistency may be linked with antipornography attitudes, while over-rewarded status inconsistency is associated with tolerant attitudes toward pornography. There is also strong evidence that demographics—another form of social variable—are related to attitudes toward pornography. There is evidence that attitudes toward pornography vary significantly with differences in gender, age, and race as well as with education, employment, ideology, religiosity, and moral rigidity (Glassman, 1978; Herrman & Bordner, 1983; Burton, 1986).

Political variables include public opinion, power, and the elasticity of the rights in question in a dispute. The first of these, public opinion, has been defined as "the complex of preferences expressed by a significant number of persons on an issue of general importance" (Hennessy, 1981, 4). As such, it is the aggregate of citizens' attitudes toward a subject. Public opinion about pornography—at least as prosecutors perceive it—influences whether or not prosecutors file criminal obscenity charges against the distributors of sexually explicit materials in their communities (Pritchard, Dilts, & Berkowitz, 1987).

Power is the ability to marshal tangible resources on one's behalf in a dispute. It includes the amount of time, money, and specialized knowledge that a disputant can bring to bear on a dispute (Galanter, 1974). Although they have the requisite specialized knowledge, prosecutors generally can devote little in the way of time or money to pornography; matters such as violent crime, property crime, substance abuse, and even white-collar crime tend to be higher on their agendas (Pritchard, Dilts, & Berkowitz, 1987). And though there are notable exceptions (see, e.g., Koenig, 1986), as a rule, prosecutors of necessity ignore pornography in their jurisdictions (Project, 1977; AGCP, 1986).

All the same, pornography is a very high priority for some citizens. Unless such citizens are highly organized, though, they are not likely to be effective antipornography crusaders (Zurcher & Kirkpatrick, 1976). Individuals, including those who claim to have been victimized by pornography, may have adequate time to engage in disputing behavior, but they are less likely to have the money and the specialized knowledge required to prevail. As Lawrence Friedman (1983, 21) noted: "The courts are stiff, formal, and expensive. Ordinary people do not like to use them, or they find them too costly or too remote."

The disputants who are most likely to have the resources and the specialized knowledge to prevail in a dispute are the producers and distributors of pornography. Pornography is a lucrative business (AGCP, 1986), and when it comes under attack those who profit from it can afford to purchase specialized knowledge. That specialized knowledge often comes in the form of an experienced lawyer, but it may also take the guise of a high-powered public-relations firm. Associations of book and periodical distributors, for instance, recently paid hundreds of thousands of dollars for a public-relations campaign explicitly intended to discredit the findings of the Meese Commission (McManus, 1986, xlvi–xlviii).

A more abstract political variable is the elasticity of the rights in question in a dispute (Wirt, 1970). The right to free expression (e.g., the right to produce, sell, and possess pornography) is elastic to the extent that its expansion does not restrict existing rights. The elasticity of the "right to pornography," however, is a matter of considerable dispute. Many serious thinkers contend that pornography infringes upon the fundamental rights of those who do not produce, distribute, or use it—especially women and children (Dworkin, 1981; Griffin, 1981; Jacobs, 1984; MacKinnon, 1984).

These lists of cultural, social, and political variables are not intended to be exhaustive. Indeed, a full inventory of factors that influence pornography regulation might well be of telephone-book proportions. Further complicating the process is the fact that there are three distinct categories of disputants in pornography regulation—the regulator (typically, legal officials), the regulated (typically, distributors of pornography), and a more diffuse category, the potential beneficiaries of the regulation, who may include not only antipornography activists but also citizens who have been (or could be) harmed by pornography. In any dispute, the cultural, social, and political attributes of each category of disputant will vary. For example, the regulator may be highly organized, the regulated poorly organized, and the beneficiaries of the regulation highly organized. In such a case, everything else being equal, the quantity of regulation would be expected to be relatively large.

But everything else is rarely equal, and there is a vast number of possible combinations among the myriad cultural, social, and political variables and the three categories of disputants. Even if, for example, there were only one important cultural variable, one important social variable, and one important political variable, and even if each of those variables had only two possible values (e.g., low and high), there would be 512 possible combinations among the nine cells of a 3 x 3 matrix such as is found in Table 1.

TABLE 1

Possible Combinations of Attributes among Categories of Disputants in Pornography Regulation

	Regulator	Regulated	Beneficiaries of the regulation
Cultural attributes	low/high	low/high	low/high
Social attributes	low/high	low/high	low/high
Political attributes	low/high	low/high	low/high

Of course, there are many important cultural, social, and political variables in pornography regulation, and—to the extent that these variables can be measured—most have more than two possible values. It should also be clear that many of these variables are not independent, but instead interact in complex and constantly changing ways.

Conclusion

This chapter has suggested that the relationship between law and behavior with respect to pornography depends upon cultural, social, and political factors that vary from time to time, from place to place, and from disputant to disputant.

Formal law does not account for variance in pornography regulation because formal law is essentially uniform throughout the United States. In other words, pornography regulation is likely to be influenced by citizen agitation and vigorous enforcement of existing law, both of which the Meese Commission recommended. Without an increase in citizen activism and heightened law enforcement, however, additional legislation—which the Meese Commission also recommended—is not likely to affect the nature of pornography regulation.

People who wish to explain and account for variance in pornography regulation—including why pornography becomes a matter of dispute in some contexts but not others, and why such disputes find their way into court in some contexts but not others—are advised to examine the cultural, social, and political attributes of the relevant individuals, groups, and organizations.

It is there that researchers will find the law in action, the *behavior* of law. And, as Roscoe Pound noted early in this century, the law in action tends to be quite different from the laws in the statute books (Pound, 1910).

REFERENCES

Attorney General's Commission in Pornography (1986). *Final Report.* Washington, D.C.: Government Printing Office.

Black, Donald (1976). *The Behavior of Law.* Orlando, Fla.: Academic Press.

Blumler, Herbert, & Hauser, Philip (1933). *Movies, Delinquency and Crime.* New York: Macmillan.

Bumiller, Kristin (1984). "Anti-Discrimination Law and the Enslavement of the Victim: The Denial of Self-Respect by Victims without a Cause." Working Paper 1984–6, Disputes Processing Research Program, Law School, University of Wisconsin–Madison.

Burton, Doris-Jean (1986). "Women, Pornography and Public Opinion." Paper presented at the annual meeting of the Midwest Political Science Association, April 1986, Chicago, Ill.

Charters, W. W. (1934). *Motion Pictures and Youth: A Summary.* New York: Macmillan.

Comment (1954–55). "Censorship of Obscene Literature by Informal Government Action." *University of Chicago Law Review* 22:216–33.

Commission on Obscenity and Pornography (1970). *Report.* Washington, D.C.: Government Printing Office.

Dworkin, Ronald (1981). "Is There a Right to Pornography?" *Oxford Journal of Legal Studies* 1:177–212.

Edelman, Murray (1964). *The Symbolic Uses of Politics.* Urbana, Ill.: University of Illinois Press.

Einsiedel, Edna F. (1986). "Public Opinion on Pornography: 1970 and 1985." Paper presented at the annual meeting of the International Communication Association, May 1986, Chicago, Ill.

Eisenstein, James, & Jacob, Herbert (1977). *Felony Justice: An Organizational Analysis of Criminal Courts.* Boston: Little, Brown.

Emerson, Thomas I. (1970). *The System of Freedom of Expression*. New York: Random House.

Friedman, Lawrence M. (1983). "Courts over Time: A Survey of Theories and Research." In *Empirical Theories about Courts*, ed. Keith O. Boyum & Lynn Mather. New York: Longman, pp. 9–50.

Galanter, Marc (1974). "Why the 'Haves' Come out Ahead: Speculations on the Limits of Legal Change." *Law & Society Review* 9:95–160.

Gitlin, Todd (1980). *The Whole World Is Watching: Mass Media in the Making and Unmaking of the New Left*. Berkeley, Cal.: University of California Press.

Glassman, Marc B. (1978). "Community Standards of Patent Offensiveness: Public Opinion Data and Obscenity Law." *Public Opinion Quarterly* 42:161–70.

Gleason, James M., & Harris, Victor A. (1976). "Group Discussion and Defendant's Socio-economic Status as Determinants of Judgments by Simulated Jurors." *Journal of Applied Social Psychology* 6:186–91.

Greenberg, David F. (1983). "Donald Black's Sociology of Law: A Critique." *Law & Society Review* 17:337–68.

Griffin, Susan (1981). *Pornography and Silence: Culture's Revenge against Nature*. New York: Harper & Row.

Gusfield, Joseph R. (1967). "Moral Passage: The Symbolic Process in Public Designations of Deviance." *Social Problems* 15:175–88.

Hennessy, Bernard (1981). *Public Opinion*. 4th ed. Monterey, Cal.: Brooks/Cole Publishing.

Herrman, Margaret S., & Bordner, Diane C. (1983). "Attitudes toward Pornography in a Southern Community." *Criminology* 21:349–74.

Herzog, Herta (1944). "What Do We Really Know about Daytime Serial Listeners?" In *Radio Research 1942–1943*, ed. Paul F. Lazarsfeld & Frank Stanton. New York: Duell, Sloan and Pearce.

Heumann, Milton. (1978). *Plea Bargaining: The Experiences of Prosecutors, Judges, and Defense Attorneys*. Chicago: University of Chicago Press.

Jacobs, Caryn (1984). "Patterns of Violence: A Feminist Perspective on the Regulation of Pornography." *Harvard Women's Law Journal* 7:5–55.

Kirkpatrick, R. George (1975). "Collective Consciousness and Mass Hysteria: Collective Behavior and Anti-pornography Crusades in Durkheimian Perspective." *Human Relations* 28:63–84.

Kittay, Eva Feder (1984). "Pornography and the Erotics of Domination." In *Beyond Domination: New Perspectives on Women and Philosophy*, ed. Carol C. Gould. Totowa, N.J.: Rowman and Allanheld.

Koenig, Richard (1986). "Success of Crusade to Rid City of Smut has Made Cincinnati a Model for Anti-pornography Forces." *The Wall Street Journal*, December 1, 1986, p. 32.

Lempert, Richard, & Sanders, Joseph (1986). *An Invitation to Law and Social Science: Deserts, Disputes, and Distribution*. White Plains, N.Y.: Longman.

Levine, James P. (1969). "An Empirical Approach to Civil Liberties: The Bookseller and Obscenity Law." *Wisconsin Law Review* 1969:153–69.

Lewis, Randy (1986). "Song Lyrics Have Little Effect on Illiterate Teens, Study Shows." *Louisville Courier-Journal*, August 8, 1986, p. C3.

Linz, Daniel; Turner, Charles W.; Hesse, Bradford W.; & Penrod, Steven D. (1984). "Bases of Liability for Injuries Produced by Media Portrayals of Violent Pornography." In *Pornography and Sexual Aggression*, ed. Neil M. Malamuth & Edward Donnerstein. Orlando, Fla.: Academic Press, pp. 277–304.

Macaulay, Stewart (1983). "Private Government." Working Paper 1983–6, Disputes Processing Research Program, Law School, University of Wisconsin–Madison.

——— (1984). "Law and the Behavioral Sciences: Is There any There There?" *Law & Policy* 6:149–87.

McClosky, Herbert, & Brill, Alida (1983). *Dimensions of Tolerance: What Americans Believe about Civil Liberties.* New York: Russell Sage Foundation.

MacKinnon, Catharine A. (1984). "Not a Moral Issue." *Yale Law & Policy Review* 2:321–45.

McManus, Michael J. (1986). "Introduction." In *Final Report of the Attorney General's Commission on Pornography.* Nashville, Tenn.: Rutledge Hill Press, pp. ix-l.

Mather, Lynn, & Yngvesson, Barbara (1980–81). "Language, Audience, and the Transformation of Disputes." *Law & Society Review* 15:775–821.

Meese Commission. *See* Attorney General's Commission on Pornography.

Meiklejohn, Alexander (1960). *Political Freedom.* New York: Harper & Bros.

Pearl, David; Bouthilet, Lorraine; & Lazar, Joyce, eds. (1982). *Television and Behavior: Ten Years of Scientific Progress and Implications for the Eighties.* Washington, D.C.: Government Printing Office.

Plato (1974). *The Republic.* Trans. G.M.A. Grube. Indianapolis: Hackett Publishing Co.

Pound, Roscoe (1910). "Law in Books and Law in Action." *American Law Review* 44:12–36.

Pritchard, David (1986). "Homicide and Bargained Justice: The Agenda-setting Effect of Crime News on Prosecutors." *Public Opinion Quarterly* 50:143–59.

Pritchard, David; Dilts, Jon Paul; & Berkowitz, Dan (1987). "Prosecutors' Use of External Agendas in Prosecuting Pornography Cases." *Journalism Quarterly* 64:392–98.

Project (1977). "An Empirical Inquiry into the Effects of *Miller v. California* on the Control of Obscenity." *New York University Law Review* 52:810–939.

Pryor, Bert, & Buchanan, Raymond W. (1984). "The Effects of a Defendant's Demeanor on Juror Perceptions of Credibility and Guilt." *Journal of Communication* 34(3): 92–99.

Reskin, Barbara F., & Visher, Christy A. (1986). "The Impacts of Evidence and Extralegal Factors in Jurors' Decisions." *Law & Society Review* 20:423–38.

Robel, Lauren (1989). "Pornography and Existing Law: What the Law Can Do." Chapter 9, this volume.

Silberman, Charles E. (1978). *Criminal Violence, Criminal Justice.* New York: Random House.

Smith, Zay N., & Zekman, Pamela (1979). *The Mirage.* New York: Random House.

Surgeon General's Scientific Advisory Committee on Television and Social Behavior (1972). *Television and Growing Up: The Impact of Televised Violence.* Washington, D.C.: Government Printing Office.

Trubek, David M.; Sarat, Austin; Felstiner, William L. F.; Kritzer, Herbert M.; & Grossman, Joel B. (1983). "The Costs of Ordinary Litigation." *U.C.L.A. Law Review* 31:72–129.

Tuchman, Gaye (1978). *Making News: A Study in the Construction of Reality.* New York: The Free Press.

Wertham, Fredric (1954). *Seduction of the Innocent.* New York: Rinehart and Co.

Wirt, Frederick M. (1970). *Politics of Southern Equality: Law and Social Change in a Mississippi County.* Chicago: Aldine.

Worden, Robert E., & Pollitz, Alissa A. (1984). "Police Arrests in Domestic Disturbances: A Further Look." *Law & Society Review* 18:105–19.

Wright, Charles R. (1986). *Mass Communication: A Sociological Perspective.* New York: Random House.

Zurcher, Louis A. Jr., & Kirkpatrick, R. George (1976). *Citizens for Decency: Antipornography Crusades as Status Defense.* Austin, Tex.: University of Texas Press.

Cases Cited

Arcara v. Cloud Books, 106 S.Ct. 3172 (1986).

Brandenburg v. Ohio, 395 U.S. 444 (1969).

Erznoznik v. City of Jacksonville, 422 U.S. 205 (1975).

FCC v. Pacifica Foundation, 438 U.S. 726 (1978).

Ginsberg v. New York, 390 U.S. 629 (1968).

Hudnut v. American Booksellers Association, 106 S.Ct. 1172 (1986), mem. aff'g American Booksellers Association v. Hudnut, 771 F.2d 323 (7th Cir. 1985).

Jacobellis v. Ohio, 378 U.S. 184 (1964).

Jenkins v. Georgia, 418 U.S. 153 (1974).

Miller v. California, 413 U.S. 15 (1973).

Near v. Minnesota, 283 U.S. 697 (1931).

New York v. Ferber, 458 U.S. 747 (1982)

New York Times Co. v. Sullivan, 376 U.S. 254 (1964).

Renton v. Playtime Theatres, Inc., 106 S.Ct. 925 (1986).

Schad v. Borough of Mt. Ephraim, 452 U.S. 61 (1981).

Wilkinson v. Jones, 107 S.Ct. 1559 (1987), mem. aff'g Jones v. Wilkinson, 800 F.2d 989 (10th Cir. 1986).

Young v. American Mini Theatres, Inc., 427 U.S. 50 (1976).

9

Pornography and Existing Law

What the Law Can Do

LAUREN ROBEL

Introduction

The vision of pornography in American law and the conclusions that flow from
that vision have recently come under intense criticism. The central legal response
to pornography has been the concept of obscenity, but new voices are being
raised that assert the inadequacy of that response. Led by feminist theorists
Catharine MacKinnon (1984, 1985) and Andrea Dworkin (1981), and fueled by
the report of the Attorney General's Commission on Pornography (1986),[1] many
people are claiming that the harm caused by pornography is entirely different,
in kind and in dimension, from the insult to moral sensibilities upon which obscenity law is premised. Those who believe that pornography is both a major
cause of violence against women and children and a heuristic device central to the maintenance of misogyny in our culture argue the irrelevance of obscenity law to their concerns and the need for new and different legal responses
to pornography. Those who oppose involving the state in further efforts to
control or suppress pornography (Burstyn, 1985; Lynn, 1986), often for complex and thoughtful reasons, match their ideological opponents in vehemence
and sincerity.

My purpose in this essay is not to attempt to resolve the deep and painful
divisions apparent in most contemporary discussions of pornography. Rather, the
question I posit is this: if one takes seriously the claims that pornography causes
various kinds of harm, what redress does existing law offer to pornography's
victims? Further, if some kinds of legal remedies are available in theory only,
what can be done to make them realistically available for those harmed by the
consumption of pornography?

178

The Problem

Proponents of new legal approaches to pornography advance a view of pornography as an organizing principle behind misogyny. Pornography is considered a key element in a variety of crimes and torts, as well as a blueprint for a system of discrimination against women in society at large. The point of such a reconceptualization of pornography is to "emphasize[] the political context of what otherwise appears as merely isolated privatized incidents of sexual violence for pleasure or profit" (Spahn, 1984–85). This view of pornography differs radically from the understanding that underlies the legal suppression of obscenity, which focuses on whether the purpose of certain explicit materials is to incite lust in ways the community finds offensive. Proponents of the view of pornography-as-organizing-principle-for-misogyny have lobbied in several cities for the enactment of ordinances defining pornography as a civil-rights violation.[2] The assumption underlying civil-rights approaches to pornography is that pornography is a cause of sex discrimination in all the areas, such as employment, housing, and access to public accomodations, with which civil-rights legislation is traditionally concerned. Yet, since the leading legislative model defining pornography as a civil-rights violation has been declared unconstitutional *(American Booksellers Association, Inc. v. Hudnut)*,[3] and the recent Attorney General's *Report* does not advocate the "civil-rights" approach, the future of such legislation looks doubtful.

What has emerged from the public hearings surrounding both the Attorney General's *Report* and the adoption of the local ordinances, however, is that many people feel that pornography is related to a number of problems ranging from sexual assault to the deterioration of their neighborhoods. Further, many of those who testified before both the local officials who considered the ordinances and the Attorney General's Commission spoke of their belief that they were without legal recourse for the harms they suffered in connection with pornography.

These testimonial discussions about the perceived lack of legal remedies for problems associated with pornography tend both to exaggerate the lack of remedies and to blur distinctions between whether existing law is adequate and whether it is adequately enforced.[4] My point here is less critical than practical. While civil-rights pornography legislation might have had the salutary effect of raising everyone's consciousness about the possible responsibility pornography bears for sexist attitudes (Brest and Vandenberg, 1987), it would be heartbreaking if the lesson many women took away from the publicity surrounding the demise of such legislation was that there is no legal recourse for any of the problems that the legislation addressed. Moreover, since it is probably easier to lobby to increase enforcement efforts under existing laws than it is to gain acceptance for a novel legal theory, it is worthwhile to examine the possibilities offered by existing laws to combat the sorts of difficulties detailed in the legislative hearings surrounding the passage of the ordinances, and in the ordinances themselves.

The Indianapolis Ordinance as Paradigm

The problems identified with pornography by proponents of the civil-rights approach fall into three broad categories. First, pornography is associated with increased violence toward women, either because pornography generally teaches men to associate sexuality and violence, or because men model specific assaultive behavior on pornography they have viewed. Second, the pornography market provides economic inducements for men to coerce or trick women into pornographic performances. Third, pornography begets an environment that is detrimental to women by picturing a world in which women willingly endure and even enjoy second-class social status and abusive behavior, and by asserting that this representation speaks the truth about how women should be treated by men.

Indianapolis, Indiana, adopted a pornography ordinance that attempted to address each of these perceived evils by using a civil-rights approach. The Indianapolis ordinance is an appropriate paradigm for the civil-rights approach in general, because Indianapolis adopted essentially in its entirety the ordinance drafted by the leading proponents of this approach, MacKinnon and Dworkin. While other approaches to civil-rights pornography legislation that might be less constitutionally problematic can be imagined (Layman, 1987), a useful way to discuss systematically the full range of problems that proponents of civil-rights legislation see in connection with pornography is to examine the structure and functions of this legislation.

The Indianapolis ordinance defines pornography as "the graphic sexually explicit subordination of women, whether in pictures or words," which also includes one of six other elements.[5] The ordinance then defines and prohibits four "discriminatory practices": trafficking in pornography, coercion into pornographic performance, forcing pornography on a person, and assault or physical attack due to pornography (Indianapolis City-County Code Section 16-5). Each prohibition is aimed at providing redress for harms described during hearings on the advisability of adopting civil-rights legislation, and each provides different remedies.[6]

My purpose here is not to critique the legislation. Rather, what I would like to do is to determine the substantive evils addressed by each of the legislation's prohibitions, canvass any available legal theories to redress those evils, and evaluate the criticisms levied against the current state of the law by those who have found it inadequate.

ASSAULT OR PHYSICAL ATTACK DUE TO PORNOGRAPHY

The ordinance defines "assault or physical attack due to pornography" as "the assault, physical attack, or injury of any woman, man, child, or transsexual in a way that is directly caused by specific pornography" (Section 16-3 [g] [7]). If a person believes that an assault was caused by specific pornography, that person can file a complaint against not only the perpetrators of the assault but also the maker, seller, exhibitor, or distributor of the offending pornography.

On the level of providing relief against the perpetrators of specific violent attacks, the ordinance offers no obvious advantages over existing tort law. Anyone who is the victim of a battery or assault may already bring a cause of action against her assailant. Moreover, the ordinance adds an extremely difficult problem of proof, that of showing a causal relationship between the assault and a specific piece of pornography.[7] While there are problems with existing tort remedies,[8] they pale in comparison to the difficulties inherent in the attempt to demonstrate causation (as opposed to imitation), as required by the ordinance.

The acts proscribed by this section are also crimes. Indeed, most of the testimony that supports this section describes criminal acts, including rape and lesser degrees of sexual assault, kidnapping, and battery.[9] Being the complainant in a criminal case is not the equivalent of being the plaintiff in a tort action; the decision about whether or not to prosecute belongs to the state, for instance, not the victimized individual. However, initiating a criminal investigation of an assault does not preclude bringing a tort action based on the same events and has the added advantage of subjecting the assailant to possible imprisonment.[10]

Supporters of the civil-rights approach argue that existing tort and criminal remedies are illusory because women's complaints about such violence generally lack credibility (in part, it is argued, because of the pervasive misogynistic mindset engendered by pornography itself). Indeed, the criminal justice system has not been historically responsive to women's injuries through sexual violence, and there is no great reason to believe that women have fared better in civil actions against their sexual assailants. As the foregoing argument implicitly recognizes, however, this relative lack of success has not (for the most part) been due to any legal exemption for sexual violence. Rather, women have failed in such actions for reasons having less to do with the adequacy of existing law than with the persistent failure of those who enforce the law to recognize and credit injury in sexual contexts, particularly in the "private" context of the marital or "quasi-marital" relationship (Breines and Gordon, 1983).[11]

Frustration with the past might understandably provoke women to lobby for new laws that would both spell out in detail how women are injured and demand that women be deemed credible.[12] However, the legal system's historic inability to recognize sexual violence as a violation of law and its similar inability to credit women's experiences might as persuasively suggest that definitional efforts of this kind are futile (SchWeber and Feinman, 1985).[13] Rather, the responsiveness of the criminal justice system has increased because women have applied political pressure on existing institutions, although gains have been hard-won and sporadic.[14] Moreover, if one believes that the prevalence of pornography causes women to be perceived generally as less credible, then an alternate way to increase women's credibility is to decrease the availability of pornography. This is the explicit goal of the trafficking section, and one to which we will return later.

The ordinance also provides for a damage action against those persons involved in the production and distribution of pornography that causes a specific assault. While the legislative materials are not entirely clear on this point, it is fair to assume that the purpose of this section is to compensate those assault victims whose attackers lack the resources to pay for the injuries they cause and to deter the production and distribution of materials that might inspire an assault. While it is theoretically possible that these goals might be achieved through other mechanisms, it is extremely unlikely that existing law will support liability against producers and distributors for harms caused by consumers of pornography. There are several reasons why this is so.

First, there are immense problems involved in showing that pornographic materials cause, in any legally relevant way, the misconduct of an assailant. Saying that a rapist copied a method depicted in a photograph is a much different thing from saying that the photograph caused the rape. While there is no more metaphysical concept in the law of torts than causation, it is the case that an act cannot be considered the legal cause of an event if the event would have occurred without it. In the case of a rapist who watches a film before he rapes, for example, the legal question is whether the rape would have occurred at all without the film. It is doubtful that such a connection could often be convincingly proven.

When one moves from the immediate assailant to the producer or distributor of pornographic materials, the difficulties grow. There is a branch of torts concerned with compensating people injured by dangerous and defective products. It has been argued that pornographic materials are such products, that is, that they present such a high risk of causing injury that the producers of pornography should be required to pay compensation for the harm the materials cause as a cost of doing business. However, no court has accepted the argument that the contents of a book, film, or magazine are the kinds of "products" that the law was intended to cover.[15] Nor have the courts been receptive to the notion that producers or distributors of expressive materials have any duty to prevent viewers from duplicating the criminal or injurious acts the materials depict.

Were it possible to demonstrate that a specific piece of pornography was the legal cause of an injury, and to overcome the other obstacles to recovery sketched above, it is still likely that the producer or distributor of the pornography could contend that the First Amendment of the United States Constitution forbids the imposition of liability. In most instances, prevailing law under the First Amendment rejects the notion that speakers should be held liable for the acts of their listeners. This is true whether the defendant is *Hustler* magazine or Walt Disney;[16] the theory is that, generally, the Constitution guarantees every person the right to speak freely without worrying about how a listener will respond. This statement begs immediate qualification. For instance, the First Amendment does not protect abusive epithets ("fighting words") hurled to provoke a brawl. Nor does it protect exhortations to criminal activity, so long as the exhortations can be said to be both directed at producing imminent lawlessness and likely to do so *(Brandenburg v. Ohio)*.

Advocates of the civil-rights approach argue that pornography implicitly advocates assaultive behavior, that is, that pornography can be said to incite crime. The difficulty with this theory, however, is that the very form most pornography takes argues against the imposition of liability under the *Branden-*

burg standard. *Brandenburg* requires both that the speaker intend to provoke immediate violence or lawlessness and that such lawlessness be likely: the paradigmatic *Brandenburg* case involves a public speaker whipping a mob into a lawless frenzy. Pornography, which usually takes pictorial or written form, is often consumed by individuals in private. It often takes the form of fantasy. Because the form of pornography requires viewer mediation, often in a relatively detached and private setting, it would be extremely difficult to satisfy the *Brandenburg* requirement that violence be immediately threatened.[17]

It is possible to argue, however, that something less than the *Brandenburg* standard should apply when the speech in question is pornographic, and the issue is whether tort liability should be allowed. The Supreme Court has hinted broadly that pornography might be considered lower-value speech for purposes of evaluating the reasonableness of allowing state controls.[18] In addition, recent Supreme Court cases have engaged in a kind of balancing of interests that gauges, on the one hand, the First Amendment value of the challenged speech (is it on a matter of public concern, for instance, or simply a private matter) against the state's interest in providing a remedy for the harm the speech has caused *(Dun and Bradstreet, Inc. v. Greenmoss Builders, Inc.)*.[19] When the speech involved in a lawsuit is pornographic, and the state's interest is in compensating for physical injury, one could argue that the balance should be struck in favor of allowing lawsuits. Nonetheless, this argument has not yet generally been made in lawsuits against media defendants, and it remains to be seen whether the combination of the Supreme Court's increasingly complex use of balancing and its increasing tolerance of legislative efforts to combat the effects of pornography will combine to make it a viable argument in the future.

At present, then, supporters of the civil-rights approach who argue that existing law is inadequate to achieve the assault section's goal of assuring compensation to victims from the producers or distributors of pornography are generally correct. However, compensation was only one of the purposes of the assault section. The other was deterrence, an explicit concern of the trafficking section. We can return to possible methods of deterrence when we consider that section.

FORCING PORNOGRAPHY ON A PERSON

The ordinance does not define "forcing pornography on a person"; instead, it simply states that it is a discriminatory practice to force pornography on anyone "in any place of employment, in education, in a home, or in any public place" (Section 16–3 [g] [6]). Reference to the legislative materials reveals many of the practices that this section was designed to combat.

It is clear, for instance, that pornography is sometimes used to attempt to intimidate and harass women, especially those who are working in nontraditional jobs.[20] The use of pornography in this way is a violation of federal law. Title VII of the Civil Rights Act of 1964[21] prohibits discrimination in employment on account of sex, and the Supreme Court has recently held that Title VII can be violated by sexual harassment that creates a hostile or offensive working environment *(Meritor Savings Bank, FSB v. Vinson)*. A hostile-environment claim involves a showing that sexual harassment is "sufficiently severe or pervasive to alter the conditions of [the victim's] employment and create an abusive working environment."[22] While it is unlikely that Title VII could be used as a vehicle to purge the workplace of all offensive pictures,[23] one court has found that pornography was an integral part of a pattern of sexual harassment that violated Title VII *(Arnold v. City of Seminole)*.

It is also possible that some uses of pornography in the workplace could give rise to a cause of action in tort for the intentional or negligent infliction of emotional distress.[24] At least one court has so held in a case in which a woman attended a business meeting at which she was told an educational film would be shown. In fact, the film was "Deep Throat," and the woman was subjected not only to the film but also to the running sexual commentary of the defendant *(Young v. Stensrude)*.

Uses of pornography in the home are more problematic. Many women testified that they were uncomfortable with their husbands' use of pornography.[25] It is possible that some domestic uses of pornography could also be actionable as intentional infliction of emotional distress, although feelings of discomfort alone are not actionable. For instance, there was testimony by a worker at a shelter for abused women in Minneapolis that one woman had been tied to a chair in front of a television by her husband and forced to watch pornographic movies on videocassettes.[26] This kind of conduct seems clearly to be so outrageous as to be actionable as the intentional infliction of emotional distress.[27]

Finally, the section makes forcing pornography on a person in a public place actionable.[28] What constitutes forcing in a public place is not entirely clear from the legislative materials. One of the authors of the ordinance makes reference to the problems experienced by neighborhoods in which pornographic bookstores and theaters have concentrated (MacKinnon, 1985), although concentrations of these "adult uses" seem more properly a concern of the trafficking section.[29]

There are, however, several ways in which public displays of sexually graphic materials might be restricted. The most obvious is through the use of zoning laws to control the concentration of businesses that specialize in sexually oriented materials. Proponents of the civil-rights approach have argued that zoning laws are ineffective in controlling or decentralizing pornographic outlets because courts have often assumed that the effect of such zoning cannot be to reduce the total number of such businesses. In *Alexander v. City of Minneapolis*, for instance, a court upheld a finding of unconstitutionality for Minneapolis's zoning ordinance because there would remain too few legal sites available to accommodate the relocation of *all* the city's existing adult businesses. The Supreme Court's recent discussion of the use of zoning to regulate adult businesses makes it clear, however, that the question for courts should only be whether the zoning provisions "effectively deny" any opportunity for such businesses to exist *(City of Renton v. Playtime Theatres, Inc.)*. Asking whether access to sexually explicit materials has been effectively denied by a city's zoning laws is a far cry from asking, as the courts have in the past, whether a zoning regulation has a substantial impact on adult businesses. Moreover, the Court noted that a claim that a zoning ordinance amounts to a denial of access cannot be premised on the argument that alternative locations for adult businesses are in fact unavailable or would be commercially disastrous, and observed that the regulated businesses would have to fend for themselves in the real estate market. Finally, the Court stated that communities need not undertake extensive studies or produce new evidence documenting the secondary effects of adult businesses, so long as whatever evidence is used is believed by the local legislators to be relevant to the problems caused by adult businesses. By allowing cities to rely on the experiences of others and on studies that have already been conducted, the Court has reduced the costs associated with adopting zoning controls of sexually oriented businesses. Thus, the *Playtime Theatres* decision is likely to make zoning of sexually oriented businesses more attractive to cities, not only because it reduces the enactment costs but also because it lessens the chance that a zoning ordinance could be successfully challenged on constitutional grounds.

Laws that restrict the manner in which sexually explicit materials are displayed for sale could also address some of the concerns of the forcing section. Perhaps because the Supreme Court has long held that states have more leeway in regulating the distribution of sexually graphic materials to minors *(Ginsberg v. New York)*, most of the recent attempts to control the display of these materials have been justified by legislative concern about their effect on minors who might come in contact with them. These laws have usually defined materials that are to be considered obscene as to minors and have required that businesses that sell these materials either do so in segregated "adults only" sections or render the materials inaccessible to children by placing them in blinder racks or sealing them in plastic.

Display laws make adult access to sexual materials inconvenient, and businesses that offer materials covered by the laws often find that compliance is cumbersome and expensive. Because the laws inevitably involve some degree of interference with the unrestrained marketing of sexual materials, they have been challenged in court by retailers and distributors who argue that the laws violate the First Amendment *(M.S. News Co. v. Casado; Upper Midwest Booksellers Assoc. v. City of Minneapolis; American Booksellers Assoc., Inc. v. Virginia; American Booksellers Assoc., Inc. v. Webb; Tattered Cover, Inc. v. Tooley)*. The laws have met with varying degrees of judicial acceptance.[30] While several courts have held display provisions unconstitutional, they have done so for reasons that are unconvincing. Courts have held, for instance, that display laws are not constitutionally permissible regulations of the place and manner of expression because the laws are triggered by the content of the material *(American Booksellers Assoc., Inc. v. Virginia; American Booksellers Assoc., Inc. v. Webb)*. However, the Supreme Court's most recent discussions of permissible regulation of sexually explicit materials have made clear that regulations of the time, place, and manner of such expression should not be considered "content-based" (and therefore unconstitutional) if they are prompted by concern about the *effects* of the materials and not motivated by a desire of the legislators simply to suppress the speech *(Playtime Theatres)*. Likewise, the concern expressed by the courts that some adults would be deterred from purchasing the materials if they were required to enter an "adults only" bookstore or section is not constitutional in magnitude. *Playtime Theatres* and other recent zoning cases have dispelled the notion that any regulation that makes access to sexually explicit materials less convenient is for that reason alone constitutionally suspect.

Probably the most substantial of the claims made by those who challenge these laws has to do with the difficulty of complying with some of the display provisions. When the laws cover not only graphic pictorial sexual representations but also any graphic written representation, booksellers are required to know the contents of the hundreds, perhaps thousands, of books contained in their inventories. For purposes of meeting the concerns of the forcing section, however, it would be enough to prohibit the display of those materials that are graphically and pictorially pornographic. One of the concerns of the section was to protect minors (and others) from unwilling exposure to pornography in public places, a concern that seems only tangentially connected to exposure to written materials. It is certainly much easier to determine whether a book contains graphic pictorial representations than it is to read an entire book to determine whether it contains passages that might fall within the boundaries of the law. Moreover, most of the concern expressed by booksellers had to do with the possibility that large percentages of the inventories of even nonadult bookstores would be covered by display laws that include any book with graphic written descriptions of sex. While much of a modern bookstore's inventory might be salacious, it is certainly not the case that most novels for adults are illustrated.

Finally, limiting the reach of these laws to pictorial representations would meet another concern expressed by the courts: that there is no basis for the belief that the kind of contact minors have with sexually oriented materials in a bookstore harms them in any way. In fact, available psychological literature supports—perhaps more strongly than any other empirical claims of pornography opponents—the view that exposure to graphic pictorial representations of pornography is harmful to children (Hearings before the Subcommittee on Juvenile Justice, 1985).

With little effort, therefore, it is possible that display laws could be adapted to withstand constitutional challenge and to meet some of the concerns of the forcing section. Most of the aims of this section could, then, be addressd by existing law.

COERCION INTO PORNOGRAPHIC PERFORMANCE

According to the ordinance, "coercion into pornographic performance" is "coercing, intimidating or fraudulently inducing any person . . . into performing for pornography. . . ."[31] The ordinance allows an action for damages against the perpetrators of the coercion or fraud and all those involved in distributing the materials, and would eventually allow a court to issue an injunction to restrain the continued distribution of a coerced performance.

Much of the testimony underlying this section was given by Linda Marchiano, who as "Linda Lovelace" was forced by an abusive husband to make pornographic movies, including the spectacularly successful *Deep Throat* (Lovelace and McGrady, 1980). Linda Marchiano gives a particularly disturbing account of how one woman was coerced into pornography, but women's sexual portrayals or nude photographs can end up in pornography—or even simply on public display—in a number of ways. Pictures are taken surreptitiously,[32] or a woman consents to being photographed by her husband or boyfriend, and the photographs end up without her consent in the public view,[33] or the photographs or films are made through physical abuse and intimidation, and the woman loses control of them.[34] In these cases, the use of the photographs might be actionable in tort as invasion of privacy.

One's privacy can be invaded in at least four ways that tort law recognizes.[35] First, the law protects against unreasonable intrusions into the solitude of another.[36] Thus, the surreptitious or coerced photographing of a woman could be actionable under this branch of invasion of privacy.[37] Second, the law forbids giving unreasonable publicity to another's life or unreasonably publicizing private facts, if the facts made public would be offensive to the reasonable person.[38] Most, if not all, unauthorized publications of pornographic pictures of private individuals would qualify under this doctrine, as would most pictures with a sexual content.[39] Thus, a woman whose nude picture was stolen and submitted to *Hustler* magazine with a forged consent form sued under a theory of public disclosure of private facts when the magazine subsequently published the picture in its "Beaver Hunt" section *(Wood v. Hustler)*.[40] Third, it is an invasion of the right of privacy to place one in a "false light" in the public eye, that is, to represent someone in a manner that distorts the truth.[41] An actress who had posed nude for *Playboy* magazine brought an action against *Hustler* magazine for the publication of several of the photographs she had consented to have published in *Playboy* but not in *Hustler*. As is typical in these cases, the person who sold the photographs to *Hustler* forged a consent form, and *Hustler* made no effort to verify the form's validity. The actress claimed that the publication placed her in a false light in two ways: first, the copy used with the photos implied that she was a lesbian; second, the appearance of the photographs "suggest[ed] she [was] the kind of person willing to be shown naked in *Hustler*" *(Douglass v. Hustler Magazine, Inc.)*. The second claim, with which the court agreed, is potentially quite useful for such plaintiffs. The court reviewed the content of *Hustler* and found that the depiction of the actress in such a magazine was degrading, and that being depicted in voluntary association with a magazine with the editorial viewpoint of *Hustler*[42] did indeed place the plaintiff in a false light. One encouraging aspect of the *Douglass* case is that the court did not find the fact that Douglass had voluntarily posed for the photographs to be relevant to its analysis of her injury.

Finally, the law forbids the appropriation of a person's name or likeness for the benefit of another, as when a person's picture is used without authorization to advertise a product.[43] The actress in the aforementioned case against *Hustler* also prevailed before the jury on a claim under this branch of privacy law (more specifically, a species of it peculiar to those whose likenesses and names have some commercial value, known as the "right of publicity").

Tort actions against publications and other media defendants are limited by the First Amendment.[44] These limitations affect most seriously those models and actresses who fall within the Supreme Court's definition of "public figures." Where the plaintiff is a public figure, and the premise of the lawsuit is a tortious publication, the First Amendment requires that the plaintiff establish a higher level of fault on the defendant's part in order to recover than if the plaintiff were a private figure. The Supreme Court has thought this heightened standard of liability necessary in order to protect the press from the self-censorship that would presumably follow should the press be held liable on the same facts as individuals, and in order to protect society from the deleterious effects of this self-censorship.

Recent cases, however, have suggested that the possibility of impairing a legitimate privacy interest through the publication of sexually oriented materials or photographs is so obvious that this heightened level of fault can be established by the plaintiff's showing that the defendant either knew that it was acting without the plaintiff's authorization in publishing the offensive material or simply did not care whether it was acting with or without authorization *(Douglass v. Hustler Magazine, Inc.)*. As this lack of care appears to be the rule rather than the exception in pornographic publications (and would certainly be the case in any instance that would fall within the terms of the ordinance), the constitutional problems associated with public-figure tort actions should not defeat an otherwise valid case.[45] Moreover, the damage awards that can properly follow from proof of a media defendant's liability in tort actions such as right of privacy cases ought to act as a deterrent against the unauthorized use of sexual materials (the appeals court in the actress's case against *Hustler* suggested that punitive damages might properly be measured by the profits of the entire issue in which the unauthorized photos appeared).

TRAFFICKING IN PORNOGRAPHY

The ordinance defines "trafficking" as "the production, sale, exhibition, or distribution of pornography" (Section 16-3 [g] [4]). The provision exempts most uses of pornography in libraries, and states that it "shall not be construed to make isolated passages or parts actionable."[46] A complainant may file an action against the "perpetrator(s), maker(s), seller(s), exhibitor(s), or distributor(s)" (Section 17-6 [6]) of the pornographic material, and it is generally not a defense to an action under this (or other) sections of the ordinance that the defendants did not know or intend that the materials were pornographic.[47]

The trafficking provision is the section of the ordinance that is most closely tailored to the goal of eliminating pornography. In some ways it is the heart of the ordinance, for it reflects the view, explicated in the legislative findings accompanying the ordinance,[48] that decreasing the availability of pornography alone could improve the status of women. Since obscenity law is also concerned with eliminating certain sexually explicit images, the question arises whether obscenity law could perform the same function as the trafficking section of the ordinance, or at least eliminate the kinds of pornographic expression that are most closely linked with adverse effects.

Proponents of new legislative initiatives voice several objections to the notion that obscenity law could be useful in eradicating the kinds of images of concern to them. Their first objection is a pragmatic one: obscenity law, they claim, simply does not work, as evidenced by the fact that the pornography industry is a growing one.[49] However, the evidence is not that pornography laws do not work, but rather that they are systematically not enforced (Attorney General's Commission on Pornography, 1986).[50] If the reason such laws are not enforced is that they are exceedingly difficult to enforce, then the difference between nonenforcement and nonexistence would be a semantic one only. But the available evidence does not support a claim that enforcement of the laws is particularly onerous. A large number of witnesses involved in law enforcement testified before the Attorney General's Commission on Pornography that they did not find the constitutional standards imposed by the leading Supreme Court case on obscenity *(Miller v. California)* to be excessively uncertain as applied or interpreted. Moreover, two major cities that chose to make enforcement of obscenity law a priority—Atlanta and Cincinnati—were successful in virtually eliminating so-called hard-core pornographic materials (Attorney General's Commission, 1986, 365; Weaver, 1985).[51]

The second objection to the use of obscenity law is political and theoretical. Catharine MacKinnon (1984) voices this objection when she states, "Their obscenity is not our pornography." Because the focus of obscenity law is "prurience" and the (moral) standards of the community, rather than the view pornography espouses about the place of women in society, and because obscenity law has in the past been used for repressive purposes such as the suppression of birth-control information, advocates of the civil-rights approach have opposed its use to combat the availability of sexually explicit materials.

As mentioned earlier, the civil-rights approach is a radical approach to the issue of pornography because it stresses pornography's political content: male domination of women. Clearly, obscenity law is not at all about domination. However, much that is legally obscene *is,* as a casual perusal of the more provocative sections of the Attorney General's report demonstrates. While enforcement of obscenity law would not achieve a rethinking of the message of pornography, it would get rid of a lot of it, as Atlanta and Cincinnati discovered. Moreover, contemporary obscenity law is not particularly suited to the repressive purposes to which it has been put in the past, because it developed as a response to just those abuses. Finally, since obscenity law is explicitly informed by community standards *(Miller v. California),* and it is at least arguable that members of a community develop such standards through public debate about questions surrounding pornography, it is possible that those who share the view of the drafters of the Indianapolis ordinance can, through open discussion of those views, incorporate them into the community's understanding of its standards. At least in Indianapolis, the public prosecutor now speaks about the sexism engendered by pornography when discussing his emphasis on obscenity prosecutions.

BEYOND EXISTING LAW

I have tried to demonstrate in this discussion that there are legal tools available to combat most of the evils exposed in hearings on the adoption of civil-rights pornography ordinances. In order to accomplish this limited goal, I have had to take apart the theoretical construct that the civil-rights pornography movement assembled. But one of the achievements of that movement was the creation of that construct, the vision that perceived a connection among the various torts, crimes, and statutory violations I have described and the social practice of pornography. While I have attempted to show that the more ambitious aspects of the recent civil-rights ordinance cannot be achieved either through existing law or through legislation that is not constitutionally problematic, the effort to enact civil-rights ordinances brought public attention to the very real problems that pornography creates. Whatever the future of such legislation, the metaphorical power of the vision that inspired it has changed the way the law must think about pornography in the future.

NOTES

1. The Attorney General's Commission on Pornography, *Final Report,* July 1986, concludes that there is a causal relationship between sexually explicit violent materials and increases in aggression toward women. The *Report* also concluded, with "somewhat less confidence," that nonviolent materials depicting domination, submission, or humiliation also increased aggressive attitudes toward women. Finally, some commission members believed that even nonviolent, nondegrading, sexually explicit materials are harmful (pp. 323–29). Cf. Special Committee on Pornography and Prostitution in Canada, 1985, 99:

> Although the Committee was frequently told that research studies clearly indicate that harms to society and to individuals were associated with the availability and use of pornography, we have had to conclude, very reluctantly, that the available research is of very limited use in addressing these questions. [T]he Committee is not prepared to state, *solely on the basis of the research and evidence it has seen,* that pornography is a significant causal factor in the commission of some forms of violent crime, in the sexual abuse of children, or in the disintegration of communities and society.

Nonetheless, the committee recommended that pornography portraying sexually violent behavior be proscribed (p. 277).

2. On December 30, 1983, the Minneapolis City Council enacted an ordinance declaring pornography a civil rights violation (see Ordinance Amending Title 7, Chs. 139 and

141, Minneapolis Code of Ordinances Relating to Civil Rights), but the ordinance was subsequently vetoed by the mayor, who expressed doubts about its constitutionality. Indianapolis enacted essentially the same ordinance in 1984. See Indianapolis, Ind., City-County General Ordinance 24 (Apr. 23, 1984), as amended by City-County General Ordinance 35 (June 11, 1984). Los Angeles considered the adoption of a modified version of the Indianapolis ordinance; the ordinance did not pass. Proponents of new legislation have also lobbied before Congress. See Hearings before the Subcommittee on Juvenile Justice of the Committee of the Judiciary of the U.S. Senate (1984).

3. For a persuasive argument that the court was correct, see Stone, 1986.

4. See Brief of Linda Marchiano and the Estate of Dorothy Stratten, Amici Curiae in Support of Appellant, *American Booksellers Association v. Hudnut*, 1985.

5. The other elements are: (1) women are presented as sexual objects who enjoy pain or humiliation; or (2) women are presented as sexual objects who experience sexual pleasure in being raped; or (3) women are presented as sexual objects tied up or cut up or mutilated or bruised or physically hurt, or as dismembered or truncated or fragmented or severed into body parts; or (4) women are presented as being penetrated by objects or animals; or (5) women are presented in scenarios of degradation, injury, abasement, torture, shown as filthy or inferior, bleeding, bruised, or hurt in a context that makes these conditions sexual; or (6) women are presented as sexual objects for domination, conquest, violation, exploitation, possession, or use, or through postures or positions of servility or submission or display. Indianapolis City-County Code Section 16-3(q).

6. Records of hearings in Indianapolis are not readily available. However, when the ordinance was challenged in court, the briefs in its support made reference to the hearings before the Minneapolis City Council in support of the ordinance there. The records of these hearings are widely available, and it is to these hearings that I shall make reference.

7. The authors of the legislation have noted that the problem of proving causation under this section are great. See Testimony of MacKinnon, Hearings before the Subcommittee on Juvenile Justice (1984). Others have noted that a pornography viewer's "wilful decision to imitate the image [could be] found to be an intervening, superseding cause of the harm," thereby precluding relief to a plaintiff under generally accepted notions of causation in tort law. Duggan, Hunter, and Vance, 1985.

8. One of the greatest problems in the past has been that these kinds of assaults frequently occur in domestic settings. Much of the testimony concerning assault modeled on particular pornography has focused on husbands' assaults on their wives. See, e.g., Hearings on Ordinances to Add Pornography as Discrimination against Women, 1983, Session II, Dec. 12, 1983, Testimony of Ms. P. Until relatively recently, the doctrine of interspousal tort immunity would have barred most civil actions against abusive husbands. This immunity has generally been abrogated, and even in the states in which it is maintained, it is often inapplicable to intentional torts. See Harper, 1986, section 8.10; Keaton, 1985, 902–903, citing *Lusby v. Lusby,* 1978 (wife raped and beaten); *Davis v. Bostick,* 1978 (intentional infliction of emotional distress).

9. Several women who testified at the Minneapolis Hearings described their rapes by men who made reference to pornography. See, e.g., Hearings on Ordinances to Add Pornography, 1983, Testimony of Ms. W., Session III, Dec. 13, 1983 (rape); Testimony of Cheryl Champion, Session III (kidnapping); Testimony of Donna Dunn, Session III (battery).

10. Indeed, pornography has often been used as evidence in criminal prosecutions. See MacKinnon, 1985, 46, n. 107 (collecting cases). Unfortunately, though much of the abuse discussed in the hearings occurred in the home, it is still not a criminal offense for a man to rape his wife in a number of states. See Note, 1986, n. 28 (listing state statutes and arguing that the marital rape exception is unconstitutional under the equal protection clause).

11. The literature on inadequate police and prosecutorial response to violence in the home is voluminous. For a critical evaluation of this literature, see Breines and Gordon, 1983.

12. The ordinance attempts to do the latter in the coercion section, by stating that it is not a defense to a charge of coercion that the person involved "consented to a use of the performance that was changed to pornography," "appeared to cooperate actively," or "signed a contract, or made statements affirming a willingness to cooperate in the production of pornography." Section 16-3(g)(5) (A) (VIII)–(XII).

13. Moreover, I find it difficult to justify a special cause of action for only those women whose assailants invoked pornography in some manner, in part because I think that it suggests that these women are somehow more worthy than other assault victims. This is not a view I ascribe in any way to the drafters of the ordinance; I merely believe that it is a negative implication of the emphasis on one sort of victim.

14. See SchWeber and Feinman, 1985, for studies on the mixed effects of legislation addressing specific issues of sexual violence. Perhaps surprisingly, law enforcement personnel have been among the most vocal in expressing the belief that pornography plays a causal role in the commission of sexual crimes. See Attorney General's Commission on Pornography, 1986.

15. See *Herceg v. Hustler Magazine, Inc.*, 1983 (contents of magazine article not "product" within meaning of sec. 402A of the Restatement [Second] of Torts); *Cardozo v. True*, 1977 (implied warranty under the Uniform Commercial Code limited to physical properties of books, not contents).

16. See *Herceg v. Hustler*, 1983 (plaintiffs' decedent accidentally killed while trying "autoerotic asphyxiation" described in *Hustler* magazine); *Walt Disney Productions, Inc. v. Shannon*, 1981 (injury resulting from attempt to reproduce sound effect from Mickey Mouse show).

17. In fact, a computer search of cases citing *Brandenburg* failed to reveal any cases in which a court found that written materials met the *Brandenburg* standard. While no court has flatly stated that it would be impossible for a publication or a broadcast to do so, several courts have rejected such arguments on First Amendment grounds. See *Olivia N. v. National Broadcasting Co.*, 1981, in which a minor plaintiff who had been sexually assaulted by several minors in a manner portrayed in a television movie entitled "Born Innocent" argued that NBC should be liable for imitation provoked by the broadcast. The court held that *Brandenburg* could not be satisfied because the broadcast did not advocate violence, nor could it be said that such violence was a likely result of the broadcast. More recently, an appellate court reversed a jury's verdict in favor of a mother who alleged that *Hustler* magazine's publication of an article explaining how to perform autoerotic asphyxiation—an article found at the feet of her dead son, who had attempted to duplicate the practice—amounted to incitement under *Brandenburg*. *Herceg v. Hustler Magazine, Inc.*, 1987. The court questioned whether *Brandenburg's* analysis would ever be an appropriate basis for the imposition of liability on written materials.

18. One might ask why the First Amendment, which prevents the government from unreasonably interfering with freedom of speech, should have any application when the context is a private lawsuit between an injured individual and a producer or distributor of pornography. The answer the Supreme Court has given is that the state is sufficiently involved, by providing both the legal mechanism that threatens speech (a tort action, for instance) and the judicial forum in which the lawsuit is prosecuted, to trigger the protections of the First Amendment.

19. For a judicial attempt to engage in this kind of balancing in the context of a tort suit against a pornographic magazine, see the dissent in *Herceg v. Hustler Magazine, Inc.*, 1987 (tort action against *Hustler* magazine to recover for child's death should be allowed; *Hustler* is low-value speech unlikely to be deterred by the possibility of private lawsuits, and policy of compensating for wrongful death is important state interest).

20. A woman who worked as a plumber testified that the walls of the lunch shacks at one job were papered with explicit pictures of naked women. When she removed the pictures, she was met with hostility, and the pictures were replaced. She testified that she believed the men hoped to run her off the job by subjecting her to pornographic pictures.

See Hearings on Ordinances to Add Pornography, 1983, Testimony of Ms. R., Session II, Dec. 12, 1983. See also Attorney General's Commission on Pornography, 1986, 826 (telephone repairwoman).

21. 42 U.S.C. sec. 2000e et seq. The law provides, in pertinent part: "It shall be an unlawful employment practice for an employer . . . to fail to refuse to hire or to discharge any individual, or otherwise to discriminate against any individual with respect to . . . compensation, terms, conditions, or privileges of employment, because of such individual's . . . sex.

22. *Meritor Savings Bank, FSB v. Vinson*, 1986, 4706 (quoting *Henson v. Dundee*, 682 F.2d 897, 904 [11th Cir. 1982]).

23. See *Rabidue v. Osceola Refining Co.*, 1984 (finding that "vulgar" language of a coworker and picures of "nude or partially clad women" displayed in coworkers' offices had "de minimis" effect on work environment). The *Rabidue* court viewed the claim that sexual harassment itself could violate Title VII as fairly novel. Courts should become more hospitable to such claims after the *Meritor* case.

24. For a description of the requirements of this tort, see generally Keeton et al., 1985, 54–66.

25. See Hearings on Ordinances to Add Pornography, 1983, Testimony of Ms. P., Session II, Dec. 12, 1983. ("During the second year of our marriage, he started reading more and more pornography. He started out reading *Playboy* and started picking up magazines like *Penthouse* and *Forum*, and as I would come home . . . from work and fix dinner, he would read excerpts from the magazines. Some of them were articles and some of them were letters to the editor, ranging from group sex, wife swapping, anal intercourse and bondage, to mention a few. I was really repulsed at the things he was reading me and I was really in disbelief.")

26. Hearings on Ordinances to Add Pornography, 1983, Testimony of Wanda Richardson, Session III, p. 68.

27. As well as false imprisonment, battery, and possibly assault.

28. The ordinance also mentions forcing pornography on a person in education. Pornography is sometimes used in medical schools to "desensitize" doctors (MacKinnon, 1985). For a case upholding the dismissal of a public school teacher for allowing the use of pornography in his class to intimidate a female student, see *Ross v. Robb*, 1983.

29. In zoning ordinances, bookstores and theaters that carry primarily sexually graphic materials are known rather euphemistically as "adult uses."

30. The Supreme Court has noted probable jurisdiction in *American Booksellers Association, Inc. v. Virginia* and so will ultimately resolve the split that currently exists over the constitutionality of these measures. See 55 U.S.L.W. 3569 (Feb. 23, 1987).

31. Indianapolis ordinance, Section 16-3(g)(5). The ordinance also states that "the injury from one coercion into pornography may date from any appearance or sale of any product(s) of such performance." The purpose of this section is to abrogate the so-called "single publication rule, under which an entire edition of a newspaper, magazine, or book is treated as only one publication. . . ." Keeton et al., 1985, 800. The advantage of abrogating the rule is that in certain cases, as where a film remains in circulation for years after its initial release, a plaintiff would not be barred by statutes of limitation from bringing a coercion action involving the material under the ordinance. Potential snares for plaintiffs under the rule have been substantially lessened by a recent Supreme Court ruling in *Keeton v. Hustler Magazine, Inc.*, in which the Court held that the First Amendment imposed no independent limitation on a state's assertion of jurisdiction over a media defendant. The effect of the ruling was to allow the plaintiff to bring a libel action in the only state in which the statute of limitations had not run out.

32. See *Cohen v. Herbal Concepts*, 1984 (nude photograph of woman and daughter used in advertisement).

33. See *Ashby v. Hustler Magazine, Inc.*, 1986 (nude photographs stolen); *Barrows v. Rozansky*, 1985 (granting preliminary injunction to Sydney Barrows, the so-called May-

flower Madam, against publication of eleven-year-old nude photographs taken by her ex-lover); *McCabe v. Village Voice, Inc.*, 1982 (woman consented to being photographed nude in her bathtub; picture ended up in the "Centerfold" section of a newspaper with a circulation of 144,000); *Myers v. U.S. Camera Publishing Corp.*, 1957 (model consented to nude photographs on condition she could not be identified; published without consent in *U.S. Camera Annual*).

34. See Hearings on Ordinances to Add Pornography, 1983.

35. See generally, Keeton et al., 1985, 849–69.

36. Restatement (Second) of Torts, Section 652B.

37. Sometimes the law recognizes that privacy can be invaded even in a public place. See *Daily Times Democrat v. Graham*, 276 Ala. 380, 162 So.2d 474 (1964) (woman photographed with her dress blown up in a funhouse).

38. See Restatement (Second) of Torts, Sec. 652D, Keeton et al., 1985, 856–59.

39. *Garner v. Triangle Publications*, 1951 (details of sexual relationship); *McCabe v. Village Voice, Inc.*, 1982 (publication without permission of plaintiff nude in a bathtub).

40. *Wood v. Hustler Magazine, Inc.*, 1984. See also *Braun v. Flynt*, 1984 (woman whose job in an amusement park included feeding "Ralph the Diving Pig" while treading water, recovered for publication of a photograph of her on the job; the picture appeared in *Chic* magazine, another publication owned by Larry Flynt, publisher of *Hustler*). As one judge has noted, "this little niche of the law of privacy is dominated by Larry Flynt's publications." *Douglass v. Hustler Magazine, Inc.*, 1985.

41. See Restatement (Second) of Torts, Section 652E.

42. The court noted that one of *Hustler*'s themes is " 'irreverence,' which has the practical meaning in *Hustler* of hostility to or contempt for racial, ethnic, and religious minorities."

43. See Keeton et al., 1985, 851–54.

44. The law of defamation, and to some extent invasion of privacy, has been increasingly constitutionalized in recent years. In *New York Times Co. v. Sullivan*, 1964, the Supreme Court held that a public official could not recover for a defamatory publication unless he proved that the defendant had actual knowledge of the falsity of the publication or acted in reckless disregard of its truth or falsity ("actual malice"). The requirement that plaintiffs show actual malice in order to recover was later extended to any public figure. The Supreme Court later expanded the reach of the actual malice rule to include plaintiffs in "false light" actions. *Time, Inc. v. Hill*, 1967. The current scope of the actual malice rule is in some doubt. In *Gertz v. Robert Welch, Inc.*, 1974, the Court held that the requirement that a plaintiff show actual malice in order to succeed in a defamation action was limited to public figures; private plaintiffs still had to establish some degree of fault in the defendant's attention to truth or falsity, if only that the defendant had been negligent. Most plaintiffs in privacy actions involving sexual materials have had little difficulty establishing negligence in the handling of consent forms. See *Wood v. Hustler Magazine, Inc.*, 1984. Moreover, in order to collect punitive or presumed damages, the plaintiff still had to establish actual malice.

To complicate matters further, states are free to require more than the constitutional minima of any plaintiff who seeks to establish media tort liability.

45. However, it should be noted that states may establish higher levels of fault than the Constitution requires. Thus, in some states, private-figure plaintiffs are required to meet the same standards as are public-figure plaintiffs. See, e.g., *Ashby v. Hustler Magazine, Inc.*, 1986.

46. The exemption for materials that are pornographic only in isolated passages or parts was apparently a concession to the perceived demands of current law under the First Amendment. One of the authors of the ordinance has stated, "[I]f a woman is subjected, why should it matter if the work has other value?" (MacKinnon, 1985).

47. A complainant under this section must prove that the defendants knew the material was pornographic in order to obtain damages, Section 16-3(g)(8). Moreover, it is a

defense to an action under this section that the materials are pornographic only by virtue of presenting women as sexual objects "for domination, conquest, violation, exploitation, possession, or use, or through postures of submission or display" in accordance with Section 16-3(q)(6).

48. Indianapolis Ordinance, Section 16-1(a)(2), Findings of the City-County Council, states:

Pornography is a discriminatory practice based on sex which denies women equal opportunities in society. Pornography is central in creating and maintaining sex as a basis for discrimination. Pornography is the systematic practice of exploitation and subordination based on sex which differentially harms women. The bigotry and contempt it promotes, with the acts of aggression it fosters, harm women's opportunities for equality of rights in employment, education, access to and use of public accommodations, and the acquisition of real property; promote rape, battery, child abuse, kidnapping and prostitution and inhibit just enforcement of laws against such acts; and contribute significantly to restricting women in particular from full exercise of citizenship and participation in public life, including in neighborhoods.

49. See, e.g., Brief of Amici Curiae Women Against Pornography et al., *American Booksellers Assoc., Inc. v. Hudnut,* #84-3147 (Court of Appeals for the Seventh Circuit) at 18–19.

50. The *Report* of the Attorney General's Commission states: "The laws of the United States and of almost every state make criminal the sale, distribution, or exhibition of material defined as obscene. . . . The enormous differences among states and among other geographic areas in obscenity law enforcement are due not to differences in the laws as written, but to differences in how, how vigorously, and how often those laws are enforced" (p. 364, footnote omitted).

51. Weaver was an assistant prosecutor in Atlanta and states that in Atlanta, "all hard-core pornography outlets were closed in 1981—the few that reopened closed again in 1984—primarily as a result of the systematic prosecution of lower-level employees, local managers, and local corporations." Weaver's experience thus contradicts another objection voiced by those who find obscenity laws ineffective, the claim that effective enforcement is possible only on a national level.

REFERENCES

Books, Periodicals, and Reports

American Law Institute (1981). *The Restatement (Second) of the Law of Torts.* St. Paul, Minn.: American Law Institute Publications.

Attorney General's Commission on Pornography (1986). *Final Report.* Washington, D.C.: U.S. Government Printing Office.

Breines, W., and Gordon, L. (1983). "The New Scholarship on Family Violence." *Signs* 8:490–531.

Brest, P., and Vandenberg, A. (1987). "Politics, Feminism, and the Constitution: The Antipornography Movement in Minneapolis." *Stanford Law Review* 39:607–61.

Duggan, L.; Hunter, N.; and Vance, C. (1985). "False Promises." In *Women Against Censorship,* ed. V. Burstyn. Vancouver and Toronto: Douglas & McIntyre.

Dworkin, A. (1981). *Pornography: Men Possessing Women.* New York: Putnam.

Harper, F.; James, F.; and Gray, O. (1986). *The Law of Torts.* Boston: Little, Brown.

Hearings before the subcommittee on Juvenile Justice of the Committee of the Judiciary of the U.S. Senate, 98th Cong., 2d Sess. (1984). *Effect of Pornography on Women and Children*. Washington, D.C.: U.S. Government Printing Office.

Hearings on Ordinances to Add Pornography as Discrimination against Women (1983). *Proceedings before the Minneapolis City Council Government Operations Committee*. Minneapolis: Organizing Against Pornography: A Resource Center.

Keeton, W.; Dobbs, D.; Keaton, R.; and Owen, D. (1985). *The Law of Torts*. 5th ed. St. Paul, Minn.: West Publishing Co.

Layman, W. (1987). "Violent Pornography and the Obscenity Doctrine: The Road Not Taken." *Georgetown Law Journal* 75:1475–1508.

Lovelace, L., and McGrady, M. (1980). *Ordeal*. Secaucus, N.J.: Citadel Press.

Lynn, B. (1986). " 'Civil Rights' Ordinances and the Attorney General's Commission on Pornography: New Developments in Pornography Regulation." *Harvard Civil Rights– Civil Liberties Law Review* 21:27–125.

MacKinnon, C. (1984). "Not a Moral Issue." *Yale Law & Policy Review*, 2:321–45.

———(1985). "Pornography, Civil Rights, and Speech." *Harvard Civil Rights–Civil Liberties Law Review* 20:1–70.

Note. (1986). "To Have and To Hold: The Marital Rape Exception and the Fourteenth Amendment." *Harvard Law Review* 99:1255–73.

SchWeber, L., and Feinman, C., eds. (1985). *Criminal Justice, Politics and Women: The Aftermath of Legally-Mandated Change*. New York: Haworth Press.

Spahn, E. (1984–85). "On Sex and Violence." *New England Law Review* 20:629–647.

Special Committee on Pornography and Prostitution. (1985). *Pornography and Prostitution in Canada*. Ottawa: Canadian Govt. Printing Centre.

Stone, G. (1986). "Comment: Anti-Pornography Legislation as Viewpoint Discrimination." *Harvard Journal of Law and Public Policy* 9:461–80.

Weaver, G. (1985). *Handbook on the Prosecution of Obscenity Cases*. New York: National Obscenity Law Center.

Cases

United States Supreme Court

Meritor Savings Bank, FSB v. Vinson, 54 U.S.L.W. 4703 (June 17, 1986).

City of Renton v. Playtime Theatres, Inc., 106 S.Ct. 925, 54 U.S.L.W. 4160 (Feb. 25, 1986).

Keeton v. Hustler Magazine, Inc., 465 U.S. 770 (1984).

Gertz v. Robert Welch, Inc., 418 U.S. 323 (1974).

Ginsberg v. New York, 390 U.S. 629 (1968).

Miller v. California, 413 U.S. 15 (1973).

Brandenburg v. Ohio, 395 U.S. 444 (1969).

Time, Inc. v. Hill, 385 U.S. 534 (1967).

New York Times v. Sullivan, 376 U.S. 254 (1964).

Lower Federal Courts

Ashby v. Hustler Magazine, Inc., 802 F.2d 856 (6th Cir. 1986).

American Booksellers Assoc., Inc. v. Virginia, 802 F.2d 691 (4th Cir. 1986), *prob. juris. noted*, 55 U.S.L.W. 3569 (Feb. 22, 1987).

American Booksellers Association, Inc. v. Hudnut, 771 F.2d 323 (7th Cir. 1985), *aff'd mem.*, 54 U.S.L.W. 3560 (Feb. 24, 1986).

Douglass v. Hustler Magazine, Inc., 769 F.2d 1128 (7th Cir. 1985), *cert. denied*, 106 S.Ct. 1489 (1986).

Upper Midwest Booksellers Assn., Inc. v. City of Minneapolis, 1780 F.2d 1389 (8th Cir. 1985).

Wood v. Hustler Magazine, Inc., 736 F.2d 1084 (5th Cir. 1984), *cert. denied*, 469 U.S. 1107 (1985).

Braun v. Flynt, 726 F.2d 245 (5th Cir. 1984).

M.S. News Co. v. Casado, 721 F.2d 1281 (10th Cir. 1983).

Alexander v. City of Minneapolis, 698 F.2d 936 (8th Cir. 1983).

American Booksellers Assoc., Inc. v. Webb, 643 F. Supp. 1546 (N.D. Ga. 1986).

Arnold v. City of Seminole, 614 F. Supp. 853 (D. Okla. 1985).

Rabidue v. Osceola Refining Co., 584 F. Supp. 419 (E.D. Mich. 1984), *aff'd,* 805 F.2d
611 (6th Cir. 1986), *cert. denied,* 107 S.Ct. 1983 (1987).

Herceg v. Hustler Magazine, Inc., 565 F. Supp. 802 (S.D. Tex. 1983), *aff'd,* 814 F.2d
1017 (5th Cir. 1987).

McCabe v. Village Voice, Inc., 550 F. Supp. 525 (E.D. Pa. 1982).

Garner v. Triangle Publications, 97 F. Supp. 546 (S.D.N.Y. 1951).

State Courts

Tattered Cover, Inc. v. Tooley, 696 P.2d 780 (S.C.Colo. 1985).

Barrows v. Rozansky, 111 A.D 2d 105, 489 N.Y.S. 481 (1985).

Cohen v. Herbal Concepts, Inc., 100 A.D. 2d 175, 473 N.Y.S. 2d 426 (1984).

Young v. Stensrude, 664 S.W.2d 257 (Mo. App. 1984).

Ross v. Robb, 662 S.W. 2d 257 (Mo. App. 1983).

Olivia N. v. National Broadcasting Co., 126 Cal. App. 3d 488 (1981).

Walt Disney Productions, Inc. v. Shannon, 158 Ga. App. 508, 281 S.E. 2d 648 (1981).

Davis v. Bostick, 282 Or. 667, 580 P.2d 544 (1978).

Lusby v. Lusby, 283 Md. 334, 390 A.2d 77 (1978).

Cardozo v. True, 242 So.2d 1053 (Fla. Dist. Ct. App. 1977).

Daily Times Democrat v. Graham, 276 Ala. 380, 162 So.2d 474 (1964).

Myers v. U.S. Camera Publishing Corp., 167 N.Y.S. 2d 771 (City Ct. 1957).

Statutes and Ordinances

Title VII of the Civil Rights Act of 1964, codified at 42 U.S.C. sec. 2000e et. seq.

Indianapolis, Indiana, City-County General Ordinance Numbers 24 and 35, codified at
Code of Indianapolis and Marion County Indiana, Chap. 16, Sections 16-1 et seq.

10

Fetishism and Hard Core

Marx, Freud, and the "Money Shot"

LINDA WILLIAMS

> There are those who believe that the come shot, or, as
> some refer to it, 'the money shot,' is the most important
> element in the movie and that everything else (if neces-
> sary) should be sacrificed at its expense. Of course, this
> depends on the outlook of the producer, but one thing is
> for sure: if you don't have the come shots, you don't
> have a porno picture. Plan on at least ten separate come
> shots . . . ten is enough to allow some freedom of
> choice.
>
> —Stephen Ziplow, *The Filmmaker's
> Guide to Pornography* (1977, 34)

Stephen Ziplow's advice to the frugal pornographer asserts what had by 1977 become the *sine qua non* of the hard-core film genre: the visual spectacle of penile ejaculation as the ultimate climax—the sense of an ending—for each of the heterosexual genital engagements figured in the expanded narrative of the now talking, now color, now quasi-legal pornographic feature. Where the earlier short, silent stag films occasionally included spectacles of external ejaculation— sometimes inadvertently—it was not until the rise of the hard-core feature-length narrative in the early seventies that the "money shot" took on the narrative function of signaling the climax of a genital event. Previously, in the primitive stag film, hard-core sequences tended to be organized as discontinuous, not entirely narrative, moments of genital show offered up in direct discourse to the stag spectator.[1]

There is much that can be said about the distinction between the stag and the feature-length narrative phases of the hard-core film genre. Although both forms are currently in circulation—present-day equivalents of the stag film can still be found in the film or video "loops" on display in private booths in "Adult" arcades—each exemplifies a particular historical phase in the cinematic hard core.[2] The silent, illegally made and exhibited single-reel stag film—or blue movie—began with the invention of cinema itself. Though it flourished during the twenties and thirties in the United States, it nevertheless continued as the dominant form of hard-core film until legal feature-length "exploitation" films began to encroach upon its subject matter and audiences in the early sixties.

Exploitation pictures capitalized on elements forbidden in mainstream cinema—usually nudity and sex—and packaged them into quickly and cheaply made feature-length narratives publicly exhibited in legitimate, but often not very respectable, movie houses. Strictly speaking, these were not hard-core films. They are important, however, in the evolution toward feature-length hard-core pornography because, in the aftermath of several Supreme Court decisions of the late sixties, the exploitation route of exhibition became the testing ground and ultimate outlet for hard-core material that had once been the exclusive province of the illegal stags.

But before stag and exploitation film merged into the new feature-length pornos, complete with sound, color, and hour-long-plus narratives, another cinematic tradition contributed to the transition. The first films to show hard-core material in public theaters were documentaries about Denmark and its then recent legalization of mass-produced forms of visual pornography: *Sexual Freedom in Denmark* (John Lamb, 1970) and *Censorship in Denmark: A New Approach* (De Renzy, 1970). Both films took immediate and clever advantage of the "redeeming social value" clause of 1966 Supreme Court rulings. Purporting to be serious exposés of the new Danish permissiveness, the films reported upon the Danish pornography industry. *Censorship in Denmark,* for example, documents a live nightclub "lesbian" sex act entitled "Olga and Her Sex Circus" and the filming of a Danish hard-core film. In both instances, the audience of the documentary film sees precisely what the audience of the live sex act and the pornographic film saw (Gordon, 1980, 118).

Audiences who might never have permitted themselves to see either Olga on stage or a pornographic film could justify the experience if it were made part of a larger quest for knowledge about the sexual activities of a different culture. The new wave of visual pornography of the late sixties and early seventies was thus not simply a celebration of "free" sex representative of the American sexual revolution. Rather, it was linked, as this revolution was itself linked, to a quest for greater knowledge about sexuality.

It is of course easy to make light of the sincerity of such a quest. Certainly films with titles like *Case Histories from Kraft-Ebbing* (Dakota Bros., 1971), compilation films of the history of the blue movie,[3] "exposés" of massage parlours,[4] or a behind-the-scenes "report" on an exploitation-film director[5] could hardly be taken seriously as advancing scientific knowledge of sexual practices. Yet these early titles suggest the aptness of Michel Foucault's argument that all forms of the modern discourse of sexuality have been marked by an intensification of scientific, truth-confessing elements, which he labels *scientia sexualis* (Foucault, 1978, 57–58).

In the transition from illicit stag film to the new legal and more pervasive hard core in such popular films of the early seventies as *Behind the Green Door* and *Deep Throat* (both 1972), a scientific "discourse of sexuality" purporting to elicit a confession of further "truths" of sex plays a major role. Whereas the stag film had been content to show its almost exclusively male audiences discontinuous moments of genital activity, the new narrative pornos organize this activity into complete dramas of arousal, excitement, climax, and satisfaction. In these extended narratives, increasingly mixed-gender audiences begin to identify with characters whose sexual pleasures are structured as narrative events rather than spectacles of genital show.

A key feature of this transition is the increased commodification and fetishization of sexual pleasures now packaged in a sixty-minute-plus narrative form. Although there are many ways of approaching the nature of this new form, I would like to concentrate here on the contrast between the characteristic shots with which each of the two types of film is likely to end its hard-core sequence. These shots are the "meat shot" of the stag film and the "money shot" of the feature-length porno.

While the stag film is content to represent the ultimate pleasure of sex in the close-up of genital penetration—in what the *Filmmaker's Guide to Pornography* would later call the "meat shot"—the feature-length hard-core film of the early seventies seems to demand a new level of "truth," signified by the emergence of a new convention in the body's confession of pleasure. The visible, external ejaculation of the penis in the "money shot" is that convention. Although the feature-length porno includes a great many "meat shots" in many of its hard-core sequences, it rarely ends these sequences with the mere evidence of genital penetration. Now it must have visual proof of the involuntary confession of pleasure that penetration obscures. The stakes of visibility have been escalated to include the precise narrative moment of (male) orgasm.

With the "money shot" we thus appear to arrive at what the cinematic will-to-knowledge had been relentlessly pursuing ever since photographer Eadweard Muybridge first threw the image of naked moving bodies on the screen of his lecture hall: the perceptual visual evidence of the mechanical "truth" of body pleasure caught in involuntary spasm; the ultimate and uncontrollable—ultimate *because* uncontrollable—confession of the body's pleasure in the climax of orgasm.

But on the other hand, this confirming close-up of what is after all only *male* orgasm, this ultimate confessional moment of "truth," might also be seen as the very limit of the visual representation of sexual pleasure. For to show the quantifiable, material "truth" of his pleasure, the male performer in a feature-length pornographic film must withdraw from any tactile connection with the genitals or mouth of the woman so that the "spending" of his semen is visible. For this the male pornographic performer is especially well paid, hence at least one source of the shot's name.

With the institution of this convention, viewers are asked to believe that the sexual performers within the film shift from a form of tactile to a form of visual pleasure at the crucial moment of the male's orgasm. It is a common conceit of much early seventies hard-core pornography that the woman prefers the sight of the ejaculating penis or the external touch of the semen to the thrust of the penis inside her. She will frequently call for the "money shot" in the familiar "dirty talk" of the newly voiced genre; she will say, for example, that she wants the man to "come all over her face," that she wants to see his semen come out of his "big hard cock," or to feel it spurt on various parts of her body. Yet at the same time, it is always quite evident that this spectacle is not really for her eyes. She may even close her eyes if the man comes on her face, and she cannot possibly see the ejaculate when he comes, as he frequently does, on her buttocks or the small of her back.

The man, on the other hand, almost always sees the "money shot"; it is clearly intended for his eyes and the eyes of the viewer. The "money shot" is thus an obvious perversion—in the literal sense of the term as a swerving away from more direct forms of genital engagement[6]—of the tactile sexual connection, replacing the relation between the performers with the more solitary (and literally disconnected) visual pleasure of the male performer and the male viewer.

Perhaps even more perverse, at least to the female viewer, is the genre's insistence that this visual confession of a solitary male "truth" coincides with the orgasmic bliss of the female. For in this case the representation of her pleasure can be said, more than his, to have been displaced onto substitute objects. Thus for the woman more than for the man, the "money shot" functions as a fetish substitute for the reality of a male-female sexual connection.

But perversion is both a very general and a very relative term. It is also a term that feminists have argued vehemently about, often using it as a blanket social and psychological epithet to describe all that is aggressive, unfeeling, objectifying, fragmented, and reified about phallically oriented heterosexuality. Indeed, as Jane Gallop has noted, there has been a general tendency within feminism to view all forms of perversion as symptoms of male sexuality and all forms of heterosexuality as tainted by perversion. In this sense, Gallop argues, many feminists end up reversing the very notion of norm and perversion to say that normal feminist sexuality is that of the lesbian—an egalitarian and tender sexuality of the "whole person"—and that heterosexuality, the ostensible norm, is actually perverse (Gallop, 1985, 13, 17).

Gallop argues that this reversal could be viewed as a failure to embrace the idea of perversion at the very moment when such an embrace might have some liberating potential for women. Abortion, contraception, lesbianism, and the feminist sexology that locates the primary source of sexual pleasure in the clitoris can all be viewed as potentially liberating "perversions" of a supposedly normal, vaginal, female sexuality yoked to patriarchal reproductive ends (Gallop, 1985, 12).

Gayatri Spivak has similarly written in this regard that male orgasmic pleasure "normally" entails an element of the male reproductive act—either semination or the production of sperm. Female orgasmic pleasure, on the other hand, does not necessarily entail any component of the female reproductive cycle—ovulation, fertilization, conception, gestation, birth. Spivak's point is that "the clitoris escapes reproductive framing."

> In legally defining woman as object of exchange in terms of reproduction, it is not only the womb that is literally appropriated, it is the clitoris as the signifier of the sexed subject that is effaced. All investigation into the definition of woman as legal object falls into varieties of the effacement of the clitoris. (Spivak, 1981, 181)

Celebration of the clitoris might constitute one way to begin to challenge the power of a phallic economy of pleasure. But it could do so only if the goal of such a celebration were not to set up an alternative organ of fetishistic worship but to dismantle the hierarchy of norm and deviation to create a plurality of pleasures accepting of difference.

The question becomes, then, just how a challenge to a phallic economy of pleasure might take place. One way in which we might begin to formulate such a challenge is through the critique of its most blatantly phallic example—the contemporary heterosexual pornographic film in which the "money shot" reigns supreme. This analysis might be useful in much the same way Luce Irigaray's reading of the phallic economy of sexuality (1986) is useful—e.g., as an empowering recognition of what that economy truly is and how it can best be challenged. For until feminists learn to read the contradictions within the phallic representation of pleasure and to construct representations of our own (different) pleasures out of these contradictions, we will find ourselves in the position of essentializing and fetishizing these pleasures, of catapulting ourselves outside the realm of all known discourse to speak normative "truths" that can easily become oppressive to someone else's "deviation."

There are reasons, however, for women to be suspicious of such arguments. For there is always the danger that such putative liberation will only further enslave women within sexual definitions that stress female sexuality as the excessive mark of difference. Rather than risk a repeat of the failures of sexual liberation, some antipornography feminists have preferred to hold on to a reversed form of this hierarchy. Fearing the moral chaos of abandoning a system of normative sexual behavior that, for all its problems, has nevertheless often functioned to protect women against patriarchal abuse, they have defensively asserted the norm of their own unfetishized pleasures against the deviation of the increasing manifestation of perversions typified by heterosexual feature-length pornography.

There is, in addition, the related problem that the male theorists most enthusiastic about the liberatory embrace of perverse pleasures—whether the outright hedonism of a Roland Barthes (1974) or the more covert hedonism of Michel Foucault's political and social analyses of power and pleasure—have had very little to say about the historical and textual specifics of the difference of female perversion. It may also not be out of place to note that for these two male homosexual theorists, the embrace of perversion does not necessarily challenge the norms of phallocentrism.[7]

Caught between the devil of buying into (even if also reversing the terms of) a normative phallic sexuality, and the deep blue sea of embracing (potentially) liberating "perversions," feminist critics of pornography need to scrutinize carefully the structure of perversions that currently reign in feature-length pornography. Perhaps even more crucially, we need to examine the theoretical discourses that we use to define such perversions as fetishism. What are the underlying concepts? Do they assume a dichotomy of norm/deviation? Are these the only alternatives? So before proceeding to an analysis of the hard core's "money shot" as the convergence of the economic and the psychosexual meanings of the fetish, we need to examine the classic Marxian and Freudian meanings of the term.

The Marxian and Freudian Fetish

In a famous passage from *Capital,* Marx (1867, 1906) defines the commodity as a "mysterious thing" in which the "social character of men's labour" appears to be "stamped" upon the very product of that labor. In an extended analogy to vision, Marx explains that just as "the light from an object is perceived by us not as the subjective excitation of our optic nerve, but as the objective form of something outside the eye itself," so we see the commodity as if it objectively possessed these qualities. But while in the act of seeing, there is "an actual passage of light from one thing to another," in the subjective perception of commodities, all is illusion. For in them, the "social relation between men" assumes "the fantastic form of a relation between things." Marx finally finds his proper analogy for the commodity in the "mist-enveloped regions of the religious world," where fetish objects of worship are "endowed with life" by the "productions of the human brain": "So it is in the world of commodities with the products of men's hands. This I call the Fetishism which attaches itself to the products of labour, so soon as they are produced as commodities, and which is therefore inseparable from the production of commodities" (Marx, 1906, 83).

In an equally famous passage written half a century later, Sigmund Freud defines the fetish as a

> substitute for the woman's (mother's) phallus which the little boy once believed in and does not wish to forego. . . . It is not true that the child emerges from his experience of seeing the female parts with an unchanged belief in the woman having a phallus. He retains this belief but he also gives it up; during the conflict between the deadweight of the unwelcome perception and the force of the opposite wish, a compromise is constructed such as is only possible in the realm of unconscious modes of thought. . . . In the world of psychical reality the woman still has a penis in spite of all, but this penis is no longer the same as it once was. Something else . . . now absorbs all the interest which formerly belonged to the penis. But this interest undergoes yet another very strong reinforcement, because the horror of castration sets up a sort of permanent memorial to itself by creating this substitute. Aversion from the real female genitals, which is never lacking in any fetishist, also remains as an indelible stigma of the repression that has taken place. One can now see what the

fetish achieves and how it is enabled to persist. It remains a token of triumph over the threat of castration and a safeguard against it. . . . (Freud, 1927, 153)

Though Marx and Freud define their fetishes very differently, both share a common will to expose the processes by which individuals fall victim to an illusory belief in the exalted value of certain objects. Both passages thus pose the illusion of an intrinsic value of an object against their authors' own greater knowledge of the social-economic or psychic conditions constructing that illusion of value. For Marx, in 1867, and for Freud, in 1927, the term *fetish* already carried a conventional opprobrium inherited from eighteenth-century studies of primitive religion.[8] The savages whom eighteenth-century travelers saw bowing down before crude, and often phallic, "stocks and stones" were not only disobeying one of the most important tenets of Protestantism in their worship of graven images; they were also so blinded by the sensuous materiality of the fetish that they forgot that they themselves had invested it with value. In its original, religious form, fetishism was thus understood as a delusion whereby the maker of the fetish fails to realize that he has given up his own productive powers to the fetish—that he worships it not simply as a conventional symbol of supernatural powers but as the literal embodiment of that power as a thing in itself.

In transposing earlier forms of the study of religion, Marx and Freud share the insight that worshipers delude themselves into thinking that the fetish object has intrinsic value. Both Marxian and Freudian fetishists locate illusory and compensatory forms of pleasure and power in the gleam of gold or the lacy frill of an undergarment. In a sense, then, both theorists offer an economic application of what in the eighteenth century had originally been a critique of religion— Marx in the direct economic terms of the investment of labor and Freud in the more indirect sense of a libidinal economy. For both, fetishization involves the construction of a substitute object to evade the complex realities of social or psychic relations.

Fetishes are thus short-term, short-sighted solutions to the real problems of power and pleasure in social relations. For Freud, however, the illusory belief in the fetish is a relatively minor perversion. He accepts as perceptual truth the "horror" and the "threat" of castration objectively located in the "real female genitals" and thus tends to sympathize with the delusion of the fetishist. He does not, like Marx, condemn the delusion as pure savagery. Rather, he universalizes the perversion as part of the natural processes of primary and infantile thought.

But where Freud tends to normalize the perversion, Marx rhetorically presses the point of a modern savagery of commodity fetishism. W. J. T. Mitchell notes that "the 'horror' of fetishism" was for Marx and eighteenth-century anthropologists alike located not simply in the "illusory, figurative act of treating material objects as if they were people," but in the transfer of human consciousness to "stocks and stones" that "seemed to drain the humanity out of the idolater" (Mitchell, 1986, 190). The horror thus lies in the perversity of an exchange in which, as Marx says elsewhere in *Capital,* persons begin relating to each other as things and things take on the social relations of persons (Marx, 1906, 73; Mitchell, 1986, 190).

We might be tempted, then, to view Marx as the theorist most inclined to employ fetishism as a term of old-fashioned, moralizing abuse. He forthrightly accuses all under the spell of the commodity of being like savages who have given up their very humanity to a thing. But it is Freud, the famous discoverer of the human rationale behind perversions, who really believes in the visual truth of what the fetishist sees when he looks at the woman's body; it is Freud who believes in the "horror of castration" of the female genitalia and who cannot see beyond them to how social relations of power have constructed them so as to appear horrifying. Since Freud's scenario of vision asserts a self-evident perceptual "truth" of female lack, his explanation itself begins in a fetishistic misrecognition of a sensuous, perceptual thing—the sight of the female genitalia construed as "lack"—followed by the creation of a compensatory substitute—the fetish. It is as if Freud trusts the fetishist's vision in its initial snap judgment of women's sexual difference as lack, but he mistrusts the fetishist's ability to continue to face the "truth" of that lack over time—hence the construction of the fetish as the denial of that truth. It is thus only in the latter part of his analysis—in the process of disavowing what he already knows to be true—that Freud does not fall victim to the very process he attempts to analyze.

Marx's narrative of explanation is, in contrast, more suspicious of sight from the outset. He looks critically at the physics of sight and the way we assume sight to originate from the object of vision when it is actually a "subjective excitation" of the optic nerve. Marx is quick to point out that this analogy is flawed; for the act of seeing at least involves a relation, an actual passage of light from the object to the eye, while there is no real relation between the physical properties of commodities and the values that accrue to them. In looking at commodities we can never see the things themselves but only the value that has been "stamped" upon them—the money they are worth rather than the social relations that have given them their value; we project the value of our own human labor onto the products of that labor.

For Marx the "horror" does not lie in the object of vision but in the subjective process of fetishization—in what happens to the idolater who fails to see his actual connection to other human producers and who therefore loses his own humanity as he invests inanimate objects with human attributes. In the Freudian fetish the idolater also invests in an inanimate object, but he retains his own humanity at the expense of the other—by turning the woman into an object even *before* he invests his desire in the substitute for her missing phallus. Thus for Freud there is an original moment of "true" vision that accepts the radical otherness of what it sees. For Marx, however, the reality of social and economic relations is a dialectical process that does not lend itself to the grasp of a single view. It is for this reason that a Marxian, political analysis of the prior *social* fact of the devaluation of women must always be factored into a discussion of the Freudian fetish.

The "Money Shot"

This sketch of the comparative structures of the Marxian and the Freudian fetish can help us to understand the relation between commodity culture and sexual pleasure in the "money shot." As the industry's slang term for the moment the hard-core film "delivers the goods" of the representation of sexual pleasure, the term seems the perfect embodiment of the illusory and insubstantial nature of late capital's "one-dimensional" "society of the spectacle"—a society that consumes images even more avidly than it consumes objects (Marcuse, 1964; Debord, 1967).

But of course it is in its connection to money proper—that ultimate obscenity—that the "money shot" is most obviously a fetish. In its convergence of money and sexual pleasure—both imagined as visible, quantifiable, sensuous, and intrinsically valuable *things* rather than as the medium for relations of exchange—the "money shot" most perfectly embodies the profound alienation of contemporary consumer society. For Marx's insight into the analogy between commodities and money and the "stocks and stones" of religious fetishes is that, although both may conveniently represent human labor in a fixed and stable form, labor is ultimately a process and cannot be so fixed. When it *is* so fixed, then this very stability and representability operate to dissolve all sense of human connection and process. Thus money comes to be seen, as Mitchell notes, not as "an 'imaginary' symbol of exchange-value, but as 'the direct incarnation of all human labor,' the 'embodiment' of value" (Mitchell, 1986, 191–192).

Once money takes on the function of representing the exchange-value of an object, the process of commodity exchange splits, as F. W. Haug observes, into the two isolated and antithetical segments of sale and purchase. The consumer uses money to obtain use-value while the seller uses use-value as a means to extract exchange-value in the form of money. The contradictory aims of consumer and producer very quickly produce a situation in which it no longer matters what the actual use-value of a commodity is so long as it *appears* useful to the consumer. Thus very early in the development of capitalism, aesthetic illusion becomes an independent function of selling. Packaging and desirability, rather than proven usefulness, begin to substitute for the tangible product (Haug, 1986, 32).

What is most characteristic of the late capitalistic form of fetishistic consumption, then, is that increasingly nothing tangible is purchased. We might compare the pleasure of viewing a contemporary porno film to the more straightforward exchange between prostitute and john, in which the consumer does, at least momentarily, possess the "goods" (or to the earlier stag film, in which the "goods" directly address the spectator as consumer). The advantage—to capital—of this new form of vicarious image satisfaction is that the very insubstantiality of the use-value purchased feeds back into the structure of needs, renewing the consumer's willingness to pay for that which will never be owned (Haug, 1986, 55).

As Haug puts it, "commodities borrow their aesthetic language from human courtship" and cast flirtatious glances at their buyers (p. 19). The effect of such commodity courtship mediated by money is that "people are conditioned to enjoy that which betrays them," even when, like the fetishist, they know that their enjoyment is founded on an illusion (p. 53). In a post-industrial society, spending (it is said) is the key to a healthy, though inflated, economy. Perhaps in the "money shot's" inflated, "spending" penis, we can see condensed all the principles of late capitalism's pleasure-oriented consumer society: pleasure figured as an orgasm of spending; the fetish not simply as commodity but as the surplus-value of orgasm.

But before we buy too far into the seductive attractions of this economic analogy, we might first explore some of the sexual assumptions that lie beneath its surface. For there is something almost too blatantly phallic about the economy of this "money shot." In the male economy of contemporary sexual pleasure, it has more typically been the woman's body that has functioned as the fetish commodity and the surplus-value of pleasure. Stephen Marcus, for example, writes in *The Other Victorians* of the "exquisite" correspondence of the "unlimited female orgasmic capacity" and contemporary consumer society (Marcus, 1974, viii–xiv).

We might ask, however, why it is the image of *female* sexuality that seems to embody so perfectly the false consciousness of a degraded and desublimated sexual pleasure? When Marcus argues that the twentieth-century image of a masturbating woman can be interpreted as the very emblem of alienated consumer culture, he states that this body directly *reflects* the alienated conditions of its economic base. But when he analyzes a contrasting image of male sexuality characteristic of nineteenth-century pornography (the proper subject of his study), Marcus offers a very different form of economic determination. The obsessive nineteenth-century focus on "male sexuality and male orgasm" does not merely reflect the limited industrial economy of scarcity and production; it also enacts a utopian fantasy of sexual abundance. This abundance is a wish-fulfilling reversal of both male physiology—its hoarding of the scarce resource of semen—and nineteenth-century economics and its limited expenditure of resources.

Marcus claims that the nineteenth-century "fantasy of pornography" is the complement of economic scarcity, "for the world of pornography is a world of plenty. In it all men are infinitely rich in substance, all men are limitlessly endowed with that universal fluid currency which can be spent without loss" (p. 22). Marcus may be right to observe that there is a fundamental shift in the representation of sexual pleasure from the nineteenth to the twentieth century. He may also be right to suggest that this shift is related to changes in the dominant economic modes of production and consumption in these periods and to male and female models of sexuality that attach to these modes. He invokes a curious double standard, however, when he offers a utopian model of a nineteenth-century (male-economic) pornography, or "pornotopia," and a merely reflective, more purely dystopian model of a twentieth-century (female-economic) pornography. He first suggests that the nineteenth-century "pornotopia" expresses utopian dreams born of limited economic and physiological realities. But in a Marxist analysis that looks back to the Frankfurt School tradition of false consciousness, Marcus views the limitless abundance of female sexuality as a frankly dystopian glut of the senses, as the false consciousness of a voracious and insatiable society of consumption.

The representation of male sexuality as active utopian longing, the representation of female sexuality as passive false consciousness—such are the paradoxes of the attempt to bring economics and history into the analysis of sexual representations. Marcus offers a dramatic illustration of the inability of a phallic visual economy to image female pleasure as anything but an insufficiency or an excess in comparison with its own limits.

Beneath this historical double standard lies the fundamental dichotomy of male subject/female object, which then generates a plethora of further dichotomies—active/passive, production/consumption, visible/invisible—each of which understands woman, as Luce Irigaray has pointed out, to be simply the absence or the negative of what man is or has: man has the phallus, woman does not; man is the logos, woman is silence; man is clearly representable, woman is the "dark continent" (Irigaray, 1986, 22, 26). Irigaray's point is that the fundamental economy—in both the Marxian sense of the commodity and the Freudian sense of libidinal desire—at work in such dichotimization is that of sameness or identity. She argues that this sameness is actually a form of male homosexuality within heterosexuality: e.g., with homosexuality understood not as the desire of man for man but as the basic phallic subjectivity that fails either to recognize or to imagine the real differences of woman (Irigaray 1985, 177).

The paradox of contemporary visual pornography and its "money shot" might therefore be described as follows: it is the obsessive attempt of a phallic visual economy to represent the difference of woman's sexual pleasure in a unitary language of sameness that cannot really imagine difference. Following Irigaray's use of Freudian and Marxist terms, we might view the "money shot" as offering the most extreme instance of the failure of a phallic signifying economy to signify anything but itself. In representing the orgasm of the couple in the active, productive, and visible orgasm of the male alone, contemporary film pornography demonstrates the mirror-speculum of a phallic desire and (speculating) economy that can see only itself, reaffirm only itself.

But even though the "money shot" offers the clearest example of the failure of the phallic economy to recognize difference, it is important to realize that the new narrative hard core nevertheless attempts to perceive the different "truth" of woman's pleasure in ways unparalleled by previous forms of film pornography. This, I think, is the real value of Marcus's attempt to sketch the shift from nineteenth-century male-centered to twentieth-century female-centered pornographic images. For the feature-length porno is almost obsessively concerned, in a way that the stag film or nineteenth-century literary pornography was never concerned, with defining the different nature of female pleasure and with defining it within narrative.

In an essay entitled "Women on the Market," Irigaray offers an extended analysis of the analogy between the Marxian definition of value as predicated on exchange and the valuation of women's bodies created in the exchange of women by men. She argues that even though women, like commodities, do have an intrinsic use-value related to their reproductive function, it is in the process of placing two women in a quantifiable relation to a third term—whether gold or phallus—that women lose their bodily specificity to become, like the commodity, an abstract and undifferentiated "product of man's labor." Thus desire, in the context of exchange, "perverts" need, "but that perversion will be attributed to commodities [marchandises] and to their alleged relations. Whereas they can have no relationships except from the perspective of speculating third parties" (Irigaray, 1985, 177). Thus woman-as-commodity exists both as a natural body with *use-value* and as a body with socially constructed *exchange-value* that mirrors masculine desire. This abstract and apparently universal value keeps women from use and exchange among themselves while they circulate as "value invested idealities"—fetish objects—within the closed homosexual economy (p. 183).

Irigaray's adaptation of Marxian economics helps explain why the contemporary pornographic film's fascination with female pleasure can never represent what this pleasure means to women. But rather than attribute this failure to the false consciousness of the commodities themselves, the real problem lies with a phallic signifying economy whose apparatus of measurement fails to count beyond the number one. For to man, women's sex is, as Irigaray's title puts it, *This Sex Which is Not One:* both unrecognizable, no sex at all, and not reducible to a single organ, to a single thing.

Without defining what woman's sexuality is, Irigaray nevertheless suggests that it is possible to recognize the existence of a non-unitary, plural economy of female pleasures in place of either/or oppositions that ultimately speak of the one and only phallic pleasure. Thus it is a question not of choosing, as Freud insists, between an active, clitoral pleasure and a passive vaginal one, but rather of the additive combination of a "multiplicity of erogenous zones"—the clitoris *and* the vagina, the lips *and* the vulva, etc. Such lists enumerating the many locations of female pleasure help to break down the either/or, active/passive dichotomies that underline phallic sexual economies.

Thus in both the Marxian economic and the Freudian libidinal sense, the fetish of the hard-core "money shot" compensates for scarcity and loss. But in its Freudian sense this fetish is peculiarly literal: in place of the psychic compromise that invests pleasure in a relatively indifferent signifier—Freud's example is the young man for whom a certain "shine on the nose" of a woman was necessary to his sexual pleasure—the "money shot" offers an image of the penis itself as substitute for the mythic phallus Freud's little boy fears to have lost in the encounter with the sexual difference of the mother. Indeed, these close-ups of excessively long, perpetually hard, ejaculating penises might seem to be nearly redundant, literal embodiments of this idealized fantasy phallus that we are all said to desire. The ejaculating penis of the "money shot" thus disavows castration by bypassing any association with the genitalia of the woman; it is as if the male fetishistic imagination could not countenance any vision of female difference at the moment of representing the orgasmic heights of its own pleasure.

In the aptly titled essay "Blind Spot of an Old Dream of Symmetry," Irigaray argues that there is an over-cathexis of vision, a "rule" of visibility and specularization in the male signifying economy that can only theorize woman as absence, lack, nothingness. If men think women are castrated versions of themselves, she argues, it is because of a fundamental castration—"a hole"—in their own limited signifying economy that can only envision woman's desire as the desire for the penis (Irigaray, 1986, 49).

The value of such an analysis is that it locates castration and fetishization where they really belong—in the presumed inadequacies of the body and mind of the male consumer of pornography. From the point of view of female empowerment, Irigaray's most hopeful pronouncement is the suggestion that the Freudian phobia aroused in men at the uncanny strangeness of the "nothing to be seen" of woman is actually the fear that she does not possess the envy that the man presumes her to possess—the fear, in other words, that she has other desires of a different nature from his own (p. 51).

Irigaray's point is that men are *blind* to women: to their different and multiple sex organs. But the solution to this blindness is not to celebrate or to fix (in turn) a single visual emblem of her difference, for this too would be to fetishize, to isolate the organ from the larger, historical dynamic of relations of exchange within which it operates.

The "money shot" could thus finally be viewed as that moment when the male "homosexual" economy most falters, most reverts to an absolute and unitary standard of value. But the import of this statement should not be to say that pornography is hopelessly phallic. It should be to say, rather, that it is hopelessly phallic in this particular way at this particular time because of pressures within its own discourse to represent the visual truth of female pleasures that it knows very little about.

In fact, from the vantage point of 1987 it is now possible to see that the "money shot" is on its way to becoming, like the convention in Westerns of good guys in white hats and bad guys in black, an unworkable and unbelievable archaism whose simplicities and limitations have become increasingly obvious.[9] As Irigaray asks, "perhaps if the phallocracy that reigns everywhere is put unblushingly on display, a different sexual economy may become possible? Pornography as 'catharsis' of the phallic empire? As the unmasking of women's sexual subjection?" (1985, 203). In the short segment of *This Sex Which Is Not One* devoted to pornography, Irigaray makes no attempt to answer these questions. But the questions themselves suggest the strategic value of a feminist attitude toward pornography that seeks the seeds of a different sexual economy in the probing of the limitations and inadequacies of the reigning one.

The questions continue: "must 'more than' always end up as 'less than?' . . . must accumulation end in discharge, disposal? . . . on the horizons of the pornographic scene is there perhaps a lingering fascination with loss? Is man admitting his incapacity to enjoy wealth? To enjoy nature?" (1985, 202). Perhaps if women can begin to pose these kinds of questions to existing pornography, we are on a path that will lead to the formulation and articulation of sexual pleasures grounded in an economy of abundance rather than scarcity, of many rather than one.

Deep Throat and the "Money Shot"

Deep Throat (Damiano, 1972) is probably the best known of the first wave of feature-length pornographic narratives to institute the convention of the "money shot." Everything in the film's narrative seems designed to motivate the requisite quantity of such shots (ten) stipulated by Ziplow in his *Filmmaker's Guide to Pornography*. A young, "swinging" single named Linda, played by Linda Lovelace, confesses to an older woman friend that she finds sex pleasant—"a lot of little tingles"—but not earthshakingly orgasmic—no "bells ringing, dams bursting or bombs going off." "Experiments" with numerous men only confirm this fact. The emphasis in these experiments, it should be noted, is primarily though not exclusively—on "meat" rather than "money" as the culminating moment of sexual engagement.

We can already note a very important difference in this scenario from that of the stag film. Where the stag film gets down to its sexual business very quickly, assuming that the act of sex is its own significance, its own fulfillment, *Deep Throat* is typical of the new wave of post-1972 hard core in that it seems to problematize this satisfaction. It is significant, therefore, that Linda confesses not to the pecadillo of sexual exploration but to what, by the early seventies—and partly as a result of new narrativizations of sexual pleasures such as these—had become much more shameful: that she does not find absolute fulfillment in that exploration.

What deserves emphasis here is that the film takes for granted a premise that is quite rare in the stag film: the possibility that sexual pleasure is not the same pleasure for everyone. Linda's older and wiser female friend puts it in terms of the well-known cliché of the seventies, "diff'rent strokes for diff'rent folks," but the point is significant. It suggests a toleration—even a welcoming and en-couragment—of a variety of sexual practices that is typical of the new seventies attitudes toward sexuality and of the pornographic film in particular.

Another cliché that marks the seventies nature of the film is the notion of therapy—what Stephen Heath (1982) has called "the sexual fix." Put simply, this is the notion that more or better sex is good for what ails us and that in matters of sexual pleasure it is always best to consult an expert. In a clinical examination that employs a telescope in place of a speculum, Linda's sexologist doctor (the ubiquitous Harry Reems) informs her that she doesn't "have one." In a phallogocentric misunderstanding that Luce Irigaray would appreciate, Linda responds, "I'm a woman, I'm not supposed to have one." What is at stake in this film, however, and, I would argue, in much feature-length pornography of this period, is precisely the question of the extent to which the phallic "one" can be used to figure and to fix the "two" (or more) of difference.

When the good doctor finally locates Linda's clitoris in her throat, he reassures her that it is at least better than having "none at all." Her concern is with the freak status it lends her—"what if your balls were in your ears!" But physiotherapy comes to the rescue, and, with a good deal of practice, beginning on the doctor himself, she learns the "deep throat" technique that leads to a climactic "money shot" whose narrative climax is enhanced by intercutting with fireworks, bells ringing, bombs bursting, and missiles firing.

The gimmick of "deep throat" thus works to naturalize what in the stag film had always been the most photogenic of all sexual practices: fellatio. Fellatio—followed by a "money shot," in which ejaculation occurs on the woman's face—becomes, in the wake of the enormous popularity of *Deep Throat,* the privileged figure for the expression of climax and satisfaction. (It reaches, for example, a kind of apotheosis in the Mitchell Bros. film *Behind the Green Door,* made later that same year.)

Finally fulfilled, Linda wants only to marry her doctor and be, as she says, his "slave." But the doctor has a more modern idea: she will become a physiotherapist. What follows is an extended parody of Masters and Johnson–style sex therapy, in which Linda administers to various mildly kinky men while still undergoing "therapy" herself with the doctor, who lands in bed with a bandage around his exhausted penis, unable to meet her demands for more sex. A final "gag" ends the film: in her work as a physiotherapist, Linda encounters Wilbur, who likes to play the role of a sadistic burglar caught in the act of spying on her. Beneath this role, however, he is sweet and gentle, the man of her dreams. When he proposes to Linda, she insists that the man she marries must have a "nine-inch cock" to satisfy the demands of her "deep throat." Wilbur instantly calls the doctor, saying he is only four inches away from happiness. The doctor reassures him, and he turns to Linda with the news that his thirteen-inch penis can be cut down to any size she wants. Little Wilbur is thus her ideal man.

In just about every sense of the word, then, *Deep Throat* fetishizes the penis. The question is how to read that fetishization. Probably the most common feminist reading would be to see it as a means of depriving women of their natural, organic forms of pleasure by imposing upon them the perversion not only of fellatio but of its gagging "deep throat" form. Gloria Steinem (1986), for example, writes that Damiano, the film's director, invented a gimmick that was "second only to Freud's complete elimination of the clitoris as a proper source of female pleasure. . . . Though his physiological fiction about *one* woman was far less ambitious than Freud's fiction about *all* women, his porn movie had a whamo audiovisual impact; a teaching device that Freudian theory had lacked." Thus the "millions of women" who were taken to the film by boyfriends, husbands, or pimps were taught how to please a man by the example of this humiliating obeisance to the fetish (Steinem, 1986, 275).

In Steinem's scenario the woman is cast in the role of Marx's savage fetishist who bows down to and gives up her own "proper source of female pleasure" to the power and pleasure of the phallus. The repeated ejaculations onto her face can thus be read as visual proof of her objectification and humiliation. Although there is a smile on that face, we know from Linda Lovelace's autobiography (1981) that this smile was a lie masking terror and pain, that she was a sex slave to the man who was her pimp and manager, and that her entire life at this time was, in the title of this autobiography, an "ordeal."

While I do not question the obvious importance for feminists to reject as inauthentic the pleasure of women portrayed in such films, I do question the notion, strongly implied in Steinem's argument, that there is a "proper" female pleasure that is repressed by the film and that is, indeed, repressed by all pornography. I would argue instead that even though *Deep Throat* elides the visual representation of Linda Lovelace's clitoris, even though its "money shot" fetish operates, in Gayatri Spivak's words, to "efface" that organ, its narrative is constantly soliciting and trying to locate the narrative moment of an invisible orgasm. So if, on the one hand, the film tries to efface sexual difference through a gimmick that renders more natural the practice of fellatio, on the other hand, this very effacement could be said to allegorize difference by actually giving it Linda Lovelace's face.

All of the film's solicitous concern for the location of the clitoris thus needs to be seen in the context of the relatively new knowledge of this organ as precisely not a diminished or lacking version of the penis—as in Freud's account of the phallic economy of the *one*—but as a new economy not reducible to that one—an economy of the *many*—of "diff'rent strokes for diff'rent folks." Even though the film's fetishization of the phallus attempts to disavow difference at the moment of orgasm and to model that orgasm on a decidedly phallic metaphor of "bombs bursting," and even though the woman is portrayed as dependent upon the *one* of the man, a contradictory plurality and difference has been registered. The very fact that the expanded narrative of the new feature-length hard-core film parodically joins with the scientific Masters and Johnson–style quest for the "truth" of the woman's difference indicates the extent to which the woman's invisible and nonquantifiable pleasure has now been brought into frame, on the scene of the obscene.

So rather than compare *Deep Throat*'s invocation of a phallic economy with Freud's, as Steinem does, we might do better to contrast their differences. In Freud, fetishization is an obvious way for the male subject to maintain the phallic economy of the one. As we saw earlier, the Freudian fetishist preserves his own humanity at the expense of stressing the freakish inhumanity—the "horror"—of the female other. I would argue that *Deep Throat* does not simply repeat this objectification of the female other. Or rather, that if it does, it does so in a way that so very blatantly puts the reigning "phallocracy" on display that it becomes possible to glimpse, in the univocal limitations of its economy of the one, the possible elaboration of an economy of the many.

Foucault writes that along with the incitement to sexuality contained in the modern age's proliferating discourses of sexuality comes an increasing tendency to identify and to address many different specialized sexual practices and in that process to "implant" these perversions (1978, 48). My point is that Linda Lovelace and her perversely implanted clitoris might be viewed not as yet another elision of and horror at the freakishness of female sexual "lack" but as something quite different: as the ambivalent and contradictory attempt of a phallic economy to count beyond the number one, to recognize, as the proliferating discourses of sexuality take hold, that there can no longer be any such thing as a fixed sexuality, male, female, or otherwise, but that there are only proliferating sexualities. For if the "implantation of perversions" is, as Foucault says, an instrument *and* an effect of power, then as discourses of sexuality name, identify, and ultimately produce a bewildering array of pleasures and perversions, the very multiplicity of these pleasures and perversions inevitably works against the older idea of a single norm—an economy of the one—against which all else is measured.

It is this breakdown of the very idea of the norm that I find most intriguing, and most useful, for a feminist reading of, and a feminist defense against, contemporary film pornography. For if there is no such thing as a "natural" pleasure independent of its production in social discourse, then one effective strategy for women concerned with the abusive intersection of power and pleasure in pornography may be to begin to understand the contradictions within the genre's production of pleasure. And similarly, if power, as Foucault says, is to be located in discourse and if resistance to power is "a multiple field of force relations" (p. 92) rather than a single revolutionary point of opposition, then the most effective resistance to the power of the fetish would not be to reestablish an essential truth against which the illusion of the fetish will be measured. To do so would only be to establish new, potentially repressive, norms as the solution to the already repressive norm of the phallus.

If the Marxian fetish of commodity capital, the Freudian fetish of the disavowal of castration, and their convergence in the "money shot" of the pornographic film can be characterized as forms of repressive power, then we need to understand that this power is not instituted from on high. The most effective way to resist these forms of fetishization, then, might not be the Marxian tradition of iconoclasm. For if we become too iconoclastic, if our only goal is to smash the abnormal and perverse idols of Mammon to destroy the false consciousness they engender, then we may fail to understand, and effectively to combat, the real appeal of capitalist and patriarchal forms of power and pleasure. On the other hand, if we, like Freud, lend too much legitimacy to the supposedly universal causes that have created the need for the (phallic) fetish, then we are in danger of becoming rational fetishists ourselves—of normalizing and justifying the fetish function in the name of universal processes of desire that elide the existence of the female subject.

We must come back, then, to the question of what is the most effective feminist use of the notion of perversion. If there can be no authentic, true, or normal position from which to resist the repression of the feminine as currently enacted in visual pornography, but only the hope of breaking out of the economy of the one, then it seems to me that the most effective strategy would be to embrace the liberatory potential contained in the "implantation of perversions."

The above does *not* mean that women should accept a phallic definition of their different sexuality as perverse. Foucault's analysis of how discourses of sexuality created the sexually "saturated" hysterical woman offers warning enough against that (1978, 104). But it does mean that we should recognize that the inevitable process of this "implantation of perversions," of fetishization itself, can be used to break down the opposition between norm and deviation upon which repressive forms of power often rely.

The lesson of *Deep Throat* would thus seem to be the following: while it is undeniable that in this film a fetishized phallic norm constantly attempts to represent the "true" nature of female pleasure, the mere fact that this pleasure cannot be represented as a singular thing within the quantifiable terms of that phallic economy forces the text to explore a range of perverse substitutions—in this case fellatio and sadomasochistic role playing—as means of getting at and fixing the elusive nature of female pleasure. In the 1972 *Deep Throat,* this range of practices is still quite limited. In subsequent feature-length pornography of the late seventies and early eighties, the range becomes wider. But each of these perverse definitions is destined to fail as the representation of the visible narrative climax of the woman's pleasure. Thus, as the feature-length form of the genre develops, it tends to multiply the opportunities to investigate wider ranges of perverse sexual practices. Feminists and moral majoritists alike have tended to see only the increased violence of these forms of sexual representation. But it is important to realize as well that the very diversity of these practices contributes to the defeat of the phallic economy's original desire to fix the sexual identity of the woman as the mirror of its own desire. And so the genre of heterosexual pornography increasingly becomes, almost in spite of itself, the occasion for the depiction of diverse sexual practices even as it seeks to represent definitive sexual identities. In the multiplication of these diverse practices, the genre undermines its original goal of fixing and representing the linear and visible narrative truth of female sexual pleasure.

A fetish is indeed, as Marx says, "a mysterious thing." Like religious icons, it mystifies. And like religious icons, it can be oppressive. But the lesson that feminism can draw from both Marx and Freud is that it needs to be understood as something more than an illusory fraud perpetrated on an unsuspecting and credulous populace. I have tried to show that the most important of these lessons must be that the "lack" disavowed by the fetish is not a true lack but only a perception based upon the prior social and economic devaluation of women. The fetish of the "money shot" typifies one short-term, short-sighted solution by the visual hard core to the perennial male problem of understanding woman's difference. But another lesson is that such solutions are fraught with contradictions that may open up possible routes to the resistance of hegemonic sexual pleasures.

NOTES

This essay is a slightly revised version of an article first published in *The Quarterly Review of Film Studies*. I wish to thank its editor, Beverle Houston, and the editors of the present volume, Susan Gubar and Joan Hoff, for their helpful comments. I would also like to thank Judith Gardiner, Julia Lesage, Chuck Kleinhans, and Paul Fitzgerald for their generous help and encouragement.

1. I discuss the stag form of the hard-core genre at some length in my forthcoming book *Hard Core: Power, Pleasure and the "Frenzy of the Visible"* (forthcoming, University of California Press).

2. Unfortunately, there is very little written about the history of either of these phases. Al Di Lauro and Gerald Rabkin's book on the stag film (1976) offers a beginning study of this form. But there is no equivalent study for the hard-core feature-length narrative. Of course there is no shortage of works about eroticism or sexuality in film in general; nor is there a shortage of theoretical or moral positions taken with respect to this new phase of the genre. In no other popular film genre has the axiom "if you've seen one you've seen them all" been taken so seriously. The brief synopsis offered here is in no sense an attempt to write in this missing history. Yet it is necessary to provide some sense of this history. In doing so I have relied mostly on my own viewings and a very brief and cavalier presentation of film pornography in a chapter of George Gordon's (1980) *Erotic Communications*. A somewhat fuller history is given in my book.

3. For example, Alex de Renzy's *History of the Blue Movie* (1970)—a sort of *That's Entertainment!* of the stag film. This film, along with *Hollywood Blue* (1971), recycled highlights from the illegal stag films as part of the process of becoming legitimate itself.

4. *Rabin's Revenge* (Mitchell Bros., 1971).

5. *The Casting Call* (Gentlemen II Prod., 1970).

6. I am using the term here in its general sense of the deviation from the organ-pleasure of genital sex toward derivative or substitute forms of pleasure. It is important to realize, however, that although the term perversion always retains the idea of "swerving away" from an instinctual norm, as early as his *Three Essays on the Theory of Sexuality* Freud (1905) was already working against the norm/deviation limits of such an understanding to theorize sexuality itself as inherently perverse.

7. It is also interesting to note that in neither Foucault's nor Barthes's many writings about sexuality and pleasure do they write as homosexuals. Their voices, as Julia Lesage pointed out to me on reading a draft of this essay, are the voices of intellectuals articulating the "truth" of sexuality from outside the place of even their *own* difference.

8. Two recent works have provided me with useful histories of the concept of fetish as it developed out of the eighteenth century and into the nineteenth. They are W. T. J. Mitchell (1986), *Iconology: Image, Text, Ideology*, and David Simpson (1982), *Fetishism and Imagination: Dickens, Melville, Conrad*.

9. This de-emphasis of the penis and the "money shot" has already taken place in the small number of hard-core films now being directed by women. See especially the work of Candida Royale—*Urban Heat* and *Femme*. It is also happening in more conventional and male-oriented hard core. Cf. the *Insatiable* series with Marilyn Chambers.

REFERENCES

Barthes, Roland (1974). *The Pleasure of the Text*. Trans. Richard Miller. New York: Hill and Wang. (Original work published 1973.)

Debord, Guy (1967). *La Société du spectacle*. Paris: Buchet/Chastel.

Di Lauro, Al, & Rabkin, Gerald (1976). *Dirty Movies: An Illustrated History of the Stag Film 1915–1970*. New York: Chelsea House.

Foucault, Michel (1978). *The History of Sexuality, Vol. I: An Introduction.* Trans. Robert Hurley. New York: Pantheon. (Original work published 1976.)

Freud, Sigmund (1905). "Three Essays on the Theory of Sexuality." In *The Standard Edition of the Complete Psychological Works of Sigmund Freud,* ed. and trans. J. Strachey, vol. 7, pp. 125–244.

———(1927). "Fetishism." In *Standard Edition,* vol. 21.

Gallop, Jane (1985?). "Feminist Criticism and the Pleasure of the Text." Unpublished essay.

Gordon, George (1980). *Erotic Communications.* New York: Hastings House.

Haug, F. W. (1986). *Critique of Commodity Aesthetics: Appearance, Sexuality and Advertising in Capitalist Society.* Trans. Robert Bock. Minneapolis: University of Minnesota Press. (Original work published 1971.)

Heath, Stephen (1982). *The Sexual Fix.* London: Macmillan.

Irigaray, Luce (1986). *Speculum of the Other Woman.* Trans. Gillian C. Gill. Ithaca: Cornell University Press.

———(1985). *This Sex Which Is Not One.* Trans. Catherine Porter, Carolyn Burke. Ithaca: Cornell University Press.

Lovelace, Linda, & McGrady, Mike (1980). *Ordeal.* New York: Berkley Publishing Corp.

Marcus, Stephen (1974). *The Other Victorians: A Study of Sexuality and Pornography in Mid-Nineteenth Century England.* New York: New American Library. (Originally published 1964.)

Marcuse, Herbert (1964). *One Dimensional Man.* Boston: Beacon Press.

Marx, Karl (1906). *Capital.* Trans. Samuel Moore and Edward Aveling. New York: The Modern Library.

Mitchell, W. J. T. (1986). *Iconology: Image, Text, Ideology.* Chicago: University of Chicago Press.

Simpson, David (1982). *Fetishims and Imagination: Dickens, Melville, Conrad.* Baltimore: Johns Hopkins University Press.

Spivak, Gayatri Chakravorty (1981). "French Feminism in an International Frame." *Yale French Studies* 62:154–84.

Steinem, Gloria (1986). "The Real Linda Lovelace." In *Outrageous Acts and Everyday Rebellions.* New York: New American Library.

Ziplow, Stephen (1977). *The Filmmaker's Guide to Pornography.* New York: Drake Publishers Inc.

11

Mitigating the Effects of Violent Pornography

MARGARET JEAN INTONS-PETERSON
AND BEVERLY ROSKOS-EWOLDSEN

As our title indicates, this chapter focuses on the reduction or neutralization of the effects of violent pornography, which we define as the portrayal of violence as a juxtaposed, often integral part of sexuality. Such a focus does not imply that we believe that violent pornography should be banned, that violent pornography invariably damages its viewers, or that violent pornography threatens social stability and order. The focus does imply a concern for educating people about the potential effects of violent pornography, effects that appear to be extensive. For example, as we review in this essay, research conducted with male subjects has consistently shown that exposure to the assaultive sexuality of violent pornography is associated with lowered opinions of women, increased tolerance of violence toward women, and increased likelihood of actual aggression against women in laboratory settings. Exposure to even nonviolent pornography may, in time, induce some societally problematic attitudes, according to some investigators. These effects emerge even with normal males who have shown no propensity for rape. If violent pornography were rarely available, the problem might not warrant attention, but that is not the case.

Violent pornography now seems to appear everywhere—in books, magazines, television, films, and videotapes. Insidiously, it pervades common forms of entertainment. It may pop up unexpectedly in the media, juxtaposing sexual activity with violence. The danger here is that its sexual themes may lull us into a sense of contented complacency, only to assail us with violence occasionally so extreme that women in these images, frequently presented as the victims, suffer serious injury or death. The message is clear: what is soothingly, sensually alluring, may be combined, even integrated with, violent aggressiveness to reach its apex, its epitome, its maximum sexual climax. This material, so prevalent in our society, is available not only to adults but also to children, for whom the impact may be especially misleading and troublesome. Children may use such depictions as a major source of sex education, a prospect that is particularly noteworthy because children frequently have difficulty separating fantasy from reality, as the National Commission on the Causes and Prevention of Violence concluded in its 1969 report. Because the negative effects of violent pornography appear to be robust and reliable, it is important to ask what measures might mitigate those effects. These are the issues that motivate this chapter.

In this essay, we review research dealing with the effects of exposure to violent and nonviolent pornography and then consider various techniques that might be used to mitigate the effects. We focus primarily on violent pornography, to the partial exclusion of nonviolent pornography, or what is often called erotica, for five reasons. First, violent pornography seems to have a greater potential for societal harm than erotica (see Donnerstein, 1984).[1] Second, violent pornography was largely overlooked by the 1970 Commission on Pornography and Obscenity. Hence, the commission's conclusion that exposure to erotica did not appear to play a significant causal role in delinquent or criminal behavior may not apply to violent pornography. Third, pornographic depictions have become increasingly violent and more likely to portray female acceptance and enjoyment of male sexual aggression (Dietz & Evans, 1982; Malamuth & Spinner, 1980; Smith, 1976a, 1976b). Fourth, violent pornography may contribute to erroneous beliefs about women, because it often depicts women as unfeeling toys designed to satisfy any and all male sexual whims (one could make a convincing case that such films also debase men). Finally, more incisive research, particularly on violent pornography, has been conducted since the commission issued its report. Our review of violent and nonviolent pornography will be brief because other, more extensive surveys have been published recently (e.g., Donnerstein, 1984; Malamuth, 1984).

For convenience, we classify pornography into three categories—erotica, pornography, and violent pornography—on the basis of their implicit and explicit aggressive components. All have a sexual theme. Erotica portrays nonaggressive sexual activity between willing, sensitive, caring partners. The partners share in the initiation and choice of activities, relatively free from the stereotypic pattern of male dominance and female subservience that characterizes much pornography. Pornography, then, presents the coercion of a less powerful person by a more powerful one. Women are the slaves, the sexual playthings, for men to use and discard. Neither women nor men are accorded much compassion or empathy, but women, in particular, are degraded and demeaned. They are represented as devoid of self-respect and feelings. Their chief interest is the satisfaction of male sexual desires and fantasies. The pornography's underlying theme of coercion and unequal status presages those of aggression, force, and sexual servitude, which define violent pornography. Violent pornography combines sexuality and violence.

Although the effects of violent pornography are our primary concern, a brief digression to examine nonviolent forms of pornography helps to set the stage for our evaluation of the effects of more violent forms of the genre. In brief, the results seem to depend on two factors: the type of material that is viewed and the duration of the exposure.

Review of the Literature on Nonviolent Pornography

In contrast to most of the research on violent pornography, studies of nonviolent pornography have yielded ambiguous results. Some of the early work reviewed by the 1970 Commission on Pornography and Obscenity suggested that exposure to nonviolent pornography might serve as a "safety valve" for sexual interests (Kronhausen & Kronhausen, 1964) or as a teaching device for resolving sexual maladjustments (Bernstein, 1982; Goleman & Bush, 1977). To illustrate the safety valve function, Kutchinsky (1973) reported that various sex crimes decreased in Denmark after the country removed restrictions on the production and distribution of erotica. Moreover, exposure to erotica has been touted as an educational device for overcoming sexual maladjustments, although the most relevant evidence indicates that the primary effect of seeing erotica is to increase the frequency of engaging in previously established sexual activities (Cattell, Kawash, & De Young, 1972; Eisenman, 1982). These effects turned out to be partly illusory, as noted in the 1970 Commission report, because the decrease in sex crimes may have been due to reduced reporting (Court, 1984), and the effects of erotic stimulation have been shown to be short-lived (Howard, Reifler, & Liptzin, 1971).

These results led the commission to reject what might be called a "cathartic" model of exposure to pornography. As an alternative to the cathartic model, the commission then examined an "imitative" model, which holds that consumers of pornography copy into their own attitudes and sexual practices the demeaning, sometimes hostile, callous opinions of women or the explicit sexual activities represented in pornographic materials. Specifically, the commission's working group asked whether exposure to nonviolent pornography would increase feelings of hostility toward women (see the commission's report for a full review). Most of the research yielded either negative or ambiguous answers, perhaps because most research used minimal exposures to mild erotica. Since then, newer investigations have increased exposure to the films as a way of mimicking the real world in the laboratory, have relied less on self-report, and have asked the subjects more detailed questions about their attitudes. This research suggests that, under some circumstances, exposure to erotica and nonviolent pornography tends to increase subsequent aggression against women (see Donnerstein, 1983; Sapolsky, 1984; and Zillmann & Bryant, 1984, for reviews). According to Sapolsky, the circumstances include factors such as whether the film is judged to be sexually arousing and pleasant or disgusting and unpleasant, the type of sexual activity depicted, its mode of presentation, and the degree of explicitness. Collectively, these factors govern the novelty, titillation, and shock value of the films.

One view of why pornography does not need regulation is that, with exposure, people will adapt to it. Part of pornography's allure may be its forbidden, secretive qualities. If these qualities are removed, pornography's magnetism will diminish. Consonant with this perspective, some researchers have found that people become increasingly bored as their exposure to nonviolent pornography increases (e.g., Howard, Reifler, & Liptzin, 1971; Mann, Sidman, & Starr, 1971; Zillmann & Bryant, 1984, 1982). For example, females and males who saw common, nonviolent pornographic films in six consecutive weekly sessions reported that, as the sessions continued, they became less sexually excited, felt less repulsion, and found the material less objectionable and more acceptable as a form of entertainment, compared to people who saw nonviolent, nonpornographic films (Zillmann & Bryant, 1982, 1984). This boredom with pornography depicting relatively commonplace sexual activity led to some unanticipated results: an increased acceptance of less common forms of sexuality, such as sadomasochism and bestiality. Zillmann and Bryant (1984, 1986) proposed that boredom with the more common forms of sexuality and pornography might prompt viewers to seek more exotic forms. To test this prediction, male participants were given the opportunity to select and watch videotapes that portrayed various kinds of sexual activities while they ostensibly waited alone for an experimenter to appear. The tapes were labeled. Viewers of pornography were more likely to select tapes about unusual sexual acts than viewers of nonpornography. This result supports their prediction.

Zillmann & Bryant (1986) examined other attitudinal changes that might accompany exposure to nonviolent pornography. They compared support for various aspects of sexuality related to marriage and family life for heterosexual viewers who had seen six films of nonviolent pornography with those who had seen six nonviolent, nonpornographic films. The films were shown over a six-week period. They found that, compared to those who saw the nonpornographic films, people who watched the pornography were more likely to accept and to tolerate pre- and extramarital sex, multiple sexual partners, and marital infidelity. They were more likely to believe that promiscuity is natural and that repressing sexual urges poses a health risk. In addition to these opinions about sexuality, the pornography viewers also were more likely to accept male dominance and female submission, to rate marriage as less significant and viable, and to want fewer children than the viewers of innocuous material.

Not all investigators have observed similar effects (e.g., Donnerstein's 1984 review), and these results should be interpreted with caution. The strongest conclusion that seems reasonable is that extensive exposure to pornography seems to affect a number of attitudes about sexual and family practices.[2]

Research on erotica and nonviolent pornography has produced somewhat ambiguous results. The quest for documentation of beneficial results was disappointing, yielding either no positive evidence or transitory effects. The quest for demonstration of negative effects has been similarly indecisive. But when we turn from erotica and nonviolent pornography to violent pornography, we find a markedly different story. Research on violent pornography yields clear, precise, and consistent results. We turn next to a review of this literature.

Review of the Literature on Violent Pornography

Accumulating evidence indicates that exposure to violent pornography has harmful effects on some individuals. To date, converging research has shown that even a few minutes' exposure to violent pornography (a) increases sexual arousal in normal and rapist males, (b) increases rape fantasies, (c) desensitizes men to the filmed pornographic acts, (d) increases aggressive tendencies and behavior, (e) decreases respect for women's rights, (f) increases the acceptance of rape myths and of violence toward women, and (g) increases tolerance for rapists (e.g., Donnerstein, 1984; Linz, 1985; Malamuth, 1984; Penrod & Linz, 1984). The extent of these outcomes depends, in part, on the psychological makeup of the individual. Some men have a greater propensity for rape and aggressive behavior than others (see Malamuth, 1984, for a review). Situational factors, such as the likelihood of being caught, also play a role. Taken as a whole, the existence of these findings reflects the seriousness of the problem.

These results differ markedly from the conclusions of the 1970 Commission on Pornography and Obscenity that pornography does not cause delinquent or criminal behavior. This contradiction is not surprising, for the commission dealt almost exclusively with nonviolent pornography, whose effects often differ from those of violent pornography (Linz, 1985). Further weakening the commission's conclusions is its reliance, in part, on a national survey that asked people if they personally had experienced more desirable than undesirable reactions to pornographic material. The respondents reported as many positive as negative reactions. These results are suspect on at least four counts. First, self-reports are notoriously unreliable, and the sensitive nature of the question is likely to exacerbate this problem. Second, the question did not define or illustrate pornography. Hence, the respondents' interpretations could have ranged from faintly erotic to violently aggressive sexual material, with concomitant variations in their reactions. Third, the definitions of "desirable" and "undesirable" reactions also were left to the subjective, idiosyncratic interpretations of the respondents. Fourth, the very wording of the question injected a bias toward reporting positive reactions. These considerations and the commission's failure to survey research on violent pornography severely limit their conclusions. Their report was deficient in another respect: it did not fully address likely individual differences in propensities to rape and in responses to pornographic material.

The importance of individual differences is underscored by findings that some individuals report a relatively stronger propensity to rape than others, and that these tendencies correlate with aggression against women in laboratory settings (Malamuth, 1981; Malamuth, Haber, & Feschbach, 1980; Malamuth & Check, 1980a, 1981, 1983; Malamuth, Reisen, & Spinner, 1979; Tieger, 1981). This evidence, combined with demonstrations that televised violence may lead to aggressive behavior (the 1972 Surgeon General's Scientific Advisory Committee on Television and Social Behavior and a similar 1980 report), suggests that exposure to violent pornography may encourage some men to devalue and even abuse women. Further, the higher the self-reported likelihood of raping, the more likely men are to hold callous attitudes about rape, to believe in rape myths, and to show relatively higher levels of sexual arousal to rape depictions (Malamuth, 1981).

Thus, the data suggest that individuals differ in their likelihood of aggressing against women. Nonetheless, even males who show no propensity toward rape display the attitudinal changes described above after exposure to violent pornography. Further, most of the research reported in this review has been conducted with males who do not appear to be rape-prone. Facilitation of such aggression, whether through pornographic films or other environmental situations, is a problem of concern to society.

We turn next to experimental evaluations of the specific effects of short-term exposure to violent sexuality on men with no known propensity toward rape. Most of the materials portray the female victims as secretly desiring the assault or as rapidly learning to desire aggressive sex. The women also tend to be shown as instruments for the satisfaction of men, as willing subordinates and sexual slaves. In short, this type of film degrades women.

THE EFFECTS OF SHORT-TERM EXPOSURE TO VIOLENT PORNOGRAPHY
Even short-term exposure (five to fifteen minutes) to violent pornography has a number of demonstrable effects on normal male viewers:

1. It may induce a level of sexual arousal that equals or exceeds the level elicited by exposure to depictions of mutually consenting sexual activities when women are shown as responding with pleasure. When watching a film that portrays the victim as becoming involuntarily sexually aroused by an assault, male viewers showed levels of sexual arousal that were as great as or greater than the arousal induced by scenes of mutually consenting sex (Malamuth, Heim, & Feshbach, 1980; Malamuth & Check, 1980a, 1980b). When the victim was not shown as sexually aroused, the arousal of male viewers was significantly lower than that of viewers of mutually consenting sex.

2. It encourages unsympathetic, unrealistic attitudes toward women. For example, in some experimentation (Malamuth, Heim, & Feshbach, 1980; Malamuth & Check, 1980a, 1983) viewers were exposed to violent pornography that depicted the female victim either as becoming sexually aroused or as disgusted and unaroused. A third group saw scenes of mutually consenting sex. They then saw a rape depiction and were asked to evaluate the extent to which the victim suffered and to estimate the number of women who would enjoy being raped. Participants who had seen a film portraying a women as sexually aroused by rape

thought that the victim had suffered less and that more women would enjoy being raped than participants who viewed disgusted and unaroused rape victims or who saw the film showing mutually consenting sex. Similarly, exposure to violent pornography increased acceptance of interpersonal violence, rape myths, and beliefs in the prevalence of adversarial sexual relations (Malamuth & Check, 1981).

3. It may also encourage aggression toward women. Other investigations have followed exposure to aggressively sexual material (depicting a female victim as becoming sexually aroused) with opportunities to aggress against accomplices of the experimenter. Regardless of whether a magazine (*Penthouse;* Malamuth, 1978) or a film (Donnerstein, 1980a, 1980b, 1983; Donnerstein & Berkowitz, 1981) was used, viewers administered more shocks to female accomplices than to male accomplices when they believed that it was acceptable to deliver shocks (in fact, no shocks were delivered, but the viewers thought that they were administering shocks because the accomplice was wired to the viewer's control box and was trained to wince on signal). In these experiments, the opportunities to shock the accomplices were presented in the guise of "teaching" the accomplices to perform experimental tasks by shocking (punishing) them when they erred. Another instructive result was that nonpornographic films that portrayed violence toward women raised the level of male aggression against female victims, but to a lesser extent than aggressive pornographic material (Donnerstein, 1983; also see Meyer, 1972; Zillmann, 1971).

In the research described above, the accomplices typically insulted the participants at the beginning of the experimental session. This procedure was used to arouse feelings of anger. This device was not necessary to elicit aggressive shocking of the female accomplices, however, for Donnerstein and Berkowitz (1981) found that nonangered males who had been exposed to violent pornography also shocked female accomplices more than their counterparts who had seen neutral, nonaggressive nonsexual scenes. Donnerstein and Berkowitz noted that, of the viewers of aggressive sexuality, the angered ones aggressed more against women than the nonangered ones. Moreover, when the film depicted an assaulted woman as protesting and suffering, only the angered viewers severely shocked the female accomplice. These results indicate that males who are aroused by exposure to sexual and violent material are likely to retaliate against a woman when the situation permits or makes possible unpunished acts of aggression. That is, the situation serves to disinhibit aggressive tendencies, as does portrayal of women ultimately desiring assaultive sex. When women are shown as suffering from assaultive sex, however, the portrayal functions as an inhibitor of abusive tendencies for men whose arousal levels are not too high (the unangered people), but ineffectively deters the aggressive tendencies of highly aroused men (the angered people).

The preceding evidence converges on the central finding that even limited exposure to violent pornography that reinforces rape myths has substantial negative effects on some adult males. Further, some males show greater inclination toward aggression than others and these individuals may be particularly likely to act out their tendencies when circumstances appear to countenance their expression (Malamuth, 1984).

Are the effects of violent pornography due to the aggressive component, the sexual component, or both components? Donnerstein (1983) addressed this question by exposing college males to one of four films. The films were selected to depict violent pornography, nonviolent pornography, violent nonpornography, or nonviolent nonpornography (the neutral condition). The two violent films were rated as equally aggressive, and the two pornographic films were judged to be equally sexually arousing, although more arousing than the nonpornographic films. The participants were angered by either a female (female-angered group) or a male accomplice (male-angered group) before exposure to their assigned film and then had an opportunity to aggress against the accomplices after the film.

The female-angered participants aggressed more against the female accomplice following exposure to the violent pornographic and violent nonpornographic films than following exposure to the two other films, with the greatest aggression occurring after exposure to the violent pornographic film. The pattern was somewhat different for the male-angered participants. Only the nonviolent pornography, compared to the nonviolent nonpornography, increased aggression, presumably mediated by general arousal.

These results and those of related experiments (e.g., Donnerstein & Berkowitz, 1981) indicate that the aggressive component of violent pornography raises the level of aggression against women more than the sexual component, although the combination of the two yields somewhat greater evidence of aggression. Exposure to nonviolent pornographic films did not increase aggression toward female accomplices compared with exposure to the nonviolent, nonpornographic film. Aggression against males is more likely to be elicited by nonviolent, pornographic material than by other combinations, probably reflecting general arousal.

THE EFFECTS OF LONG-TERM EXPOSURE TO PORNOGRAPHY

The preceding work described effects of exposure to violent pornography for short intervals of time, up to about fifteen minutes. We now consider the effects of longer-term exposure on nonrape-prone men. One possibility is that people will become less sensitive, even inured to violent pornography with repeated exposures (a process called desensitization, adaptation, habituation, or satiation). Alternatively, extended exposure might further counteract inhibitions of aggressive tendencies. Under extended exposure these tendencies could generalize to other persons, objects, and responses, such as increased callousness toward all women, not just rape victims.

Zillmann and Bryant (1982, 1984) found that exposure to *nonviolent* pornography for four hours and forty-eight minutes in a six-week period yielded more toleration of bizarre and violent forms of pornography, less support for equality of the sexes, greater leniency in sentencing rapists, and increased tendencies to accept statements about callousness toward women, such as "A man should find them, fool them, fuck them, and forget them," "A woman doesn't mean no until she slaps you," "If they are old enough to bleed, they are old enough to butcher." One problem with this research is that specially prepared pornographic film clips were used, rather than commercially available materials, so that Zillmann and Bryant's stimulus films were not necessarily comparable to either those used by many other researchers or those commonly available.

Linz (1985) also examined the effects of long-term exposure to pornographic materials. His first study compared the effects of five days of exposure or nonexposure (the control group) to violent pornography (R-rated slasher films) on judgments about a victim and a rapist in a mock rape trial. The viewers of violent pornography rated the films as significantly less violent over the five days, despite the fact that half of them saw the films in one order and the other saw them in the reverse order. This desensitization to film violence tended to generalize to the rape trial judgments: the viewers of violent pornography judged the victim to be less injured and less worthy than the control subjects who did not see the films. Apparently, some desensitization or habituation occurs under sustained exposure to pornography, but the effect of the desensitization is to reduce self-ratings of violence and to increase ratings of callousness toward women.

Linz's second study (1985) compared the effects of long-term exposure to the slasher films with exposure to two types of nonviolent films that may be degrading to women: nonviolent, sexually explicit films that typically portray women as willing to engage in virtually any sexual activity requested by men and nonviolent R-rated "teen sex" films. The "dosage" also was manipulated, so some participants saw two films of their assigned type and others saw five. These exposures were followed by the mock rape trial and questions about it.

Regardless of the number of exposures to the violent pornographic films, viewers showed desensitization, reporting a decline in feelings of anxiety, in perceived violence, and in their ratings of how degrading the material was to women. These viewers also rated the rape victim as less injured and as less worthy than the viewers of nonviolent materials. Again, dosage made no difference. These experiments indicate that exposure to two slasher films is sufficient not only to desensitize viewers to their initial anxiety and repulsion toward the material but also to induce greater callousness toward women.

The results described above are not surprising, for they represent the operation of a number of well-known principles in psychology. These principles provide some insight into the questions of why some men rape whereas others do not. As indicated by Malamuth's research (1984), some men are more rape-prone than others, and a confluence of psychological-cultural factors may precipitate attacks by rape-prone individuals that would not do so for less rape-prone individuals. These factors include the following. First, exposure to juxtaposed scenes of violence and sexuality may, through simple conditioning, result in the association of sexuality with aggressive acts. Sexual arousal to aggressive situations would be increased, with concomitant changes in the contents of sexual fantasies and even in sexual behavior.

Second, violent pornography frequently portrays the victim as secretly desiring or seeking the assault and as deriving sexual pleasure from it (Malamuth, 1984; Malamuth, Heim, & Feshbach, 1980; Smith, 1976a, 1976b). For those individuals who already believe in rape myths, these depictions may serve to validate their attitudes,[3] setting the stage for a third psychological-cultural factor, the approval or acceptance of aggressive sexuality implicitly suggested by its appearance in standard forms of the media, such as television, videotapes, and movies.

The first factor presumably interacts with individual inclinations to aggress in a manner described by a *general arousal model* (e.g., Bandura, 1973; Baron & Bell, 1973; Donnerstein, 1983; Zillmann, 1971). This model states that when aggression is a dominant response to arousal, any source of moderate emotional arousal (such as that induced by exposure to pornography) will tend to increase aggressive behavior. The second and third factors relate to self-control or inhibition of aggressive behavior. Under many circumstances, normal inhibitions will deter individuals from committing antisocial acts, but these inhibitions may be vitiated by so-called disinhibitory messages. One such message is that conveyed by the mere presence of aggressive pornography. This material is available, the person thinks, so it must be condoned, at least in certain circumstances. As has been noted frequently, the media often depict violence as acceptable if it serves some socially approved end, such as killing or incarcerating a criminal. The media play the same disinhibiting role when they present images of women responding favorably to male aggression. Lest the reader think that the disinhibitory role of the media is overblown, numerous studies have indicated that both children and adults have difficulty distinguishing media portrayals (fantasy) from reality (Gerbner, Gross, Eleey, et al., 1977; Gerbner, Gross, Morgan, et al., 1982). Moreover, depictions of sexual violence are likely to be influential even when the viewer knows that they are fictional. For example, participants asked to imagine an event that they knew was totally fictitious were more likely to believe that it would actually occur than a group that was not asked to imagine the event (Carroll, 1978).

A somewhat different approach is taken by McFall (1982) in his information-processing model of social competence. In this model, three processes support the transformation of cues (information) from the environment into responses to those cues. Decoding processes are used to perceive and interpret the initial information; decision processes are used to generate and to assess the utility of each possible response; and execution processes contribute to the effective production of the chosen response. All types are necessary for competence; hence failures at any stage may produce maladaptive responses. Applying this model to rape, Lipton, McDonel, and McFall (in press) hypothesized that rapists may misconstrue the social information they receive from women, perhaps by interpreting women's negative cues as positive, as "come ons." They tested the ability to interpret correctly interpersonal cues from women and men using groups of rapists, violent nonrapists, and nonviolent nonrapists. As predicted, the rapists were particularly deficient in correctly interpreting women's interpersonal cues. Their results and the model encouragingly imply that rape-prone individuals might be helped through training to more realistically assess the cues given by women to encourage or discourage male attention.

Most important, the models described above apply generally to human behavior. Their guidance may lead to a deeper understanding of the factors that predispose men toward sexual aggression and to the development of effective remedies.

Although the effects of exposure to violent pornography in laboratory settings have been studied extensively, no evidence indicates that viewing violent pornography actually precipitates rape. Moreover, no direct experimental evidence is likely to be sought, because ethical considerations prohibit such research even under tightly controlled conditions.[4] In fact, contemporary researchers try to select participants who do not seem to be at particular risk by using likelihood-of-rape questions and scales that measure hostility and psychoticism (e.g., Linz, 1985), despite the fact that these precautions may reduce the expected impact of the films. They conscientiously and fully warn their subjects about the possible effects of violent pornography. These precautions do not accompany the viewing of pornography in the real world, however. As a result, many researchers now are searching for effective mitigators of the effects of routine, nondebriefed exposure to representations of aggressive sexuality. In the rest of this chapter we consider the techniques that have been tested.

Mitigators of the Effects of Violent Pornography

Four general techniques have been proposed to lessen or eliminate the harmful effects of exposure to aggressive sexuality: prohibitive legislation, teaching critical viewing skills, debriefing after exposure, and briefing before exposure.

One obvious possibility, simply banning the distribution and sale of these materials, does not seem to be feasible, according to legal scholars, who agree that legal remedies would not achieve the intended purpose (e.g., Dworkin, 1985; Jacobs, 1984; Penrod & Linz, 1984; Tigue, 1985; also see other chapters in this book). Current laws provide some controls through obscenity statutes and the like, but more comprehensive laws would be needed to control the dispersion of aggressive pornography. Such laws are likely to violate the First Amendment and, as a consequence, be unconstitutional. Thus, this method of combating the effect of violent pornography does not appear to be particularly desirable, practical, or feasible.

CRITICAL VIEWING SKILLS

The development of critical, informed approaches to viewing the media has obvious promise. In the first place, these skills might generalize to other aspects of the individuals' lives, helping them to become more discriminating, discerning consumers of information. An impressive demonstration of the effectiveness of such skills was provided by Huesmann et al. (1983) when they showed that the aggressive behaviors of first- and third-grade children could be modified by changing their attitudes toward televised violence. To date, critical viewing skills have not been applied to violent pornography, although Donnerstein (personal communication) is currently working on such a test. In the meantime, to describe the procedures, we present the method used with aggressive material.

Huesmann et al. (1983) selected children who regularly watched at least six highly violent television shows. Half of the children were randomly assigned to the experimental group, and half to the "placebo" group. The training sessions for the experimental groups were designed to teach them "(a) that the behaviors of the characters on these shows do not represent the behaviors of most people, (b) that camera techniques and special effects are giving the illusion that the characters are performing their highly aggressive and unrealistic feats, and (c) that the average person uses other methods to solve problems similar to those encountered by the characters" (p. 902). These principles were taught through the use of stories about how most people handle the problems, demonstrations of special media effects, discussions about the unreality of the film depictions, etc. The placebo group spent an equivalent amount of time in discussions about nonviolent television programs.

Reactions were tested both immediately after the end of the experimental sessions and three months later. The pretests had been administered approximately nine months before the experimental sessions began. At the end of two years, the experimental participants were less aggressive than the placebo students. Moreover, the experimental youngsters were rated as significantly less aggressive by their peers than the placebo youngsters. These encouraging results suggest that the violent aspects of aggressive pornography might succumb to the scrutiny of critical viewing skills. We do not yet know whether the same will be true for explicit sexuality or for the conjunction of violence and sexuality. Nor is it clear that consumers of violent pornography would adapt and apply such techniques. The approach presumably would be to teach critical viewing skills that could be generalized to different kinds of materials.

DEBRIEFING

Five recent studies have explicitly addressed the effectiveness of post-experimental warnings, usually called debriefings, and all have found that debriefing following exposure to a depiction of violent pornography reduced acceptance of rape myths. In most of the work, precautions were taken to dissociate the exposure to aggressive sexuality or related materials and debriefings from the test for acceptance of rape myths. These precautions were designed to reduce the chance that subjects are responding in ways that they think are appropriate or are what they believe the experimenter expects.

In one report, Donnerstein and Berkowitz (1981) sent a rape myth questionnaire two weeks to four months after participation in the main experimental session. Males who had seen nonaggressive erotic films or aggressive erotic films that depicted the female as either enjoying or not enjoying the sexual assault were debriefed about the likely negative effects of exposure to pornography. These debriefed subjects were less likely to accept rape myths than subjects who saw neutral films and were not debriefed. Unfortunately, the report does not state whether or not the groups had comparable initial beliefs about rape myths.

In other work, Malamuth and Check (1984) asked both female and male undergraduates to read stories about a forcible rape or about mutually consenting intercourse. The rape stories indicated pain or no pain and victim arousal or victim disgust. After reading one of the rape stories, the students read a rape-related debriefing designed to counter rape myths. Subjects who read about consensual intercourse had a debriefing that described the benefits of research about human sexuality. The two messages were about the same length.

Both groups were tested for espousal of rape myths and opinions about the causes of rape by asking them to answer questions about a newspaper article that described a rape. This article, embedded in other newspaper articles to conceal the purpose of the research, was administered about ten days later as part of a "Public Survey." Subjects who had been exposed to the rape debriefing following a rape depiction were less likely to accept rape myths than were subjects exposed to a debriefing given after exposure to consensual intercourse.

Similarly, Malamuth and Check (1980b) and Malamuth, Heim, and Feshbach (1980) have found that exposure to rape depictions followed by a debriefing that debunks rape myths tends to reduce subsequently tested expression of those myths.

Linz (1985) used three debriefings tailored to the films seen by the participants: R-rated violent films, R-rated nonviolent films, and X-rated nonviolent films. These subjects all took Burt's Rape Myth Acceptance (1980) test before beginning their initial participation in the study and almost six months after debriefing. All groups showed a significant reduction in their espousal of rape myths, with the R-rated violent group showing the greatest decline.

These results suggest that, following exposure to aggressive pornography, debunking-type debriefings may reduce acceptance of rape myths below that shown by control subjects. Some investigators (e.g., Malamuth & Check, 1984) have proposed that such debriefings may be an effective tool for combating the antisocial effects of violent pornography. These conclusions are premature, however, for the experimental groups have been exposed to pornographic film–debunking debriefing combinations, whereas control groups have heard a debriefing that describes the value of scientific investigations of sexuality after seeing a film showing consensual intercourse. Thus, both the combinations of materials and the contents of the manipulations differed for the experimental and control groups. This confounding means that it is impossible to determine what produced the decline in rape-myth acceptance in the experimental group. The decline could have been due to the nature of the experimental debriefings or to the combination of the experimental debriefing and the pornography. The latter might have sensitized or alerted subjects to excessive violence or violent sexuality. Also unresolved is the question of whether rape-related debriefing could, by itself, reduce the acceptance of rape myths.

Check and Malamuth (1984) addressed these problems by giving some subjects in the control group the rape-related debriefing and other subjects the consensual intercourse debriefing. A third group received the rape-related debriefing after reading a rape depiction. They found that, although the rape-related debriefing increased the perception of pornography as a cause of rape compared to the sexuality-related debriefing, the rape-related debriefing was most effective when it followed exposure to violent pornography. Two explanations are offered for this interesting result. According to the first, the rape exposure/rape debriefing provides a "corrective experience . . . [in which] . . . research participants [gain] new insights about how they may unwillingly accept rape myths" (Check & Malamuth, p. 16). The other explanation, the inoculation effect (McGuire & Papageorgis, 1961), is that the subjects are immunized against uncritical acceptance of rape myths by hearing counterarguments that discredit a portrayal of a rape victim as a willing sexual participant. These two explanations may well be indistinguishable.

Check and Malamuth (1984) also manipulated the type of rape depiction (stranger or acquaintance) read by the participants. Other subjects read about consensual intercourse. Check and Malamuth reasoned that the readers would attribute the most pleasure and the least pain to consensual intercourse. They would assign the most pain and the least pleasure to the stranger rape situation, with assessments of the acquaintance rape depiction in between. The data validated these expectations. Nonetheless, the differences in the type of rape did not interact with the type of debriefing.

In summary, the debriefing experiments permit several conclusions. First, debriefings that counter rape myths are effective in dispelling the myths to a greater extent than debriefings that discuss the value of research on sexuality. Second, these effects persist at least as long as six months (Linz, 1985). Third, rape-related debriefing more effectively reduces rape myths when it is preceded by a depiction of violent pornography than when it is preceded by a depiction of mutually consenting intercourse. Fourth, rape-related debriefing is effective following depictions of both stranger and acquaintance rapes.

Despite these salutary effects, a central problem with the principle of debriefing is that it is not feasible to append debriefings to all or most exposures to aggressive pornography. Producers and sponsors would fight the inclusion of such a message because it adds expense and might discourage some viewers. Many producers would not include the message unless they were legally forced to do so. Then, too, some assaultive sexuality, such as that described in literature, comes in a form that does not lend itself to debriefing messages. Thus, debriefing remains one method for reducing the negative effects of violent pornography, but it has somewhat limited utility.

BRIEFING BEFORE EXPOSURE

Of potentially wider applicability are various methods of briefing or "inoculating" people before they are exposed to violent pornography. Basically educational in nature, one variant explicitly warns people of the possible effects of exposure to violent pornography (e.g., Bross, 1984). This approach is much like presenting a debriefing before rather than after a pornographic film, and, as used to date, deals specifically with likely desensitization and callousing effects of exposure to aggressive sexuality. Other, more general methods include sex education programs that present the similarities and differences of female and male sexual responses, differences in what the two sexes consider to be sexual signals, communication skills, consideration for one's partner, and the like. The purpose of these programs is to develop sexually educated individuals whose knowledge will make them less susceptible to myths encountered in the media and other places.

The above approaches are designed for individual or small-group administration. Other techniques focus on large audiences. For example, the movie *The Hottest Show in Town* was designed to depict mutually consenting erotica with partners of approximately equal power. Such a film might replace more violent fare. Unfortunately, Malamuth (1984, 45) tells us that, "Ironically, this movie was sometimes shown in adult theatres as part of a double feature with such films as *Femmes de Sade,* which focused on sadomasochistic relationships between women." Recent media programs about rape *(Cry Rape, Why Men Rape, A Scream of Silence)* and aggressive pornography *(Not a Love Story)* are designed to raise the awareness and the understanding of the audience about these topics. While these programs may have the intended effect of educating people about the damage of rape and other forms of forced sexuality, they also may have the opposite effect of stimulating those individuals who are particularly excited by scenes of violent sexuality. Programs pitched at a mass audience do not lend themselves to tailoring to the needs of special groups.

Experimental investigations of educational interventions are limited. In two experiments, Bross (1984) studied the effects of prefilm briefings. The rationale for this procedure was that advance warnings about the content of aggressive pornographic films and the likely consequences upon attitudes and behavior might increase sensitivity toward a female rape victim. Bross used two written prefilm messages that were presented aurally with or without a simultaneous reading of the message. One briefing presented a description of the film. Another briefing described how viewing slasher films could produce desensitization to filmed violence, particularly when scenes of violence are juxtaposed with those of sexuality. Both briefings were quite short and both were specific to the following pornographic film. Their brevity reflected Bross's interest in mimicking the type of warning occasionally used on television (similar to warnings about smoking cigarettes).

After exposure to the prefilm message and to a violently pornographic film, all participants were shown a mock rape trial and subsequently asked for their evaluations of the harm suffered by the victim, their sympathy for her, and so on, in addition to other questions designed to obtain self-reports of sexual arousal, and evaluations of the technical and artistic merits of the film. A third group differed from the others only by not seeing any prefilm message.

The results were essentially negative, regardless of whether the message was read while hearing it. The prefilm briefings had little influence on perceptions of the slasher film or of a rape victim. The descriptive message, however, did increase the level of fear felt while watching the slasher film.

Why were the briefings largely ineffective? The most likely explanation is that both of the messages represented a minimal intervention. Even the "effects" message was stated in a relatively bland and abstract way that could have been easily dismissed by the viewers as not relevant to themselves.

Recent Research on Prefilm Briefing

We recently tested more general prefilm briefings.[5] Videotapes were prepared to present two types of briefings. One briefing dealt with general matters of interpersonal relations and sexuality, and the other focused on information about rape that is often not known. Thirty men saw each of these videotapes. A third group of thirty men saw no prefilm videotape. The groups then were trifurcated. One-third of each group saw a violent pornographic movie, another saw a movie depicting nonviolent, mutually consensual sex, and the remaining third saw a nonviolent nonpornographic movie. These movies are regularly available, commercial ones. All participants were tested for their acceptance of myths about rape before the briefing, after exposure to the movie, and again two weeks later at a second session. The test for rape-myth acceptance, developed and standardized by Burt (1980), contained eleven questions such as "In the majority of rapes, the victim is promiscuous or has a bad reputation," and "A woman who is stuck-up and thinks that she is too good to talk to guys on the street deserves to be taught a lesson." The questions from this test were embedded among others that asked about the contents of the various films, evaluations of the esthetic qualities of the films, and the viewers' own emotional-physiological reactions to the films. The session ended with a debriefing film, which was designed to warn the participants about the possible effects of exposure to violent sexuality.

Our first concern was whether or not the participants understood commercial films. Clearly, the films would not be expected to have an effect unless the participants paid attention to them. In general, they answered correctly most questions about the films. They also answered questions about briefings they had seen but were close to chance in their responses to briefings that they had not seen. These results indicate that the men attended to the presentations and that the information provided by our briefings was not widely known to our participants.

If the briefing moderated the effects of exposure to violent pornography, rape-myth acceptance should decline more from its initial level for the groups who saw the briefing videotapes before seeing violent pornography than for the counterpart group that had no briefing. This is exactly what we found. The briefed groups showed a marked, and almost equivalent, decline in their acceptance of rape myths, as measured by the rape-myth acceptance scale, whereas the nonbriefed group showed an *increase* in rape-myth acceptance. This latter finding corresponds to the typical result described earlier, namely that exposure to violent pornography increases the acceptance of myths about rape. These outcomes suggest that education briefings can mitigate at least some of the negative effects of exposure to violent pornography.

Still other groups of participants saw nonviolent pornographic or nonviolent nonpornographic movies after being briefed with one of the two briefing videotapes or not being briefed. These groups showed generally lower acceptance of rape myths than the groups exposed to violent pornography, but the effects of the briefings yielded the same pattern: acceptance of rape myths decreased more for the briefed groups than for the nonbriefed control.

Thus, the briefing videotapes appeared to mitigate an important effect of exposure to violent pornography: acceptance of erroneous myths about rape. Further, the final testing of rape-myth acceptance two weeks later indicated that acceptance of these myths had declined even more. These effects, then, are sustained over at least a two-week interval.

These results were obtained with a slightly more varied sample of participants than is usually the case. Our respondents, all males, ranged in age from 21 to 38, with a mean of 24.03 years. Their educational background extended from high school graduation to graduate training.

In addition to rape-myth acceptance, we examined attitudes toward and opinions about a rape victim and a rapist described in a mock rape trial. The trial described an ambiguous situation, so the subjects were relatively unconstrained about how they interpreted the guilt or responsibility for an unwanted sexual assault. The rationale for introducing this measure was that attitudes induced by the briefings (or their absence) and the commercial films might influence their judgments as potential jurors in a rape trial. We hypothesized that, if the influence of the briefing videotapes carried over to this situation, the briefed men should be more supportive of the rape victim and more disapproving of the rapist than nonbriefed men. These results also obtained. Compared to the nonbriefed participants, briefed men were more likely to describe the victim positively, to attribute less blame to her, to have greater compassion for her, and to consider the rapist guilty. These reactions generally did not differ as a function of the commercial film they saw.

Our results provide a straightforward answer to our question: briefings about concern for one's sexual partner or rape education mitigate some effects of exposure to violent pornography. Moreover, the rape information and the general sex responsibility briefings appeared to be about equally effective mitigators. We find these results to be encouraging, for the kinds of information incorporated in our briefing films should be easy to present to other groups.

Not only may briefings sensitize people to rape myths and make them less susceptible to the callousing effects of violent pornography, but they also should have the salutary effect of providing more information about sexuality and its interpersonal components. Although the wisdom of widespread exposure to sex education occasionally is challenged, the evidence both here and in other countries, including Scandinavian ones (e.g., Fact Sheets on Sweden, 1982; Jones et al., 1985; Zabin et al., 1986), suggests that exposure to sex education is associated with reduced rates of unwanted pregnancies, abortion, aggravated sexual assault, and other forms of sexual abuse and illegal sexual activities.

Another confirmatory study recently appeared. Furstenberg, Moore, and Peterson (1985) reported that fifteen- and sixteen-year-olds who had had sex education were less likely to have had sexual intercourse (17 percent) than their peers who had not had sex education (26 percent). Moreover, both talking with parents and taking sex education courses reduced the percentages of sexually active teens. For example, 31 percent of the students who had neither taken sex education courses nor talked with their parents were sexually active, in contrast to 21 percent who had talked with their parents, and 17 percent who had taken sex education courses. Talking with parents and taking sex education lowered the rate to 16 percent.[6]

In sum, educational briefings both before and after exposure to violent pornography reduce the negative effects of such exposure. The development of critical viewing skills may function the same way, but no data are yet available that deal specifically with modification of attitudes induced by exposure to violent pornography.

If measures are sought to counteract some effects of exposure to violent pornography, we know that at least two effective tools currently exist: debriefing after exposure or briefing before exposure. Both of these techniques are designed to educate viewers to make them less susceptible to the subtle influences of media that systematically degrade one gender.

NOTES

We wish to thank Susan Gubar, Joan Hoff, David Pritchard, Lauren Robel, Mary Jo Weaver, and other members of the Seminar on Violent Pornography who shared their knowledge with us and who provided the incentive to conduct the research described herein, and three perceptive, persistent critics of the manuscript, Bruce Berg, David Houston, and Richard McFall.

1. It is important to note that Baron and Bell (1973), Donnerstein, Donnerstein, and Evans (1975), Malamuth, Feshbach, and Jaffe (1977), Zillmann (1971, 1979), and Zillmann and Bryant (1984) have reported negative effects of extensive exposure to nonviolent pornography.

2. We should note, as well, that the extant research does not indicate how these attitudes affect behavior, although the results of interviews (Russell, 1983) indicate that pornography viewers occasionally request that their partners emulate the sexual activities portrayed by the films or other media.

3. Of course, the depictions may contribute to the attitudes, so that the process operates in both directions.

4. Some quasi-experimental analyses of this problem may be possible (see Lipton et al., in press).

5. This research was supported in part by the Kinsey Institute for Research in Sex, Gender, and Reproduction and by the Women's Studies Program at Indiana University. We gratefully acknowledge the assistance of June Reinisch, Director of the Kinsey Institute; Stephanie Sanders, Mary Davis, and Susan Straub, members of the staff of the Kinsey Institute; and Mary Ellen Brown, Director of Women's Studies. We wish to thank the male experimenters who made this research possible, David Roskos-Ewoldsen, Kevin Murnane, Bruce Berg, and David Horner. Our greatest indebtedness is to Dafna Blut, Mary Shirley, and Laura Thomas for their assistance in designing the experiment, writing the scripts, conducting the experiment, and analyzing it.

6. There is the possibility of "self-selection" of the groups in this kind of research. For example, those students who are less sexually active may be more willing to talk to their parents about sex.

REFERENCES

Bandura, A. (1973). *Aggression: A Social Learning Analysis*. Englewood Cliffs, N.J.: Prentice-Hall.

Baron, R. A., & Bell, P. A. (1973). "Effects of Heightened Sexual Arousal on Physical Aggression." *Proceedings of the 81st Annual Convention of the American Psychological Association* 8:171–72.

Bernstein, S. (1982). Editorial. *Puritan* 9:1.

Bross, M. S. (1984). "Effect of Pre-film Messages on Viewer Perceptions of Slasher Films." Master's thesis, University of Wisconsin–Madison.

Burt, M. R. (1980). "Cultural Myths and Supports for Rape." *Journal of Personality and Social Psychology* 38:217–30.

Carroll, J. S. (1978). "The Effect of Imagining an Event on Expectations for the Event: An Interpretation in Terms of the Availability Heuristic." *Journal of Experimental Social Psychology* 14:88–96.

Cattell, R. B.; Kawash, G. F.; & De Young, G. E. (1972). "Validation of Objective Measure of Ergic Tension: Response of the Sex Erg to Visual Stimulation." *Journal of Experimental Research in Personality* 6:76–83.

Check, J. V. P., & Malamuth, N. M. (1984). "Can There Be Positive Effects of Participation in Pornography Experiments?" *Journal of Sex Research* 20:14–31.

The Commission on Obscenity and Pornography (1970). *Report of Commission on Obscenity and Pornography*. Washington, D.C.: U.S. Government Printing Office.

———(1971). *Technical Report*. Vol. 8. Washington, D.C.: U.S. Government Printing Office.

Court, J. H. (1984). "Sex and Violence: A Ripple Effect." In *Pornography and Sexual Aggression*, ed. N. M. Malamuth and E. Donnerstein. Orlando, Fla.: Academic Press.

Dietz, P. E., & Evans, B. (1982). "Pornographic Imagery and Prevalence of Paraphilia." *American Journal of Psychiatry* 139:1493–95.

Donnerstein, E. (1980a). "Aggressive Erotica and Violence against Women." *Journal of Personality and Social Psychology* 39:269–77.

———(1980b). "Pornography and Violence against Women." *Annals of the New York Academy of Sciences* 347:277–88.

———(1983). "Erotica and Human Aggression." In R. G. Geen and E. I. Donnerstein, eds., *Aggression: Theoretical and Empirical Review*. Vol. 2. New York: Academic Press.

———(1984). "Pornography: Its Effect on Violence against Women." In *Pornography and Sexual Aggression*, ed. N. M. Malamuth and E. Donnerstein. Orlando, Fla.: Academic Press.

Donnerstein, E., & Berkowitz, L. (1981). "Victim Reactions in Aggressive Erotic Films as a Factor in Violence against Women." *Journal of Personality and Social Psychology* 41:710–24.

Donnerstein, E.; Donnerstein, M.; & Evans, R. (1975). "Erotic Stimuli and Aggression: Facilitation or Inhibition." *Journal of Personality and Social Psychology* 32:237–44.

Dworkin, R. (1985). "Do We Have a Right to Pornography?" In *A Matter of Principle,* ed. R. Dworkin. Boston: Harvard University Press.

Eisenman, R. (1982). "Sexual Behavior as Related to Sex Fantasies and Experimental Manipulation of Authoritarianism and Creativity." *Journal of Personality and Social Psychology* 43:853–60.

Fact Sheets on Sweden (1982, August). *Legislation on Family Planning.* Sweden: The Swedish Institute, FS 73: Vn.

Furtstenberg, F. F.; Moore, K. A.; & Peterson, J. L. (1985). "Sex Education and Sexual Experience among Adolescents." *American Journal of Public Health* 75:1331–32.

Gerbner, G.; Gross, L.; Eleey, M. F.; Jackson-Beeck, M.; Jeffroes-Fox, S.; & Signorelli, N. (1977). "TV Violence Profile No. 8: The Highlights." *Journal of Communication* 27:171–80.

Gerbner, G.; Gross, L.; Morgan, M.; & Signorelli, N. (1982). "Charting the Mainstream: Television's Contributions to Political Orientation." *Journal of Communication* 32:100–26.

Goleman, D., & Bush, S. (1977). "The Liberation of Sexual Fantasy." *Psychology Today* 11:48–49, 51–53, 104, 106–107.

Howard, J. L.; Reifler, C. B.; & Liptzin, M. B. (1971). "Effects of Exposure to Pornography." In *Technical Report of the Commission on Obscenity and Pornography* (Vol. 8, pp. 97–132). Washington, D.C.: U.S. Government Printing Office.

Huesmann, L. R.; Eron, L. D.; Klein, R.; Brice, P.; & Fischer, P. (1983). "Mitigating the Imitation of Aggressive Behaviors by Changing Children's Attitudes about Media Violence." *Journal of Personality and Social Psychology* 44:899–910.

Jacobs, C. (1984). "Patterns of Violence: A Feminist Perspective on the Regulation of Pornography." *Harvard Women's Law Journal* 7:5–55.

Jones, E. F.; Forrest, J. D.; Goldman, N.; Henshaw, S. K.; Lincoln, R.; Rosoff, J. I.; Westoff, C. F.; & Wulf, D. (1985). "Teenage Pregnancy in Developed Countries: Determinants and Policy Implications." *Family Planning Perspectives* 17:53–69.

Kronhausen, D., & Kronhausen, P. (1964). *Pornography and the Law.* Rev. ed. New York: Ballantine.

Kutchinsky, B. (1973). "The Effect of Easy Availability of Pornography on the Incidence of Sex Crimes: The Danish Experience." *Journal of Social Issues* 29:163–81.

Linz, D. G. (1985). "Sexual Violence in the Media: Effects on Male Viewers and Implications for Society." Ph.D. diss., University of Wisconsin–Madison.

Lipton, D. N.; McDonel, E. C.; & McFall, R. M. (in press). "Heterosocial Perception in Rapists." *Journal of Consulting and Clinical Psychology.*

McFall, R. M. (1982). "A Review and Reformulation of the Concept of Social Skills." *Behavioral Assessment* 4:1–33.

McGuire, W. J., & Papageorgis, D. (1961). "The Relative Efficacy of Various Types of Prior Belief-Defense in Producing Immunity against Persuasion." *Journal of Abnormal and Social Psychology* 62:327–37.

Malamuth, N. M. (1978). "Erotica, Aggression, and Perceived Appropriateness." Paper presented at the 86th annual convention of the American Psychological Association, Toronto, Canada, September 1978.

———(1981). "Rape Proclivity among Males." *Journal of Social Issues* 37:138–57.

———(1984). "Aggression against Women: Cultural and Individual Causes." In *Pornography and Sexual Aggression,* ed. N. M. Malamuth and E. Donnerstein. Orlando, Fla.: Academic Press.

Malamuth, N. M., & Check, J. V. P. (1980a). "Penile Tumescence and Perceptual Responses to Rape as a Function of Victim's Perceived Reactions." *Journal of Applied Social Psychology* 10:528–47.

———(1980b). "Sexual Arousal to Rape and Consenting Depictions: The Importance of the Woman's Arousal." *Journal of Abnormal Psychology* 89:763–66.

———(1981). "The Effects of Mass Media Exposure on Acceptance of Violence against Women: A Field Experiment." *Journal of Research in Personality* 15:436–46.

———(1983). "Sexual Arousal to Rape Depictions: Individual Differences." *Journal of Abnormal Psychology* 92:55–67.

———(1984). "Debriefing Effectiveness Following Exposure to Pornographic Rape Depictions." *The Journal of Sex Research* 20:1–13.

Malamuth, N. M.; Feshbach, S.; & Jaffe, V. (1977). "Sexual Arousal and Aggression: Recent Experiments and Theoretical Issues." *Journal of Social Issues* 33:110–33.

Malamuth, N. M.; Haber, S.; & Feshbach, S. (1980). "Testing Hypotheses Regarding Rape: Exposure to Sexual Violence, Sex Differences, and the 'Normality' of Rapists." *Journal of Research in Personality* 14:121–37.

Malamuth, N. M.; Heim, M.; & Feshbach, S. (1980). "Sexual Responsiveness of College Students to Rape Depictions: Inhibitory and Disinhibitory Effects." *Journal of Personality and Social Psychology* 38:339–408.

Malamuth, N. M.; Reiin, I.; & Spinner, B. (1979). "Exposure to Pornography and Reactions to Rape." Paper presented at the 86th annual convention of the American Psychological Association, New York.

Malamuth, N. M., & Spinner, B. (1980). "A Longitudinal Content Analysis of Sexual Violence in the Best-selling Erotic Magazines." *The Journal of Sex Research* 16:226–37.

Mann, J.; Sidman, J.; & Starr, S. (1971). "Effects of Erotic Films on Sexual Behavior of Married Couples." In *Technical Report of The Commission on Obscenity and Pornography* (Vol. 8). Washington, D.C.: U.S. Government Printing Office.

Meyer, T. P. (1972). "The Effects of Sexually Arousing and Violent Films on Aggressive Behavior." *The Journal of Sex Research* 8:324–33.

National Commission on the Causes and Prevention of Violence (1969). *Report.* Washington, D.C.: U.S. Government Printing Office.

Penrod, S., & Linz, D. (1984). "Using Psychological Research on Violent Pornography to Inform Legal Change." In *Pornography and Sexual Aggression,* ed. N. M. Malamuth and E. Donnerstein. Orlando, Fla.: Academic Press.

Russell, D. E. H. (1983). "Research on How Women Experience the Impact of Pornography." In *Pornography and Censorship,* ed. David Copp and Susan Wendell. Buffalo, N.Y.: Prometheus Brooks.

Sapolsky, B. S. (1984). "Arousal, Affect, and the Aggression-moderating Effect of Erotica." In *Pornography and Sexual Aggression,* ed. N. M. Malamuth and E. Donnerstein. Orlando, Fla.: Academic Press.

Smith, D. G. (1976a). "Sexual Aggression in American Pornography: The Stereotype of Rape." Presented at the annual meetings of the American Sociological Association, New York.

———(1976b). "The Social Content of Pornography." *Journal of Communication* 26:16–33.

Surgeon General's Scientific Advisory Committee (1972). *Television and Growing Up: The Impact of Televised Violence: Report to the Surgeon General.* U.S. Public Health Service, Department of Health, Education, and Welfare Publication N. HSM 72-9090. Rockville, Md.: National Institute of Mental Health.

Tieger, T. (1981). "Self-reported Likelihood of Raping and the Social Perception of Rape." *Journal of Research in Personality* 15:147–58.

Tigue, R. D. B. (1985). "Civil Rights and Censorship—Incompatible Bedfellows." *William Mitchell Law Review* 11:81–118.

Zabin, L. S.; Hirsch, M. B.; Smith, E. A.; Streett, R.; & Hardy, J. B. (1986). "Evaluation of a Pregnancy Prevention Program for Urban Teenagers." *Family Planning Perspectives* 18:119–26.

Zillmann, D. (1971). "Excitation Transfer in Communication-mediated Aggressive Behavior." *Journal of Experimental Social Psychology* 7:419–34.

———(1979). *Hostility and Aggression.* Hillsdale, N.J.: Erlbaum.

Zillmann, D., & Bryant, J. (1982). "Pornography, Sexual Callousness, and the Trivialization of Rape." *Journal of Communication* 32:10–21.

———(1984). "Effects of Massive Exposure to Pornography. In *Pornography and Sexual Aggression,* ed. N. M. Malamuth and E. Donnerstein. Orlando, Fla.: Academic Press.

———(1986). "Effects of Pornography Consumption on Family Values." Manuscript.

CONTRIBUTORS

Doris-Jean Burton, adjunct assistant professor of Political Science at Indiana University, Bloomington, is the assistant to the chair of Political Science. She has published articles on the status of women in political science and on student evaluations of classes and teaches courses on women and the law and families and public policy.

Edna F. Einsiedel, professor and associate director of the Communication Studies Programme, University of Calgary, served as staff social scientist for the 1986 Commission on Pornography with sole responsibility for the Social Science Findings section of the *Final Report* and for various background papers on social science issues for the commission. Her recent research is on science and the mass media, public information campaigns, and social science and public policy.

Susan Gubar, professor of English and Women's Studies at Indiana University, is coauthor with Sandra M. Gilbert of *The Madwoman in the Attic, The War of the Words,* and *Sexchanges.* She is coeditor, also with Sandra M. Gilbert, of *Shakespeare's Sisters: Feminist Essays on Women Poets* and the *Norton Anthology of Literature by Women.*

Joan Hoff, executive secretary of the Organization of American Historians and professor of History at Indiana University, has published books and articles on women and twentieth-century U.S. history. She is the author of the forthcoming work *Too Little—Too Late: Changing Legal Status of U.S. Women from the American Revolution to the Present.* Her current research is focused on a reevaluation of the Nixon presidency.

Margaret Jean Intons-Peterson, professor of Psychology and adjunct professor of Women's Studies at Indiana University, regularly teaches a course on the psychology of women. She is the author of two forthcoming books, *Children's Concepts of Gender* and *Gender Concepts of Swedish and American Youth.*

Richard B. Miller, assistant professor in the Department of Religious Studies at Indiana University, specializes in social ethics. His teaching and research make reference to traditional and contemporary theories about violence in Western religions. He is currently concentrating on such ethical issues as social justice, pacifism, the just-war tradition, nuclear deterrence, and civil conflict. His articles have appeared in *Journal of Religion, Horizons, Theological Studies,* and *Soundings.*

David Pritchard, assistant professor, School of Journalism at Indiana University, was one of the original members of Indiana University's Task Force on Pornography. He is also a member of the advisory committee for the Indiana University Center for the Study of Law and Society. His principal research interest is social control and the media, and he has published articles in *Public Opinion Quarterly, Journal of Communication, Journalism Quarterly,* and *Communications and the Law.*

Lauren K. Robel, assistant professor of Law at Indiana University, teaches Constitutional Law and Civil Rights.

Beverly Roskos-Ewoldsen, a graduate student at Indiana University, specializes in cognitive psychology, with a minor in Women's Studies.

Mary Jo Weaver, professor of Religious Studies at Indiana University, is also a member of the Women's Studies faculty. Her first two books were on religious modernism in late nineteenth-century British Catholic thought, and her more recent research on the women's movement in the American Catholic church appeared in *New Catholic Women: A Contemporary Challenge to Traditional Religious Authority.* She is currently working on a book on gender and spirituality.

Robin West, professor of Law at the University of Maryland School of Law and visiting research fellow, Center for Philosophy and Public Policy, University of Maryland, College Park, has published several articles on feminist legal theory, the expanding field of law and literature, and liberal jurisprudence. Her writings have appeared in such publications as *The American Bar Foundation Research Journal, The Wisconsin Women's Law Journal, The Chicago Law Review,* and *Mercer Law Review.*

Linda Williams, associate professor of English at the University of Illinois, Chicago, is the author of a book on surrealist film, *Figures of Desire,* and coeditor of *Revision: Essays in Feminist Film Criticism.* Her forthcoming book on film pornography is entitled *Hard-Core: Power, Pleasure and "The Frenzy of the Visible."*

INDEX

Abortion, opinions on, 139, 141–42
"Abusive Images of Women in Mass Media and Pornography," 147–48, 160 n.1
Adult men's magazines, 89–90, 103 nn.1, 2, 144, 182, 192 nn.15, 16, 17; examples of violent pornography from, 147–48; relationship between circulation rates and rape rates, 90, 93, 103 n.6. *See also* magazines by name
"Adults-only" establishments, 168, 184–86, 199
Aesthetics, 48–49, 52–54, 58, 148–50, 155–60, 161 n.3
Aesthetics of Pornography, The (Michelson), 56
AGCP. *See* Attorney General's Commission on Pornography
Age: as factor in opinion on pornography, 136–38, 142
Aggression/aggressive behavior, 227, 228–29; affected by exposure to sexually explicit materials, 91–93, 94–95, 222, 224–26; toward women, 170, 190, 220–21, 223
Alexander v. City of Minneapolis, 184
Alexandrian, Sarane, 65 n.6
American Booksellers, Inc. v. Hudnut, 9, 179
American Booksellers Assoc., Inc. v. Virginia, 185, 193 n.30
American Civil Liberties Union (ACLU), 31, 34, 167
Angel Heart (film), 5–6, 7, 11
Anticensorship feminists, 10, 48, 120; FACT, 10, 33–34, 104 n.9, 109, 167
Antipornography feminists, 76, 90, 101, 109, 120, 178; and Christian tradition, 82, 83 n.10; public support for, 144–45; and religious conservatives, 68–70; on sexuality, 202–3
Antipornography laws, 8, 10, 32, 179, 190–91 n.2; as drafted by feminists, 31, 48, 65 n.4; Indianapolis ordinance, 3, 8–9, 145, 180–90, 191 n.2; Minneapolis ordinance, 48, 65 n.4, 190–91 n.2; 1986 Commission support for, 163, 164–65, 174; public opinion on, 103 n.3, 134–45. *See also* Pornography regulation
Art, 22, 49–54; relationship to pornography, 48–49, 54, 56–60
Assault, 111–12, 180–83, 192 n.13
Atlanta, Ga.: enforcement of obscenity law, 189, 195 n.51
Attitudes: relationship to behaviors, 92–93, 95, 103 n.4
Attorney General's (Meese) Commission on Pornography (AGCP) (1986), 17–18, 87, 89–92, 94–96, 129 n.6; findings, 9, 29, 31, 89, 92–94, 101–2, 172, 178, 179, 190 n.2; as public forum for victimized women, 108, 129 n.1; and public opinion polls, 143, 145; on regulation of pornography, 163, 164–65, 168, 174, 189, 195 n.50; use of social science research, 88–89, 92–98, 99–100
Atwood, Margaret, 35, 36
Authoritative world view, 115, 117, 118–19, 122–23
Autoerotic asphyxiation, 192 nn.16, 17

Bakhtin, Mikhail, 18, 19–20, 23, 24, 65 n.1
Baron, L., 90, 93, 103 n.6

Barrows, Sydney, 193–94 n.33
Barry, Kathleen, 55
Barthes, Roland, 56, 66 n.10, 202, 216 n.7
Behavior, 92–93, 118, 122–23; relationship to law, 164–65, 173–74. *See also* Sexual activities
Behind the Green Door (film), 200, 212
Belief clusters, 115–16, 117
Bell, Rudolph, 73, 76
Berger, John, 53
Berkowitz, L., 224, 229–30
Bernard of Clairvaux, 78
Bessmer, Sue, 144
Billings, V., 90
Bird, Phyllis, 74, 83 n.7
Black, Donald, 166, 169–70
Bloom, Alexander, 69
Blue movie, 199, 216 n.3
Blue Velvet (film), 5–7
Body, 70, 73, 75–86, 207
Bondage and Discipline Quarterly, 148
Boredom, 150, 221
"Born Innocent" (TV film), 192 n.17
Bouteille, La (Magritte), 39, il. 51
"Boy loving," Greek practice of, 39 n.7
Brandenberg v. Ohio, 182–83, 192 n.17
Breton, André, 52, 63
Briefing before exposure (prefilm briefing): as mitigating technique, 228, 231–35
Bross, M. S., 231, 232
Brownmiller, Susan, 57
Bryant, J., 221, 225–26
Buddhism: treatment of women, 74

Cannibal Feast (Oppenheim), 49, 64, il. 50
Capitalism, 27, 37 n.3, 115–16, 122, 206–7
Capture fantasies, 120, 123
Carnal Knowledge (film), 168
Carnival and the grotesque, 19, 23, 24
Carter, Angela, 56–57, 58
Castration, 60–61, 74, 203–5, 210, 214
Catharsis (purgative, safety-valve) model, 29–30, 91, 101, 104 n.11, 151–52, 154, 155; 1970 Commission on, 220; public opinion on, 134, table 135; & tensions created by social change, 159
Caught Looking (publication), 33–34
Caws, Mary Anne, 49
Censorship, 22, 35, 48, 56, 103 n.6, 147, 164; literary critics on, 54–56, 57. *See also* Anticensorship feminists
Censorship in Denmark: A New Approach (film), 199
Chadwick, Whitney, 49
Check, J. V. P., 98, 230–31
Chic, 194 n.40
Child pornography, 57, 122, 168
Children, 172, 178, 185, 186, 219, 228–29; sexual abuse, 57, 104 n.11, 112
Chodorow, Nancy, 61
Christ, Carol P., 74
Christianity, traditional, 69–72, 75–78, 81, 83 n.1; pornography linked with failure to follow teachings of, 69, 72, 77; teachings on sex, 69–73, 75

242